Asia-Pacific in the New World Order

In loving memory of two remarkable women –
Elizabeth Brook (1913–1997)
Margaret Mary McGrew (1922–1997)

This book is part of a series produced in association with The Open University. While each book in the series is self-contained, there are also references to the other books. Readers should note that references to other books in the series appear in bold type. The list of other books in the series is:

Economic Dynamism in the Asia-Pacific, edited by Grahame Thompson

Culture and Society in the Asia-Pacific, edited by Richard Maidment and Colin Mackerras

Governance in the Asia-Pacific, edited by Richard Maidment, David Goldblatt and Jeremy Mitchell

The Asia-Pacific Profile, edited by Bernard Eccleston, Michael Dawson and Deborah McNamara

The books form part of the Open University course DD302 *Pacific Studies*. Details of this and other Open University courses can be obtained from the Call Centre, PO Box 724, The Open University, Milton Keynes, MK7 6ZS, United Kingdom: tel. +44(0)1908 653231, e-mail ces-gen@open.ac.uk.

Alternatively, you may visit the Open University website at http://www.open.ac.uk where you can learn more about the wide range of courses and packs offered at all levels by The Open University.

For availability of other course components, contact Open University Worldwide Ltd, The Berrill Building, Walton Hall, Milton Keynes MK7 6AA, United Kingdom: tel. +44(0)1908 858785; fax +44(0)1908 858787; e-mail ouwenq@open.ac.uk; website http://www.ouw.co.uk

Asia-Pacific in the New World Order

Edited by Anthony McGrew and Christopher Brook

London and New York

in association with

The Open
University

First published 1998 by Routledge. Reprinted in 2000, 2002, 2003
11 New Fetter Lane, London EC4P 4EE

Simultaneously published in the USA and Canada
by Routledge
29 West 35th Street, New York, NY 10001

© The Open University 1998

Edited, designed and typeset by The Open University

Printed in the United Kingdom by The Alden Group, Oxford

British Library Cataloguing in Publication Data
A catalogue record for this book is available from The British Library

Library of Congress Cataloging in Publication Data
A catalogue record for this book has been requested

ISBN 0-415-17271-3 (hbk)
ISBN 0-415-17272-1 (pbk)

1.4

CONTENTS

Series preface

The five volumes in this series are part of a new Open University course, *Pacific Studies*, which has been produced within the Faculty of Social Sciences. The appearance of *Pacific Studies* is due to the generous and enthusiastic support the course has received from the University and in particular from colleagues within the Faculty of Social Sciences. The support has been especially remarkable given that this course has ventured into relatively uncharted scholarly waters. The potential risks were readily apparent but the commitment always remained firm. I am very grateful.

There are too many people to thank individually, both within and outside of the Open University, but I must record my appreciation for some of them. Within the University, I would like to acknowledge my colleagues Anthony McGrew and Grahame Thompson. *Pacific Studies* could not have been made without them. Their role was central. They were present when the course was conceived and they lived with it through to the final stages. They also made the experience of making this course both very enjoyable and intellectually stimulating. Christopher Brook and Bernard Eccleston made an enormous contribution to the course far beyond their editorial roles in two of the books in the series. They read the successive drafts of all chapters with great care and their perceptive comments helped to improve these volumes considerably. David Goldblatt and Jeremy Mitchell, because of their other commitments, may have joined the Course Team relatively late in the production process, but their contributions, especially to *Governance in the Asia-Pacific* have been much appreciated. Michael Dawson played an especially important role in the production of *The Asia-Pacific Profile* and his calm and genial presence was valued as always. Jeremy Cooper and Eleanor Morris of the BBC were responsible for the excellent audio-visual component of *Pacific Studies*. Anne Carson, the Course Manager of *Pacific Studies*, was consistently cheerful and helpful. All of the volumes in this series have been greatly improved by the editorial craftsmanship of Stephen Clift, Tom Hunter and Kate Hunter, who have been under great pressure throughout the production of this course, but nevertheless delivered work of real quality. The striking cover designs of Richard Hoyle and Jonathan Davies speak for themselves and the artwork of Ray Munns in all five volumes has been most impressive. Paul Smith, whose recent retirement from the University will leave a very real gap, made his usual remarkable contribution in providing unusual and interesting illustrations. Giles Clark of the Copublishing Department was a constant source of encouragement and in addition his advice was always acute. Our colleagues in Project Control, especially Deborah Bywater, and in the Operations Division of the University, were far more understanding and helpful than I had any right to expect. Anne Hunt and Mary Dicker, who have been responsible for so much of the work in this Faculty over the past several years, performed to their usual exacting standards by preparing the manuscripts in this series for publication with remarkable speed and accuracy. They were very ably assisted by Chris Meeks and Doreen Pendlebury.

Pacific Studies could not have been made without the help of academic colleagues based in the UK as well as in the Asia-Pacific region. This series of books has drawn on their scholarship and their expertise but above all on their generosity. I must record my appreciation to all of them for their participation in this project. The Course Team owes an especially large debt to Dr Gerry Segal, Senior Fellow at the International Institute of Strategic Studies, who was the External Assessor of *Pacific Studies*. He was both an enthusiastic supporter of this project as well as a very shrewd critic. His wise counsel and tough advice have greatly improved the volumes in this series. It has been a pleasure to work with Professor Colin Mackerras, Director of the Key Centre for Asian Studies and Languages at Griffith University in Australia. Griffith University and the Open University have collaborated over the production of *Pacific Studies*; an arrangement that has worked extremely well. The success of this collaboration has been due in no small part to Colin. Over the past three years I have come to appreciate his many qualities particularly his immense knowledge of the Asia-Pacific region as well as his patience and courtesy in dealing with those of us who know far less. I would also like to thank all of those colleagues at Griffith who have helped to make this collaboration so successful and worthwhile, especially Professor Tony Bennett, who played a key role during the initial discussions between the two universities. Frank Gibney, President of the Pacific Basin Institute, was always available with help, advice and encouragement. It was one of the real pleasures of this project to have met and worked with Frank and the PBI. This series has also benefited considerably from the enthusiasm and insight of Victoria Smith at Routledge.

The production of *Pacific Studies* was helped greatly through the assistance of several foundations. The Daiwa Anglo-Japanese Foundation awarded this project two grants and its Director General, Christopher Everett, was a model of generosity and support. He invited the Course Team to use the attractive facilities of the Foundation; an invitation which was accepted with enthusiasm. The grant from The Great Britain Sasakawa Foundation was also greatly appreciated as was the advice, encouragement and the shrewd counsel of Peter Hand, the Administrator of the Foundation. Mr Tomoyuki Sakurai the Director of the Japan Foundation in London was always interested in the development of *Pacific Studies* and I have no doubt that this resulted in a generous grant from the Foundation. Mr Haruhisa Takeuchi, formerly Director of the Japan Information and

Cultural Centre, was most supportive during the early stages of this project and his successor at the Centre, Mr Masatoshi Muto has been no less helpful. Finally, I must record my thanks to the British Council in Australia for their assistance which was much appreciated.

Richard Maidment
Chair, *Pacific Studies*
Milton Keynes, November 1997

Asia-Pacific in the New World Order: preface

Many individuals contributed to the production of this volume. In particular we would like to thank Grahame Thompson, Bernie Eccleston, Richard Maidment and Gerald Segal for their considerable advice on numerous drafts. The authors of individual chapters proved exceptionally efficient in working to a demanding schedule and taking into account the diverse comments from the Course Team and Editors. Without Anne Hunt and Mary Dicker the final manuscript would not have been typed and presented so professionally. Stephen Clift, Tom Hunter and Kate Hunter did a marvellous job of editing individual chapters and to a very tight schedule.

During the completion of this volume both our Mothers took seriously ill and subsequently died. The volume is therefore dedicated to the memory of two rather remarkable women: Elizabeth Brook (1913–1997) and Margaret McGrew (1922–1997).

Tony McGrew
Chris Brook
Walton Hall, November 1997

Introduction

Anthony McGrew and Christopher Brook

Sealed by a dramatic public ceremony and a choreographed transfer of power the return of Hong Kong to Chinese sovereignty, on 30 June 1997, symbolized a historic moment in the West's relations with the Asia-Pacific. Not only did it represent the end of the Imperial era in East Asia but also a recognition of the Asia-Pacific's ascendance in the hierarchy of global power. Like the Petronas Towers in Kuala Lumpur, now the world's tallest buildings, the symbols of the inexorable 'rise of the Orient' constitute, for some, the arrival of the 'Asia-Pacific Century' (Fernandez-Armesto, 1995; Mahbubani, 1995). But several times this century already the Asia-Pacific idea has fallen prey to its own hubris (Korhonen, 1996). What is distinctive today, however, is the spectacular economic dynamism of the region; a dynamism which defines a historic shift in the global balance of economic power. For by the twenty-first century the Asia-Pacific will be home to the world's three largest economies: the USA, Japan, and China. In this respect understanding the contemporary global condition, and the prospects for global stability and prosperity, demand an understanding of the international politics of the Asia-Pacific. This, amongst other objectives, is a primary purpose of this volume.

To speak of the 'Asia-Pacific' is somewhat problematic since it is not so much a geographically defined entity as a 'socially constructed' one. What constitutes the 'Asia-Pacific', whether it is a coherent region, or how far it can be understood as a distinctive 'community of nations', are all deeply contested matters (Segal, 1990). Although these matters are confronted in subsequent chapters there is general agreement amongst the authors that, for most purposes, the term Asia-Pacific refers to the member countries of the forum for Asia-Pacific Economic Co-operation (APEC). Constructed in this way it embraces the countries of East Asia (North and South), the Antipodes, North America, the Pacific Islands and some Pacific Rim countries of South America (see Chapter 4, Figure 4.2). Whilst, to a degree, this constitutes a very particular ideological construction of the 'Asia-Pacific' it is one which finds great resonance in the academic and political discourses on the region.

Given this delimited focus the contributions to this volume seek to describe and explain:

- the ascendancy of the Asia-Pacific in the global political economy;

- the international and transnational politics of trans-Pacific relations;

- the dynamics of, and prospects for, growing regional co-operation; and

- the challenges the Asia-Pacific presents to the principles and form of the contemporary world order.

1   Analysis, structure and argument

In seeking to address these issues the authors draw upon a range of theoretical approaches from the study of international relations, security studies, and global political economy. Such approaches embrace *neo-realism*, *neoliberal-institutionalism*, and middle-range theories and concepts. In this context *neo-realism* is broadly interpreted as an explanatory framework which seeks to understand the Asia-Pacific through an analysis of the regional/global structure of power (both economic and military-political), power politics amongst the dominant regional actors, the primacy of the state and inter-state (intergovernmental) relations, and the dominant patterns of regional conflict and co-operation (Waltz, 1979; Buzan in Chapter 4). *Neoliberal-institutionalism* is more concerned with seeking to explain the necessary conditions for, and patterns of, trans-Pacific co-operation and collaboration, the growth of regional economic and security interdependence, the extent to which security and economic relations in the region are becoming institutionalized or managed, and therefore the degree to which such institutionalization prefigures the emergence of a Pacific 'community of nations' (Keohane, 1984; Ravenhill, 1995). Middle-range theories and concepts (for example, the *balance of power*, *co-operative security*, *strategic uncertainty*, and *strategic culture*) are also deployed in an effort to explain the dynamics of intra-regional politics and to analyse the policies of the major regional powers. In many respects the chapters reflect an evolving conversation between *neo-realism* and *neoliberal-institutionalism* so providing a common intellectual thread weaving together the concerns and subject matter of individual chapters.

The underlying narrative of the volume reflects a division into three major parts, each one presenting a discrete aspect of the Asia-Pacific story. Part 1, 'Evolution', describes the historical evolution of the international relations of the Asia-Pacific from the nineteenth century to the post-Cold War era. Part 2, 'The New Regional Order', examines the nature and dynamics of the post-Cold War regional security order and the related restructuring of the foreign and defence policies of the major (and middle-ranking) regional powers. Part 3, 'A Pacific Community?', seeks to explain the apparent intensity of regional co-operation and collaboration, whether this defines the contours of an evolving regional community of nations, and the consequent global challenges presented by the Asia-Pacific's ascendancy.

In Part 1, the three chapters chart the rise of the Asia-Pacific to global prominence and its shifting patterns of international politics in the period since the ending of the Pacific War in 1945. In the first chapter Frank Gibney offers a historical panorama of trans-Pacific relations since the late nineteenth century concentrating on US–East Asian relations. By placing contemporary developments in a historical perspective the question of whether or not contemporary trends define an emerging Pacific 'community of nations' is critically posed. Colin Mackerras contributes further to this historical picture through an examination of the shifting patterns of power politics in the Asia-Pacific from the inter-war period

Symbols of a global power shift: the Hong Kong flag is lowered for the last time during the British farewell ceremony, 30 June 1997; and the Petronas Towers, Kuala Lumpur, Malaysia

through to the end of the Cold War. He highlights the distinctive features of the contemporary configuration of power relations within the region in as much as, for the first time in modern history, regional security and stability depend overwhelmingly upon the actions and policies of the three dominant Pacific powers: the USA, Japan, and China. Finally, Javed Maswood reviews the sources of Asia-Pacific economic dynamism and the region's ascendancy in the global political economy. In analysing critically the 'Asia-Pacific century' thesis Maswood explores the regional problems and global challenges posed by the rise of the Asia-Pacific.

The chapters in Part 2 examine systematically the evolving form of the post-Cold War regional order and the changing international relations of the Asia-Pacific at the end of the 1990s. Although the USA remains a key regional actor, its hegemonic power has been eroded by the countervailing power of Japan and the People's Republic of China. The nature of power politics in the region is changing and this has significant implications for regional and global security.

Barry Buzan launches this discussion, in Chapter 4, with an exploration of the concept of 'regionness' and the question as to whether the Asia-Pacific constitutes a delimited region in the global political economy. He argues that the rhetoric of an 'Asia-Pacific region' receives only weak support when the evidence is scrutinized, while a rather stronger case can be made for a distinctive East Asian region. Even so the search for regions and regionness can lead to oversimplification. Buzan makes a case for viewing the United States of America as a global power in the Pacific rather than an Asia-Pacific power *per se*. Furthermore he argues that the USA is pursuing an anti-regional strategy towards the Asia-Pacific, obstructing the emergence of a true regional community of nations, in order to preserve American influence in East Asia as well as to prevent the emergence of rival centres of global power.

The focus of Chapter 5 is on mapping the complex web of power politics and security relations developing in the Asia-Pacific. In it Joon Num Mak explores the security dilemmas confronting core states (USA, China and Japan) as they attempt to extend, or safeguard, power and influence. Mak notes that from a military and security standpoint North-East Asia and South-East Asia appear to be following rather different paths, and uses the middle-range theory of *strategic culture* to shed light on these differences. His analysis is that North-East Asia is marked by inter-state tension and a strategic culture which places strong emphasis on military power and conflict resolution through strength. In contrast the strategic culture of South-East Asia, with the exception of the Indo-China states, appears to place more emphasis on co-operation and seeking common ground. Mak argues that such differences are also reflected in the levels and character of the arms build-up, in so far as the expansion of military capability is much greater in the North-East and the intent more hostile and reactive. Nevertheless Mak is at pains to point out that security issues in the region cannot be explained through a single theory. Indeed it is often only by utilizing a combination of theoretical 'lenses' that we can begin to perceive the complexity of relations involved.

The next five chapters focus on the interests of particular states or groupings of states. In each case there is a different set of regional interests to consider, a product of a different set of historical and regional circumstances and relationships. Chapters 6, 7 and 8 consider the three main players in post-Cold War Asia-Pacific security, Japan, China and the USA. In the first of these chapters Kenneth Pyle examines Japan's role as a potential regional hegemonic power and explores its changing relations with the USA and other regional powers. Of particular interest is the way foreign and defence policies are being reshaped to confront the post-Cold War strategic environment in the region, and the interplay between national, regional and global forces in determining its evolving 'national mission'. Pyle notes that while Japan's economic strategies are well developed and co-ordinated, its record on foreign and defence policies remains marked by caution and circumspection. While Japan has become more involved in issues of international and regional security and in its support of UN missions, such involvement often appears tentative and fragile. Also its desire to develop a more equal security partnership with the

USA remains undermined by economic tensions and constitutional barring of collective defence by the Japanese state.

The situation facing the People's Republic of China is rather different. The PRC's reforms and increasing participation in the regional and global economies have brought anticipation that it could become the dominant regional power. Its increasing military as well as economic status is much prized by the country's leaders but has also heightened fear of regional confrontation, given the PRC's declared ambition to re-establish a 'Greater China'. In Chapter 7 Denny Roy explores the PRC's growing power and regional security impact as the new millennium approaches. Roy stresses the importance to the PRC leadership of linking internal issues with external pressures and influences, and in developing a foreign policy which reflects these connections and concerns. He also examines what impact an increasingly powerful China might have on the regional security order. Does the PRC's increased status represent a threat to regional security or can its regional ambitions be pursued more benignly through international diplomacy and the power of the market? To Roy and many others this could be the most important security issue of our time.

Whatever the outcome much will depend, directly or indirectly, on the changing role and influence of the USA. In Chapter 8 Anthony McGrew examines the dynamics of US Asia-Pacific policy and its inherent contradictions. He discusses the underlying motivations and processes informing US policies towards the region and the form of post-Cold War regional order which the USA is seeking to construct. Taking issue with Buzan (Chapter 4) McGrew argues that the USA is very much an Asia-Pacific power rather than a global power in the Pacific.

In the next chapter the focus switches to what are sometimes termed 'middle powers' of the region. Here Nikki Baker examines the regional strategic interests of three states, Indonesia, Singapore and Australia. Baker shows how the notion of *strategic uncertainty* offers a purchase on the security predicaments of these three very different states. For Indonesia the principal concern is internal stability, while Singapore's uncertainty is linked more to size and location – it fears getting caught up in the internal affairs of its larger neighbours, Malaysia and Indonesia, and is concerned to maintain its strategic advantage as a trading centre. In the case of Australia the uncertainty appears more ambivalent, on the one hand there is concern to be viewed as part of the East Asian economic miracle and not as a white outpost, while the government is also anxious to strengthen US military security relations. Baker's discussion cautions against overuse of 'middle power' as a generic term; such states are marked as much by their differences as by a common character and interests.

The final chapter in Part 2 focuses on the Pacific Islands. Richard Herr stresses two themes: the search for 'unity in diversity', and the problems of micro-state sovereignty in the post-Cold War era. The Islands are marked by great ethnic and cultural heterogeneity which has been complicated further by an uneven decolonization process. Inevitably these differences have made it more difficult for Island states to co-operate in a sustained and meaningful way to confront shared issues like economic uncertainty, the growth in drug trafficking and environmental degradation. And yet their small size and vulnerability to external influence have demanded a common approach. Herr notes how support for regional initiatives in the South Pacific has come from both inside and outside the area, with Australia and New Zealand both intimately involved. However, in the post-Cold War era regional co-operation has come under increased pressure, with Western financial support less certain and Asian interests unclear on the benefits of assistance. Herr shows that the external threats to the Islands in the post-Cold War era are more complex and diffuse, while the pressure for a collective response has become greater. While many of these threats are not particular to the South Pacific, the fragility of these economies and reduced external support limit the foreign policy options available.

A key debate running through this book concerns the question of regional co-operation and the extent to which the countries of the Asia-Pacific are developing a common identity or building the foundations of a regional community. Previous chapters focused in some depth on the way security needs and issues are perceived by particular states or groupings of states. The five chapters of the final part – Part 3 – seek to explain the dynamics of regional co-operation and its implications for global relations. Here the idea that countries of the Asia-Pacific are becoming a regional community of nations is strongly contested, though the imperatives for more intensive and extensive forms of regional co-operation are growing as the region is being made 'smaller' and more interdependent in so many ways.

Underlying attempts to expand regional co-operation is a battle for regional supremacy. Regional collaboration provides opportunities for states to extend influence and increase status in the region. There is significant rivalry not only between Asia-Pacific institutions, such as APEC and ASEAN (Association of South-East Asian Nations), but also within them, as states and other interests engage in a struggle for power and influence. Accordingly, while there are strong imperatives for increased regional co-operation, there are powerful forces undermining such arrangements particularly given the increasingly competitive economic environment.

Developments in the Asia-Pacific must also be viewed in a wider world context. Economies and societies around the world are becoming more and more interconnected, and this *globalization* of affairs acts both to undermine and stimulate the development of common regional interests and identities. It undermines in the sense that the varied character and interests of Asia-Pacific states are reflected in their diverse networks of global connections and relations. Any attempt to increase regional collaboration and develop a shared identity may be resisted by groups with economic interests and cultural ties outside the Asia-Pacific.

The importance of viewing patterns of Asia-Pacific collaboration in a global context is the central theme of Chapter 11. Here Christopher Brook considers two frequently presented accounts of the emerging world order: a world carved up into a number of regional blocs; or a more global system of governance. Brook examines the degree to which developments in the region can be understood and explained in the terms of these contrasting accounts. He argues that neither account, by itself, is entirely convincing. While there are fast growing economic ties across the region, the patterning of these linkages remains very uneven and there is little practical sign of an emerging regional identity or deeper co-operation on a region-wide basis. There is also some doubt over the extent to which the Asia-Pacific is being drawn into a more global politics. The dominant globalization pressures are Western-led, as are the emerging *international regimes* of governance which attempt to manage these pressures. For many East Asian states there is unease at becoming part of a Western-inspired world order, reflected in the debate over 'Asian values' and the notion of an alternative East Asian-led globalization. It is clear that not only are the forces of regional and global integration very uneven, but each set of forces act both to promote and frustrate the development of the other.

Developing the theme of regional co-operation, Chapter 12 seeks to explain the underlying imperatives driving regionalism and the prospects for a more institutionalized system of regional co-operation and dialogue. John Ravenhill explores the increased interest in regional collaboration in the decade from 1985, when previously there had been a relative absence of such collaboration. Ravenhill draws on ideas from international relations and economics to frame his analysis, focusing on three theoretical perspectives – *economic functionalism*, *neo-realism* and *liberal-institutionalism*. He argues that increased interest in regional collaboration must be linked to changes in the wider global environment; specifically the complexities of negotiating trade liberalization at a global level (as borne out by the Uruguay Round of the General Agreement on Tariffs and Trade/World Trade Organization talks) and the security uncertainties brought by the end of the Cold War have increased the perceived utility of regional-level arrangements. That said, Ravenhill sees little sign of collaborative forums such as APEC or the ASEAN Regional Forum (ARF) being extended to a set of more institutionalized arrangements, or of the emergence of an Asia-Pacific identity.

By contrast Lawrence Woods examines the growing significance of transnational forces (non-governmental organizations) in the politics of regional co-operation and institution building. Taking a historical perspective he offers a critique of the conventional account of the role of transnational forces in the APEC 'project'. He argues that the development of transnational solidarity amongst a coalition of citizen's groups and social movements presents a direct challenge to the 'top down', inter-governmental form of regionalism promoted by APEC.

In the next chapter Michael Smith adopts an external perspective and concentrates on the European Union's attempts to construct an inter-regional dialogue and institutionalized co-operation with ASEAN. Smith examines the EU's new strategy towards the region and considers some of the issues and challenges that have arisen in developing this strategy. For instance, the EU lacks the superpower status and political coherence of the USA, and this has made it more difficult to apply leverage when trying to resolve economic tensions. Past colonial influences by countries like Britain and France have also left their mark. Smith follows Chapter 11 in setting EU–Asia-Pacific relations in a global context, exploring the influence of global economic pressures dominated by the EU–USA–Japan triangle, and the significance of global multilateral institutions. The chapter also examines the interdependent character of global networks focusing on the impact of East Asian business and investment on Europe, what Smith refers to as 'Asia-Pacific in Europe'. He concludes that relations between the EU and the Asia-Pacific are multilayered, with influences operating at a variety of intersecting levels – global, regional, and transnational.

In the final chapter Gerald Segal explores the implications of the region's development for the structure of global power relations into the twenty-first century. This draws Segal into debates over the nature of the challenge(s) brought by the region's ascendancy and what this means for the agenda and future governance of global society. A number of specific issues run through the chapter. First Segal considers the sustainability of the Asia-Pacific challenge and whether the forces promoting regional dynamism can be maintained. He draws the distinction between 'values in Asia-Pacific' and 'Asia-Pacific values' and puts the hotly contested case that the values that explain the region's economic success are not particular to Asia-Pacific society; he argues, on the contrary, that a broadly similar set of values existed in eighteenth- and nineteenth-century Atlantic societies. This provides a sharp focus for debate about the distinctiveness of Asia-Pacific cultures and how far one can conceive of East Asian dynamism as qualitatively different in character to Western development. A second issue explored by Segal is the significance of difference and diversity across the region. How reasonable is it to view East Asian economic development as a unified force constituting a single challenge to the West? On the security front Segal points to the difficulty of establishing region-wide stability given the focus by East Asian governments on more local security needs. Segal concludes by exploring some of the challenges a globally ascendant East Asia, and particularly the PRC, poses to the stability and security of Asia-Pacific and the nature of the future world order.

2   Three themes

Three organizing themes find expression in the subsequent chapters: *dynamism*, *differences*, and *disjunctures*. Each of these themes is itself reflected in the diverse literature on the Asia-Pacific and together they represent the dominant motifs of the Asia-Pacific academic discourse. As articulated here they are understood in the following terms:

- DYNAMISM – the secular process of rapid economic, social, and political transformation of the nations and economies of this region.

- DIFFERENCE – the distinctive (exceptional) forms of modernity associated with this region and its tremendous cultural, economic, and social diversity.
- DISJUNCTURES – the contradictions between the underlying socio-economic dynamism and the maintenance of regional stability and security.

Each of these themes, in different ways, is directly confronted in the following chapters. The question of whether, and in what form, the dynamism of the Asia-Pacific region signifies a shift in geopolitical terms is a key focal theme for the entire book. The sources of dynamism are introduced as is the issue of its limits. The theme of differences is reflected in the discussions about the 'Asian way' of regional co-operation and the unique configuration of power politics in the region; the question of whether the Asia-Pacific constitutes a global region; whether there are processes of regional integration taking place; and the enormous regional diversity as expressed in the regional hierarchy of power, regional economic and military inequalities. The theme of disjunctures is given expression in, amongst other issues: discussion of the economic dynamism of this region and the underlying militarization, tensions and unresolved conflicts, which threaten regional stability and security; the tensions between globalization and regionalization; and the contradictory imperatives of regional integration and regional fragmentation.

3 Conclusion

The following chapters critically explore the notion that a distinctive regional power bloc is developing linking countries bordering the Pacific, with East Asia at its core. They shed light on the complex interplay between global, regional and national forces which have transformed the Asia-Pacific arena into one of the most vibrant and economically successful regions in the world. Historical narratives alongside geopolitical and geoeconomic perspectives are deployed to examine the shifting pattern of power relations and security structures across the region, set within a wider global context. The contributions to this volume deliver substantive responses to four key questions which dominate the contemporary study of Asia-Pacific relations:

- Why is the Asia-Pacific viewed as a dynamic new power complex within the contemporary world system?
- What are the primary security problems of the region and how are these being resolved?
- Is the Asia-Pacific becoming a real community of nations?
- Does the emergence of the Asia-Pacific pose a significant challenge to existing structures of world order?

As you read and study each chapter we hope you will develop your own answers to these fundamental questions.

References

Fernandez-Armesto, F. (1995) *Millennium*, London, Bantam.

Keohane, R.O. (1984) *After Hegemony*, Princeton, Princeton University Press.

Korhonen, P. (1996) 'The Pacific age in world history', *Journal of World History*, vol.7, no.1, pp.41–70.

Mahbubani, K. (1995) 'The Pacific impulse', *Survival*, vol.37, no.3, pp.105–21.

Ravenhill, J. (1995) 'Bringing politics back in: the political economy of APEC', Third Conference on Asia-Pacific Co-operation, Seoul, South Korea.

Segal, G. (1990) *Rethinking the Pacific*, Oxford, Oxford University Press.

Waltz, K.N. (1979) *The Theory of International Politics*, Reading, Mass., Addison-Wesley.

Evolution

Pacific ties: the United States of America and an emerging 'Pacific community'?

Frank Gibney

1.1 Introduction

Since the early decades of the nineteenth century, peoples on opposite sides of the Pacific have come to regard each other with paradoxical mixtures of admiration and disgust, curiosity and aversion, spiritual selflessness and basic economic greed. Their cultural collisions have been punctuated by intermittent warfare. The threatening gunboats of Commodore Perry's black ships off the Shogun's port of Uraga, the march of US marines to capture Beijing from the Boxers and the bloody colonial struggles of American colonialists in the Philippines were climaxed with the titanic sea, air and land battles of the Second World War – only to be followed by more war in Korea and Vietnam. Yet throughout the past half century American technology acted as a spur to the world's second industrial revolution in East Asia, while American consumers stood happily in line to buy the resultant Asian products. Americans proved alternately fascinated and repelled by traditional 'exotic' Asian cultures. Yet the echo of 1776 and America's own enlightenment revolution served to inspire young Asian revolutionaries to modernize, while their intellectuals continued to deplore the assertiveness of American 'individualism'.

Historians have had an easier time analysing the centuries-long face-off of Europeans and Asians that began in the 1500s and continued up to the Second World War. The Europeans came not only as traders and missionaries. They were avowed political hegemons, with colonization as the ultimate aim of many. Through most of the twentieth century, the relationship of Europeans to Asians was that of masters to apprentices or servants. Japan's conquest of the West's colonies early in the Second World War changed this relationship for good. One way or another, however, Asians and Europeans always knew more or less where they stood. With the Americans things were different. No strangers to imperialism and colonialism themselves, they none the less preserved the strong impulses of democracy and internationalism that was their heritage as the enlightenment country. Along with the professed one-worldism of the Americans, however, came deep-rooted racial prejudices and a kind of hometown arrogance that was peculiarly offensive. Dealing with the Americans, over the decades, Asians were never quite sure which mood would predominate.

As we enter the twenty-first century, the ties across the Pacific have intensified. Geographic barriers have been significantly reduced by technology and instant communication. Intercultural contacts – or collisions – greatly increased due to successive US occupation of Asian countries and an ever rising tide of Asian emigration to the USA. If many have proclaimed the twenty-first century as the 'Asian century', it is also becoming 'America's Pacific century'. For all their Eurocentric roots, Americans have taken to the idea that their country is a Pacific power. It is no accident that American initiatives at the international Asia-Pacific Economic Co-operation (APEC) organization have succeeded the original impulses from Japan, Australia and Korea that set off the idea of the Pacific Basin. Since the 1960s, also, the United States has been the engine of growth for the so-called 'miracle economies' of East Asia. Understandably, Americans have taken the lead in demanding a 'level playing field' for exports and imports across the water, over the opposition of Asian countries, still in a development mode, where mercantilism remains a lively practice.

Cultural paradoxes abound. Even more than in Europe, young East Asians have taken to all the trappings of America's pop culture – rock, rap, blue jeans, Hollywood, television sitcoms and fast food combined. 'Pop' popularity has accelerated the backlash of Asian intelligentsia warning against the spread of materialist and 'immoral' American ideas among them. Party bosses denouncing spiritual pollution in China are not alone in this. Similarly, after the collapse of Russia, America remains the one powerful guarantor of security in Asia – at least enforcing a rather lopsided balance of power. Yet the very power of the American military has provoked reactions ranging from apathy to outright anger among various Asian populations. The triangular rivalry of China, Japan and America, has intermittently continued over the past century and a half – and nowhere more than now.

None the less, there is a cultural uncertainty about Americans – as distinguished from their European cousins – that made them more outgoing and receptive to Asian ideas of doing things. This was matched by the nervous uncertainty of two generations of Asian revolutionaries – political and economic – who were putting on the habiliments of Western democracy, science and parliamentary institutions without really having tested them for size. This double uncertainty paradoxically made for a certain comity across the Pacific.

1.2 First encounters

Americans first appeared in the Pacific in the role of the Yankee trader. Commerce and profit were the instruments that drove American clipper ships across the Pacific and inspired their merchants to set up their counting houses in southern China, on the heels of their friendly enemies, the British. In 1784, only a few years after America had become a nation-state, the 'Empress of China' dropped anchor off Canton (Guangzhou). She was the first in a long series of traders between the New England sailors and the China coast. Elias 'King' Derby from Massachusetts' old seaport Salem, who died in 1799, was only the first American to make his million in the China trade. Soon Yankee firms like Perkins and Russell were crowding into what had once been a cosy British monopoly. During the season of 1833–34, for example, some 70 American ships put in at Canton, compared with 101 vessels of British or Indian registry, with considerably lesser numbers from other European countries. The merchants were acquisitive and single-minded. As the Massachusetts expatriate Robert Bennett Forbes once observed: 'I had not come to China for health or pleasure and I should remain at my post as long as I could sell a yard of goods or buy a pound of tea'.

When British trading companies began to sell opium to China, American traders were quick to cash in on the business with their own brands. Its benefits were widely distributed. While housewives in Boston and New York filled their mantelpieces and china closets with prized items of *chinoiserie*, New England sea captains rounded the 'Horn' and sailed into the Pacific with their lethal cargoes of opium. The best families were involved. Peabodys, Russells, Forbes, Lowes and Delanos all happily shared in the take. One of the leading opium profiteers, in fact, was Warren Delano – in other respects a God-fearing Christian. The grandfather of Franklin Delano Roosevelt, he was a leading figure in the American firm of Russell and Co. 'This has been a fair, honorable and legitimate trade ... ' he once noted, 'besides all the best people did it'.

The opium trade arose from one of the first East–West trade imbalances. British traders who had established strong footholds in India had trouble selling to China. Although Chinese goods were very much in demand in Europe and the new United States, the Chinese were not really interested in buying the Manchester textiles and other products which the British and the Americans had to offer. They preferred local brands. Someone made the happy discovery, however, that the huge cakes of opium bulging the East India Company's warehouses in Patna could be sold to China at a heavy profit. It mattered not that the opium trade was illegal in China. Royal Navy squadrons came to back up the merchants. The infamous Opium War of 1841 forced the opium trade down the throats of the Chinese mandarins, and not so incidentally, gave the British Hong Kong. Most Englishmen supported this trade. It remained for a young politician named William Ewart Gladstone to denounce merchants and his government in a speech in Parliament: 'Justice in my opinion is with them and whilst they are pagans, the semi-civilized barbarians have it on their side, we the enlightened and

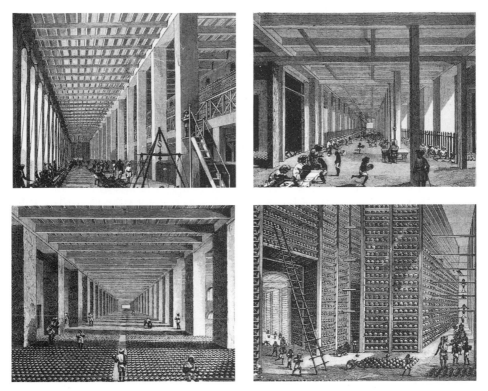

An opium factory at Patna, from left to right, top: the examining hall and balling room; bottom: the drying and stacking rooms

The Opium War: bombardment of Canton, 1840

civilized Christians are pursuing objects at variance both with justice and with religion.'

The net effect of the Opium War was to solidify a permanent anti-Western antipathy in whatever establishment was running China, one which was extended to all Europeans and Americans as well as British. This was to play a great part in the years to come, down to the present day, where the Beijing government sponsors nationalistic films highlighting the Western traders' excesses of 150 years ago.

With Americans, as with Britain, the flag followed the traders. A Pacific squadron of the American navy has existed since 1822. In the early 1800s American whalers were already wintering at Lahaina Roads in the Hawaiian Islands. By mid century, in fact, there was a substantial American colony in Honolulu with a variety of shops, taverns and inns catering to the considerable numbers of merchants, sailors and whaling men visiting what many Americans called the harbour of 'Owhyhee'.

The memorable opening of Japan by Commodore Matthew Perry in 1853 was not so much a case of early imperialism. He sailed there primarily to smooth the way for American traders. Whaling ships were particularly active in North-Eastern Pacific waters. Whaling had become an important industry. The age of steam had now begun and one of its by-products was a new demand for coaling stations for the Pacific trade. Japan then was still locked in the isolation of the Tokugawa Shogunate. American sailors shipwrecked on Japanese shores did not have a happy time of it. But Japan was known to the West as a country of coal mines as well as samurai. Perry's charter was to expand trade and secure coaling bases, along with a hospitable atmosphere for American sailors. Although his mission was avowedly a friendly one, it succeeded due to the military threat which his 'black ships' dramatized.

Other Americans now began to interest themselves in Asia. Protestant missionaries, full of zeal for spreading the gospel, were quick to think of the vast opportunities for proselytizing 'the heathen Chinese'. In 1820 a group of Congregational missionaries, fresh out of Boston, landed in Honolulu. A few years later, the Reverend Peter Parker MD, opened hospitals for the 'natives' at Canton and Macau. There was a good bit of the missionary urge in Perry's mission as well. He brought with him various products of current American civilization – a small steam locomotive among them – in his zeal to teach the Japanese something of American culture.

The move westward had another impetus. The discovery of gold in California in the mid nineteenth century impelled a vast westward migration of amateur miners, business entrepreneurs and others. The Gold Rush added to the maritime traffic around Cape Horn and into the Pacific, making the entire country aware of its Pacific future. In the years to come, confident Christian missionaries expanded their bridgeheads in Hawaii and China, their mission now to convert the 'masses' of the East on their home grounds. Perry may have opened Japan by the implied threat of his gunboats – the 'black ships' quickly became famous in Japanese pictures and stories. Americans, however, were slow to establish the kind of political colonialism widely practised by the Europeans.

Pacific sea-faring become popular, and in the best tradition, trade furthered technology. With business expanding, a ship's speedy turn-around time meant money. To meet this pressure New England designers developed the clipper ship. With its sleek hull and expanded sail area, the clipper could beat normal sailing times by more than a third. Some could make from 17 to 20 knots with the right winds. The far-ranging clippers helped build a new mystique of the Pacific in the American mind. Its laureates were Herman Melville, who dramatized its romance and harsh-ness in books like *Moby Dick* and *Typee*, and the more prosaic Richard Henry Dana (*Two Years Before the Mast*). As early as the 1850s the newly crowded harbour of San Francisco was hailed as 'the sole emporium of a new world, the awakened Pacific'.

One American initiative brought dramatic, if unexpected results. Perry's arrival in Japan was the catalyst for that most remarkable and unique of self-modernizations, the Meiji Restoration. Meiji was more a cultural revolution than the proclaimed 'restoration' of imperial power. The men who restored the Meiji emperor to power – mostly young samurai bureaucrats who worked in Japan's clan (han) capitals – were activated by a threat and a promise. The threat was obvious and it went far beyond Perry. By the mid nineteenth century Europeans were setting up their 'treaty ports' as independent enclaves in China. Japanese visiting Shanghai were shocked at the subservience of Chinese to European merchants, soldiers and officials. Japan's first order of business, as they saw it, was to arm itself. But to get the guns one had to have foundries and steel mills and banks. Step-by-step the young reformers found themselves drawn into an enforced modernization of their country.

The American role in Japan's early modernization was prompted by idealism as well as expediency. Teachers, technical experts and missionaries followed Commodore Perry, who displayed a good bit of teaching zeal himself. From that early day the Americans came to be known as 'the people to learn from'. But the Japanese – quick, adaptive learners – soon wanted to take over teaching and technology themselves.

From the late nineteenth century there developed a curious ambiv-alence of feeling between Japan and America which has continued to this day. Japanese troops had marched with the other 'allied' Western contin-gents when the foreigners invaded Beijing to quell the Dowager Empress's anti-foreign Boxer Rebellion. By 1905, with its victory over the Russians, Japan had established itself as one of the big world powers. It is significant that Americans were largely supportive of Japan in that conflict. President Theodore Roosevelt, in fact, offered services as an arbitrator between the two countries. The treaty that ended the Russo-Japanese War was signed in Portsmouth, New Hampshire.

Although the Japanese had won militarily, Japan's statesmen realized that they lacked the economic resources to continue the fighting much longer. So they were quietly grateful for American intervention. On the other hand, the Japanese public, influenced by its new popular press, were quick to denounce the Americans for their rude 'interference'. Such shifts of opinion were to come often on both sides of the ocean.

1.3   The USA: a Pacific power

At the beginning of the twentieth century, the United States of America had established itself as a Pacific power. The Hawaiian Islands were first taken over as an American protectorate and then finally annexed by the Republic in 1898. The annexation of Hawaii was bitterly resisted by many Americans as an undemocratic intrusion on the lives of the people there – which it certainly was. In general, the Democrats were opposed; Grover Cleveland refused to sanction the annexation while he was President. William McKinley did; and after McKinley won a second term in 1900, defeating William Jennings Bryan, a strong anti-imperialist, annexation of the newly conquered Philippines followed. Just after the turn of the century, American warships and troop transports were landed in the Philippines to suppress the local independence movement that had briefly succeeded Spanish rule. American colonialism had begun.

In the autumn of 1892, a young University of Wisconsin history professor named Frederick Jackson Turner put the finishing touches on the draft of a paper he was going to read at a scholarly meeting the following year. Its title was *The Significance of the Frontier in American History*. Its theme was to become a classic: that the constant westward expansion of Americans, taming new frontiers as they went, had played a major part in shaping the national character and building the national society. 'It is to the frontier', Turner wrote,

> that the American intellect owes its striking characteristics. That coarseness of strength combined with acuteness and acquisitiveness, that practical and inventive turn of mind, quick to find expedience ... that masterful grasp of material things, lacking in the artistic but powerful to effect great ends, that restless, nervous energy, that dominant individualism working for good and for evil ...

(Turner, 1920)

Turner argued that the whole national character was built up on the pioneer premise – there was always land, work and adventure to be had by mining the west. By the time he wrote, national boundaries had long since reached the Pacific. The physical frontier – the frontier of the Wild West and the covered wagon – was no longer available. Turner was right and he was wrong. He was right about the power of the frontier mystique, but wrong about its closure. In fact, just as he was drafting his paper, forces were at work which were to push the frontier further westward across the Pacific.

Within ten years after Turner wrote his essay, the USA had formally annexed the Hawaiian Islands, and further to the west, American Samoa. The Philippine Islands were added in 1899 along with Puerto Rico and

Guam, as US possessions, following America's victory in the Spanish American War. In 1902, Congress passed legislation authorizing the government to build a canal across the isthmus of Panama.

After belatedly joining the European powers and Japan, American imperialism was aggressively on the march through the Pacific. In fact, the early Pacific strategy of Commodore Perry and the Boston merchants in Canton had been temporarily interrupted only by the Civil War. William Seward, Lincoln's Secretary of State, and a strong Pacific power advocate, had purchased Alaska from Russia in 1867 as part of a policy that was far ahead of its time. The same chauvinistic 1840s idea of 'Manifest Destiny' which was used to justify the war with Mexico, now widened its scope. By the early 1900s three prime factors were apparent in this gathering American expansionism:

1   the urge to trade;

2   the missionary urge to convert (and 'westernize'); and

3   latest of all, the urge to dominate as a colonial power.

'The Philippines are ours forever', the prominent Indiana Republican, Senator Albert Beveridge, orated in 1898, 'and just beyond the Philippines are China's illimitable markets. We will not retreat from either ... the Pacific is our ocean ... and the Pacific is the ocean of the commerce of the future'.

Powerful dissenters continued to denounce the new imperialism. Against Democratic opposition, Republicans were barely able to get the annexation of the Philippines through the Senate. Prominent non-political Americans attacked territorial expansion – President Charles Eliot of Harvard among them – just as Gladstone had denounced the British incursion in the Opium War 75 years before.

Two people were primarily responsible for heading America into the Pacific: a studious navy captain named Alfred Thayer Mahan and an up-and-coming politician named Theodore Roosevelt. Mahan, who later became head of the US Naval War College, was an intense student of naval history. With his book, *The Influence of Sea Power on World History*, he became for naval strategy what Karl von Clausewitz had been to the military. To Mahan, mastery of the seas meant control of commerce and with it, political hegemony.

No one was more attracted to his new ideas than Theodore Roosevelt. As Assistant Secretary of the Navy, Roosevelt had personally ordered Admiral Dewey on to Manila at the beginning of the Spanish American War. He was thus directly responsible for the American victory there. As President, Roosevelt developed a methodical policy of advancing American interests by sea power: 'The guns of our warships', he said, 'have awakened us to new duties'. He more than justified Mahan's hopes for an immediate navy build up. In 1903 he strong-armed Colombia into accepting the independence of Panama – and Panama into accepting an American-owned canal zone for his cherished route across the isthmus. The canal, opened finally in 1914, became the indispensable artery for the American's two-ocean navy.

Acquisition of the Philippines, however, proved to be a very bloody undertaking. American troops fought for years before Filipino fighters under General Emilio Aguinaldo, who wanted independence, not American annexation, finally surrendered. The Americans then studiously trumpeted the new 'Open Door Policy' towards China. First enunciated by Secretary of State John Hay in 1900, the Open Door Policy insisted that no foreign country should set itself up as a colonial occupier in China, leaving that country free to trade with anyone – Americans principally – who wished to do so.

Hay's Open Door Policy was little more than a restatement of past American initiatives to keep the trade lanes open. As the historian, Tyler Dennett (1922) once wrote, 'the corollary of the Open Door Policy was to promote an Asia strong enough to be its own door keeper'. This policy was strictly economic. There was almost no political or military bite behind the American traders' bark. For most of the nineteenth century, this 'economics first' policy sheltered in the lee of the political power represented by the British fleet in Asian waters and the obvious strength of the European colonial powers. Ironically enough, the American Pacific role in the nineteenth century most strikingly prefigured that of 'economics only' Japan in the latter part of the twentieth. The political cover in Japan's case was supplied by American sea and air power.

With 'pacification' of the Philippines almost complete, Roosevelt proceeded on a huge naval build up. By 1907, when he dispatched the 'Great White Fleet' on its 'round the world cruise', the USA was recognized as a leading naval power. Roosevelt was the first American statesman to appreciate the growing strategic importance of Japan, a country he alternately feared and admired. With the callous hand of a veteran big power diplomat, he gave Japan a free hand in Korea in return for Japan's acquiescence in American dominion over the Philippines. In 1907, the resultant Root–Takahira Agreement, which stabilized Japanese–American relations in Asia, guaranteed unrestricted commerce with East Asia, China included, for the next 15 years.

For the average American, however, East Asia still remained a series of odd remote countries and colonies. The American colony in the Philippines finally achieved some form of stability – and was promised independence before the beginning of the Second World War. The Americans behaved in many ways like the European colonial powers. American business domination of the Philippines economy, for example, was quite thorough. Yet it had its own peculiar characteristics. For one, Americans determinedly tried to educate the Filipinos. Even though the children were brought up on American school books – hardly suitable to their background and area – the Philippines developed into a comparatively literate Asian country. Widespread education and the promise of independence was one reason why the majority of Filipinos – in contrast to Indonesians, Vietnamese and

Malaysians, resisted the Japanese invasion and stayed on the American side throughout the war.

1.4   The impact of the world wars

After Roosevelt left the presidency in 1909, Americans tended to concentrate on domestic affairs. There was at first no enthusiasm for entering the First World War, which Americans quite understandably considered Europe's problem. The Democrat Woodrow Wilson, elected President in 1912, helped win re-election in 1916 with the slogan, 'He kept us out of war'. Ironically, Wilson's indignation at Germany's unrestricted submarine warfare against commerce proved a major factor in American entry into the war in 1917.

Wilson, an idealistic internationalist, assumed a dominant role in the 1919 Versailles peace negotiations, advocating a 'peace without victory' and self-determination for all peoples. His lofty proposals, however, were frustrated by the strong nationalism of the European victors, especially the French, and he was forced to give ground on his principles. Japan was allowed to keep its gains in the Shandong Peninsula at the expense of China and tacitly confirmed in its occupation of Korea by the other colonial powers. Although European concerns dominated the peace conference, the colonialism supported by the majority of victors left deep scars in Asia. The May Fourth movement in China and the March First independence demonstrations in Korea – both took place in 1919 – were reactions against Versailles' denial of self-determination rights in Asia. The refusal of the powers to ratify a clause in the Treaty against Racial Discrimination – proposed by Japan – added to Asia's ill feelings.

The League of Nations, designed by Wilson as a plan to guarantee world security, was adopted with many reservations by the Allied Powers, but in the end refused ratification by the US Senate in 1920. Wilson's internationalism was thus denounced and side-tracked by his largely Republican opposition. The defeat of the League marked the high-tide of internationalist sentiment in the USA. Under his successor Warren Harding, Americans returned to their pre-war isolationism. The country as a whole remained for two decades largely 'isolationist', equally immune to the appeal of Wilsonian 'one-worldism' and Theodore Roosevelt's balance-of-power imperialism. While American statesmen, for example, continued to denounce Japan's militarist assault on China in the 1930s, it became obvious to all concerned that the Open Door Policy lacked any enforcement or will power.

There remained a colonialist condescension in the American attitude toward Asian peoples. William Howard Taft served as governor general of the Philippines before becoming President in 1909. It was he who coined the phrase, 'our little brown brothers' – his words aptly summarizing the curious mixture of paternalism and condescension with which America governed its few colonies. American colonialists, however, were somewhat more concerned than the British, French or, certainly, the Dutch, in their feelings of some obligation toward their charges. And with all its faults, the American occupation of the Philippines was a contrast to the brutal Japanese colonization of Korea, begun after Japan's success in the Russo-Japanese War.

After Hitler's rise in Germany, with the Second World War increasingly imminent, another Roosevelt, Franklin D. – like his cousin an internationalist and 'big navy' man – tried to arouse the US public from its complacency. Now alarmed by the gathering aggression of General Hideki Tojo's Japan as well as the strength of Nazism in Europe, the Roosevelt Administration repeatedly warned Japan against extending its incursions into South-East Asia as well as China. To the Tokyo leadership, the American and Allied Powers' embargo on oil shipments to Japan was an incitement to war. None the less it took the Japanese attack on Pearl Harbor to end isolationist sentiment in the USA.

With the Second World War, a generation of young Americans went off to battle, their anxious families knowing only that they would be 'somewhere in the Pacific'. Once unknown names now filled the American map – Bataan and Midway, Guadalcanal, Tarawa, Port Moresby and the Burma Road (see **Eccleston et al., 1998**). Then, as US forces pushed westward, Leyte, Saipan, Iwo Jima and Okinawa came into the news. In the end Hiroshima and Nagasaki were partly obliterated by the A-bomb. Tokyo was barely visible through the haze of B29 carpet bombing.

While the war in Europe was intensified by the horrors of Nazism and the concentration camps, the Pacific War had a peculiar savagery of its own. It was a war in which few prisoners were taken. It began with the tactically unsuspected (but strategically logical) 'sneak attack' on Pearl

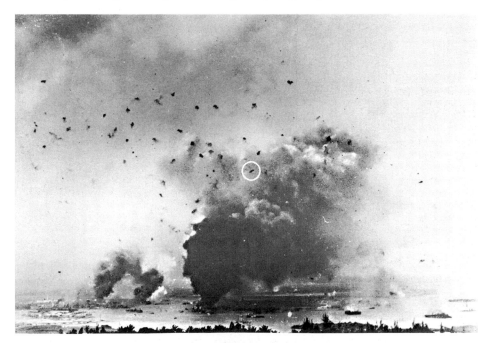

A US Navy photograph of the Japanese attack on Pearl Harbor, 7 December 1941

Harbor by the carriers of Japan's Combined Fleet. (Interestingly enough, the surprise attack in 1941 strongly resembled the earlier attack which Japanese navy units had made on the Russian Asiatic fleet off Port Arthur at the beginning of the Russo-Japanese War.) Japan's instant apparent success at Pearl Harbor barely concealed a long-term blunder. For by concentrating his attack on 'battleship row' – the major American carriers were off on manoeuvres – and over cautiously calling a second strike back after the first had succeeded, Admiral Chuichi Nagumo neglected to bomb the huge oil reserve tanks in Hawaii. Their loss would have held back the American fleet for a far longer period.

The sheer competence of the surprise attack served to inflame Americans more. So did stories of Japanese atrocities on the Bataan Death March after Japanese troops had defeated American forces in the Philippines. Early in the war, enough information leaked out to show the purposeful cruelty of the Japanese military toward British, American and Australian prisoners, not to mention the helpless civilian non-combatants in the Asian countries Japan invaded. Actually, Japanese troops of an earlier generation had behaved well toward their enemies and conquered populations, both in the Russo-Japanese War and during Japan's intervention in the Boxer Rebellion at the turn of the century in China. But attitudes had changed radically during the unbridled ascendancy of the Japanese militarists. Throughout the 1930s, the officers' cliques – who dramatized their rise to power by the assassination of some of Japan's most prominent civilian leaders – foisted on the Japanese people a single-minded devotion to the reconstituted ideals of Bushido and the so-called 'samurai spirit'. This left no room for even the conventional mercies of the Geneva Convention.

Japanese wartime atrocities rekindled a streak of racism in the popular American psyche. For all the pious talk about converting the heathen and the very real good works of the missionaries, racial prejudice remained a constant factor. It had its roots in the mid nineteenth century. Thousands of poor Chinese had emigrated to the USA, to work under virtual slave conditions building the transcontinental railroads. (The very word 'coolie' is an Anglicization of the Chinese *kuli*, meaning 'hard labour'.) The Chinese were poor and uneducated. Totally alien to their surroundings, their only wish was to return to their families in China with their savings. Generally unable to communicate in English, they soon became the target for the most vicious kind of American nativism. They were beaten, robbed and even lynched by American mobs. In San Francisco a local political party was organized with the battle cry, 'the Chinese must go!' Labour union bosses, worried about cheap competition, denounced all 'Orientals'. In 1882, Congress passed the infamous Chinese Exclusion Act, following a California state election with a heavy pro-exclusion vote.

After the First World War, however, it was Japan's increasing power and prominence that drew the indignation of American racists. As with the Chinese, the ill feeling was raised by Japanese emigration to the west coast of the USA. This was seen as a threat to American labour – not to mention 'cherished' American institutions. As with the Chinese before them, San

Francisco became the centre of anti-Japanese agitation. President Theodore Roosevelt endeavoured, unsuccessfully, to persuade local school boards in California to nullify or at least abridge their prohibitions against enrolling Japanese children. From the street gangs in San Francisco to state legislators in Sacramento, the word was out to 'get the Japs'.

On 1 July 1924, both the US House of Representatives and the Senate overwhelmingly passed a restrictive immigration bill, incorporating an exclusion clause specifically directed against Japan. The weight of opinion in favour of exclusion was heavily regional. (While 80 per cent of west coast newspapers came out for exclusion, only 5 per cent of eastern editorialists were so disposed.) Yet few legislators in Washington felt strongly about opposing it.

For their part the Japanese had developed a considerable head of anti-American steam. Their exports were hopelessly at the mercy of American consumers. The US Depression of 1929 and the early 1930s devastated the silk industry, then Japan's principal overseas earner. America's record of anti-Japanese immigration policies was readily exploited by Japan's nationalists, who scornfully contrasted them with Washington's moral preachments against Japan's advances into China.

All of this stored prejudice inflamed people on both sides of the Pacific. As the war progressed, all Americans wanted was to avenge Pearl Harbor and Bataan. The ingenuity and hustle of the Yankee trader now went into the manufacture of guns, tanks and aeroplanes. The tension of the past four decades between America's 'moral universalism and political parochialism' as Akira Iriye (1967) trenchantly put it, no longer existed. At the start of the Second World War, some 120,000 Japanese-Americans on the US west coast were rounded up and bundled into 'relocation centres' that were little more

Japanese-Americans arrive at the Alien Reception Center, Manzanar, California, March 1942

than concentration camps. This was done allegedly for security reasons. (By contrast, nothing whatsoever was done to restrict recent immigrants from Italy or Germany in similar situations.) Hardly anyone protested against the wrongs done to these people, almost all of them, as they proved to be, loyal Americans.

Throughout the war, Japan's military behaved atrociously. No amount of post-war Japanese 'revisionist' explanation can erase the horrors of the Bataan Death March and the Burma Railway, the *kempeitai* tortures in Manila's Fort Santiago and Singapore's Changi Jail, the brutal slaughter of Chinese and other Asian civilians, the exploitation of Korean and Indonesian forced labourers or the beheadings of captured American airmen. Americans reacted in kind. Later, the massive fire-bombings of Tokyo and other major cities, worse than the A-bombs in their toll of Japanese civilians, were atrocities of their own.

From a military point of view, the Second World War held some valuable lessons. Mahan's theories about the strategic importance of sea power – now supplemented by air power – were graphically borne out by the American counter attack across the Pacific. The steady 'island hopping' reduction of Japanese strongholds by amphibious invasion would have been impossible without the naval and air supremacy which a rearmed US fleet gradually secured. The Battle of Midway in 1942 was the turning point of the war. There a contemplated Japanese invasion was smashed by American carrier planes, with heavy losses on both sides. It was followed shortly thereafter by American forces, supplied from Australia, landing on Guadalcanal. With Douglas MacArthur, rescued from his shattered Philippine proconsulship, available to lead them, American ground forces began a steady march northward.

America's once piecemeal support of the Chinese now also became a wartime alliance. Although China's Nationalist (Kuomintang) government under Chiang Kai-shek had been forced back deep into the Chinese hinterland, Americans gave what assistance they could. Fighting wide-spread national corruption, General Joseph Stillwell tried with varying degrees of success to equip a new Chinese army. Elements of this army fought against the Japanese in Burma. Ultimately, MacArthur invaded the Philippines. At the end of the war, after the successful capture of Okinawa, a Japanese home prefecture, US army and marine forces were poised for the invasion of the Japanese home islands. For all the ground fighting, the issue in the end was decided by Admiral Nimitz's planes and ships. After overwhelming American sea and air power had nullified Japan's early naval advantages, the US submarine fleet effectively isolated Japan in a blockade that ultimately saw ships being sent to the bottom within sight of the Japanese home islands.

Although Britain, Australia and New Zealand participated as much as they could, the Pacific War was essentially an American show. The first Japanese successes permanently destroyed the illusion of superiority once flaunted by the European colonialists. Even after the Allied victory, colonial relationships stayed shattered. Indeed, wartime exigencies even destroyed the basic dependence of Australia on the United Kingdom. Americans used Australia as a base for their Pacific counterattacks – MacArthur was universally welcomed as the saviour of Australia as well as the Philippines.

With the end of the war, Americans were faced with a curious set of contradictions. Should the USA act as the harbinger and exemplar of democracy throughout East Asia – buttressed by the Christianity which Americans had long begun to export to China, Korea and other Asian countries? Or should America hold firm with its European allies and help shore up the damaged bastions of white supremacy in East Asia? The answer was a ragged compromise, which satisfied few.

1.5 Pax Americana

After first supporting the returning Dutch, the Americans gradually put heavy pressure on them to deliver the East Indies to the newly independent government of Indonesia. It was America's threat of withdrawing Marshall Plan aid that finally forced the Dutch to cede the territory back to the Indonesians. First American contacts with Vietnam seemed rather promising. Office of Strategic Services' officers brought aid and advice to Ho Chi Minh's newly energized Viet Minh revolutionaries. There was little sympathy with French efforts to re-conquer their Indo-Chinese colonies. If Franklin D. Roosevelt had lived, this anti-colonialism might have become a firmer American policy. In the event, however, Americans remained faithful to what they felt was their major European commitments. Although rejecting French demands for US carrier aircraft to save the beleaguered base at Dien Bien Phu in 1954, the USA none the less pitched in on the side of French colonialism. Ultimately, to the country's later regret, they replaced the French as principal antagonists of revolutionary (and communist) Vietnam.

In Korea, a Japanese colony for 40 years, Japan's defeat in 1945 brought an uneasy partition between the Soviet Union and the USA. To no one's surprise, the Soviet occupiers moved quickly to communize their occupation zone in the north. They set up a Korean protégé, Kim Il Sung, as a virtual dictator. The Americans, who knew little or nothing about the country, occupied Korea south of the 38th parallel. There the ham-handed efforts of an inept US military government to further Korean independence resulted in a country far less prepared than it might have been to resist the communist invasion which came in 1950.

In Japan, by contrast, the American mixture of power and democracy largely worked. The US occupation of Japan, with the imperious military leader Douglas MacArthur as its proconsul, accomplished what many Japanese regarded as a 'second opening' of their country, in which the earlier promise of the Meiji modernization was revived.

After Japan's Meiji Restoration of 1868, a tense if partly sub-surface battle had taken place between reformers who wanted Japan to become a true parliamentary democracy – and there were many – and traditionalists who wanted Japan to become a militarist, emperor-worshipping colonial power. The young samurai bureaucrats who provoked Meiji's cultural revolution were themselves divided. There was a huge gap between the militarism of General Aritomo Yamagata and the populism of men like Taisuke Itagaki and Yukichi Fukuzawa. Japan did enjoy a brief period of democratic rule in the 1920s. The so-called 'Taisho Democracy', did not last, however. The hardliners ultimately won; and with the 1930s annexation of Manchuria, Japan's China War began.

The post-1945 US occupation was at first designed merely to demilitarize Japan. It went on to produce something like a rebirth of democracy. Considerable preparation lay behind this policy. In contrast to the neglect of other areas of Asia, staff officers and other area experts in Washington had worked on plans for a Japanese occupation throughout the Second World War. When MacArthur landed at Atsugi airport, he had more than a blueprint to go on. A group of relatively young 'new dealers' from the USA, working under the authority of the Supreme Commander of the Allied Powers, took over the governance of Japan. A new constitution with its famous anti-war clause, Article 9, was written for the Japanese. It included sweeping guarantees of human rights – including women's suffrage – that the Japanese had never enjoyed before. Occupation-dictated labour laws favoured the development of a Japanese trade union movement. Land reform set the agricultural economy on its feet, albeit with considerable hardship to landowners whose lands were expropriated.

Later, as the Cold War with international communism intensified, a 'reverse course' set in. Washington became more anxious to develop an economically sound – and anti-communist – Japan than to foster a Japanese American-style democracy. Yet many of the early reforms remained. They included, most significantly, the MacArthur Constitution. Along with them came a Security Treaty in which the USA undertook to defend Japan, with the implicit promise that Japanese political and diplomatic policy would faithfully follow America. The Security Treaty was a product of the Cold War. Its *de facto* alliance terms conflicted with the American-inspired anti-war constitution. None the less, the Security Treaty acted for many years as a source of regional stability. Despite the capture of the Chinese mainland by Mao Zedong's communists in 1949, American sea and air power remained the arbiter of the Pacific.

It is ironic that for 30 years into the so-called 'post-war' period in Asia, the USA was involved in two major wars: Korea and Vietnam. Both exploded because of the deepening Cold War antagonisms between the USA and the then Soviet Union, but their intensity was fuelled by bitter cross currents left over from the colonial regimes of the past century. North Korea's invasion of South Korea (the Republic of Korea) on 25 June 1950, was the result of two miscalculations. The first was the American failure to set the Republic of Korea solidly within the US strategic sphere of influence. The second, which resulted from the first, was the ill-advised gamble of Kim Il Sung, by then solidly entrenched in power. Kim calculated that his Soviet-trained troops could overwhelm the badly prepared army of the

South in a lightening attack, without risking American interference or retaliation. Kim first convinced the ever-cautious Josef Stalin to support his intervention in a limited way – because it seemed sure of success. He gained the further support of Mao Zedong. Fresh from his victory over the US-supplied Nationalists, Mao wanted Americans out of Asia on principle.

After a series of embarrassing reverses, a revitalized Eighth Army under General Matthew Ridgeway recaptured Seoul and stood poised to roll back the communist advance even further. The American public was growing war-weary, however, following the campaign promises of President-elect Dwight Eisenhower: 'I shall go to Korea' – with the implied prospect of peace. The USA and its UN allies agreed to a cease fire along a line only slightly north of the original 38th parallel boundary between the North and South. This decision seemed admirable at the time, but it left the South Korean capital of Seoul perilously close to a border which North Korea increasingly fortified. Kim Il Sung's singular dictatorship, its army now revived, grew more belligerent, with continuing acts of armed provocation. Thus the threat of a second invasion constantly hung over the economically recovering country to the south.

The USA went to war in Vietnam in the mid 1960s through a series of miscalculations. On a debatable premise – the so-called 'domino' theory that one East Asian country falling to communism would provoke the rise of communism in its neighbours – the Johnson Administration began to commit sizeable numbers of US troops. For it soon became clear that the South Vietnamese were unable to cope with the southern Viet Cong rebels – who were led, supplied and reinforced from the communist North.

The American military now intervened in force, albeit limited by concerns that taking the war north would provoke retaliation from both China and the USSR. US troop strength soared to 500,000 by 1968. Yet it was not enough to secure the Republic of Vietnam against an increasingly competent and dedicated enemy. Following the widely publicized 'Tet' offensive of 1968 (in which, contrary to general American belief, the invading North Vietnamese suffered near crippling losses), American distaste for the war mounted a veritable tidal wave of anti-war public opinion. This produced profound domestic repercussions in the USA. Unable to sustain an unpopular and not very competently waged war, the USA ultimately evacuated Vietnam in 1973 after a dubious truce was made with the communists. The truce was later broken by a final invasion from the North, which unified the country under the communist regime.

Despite the communist victory in Vietnam the 'domino' drop did not occur. If it did, it happened in reverse. The six nations of ASEAN (Association of South-East Asian Nations) developed stable and determinedly anti-communist regimes – their long-standing union impelled originally by fear of Vietnamese communists. In addition the American overtures to China in 1972 by President Richard Nixon, welcomed by an ailing and anti-Soviet Mao Zedong, more or less stabilized the situation. Later, Chinese troops clashed with Vietnamese in an intra-communist struggle. The sea and air power of the US Seventh Fleet, backed by American strategic military reserves, remained the arbiter of security in East Asia. It was buttressed by the post-war Japan–US security treaty – renewed in 1960 and thereafter – whereby the USA agreed to intervene in any attack on Japan.

1.6 The Asia-Pacific economic miracle

Even as the Vietnam fighting went on, however, the focus of American–East Asian relations had turned to trade and investment. Freed from political responsibilities – for most of the century, Japanese diplomacy meekly followed the American initiative – Japan turned its attention wholeheartedly to business. Spearheaded by extraordinary technology and leadership in the electronics and automotive sectors, Japanese sales people found willing customers in the USA and, to a lesser extent, in Europe, South-East Asia and the rest of the world. Japan's trade balances soared, while US imbalances went ever deeper into the red. American business people became increasingly restive, demanding a 'level playing field' against a Japan dominated by an aggressive industrial policy forged in an alliance of business and bureaucracy. However, the trade-off of Japanese Cold War political support for America's economic passivity remained in place until well into the 1980s. Meanwhile, Japanese competition proved a useful, if very abrasive, remedy for an American industry which had grown flabby with post-war success in the 1950s and 1960s.

A succession of US trade representatives, backed more or less intensely by their Presidents, pounded on the doors of Japanese protectionism. By the 1980s, however, American and Japanese business had become hopelessly intertwined. Meanwhile Japan's huge trade surpluses had made this country an international arbiter in investment. By 1996 fully 60 per cent of the world's investment capital came from Japan. Japanese investors continued to own a great deal of the US government debt, which had multiplied under the Reagan Administration.

By the mid 1990s the Pacific economic pattern had rearranged itself. The enforced liberalization of the Japanese economy rendered the old rule of the bureaucracy far less stable. Worried about 'Japan bashing' and other US protectionist tendencies, as well as the increasingly high labour costs in Japan's affluent society, Japanese companies began to move manufacturing to the USA as well as to other countries in South-East Asia and Europe. American state governments, in turn, vied eagerly to secure new Japanese plant investments – which meant additional jobs to their citizens.

As the century nears its end, many of Japan's competitive practices remained in place, particularly its restrictive protectionism through non-tariff barriers. Having caught up with the rest of the advanced nations, however, Japan has become part of an international economy. Nor was the USA any longer either able or willing to practice the counter-protectionism, as typified by the 'Nixon shock', of bans on various Japanese exports in the 1960s.

A major new actor had emerged in the Asia-Pacific region – economic, political and strategic. Basing his policy on the Four Modernizations he had once sponsored with Zhou Enlai, Deng Xiaoping, China's new communist leader, had solidified his power by 1981. Deng did away with the Maoist tyrannies of the Cultural Revolution and ostentatiously opened China to the world. Beginning in the 1980s, American companies began to move into China in what for a time seemed a feeding frenzy. Business people jostled one another in the rush to provide consumer goods to China's billion plus potential customers. By the 1990s, firms trading and investing in China had vastly expanded their bridgeheads. Not so incidentally, they formed a strong pressure bloc advocating the expansion of trade with China, whatever problems the USA might have had with human rights violations by China's still hardline communist government.

The conflict between trade profits and democratic advocacy was dramatized and exacerbated by the June 1989 massacre of student demonstrators and workers at Beijing's Tiananmen Square. Deng Xiaoping had personally ordered the People's Liberation Army troops to fire on the crowds, fearful of the chaos that would result from this obvious threat to party rule. Despite the wave of revulsion that filled the USA from viewing television images of tanks confronting students in the Beijing streets, American businesses once more rallied to the support of a new 'open door' policy in dealing with the Chinese. Deng later swung back into action with a last dramatic appeal for an expanded free (or almost free) economy.

By the late 1990s, America's trade deficit with China had risen close to that with Japan, and China's nervous post-Deng succession of communist leaders, unlike the Japanese, proved harshly resistant to American pressure for human rights freedoms. China's belligerence toward Taiwan typified a new hardness of policy. Following the election of Taiwan's first native Taiwanese President, Lee Teng Hui in 1996, the People's Liberation Army actually staged several provocative test missile firings in the Taiwan Straits, threatening an invasion if there was any obstacle to the reunification of China – Taiwan included – on Beijing's terms. This forced the USA to send two aircraft carriers to the area.

While this had a dampening effect on Chinese belligerence towards Taiwan it dramatized, as little else could, the conflicts between America's role in East Asia. For all the successes of the Yankee trader and investor in East Asia – coupled with the satisfaction of American consumers of Japanese, Chinese and other East Asian goods – the image of the USA as defender, instigator and supporter of democracy and human rights did not fade. The Clinton Administration vacillated between demands that China observe the rule of law and emphasis on augmenting trade relations. This reflected a deep division within the American public, for American democracy had played just as big a role in East Asia's development as economic relationships.

Since the mid 1980s a rising Asian middle class, justifying the predictions of many American scholars and political observers, had demanded an increasing share of its own government. The mass demonstrations in Manila in 1986 and Seoul in 1987 toppled the Marcos dictatorship in the Philippines and enforced a relaxation of the semi-military government of South Korea in the direction of an honest parliamentary democracy. The same could be said of Taiwan. Before his death, Chiang Kai-shek's son, Chiang Ching-kuo had revoked the martial law that was a legacy of the Kuomintang's forcible occupation of Taiwan in 1947. Taiwan greatly expanded popular freedoms; and what was once a rigid one-party government had become an effective, if noisy democracy. The same tendency was observable elsewhere. In Thailand, popular indignation forced at least a relaxation of the once powerful military government, while in Indonesia similar pressures began to work against the continuance of the Suharto 'velvet glove' dictatorship.

None the less, the challenges of democratization – and political succession – were pressing. America remained 'the country to learn from'. There was no better statistic in support of this than the fact that almost all of China's communist ruling hierarchy sent its children to the USA for their college education (including Deng Xiaoping's own children). Still, many Asian students grew increasingly strong in their insistence that how they applied the lessons America had to teach was strictly their own affair. China's insistence that autocratic rule of its communist hierarchy need not be any handicap to economic expansion, ran directly counter to long-standing American tradition and prejudice. In addition, the dictatorship of Lee Kuan Yew in Singapore and his spirited defence of 'Asian values' attempted to draw the line between the 'unbridled individualism' of the Americans and Asian populations who were allegedly content under authoritarian rule, as long as the economy was good. This conflict has yet to be solved. Despite the apparent economic prosperity of the Asian 'miracle economies', many Americans were worried not merely by China's growing belligerence but by the prospect of a clouded future after Hong Kong was returned to communist rule.

1.7 A Pacific community?

Two forces were at work as the end of the century came. They had dominated the world for some years. The first was the extraordinarily contagious effect of what one might call techno-civilization, a materialistic world of creature comforts, super-communication, mass transportation and fast car wizardry. The rapid spread of techno-civilization throughout the Asia-Pacific's great cities was evident – a world of television, cellular phones and instantaneous, international investment. It is easy to agree that the sheer prevalence of creature comforts, leisure and ample opportunities for education was developing a thinking middle class, anxious to preserve its independence.

This view, however, neglected the other great force at work in the world – the influence of long-established traditional cultures. Although driven underground, ostensibly by the success of material civilizations, cultures have deep roots. In the case of the East Asian countries, long exposure to

Confucianism had fostered the sense of a society primarily motivated by the welfare and mutual esteem of its groups. This is hugely different from the 'self esteem' cult which has come to be the boast of individualistic Americans. All societies have social consciences, but there is quite a difference between what used to be known as the individualist 'guilt' culture of the West and the 'shame' culture of the Confucians.

Confucian societies had developed a long immunity to political activism, as long as the basic family core units were not disturbed. This fact was very clear in China. While the American public was aroused by the repression of the student protesters at Tiananmen, the average Chinese did not care overmuch about the government, as long as his or her group was not particularly interfered with. It may be that the communists have here discovered a way to put democracy in the freezer for an indefinite period of time.

For many years both the brilliance and the persistence of the revolutionary 'catch-up' economics of East Asia had been undervalued by both the US government and American businesses. The US economy, as the century neared its end, continued to be strong – far stronger, for example, than the depression-ridden Japanese economy, now hampered rather than supported by its burden of bureaucratic guidance. Yet Americans remained very much concerned with exports and trade balances. By 1996 trade with Japan – imports balanced against exports – still showed an imbalance of about US$45 billion. While the deficit with the newly-industrialized countries (NICs), principally Taiwan, Hong Kong and Singapore had climbed to more than US$20 billion.

The North American trade bloc, with Canada and Mexico joining the USA (NAFTA, North American Free Trade Agreement), had been pushed by Washington, originally out of fear that an East Asian trade bloc might emerge – the sort of Japanese dominated regional economy which might recall the wartime Greater East Asia Co-Prosperity Sphere. Fears on which this was based turned out to be groundless. Indeed, there was much pressure on both sides of the ocean to work in the direction of an all-Pacific trade and investment bloc. In many ways this would be a case of political action following economic fact – since the linkages of both trade and investment across the Pacific are by now far too complex and difficult to untangle by governments' decrees.

In the end a new kind of Pacific community, an international condominium of sorts, seemed to many the best answer. The revolution of rising expectations, so-called, has brought a new middle class into existence in the East Asian countries. This emerging Asian middle class has some strong international common denominators, and it has been enough to force peaceful political revolutions, as I have noted, throughout the East Asian countries. Despite underlying cultural differences, the Asian middle class shares a great deal in common with the North American middle class across the Pacific. Similarities of lifestyle and politics among these culturally different peoples bring added meaning to a sense of Pacific community.

The first ideas of Pacific co-operation, as with similar movements in Europe, came from generally realized economic necessity. It was a Japanese economist, Kiyoshi Kojima, who sketched out the idea of a Pacific community as early as 1966, when he advocated a Pacific free trade area. Some years later, spurred by the political support of Japan's Prime Minister Masayoshi Ohira and Australia's Prime Minister Malcolm Fraser, the Pacific Economic Co-operation Council – now known by the acronym PECC – was founded in 1980. PECC has become an organization of more than 20 Pacific nations. The constant interaction of the past 20 years has developed a certain internationalist 'Pacific' point of view. Pacific nations have gone on to explore common problems in energy, natural resources, communications, the environment and human development – as well as the more obvious issues of trade and investment.

The Asia-Pacific Economic Co-operation forum (APEC) began to organize in 1989, again on an Australian initiative. Backed heavily by the US President, Bill Clinton, who organized the first APEC heads of government meeting, this organization has become a strong factor in Pacific affairs. Because of economic as well as strategic interests, the USA will remain a powerful regional force. While tensions remain about political succession crises and a general nervousness about security pervades – largely prompted by China's new found diplomatic truculence – it seems most probable that the obviously mutually profitable economic interrelationships of this area will develop into stronger cultural and social co-operation. This trend is powerfully enhanced on the American side by the heavy emigration of East Asians to the west coast of the USA. In such a Pacific relationship China, Japan and the USA will remain – as they have for the past century and a half – the most powerful and critically interlocking factors.

References

Dennett, T. (1922) *Americans in Eastern Asia in the Nineteenth Century*, New York, Macmillan.

Eccleston, B., Dawson, M. and McNamara, D. (1998) *The Asia-Pacific Profile*, London, Routledge in association with The Open University.

Iriye, A. (1967) *Across the Pacific: a History of American–East Asian Relations*, Cambridge, Mass., Harvard University Press (rev. edn, 1995, Chicago, Imprint Publications).

Turner, F.J. (1920) *The Significance of the Frontier in American History*, New York, Henry Holt.

Further reading

Godement, F. (1997) *The New Asian Renaissance*, London, Routledge.

Iriye, A. (1967) *Across the Pacific: a History of American–East Asian Relations*, Cambridge, Mass., Harvard University Press (rev. edn, 1995, Chicago, Imprint Publications).

Spence, J.D. (1990) *The Search for Modern China*, London, Hutchinson.

Thompson, J.C., Stanley, P.W. and Perry, J.C. (1981) *Sentimental Imperialists: the American Experience in East Asia*, New York, Harper & Row.

Yahuda, M. (1996) *The International Politics of Asia Pacific 1945–1990*, London, Routledge.

CHAPTER 2

From imperialism to the end of the Cold War

Colin Mackerras

2.1   Introduction

This chapter traces the evolution of the international relations of the Asia-Pacific over the critical half-century from the early 1930s to the 1980s. It will identify some central features of the international politics of the region in the period leading up to the Second World War and discuss the changes in the configuration of relationships during the period of the Cold War, with the emphasis on regional security and economics. It is designed as narrative background to the period after the Cold War, showing how the great powers have contributed to shaping the region.

Several points are of particular note in the history of the international relations of the Asia-Pacific region during this period. They include:

- the progress of most of the countries of East Asia (defined as including North-East and South-East Asia) from colonial to independent status;

- the emergence of two superpowers, the USA and the Soviet Union, in the post-1945 era and the superpower rivalry which dominated the world, including this region;

- the collapse of colonial empires in the wake of Japan's defeat in the war;

- the emergence of a strong and assertive China in the region, despite its ideological instability; and

- the rise of Japan as an economic power and the long-term economic growth in the Asia-Pacific to bring its countries from an impoverished, mostly colonial or semi-colonial status in 1930, to one of the world's power hubs by the late 1980s.

2.2 The world of Western colonialism and the impact of Japanese imperialism

As the period of concern to this chapter dawned, European colonialism was in decline, while Japanese imperialism was still on the rise. Nationalism, spawned in reaction to imperialism and colonialism, had begun to become a force in the Asia-Pacific region. I will begin by asking just what such terms mean.

The word *imperialism* is connected with empire and its adjective imperial. It means the state policy or practice of extending power and domination, with one country appropriating political or economic control outside its own territorial borders. There is nothing new about imperialism, the ancient world seeing a succession of empires. However, the modern form of imperialism dates from the late eighteenth century, when Western Europe's industrial revolution gave it both the means and desire to extend its power overseas. Yet modern imperialism is not exclusive to Europe, Japan being a major example of a modern imperialist power. Japan industrialized so rapidly that it became both able and willing to force its power on to nearby countries.

Colonialism is similar to imperialism in that it involves the domination of one country over another. But the essential difference is that one country actually both determines and makes up the government of another. In the days of modern colonialism, the European powers and Japan conquered and took over the government of other places, sometimes taking over territories which lay beyond their seas and calling them part of their own country.

Nationalism is a reaction to both imperialism and colonialism. However, in contrast to imperialism, nationalism is a modern phenomenon, because it is based on the concept of 'the nation', which derives from modern Europe. A nation implies that group of peoples who dwell within defined borders and owe loyalty to the state which rules that territory. Nationalism is much more than the simple love of a country we call patriotism. The loyalty of the people belonging to the nation goes primarily to the state which represents that nation. Personal loyalties such as to monarchs may be important but are subordinate to loyalty to the nation as a whole.

The concept of nation or nationalism was foreign to the peoples of East Asia before the age of European imperialism and colonialism. Loyalties were to family, to individual lords, to kings or emperors, or to religious leaders, not to nations. So it was ironical that by introducing the ideology of nationalism, the European powers actually created the seeds of the decline of imperialism and colonialism in Asia. In reaction against imperialism, nationalists arose who demanded loyalty to their own nation, not to any foreign European power.

In the 1930s, almost all the countries of North-East and South-East Asia were colonies of a European country or of Japan. The largest colony of the Netherlands was the East Indies, while France occupied Indo-China, including Vietnam, Cambodia and Laos. Britain's colonies in South-East Asia included Burma, Malaya and Hong Kong, and at the end of the nineteenth century the Americans took over the Philippines. Japan, although a relative newcomer among colonial powers, gained Taiwan and other parts of China from its victory in the Sino-Japanese War of 1894–95, and in 1910 took over the whole of Korea as well (Figure 2.1).

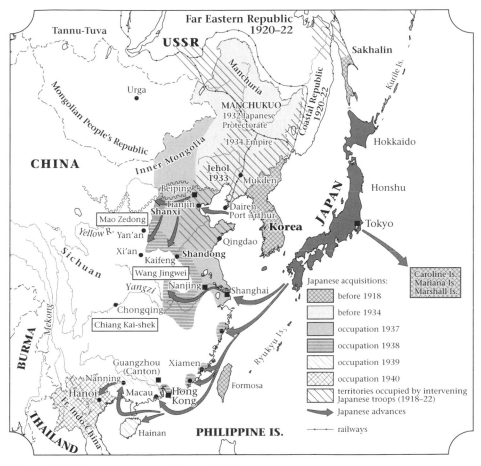

Figure 2.1 *Japanese expansion to 1941*

Source: Kinder and Hilgemann (1978, p.174)

Indeed, among the states of East Asia, only a few were not colonies of other countries. Other than Japan itself, they included Thailand and most of China. Thailand, called Siam until 1932, remained free largely because of Anglo-French rivalry in the locale, but nevertheless was subjected to various unequal treaties and ceded some territory to the colonial powers. China, with its enormous territory and population, saw major enclaves taken over by the powers. In the nineteenth century, the first was Hong Kong, ceded to Britain through the Treaty of Nanjing (1842), followed by a series of other 'treaty ports' handed over to various colonial powers.

Although the British, French and Dutch still exercised enormous power in South-East Asia in the 1930s, in East Asia, it was the Japanese who were the main imperialists. In 1931, Japanese troops moved into Manchuria, setting up the puppet state of Manchukoku, or Manchuria, the following year. Throughout the 1930s the Japanese continued to encroach on Chinese territory, especially in the northeast, where they moved south from Manchuria towards Beiping (now called Beijing). On 7 July 1937 Japanese troops attacked a town just south of the ancient Marco Polo Bridge outside Beiping, sparking off the second Sino-Japanese war (1937–45), which the Chinese generally know as the War of Resistance Against Japan but which Western thinking usually regards as part of the Second World War.

Colonialism and imperialism gave rise to nationalist movements in all the countries of East Asia. In May 1930, the communists under Ho Chi Minh (1890–1969) and others organized large-scale uprisings against the French in Vietnam, but were quickly suppressed with many people killed or imprisoned. Other than Ho Chi Minh, the main South-East Asian nationalist to emerge about this time was the Dutch-educated Sukarno (1901–70), who blended Indonesian nationalism with an idiosyncratic mixture of traditional Javanese, Islamic, and Marxist and other Western ideas. Religion was a spur to nationalism in several parts of Asia, including Malaya where Islam and the wish to preserve traditional Malay culture in the face of Chinese and Indian immigration were more important than hostility to British colonialism.

Meanwhile in China, there were various forms of nationalism, both of the left and the right. If they had one aspiration in common it was to resist Japanese encroachment and to oppose European colonialism and imperialism. Another, but related, common aim of Chinese nationalism was to preserve, or regain, national unity. In Korea, the Japanese police could keep nationalism in check through brutal repression but not quieten the bitter resentment the people felt against them.

2.3 The anti-Japanese war

With the military growing in influence in the government, Japan had developed its own form of ultra-nationalism, based on a highly conservative form of Confucianism called the Imperial Way. It expressed itself in a plan to establish the 'Greater East Asia Co-prosperity Sphere', which was also motivated by economic imperatives. A document produced in January 1942 by the Total War Research Institute for the Japanese army and cabinet describes Japanese objectives:

> *The Plan.* The Japanese empire is a manifestation of morality and its special characteristic is the propagation of the Imperial Way ... It is necessary to foster the increased power of the empire, to cause East Asia to return to its original form of independence and co-prosperity by shaking off the yoke of Europe and America, and to let its countries and peoples develop their respective abilities in peaceful co-operation and secure livelihood.

(Tsunoda *et al.*, 1958, pp.801–2)

The trouble was that the doctrine led to anything but peace and prosperity. The Japanese may have portrayed themselves as being on the side of the Asians, and against the colonialists of Europe and America, so that Japanese nationalism coalesced into Asian nationalism. But the reality was quite different: it was an occupation of extreme barbarism.

One of the first – and worst – single acts of cruelty occurred early in the war. The Japanese occupied the Chinese capital on 13 December 1937 and almost immediately began the infamous 'rape' of Nanjing, which lasted about three months. They murdered people in large numbers – 200,000 Chinese men according to the 1946–47 Asian war crimes trial in Tokyo – by bayoneting them, burying them alive or using them for machine-gun practice. They raped women of all ages – 20,000 according to the war crimes trial – and set fire to the districts they had looted, destroying about one-third of the city (Behr, 1987, p.241).

The seizure of Nanjing forced the Chinese to move their capital inland to Chongqing in Sichuan province. The Japanese continued to expand their occupation, and in March 1940 inaugurated Wang Jingwei as the head of a puppet Chinese regime, with Nanjing as its capital. Wang Jingwei, whom most Chinese regard as a traitor and collaborator, died in Japan in November 1944, so his regime did not last long.

Despite their success in establishing a puppet regime, the Japanese did sustain defeats in China. For example, they made three unsuccessful attempts to seize Changsha, the capital of Hunan province in southern China, in 1939, 1941 and 1942. However, from April to November 1944, they undertook a vast trans-continental offensive across China during which they captured many Chinese cities for the first time, one of them being Changsha, which fell in June. Even more important, they established a railway linking Vietnam through China to Korea. There was great irony in the fact that they achieved their greatest victories not long before their final defeat in 1945.

China was by far the biggest country the Japanese occupied, but there were many others. In September 1940 they occupied Vietnam, where, until near the end of the war, they left the French to govern on their behalf. In December 1941 Japan made the mistake of attacking Pearl Harbor in Hawaii, almost destroying the American Pacific fleet stationed there, and thus brought the USA into the Pacific War. This did not prevent them from occupying virtually the whole of South-East Asia, invading the Philippines two days after the attack on Pearl Harbor and later Thailand, Malaya, Singapore and Indonesia, where the Dutch colonial forces surrendered on 8 March 1942.

The horrors of Japanese occupation spawned anti-Japanese nationalism in most parts of East Asia. However, the Japanese themselves appealed to their own Asianness as a reason why their conquests should spark pride against Western imperialism, so the Japanese occupation did provide a spur to anti-Western nationalism as well. In the Philippines most politicians were prepared to collaborate with the Japanese against American colonialism. The fall of Singapore exposed the weakness of British imperialism while Japanese occupation had the effect of destroying the power of Dutch colonialism in the East Indies. In Vietnam, the Japanese overthrew the French colonial administration in March 1945 and disarmed its troops.

The tide turned against Japan very soon after their South-East Asian victories. In particular, in June 1942, they were defeated at the naval Battle of Midway in the Pacific, largely by the very American aircraft carriers which had been out on patrol – and thus escaped bombing – on the day the Japanese had attacked Pearl Harbor. Although the war dragged on for three years, there was little possibility of Japanese victory in the Pacific War after the Battle of Midway.

The Pacific War went a long way towards establishing the strategic importance of the Pacific Ocean in world affairs. The Battle of Midway may have been the most important of the encounters in the Pacific Ocean, but it was by no means the only one. Apart from the Japanese victories at the beginning of the Pacific War, there were the highly significant Battle of the Coral Sea in May 1942 and the lengthy battle for the nearby Japanese garrison at Guadalcanal in the Solomons, which lasted from August 1942 until February 1943. And towards the end of the war, the battle for the Philippines in March 1945 was of crucial importance in the Allied victory.

The end came in 1945, hastened by the dropping of atomic bombs on Hiroshima and Nagasaki on 6 and 9 August respectively. The Soviet Union formally declared war against Japan, sending a large force into the puppet state of Manchukoku. Japan surrendered a few days later, with a formal ceremony marking the Allied victory at the beginning of September 1945.

2.4 The emergence of the Cold War and the nuclear age

What shaped the configuration of world affairs, and especially in the Asia-Pacific region, in the aftermath of the Second World War was the Cold War between the two superpowers: the USA and the Soviet Union. The Soviet Union saw the USA as an imperialist power, with visions of world hegemony. The USA, on the other hand, saw the Soviet Union as an aggressive power bent on spreading its communist ideology throughout the world and on using its ideology to achieve global dominance. In the USA the policy of containment gained currency, meaning that the USA sought to contain militarily and politically Soviet aggression and expansionism and to prevent the growth of communism.

Historians still debate whether the atomic bombs were really necessary to force a Japanese surrender, and whether they should best be seen as the last act of the Second World War or rather the first move in the Cold War. Certainly one result of the dropping of the two atomic bombs was to introduce a long period in which the existence of nuclear weapons was one of the central realities of international relations and of the Cold War. Another important result was that post-war Japan followed a consistently pro-American foreign policy and sided with the USA in the Cold War. It was the USA which occupied Japan, and took the primary initiatives in the formal San Francisco Treaty of 8 September 1951 which ended the Pacific War. The Soviet representative at the preceding Peace Conference argued that the Treaty 'provides for the conversion of Japan into an American military base' (Lach and Wehrle, 1975, p.156). These words were an exaggeration but they were by no means ridiculous. A few hours after the representatives of about 50 countries had signed the Treaty, the USA and Japan signed a Security Treaty which, although providing for the withdrawal of the American occupation troops, also gave the USA the right to station armed forces 'in and about' Japan.

The collapse of Japan had brought an immediate nationalist upsurge throughout East Asia. On 15 August 1945 the Korean nationalist Lyuh Woon-hyung agreed to head a new administration which would be called the People's Republic of Korea. The Vietnamese nationalist Ho Chi Minh declared the establishment of the Democratic Republic of Vietnam on 2 September. Although he had collaborated with the Japanese occupation, Sukarno announced an Indonesian republic independent of the Dutch two days after the Japanese surrender, with himself as President.

The US President, Franklin Delano Roosevelt, had declared himself opposed to any return of European colonialism to Asia after the war, but he died early in 1945 and his successor Harry Truman was much more equivocal on this issue. The Americans granted independence to the Philippines in 1946, the Republic of the Philippines being proclaimed on 4 July that year. The British regained control over Malaya and Singapore, the former not gaining independence until 1957, and the latter in 1959. In Indonesia, with British and American support, the Dutch carried out a 'police action' trying to restore their rule in the islands. By 1948, they had indeed gone a long way towards achieving their aim, as well as having captured Sukarno. However, the tide then turned for a variety of reasons, including the withdrawal of American support, and the Dutch were forced to grant independence to Indonesia at the end of 1949 (see Figure 2.2).

In Asia the place where Soviet–American Cold War rivalry expressed itself most quickly and forcefully on Japan's surrender was in Korea. A few days before the surrender Soviet troops moved from Manchuria into the northern part of Korea where they put in power the long-time anti-Japanese Marxist–Leninist nationalist Kim Il Sung (1912–94). On 8 September American troops occupied the south under Lieutenant-General John Hodge, so that in effect the country was divided along the 38th parallel. Over the next few months the division into north and south became solidified. Despite various half-hearted attempts at reunification, the south saw the establishment of a pro-American state called the Republic of Korea (ROK) in mid 1948, headed by the right-wing nationalist Syngman Rhee (1875–1965), the north following suit three months later with the Democratic People's Republic of Korea (DPRK) under Kim Il Sung. The Soviet troops withdrew from North Korea completely in 1948, while the Americans did the same from South Korea the following year, although about 500 advisors remained.

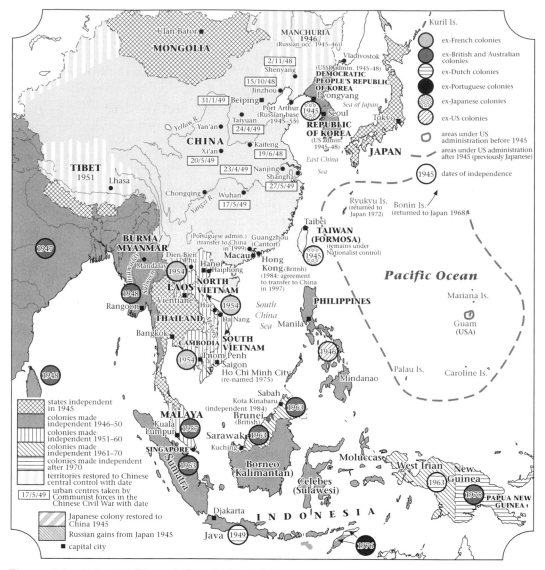

Figure 2.2 *Retreat of imperialism in East Asia*

Source: Moore (1983, p.161)

In China the situation was even more complicated. The Nationalist Party led by Chiang Kai-shek (1887–1975) and the Chinese Communist Party (CCP), led by Mao Zedong (1893–1976), both claimed the mantle of patriotism, having fought victoriously against the Japanese. Stalin signed a Treaty of Friendship with Chiang Kai-shek's government in August 1945, at the same time as Japan's surrender and a few days after Soviet troops had invaded Manchuria. Meanwhile, Chinese communist troops expanded their power in Manchuria, where they were particularly strong.

Civil war broke out between Chiang's and Mao's forces in the middle of the following year. After completing the seizure of Manchuria early in November 1948, the communists went on to seize territory further south, taking the nationalist capital Nanjing on 23 April 1949. By the end of that year, they had gained total victory in the civil war, Mao setting up the People's Republic of China (PRC) on 1 October 1949 and Chiang making his final departure from the Chinese mainland for Taiwan on 10 December.

The Korean War (1950–53) and its impact on the configuration of power in Asia-Pacific

Late in June 1950, only a few months after the PRC's establishment, war broke out very close to China's borders, when Kim Il Sung's troops carried out a major attack on South Korea, seizing the capital Seoul on 28 June and quickly extending control over almost the whole country. Washington reacted with surprise and anger, charging that this was a clear case of communist aggression. The communists considered the attack as an attempt to close the five-year-old division of the country, and also argued that the first shots had actually been fired by the South, not the North.

International reaction to the crisis was very swift, the United Nations immediately deciding to send an expeditionary force on the side of the ROK. The Soviet Union failed to use its veto in the UN Security Council to prevent this action, since it was boycotting the Council in protest against the continued seating of Chiang Kai-shek's government in the United Nations China seat. Although under the UN banner, and including troops from Australia and New Zealand, in fact the expeditionary force was predominantly American, both in its leadership and composition.

The UN force very quickly defeated the North Korean forces in the South. MacArthur pushed the attack northwards, right to the borders with China. In addition, he issued threatening statements about bombing supply bases and power stations on the Chinese side. Indeed, in August 1950 Chinese Premier Zhou Enlai cabled the American Secretary of State, Dean Acheson, protesting against bombing in China's territory near the border with Korea and demanding that the USA compensate for all losses. MacArthur's actions had the effect of convincing the Chinese leadership that China itself was under threat, since the USA was making no secret of its hope that the CCP would soon be overthrown. Mao Zedong decided that China must intervene in its own interests and to save the Marxist–Leninist regime of Kim Il Sung. In October Chinese troops moved into Korea, retaking Seoul on 4 January 1951 and moving on deep into the south.

At the beginning of February 1951 the United Nations General Assembly adopted an American resolution condemning China for aggression in Korea. Zhou Enlai responded by denouncing the condemnation the next day. The issue of Chinese aggression remained important in American foreign policy for some 20 years. It is notable that the Chinese continuously and consistently charged the USA with the same crime. Of course the term may be subject to different interpretations, but it is notable that the first foreign troops in Korea since June 1950 were American, not Chinese. The initial major attacks were carried out by the North Koreans against the South, but they were at least Korean, and when politicians charge another country with aggression, they usually refer to encroachments against a foreign country.

The United Nations sent reinforcements to push the Chinese and North Koreans north of the 38th parallel. In mid 1951, the Soviet Union proposed negotiations for a truce. From this point on, most of the fighting was in the territory near the 38th parallel. Casualties continued to be high, but in fact the war had reached a stalemate.

Finally, in July 1953, Chinese, North Korean and UN delegates signed the Korean armistice. There was no comprehensive peace agreement (and only in 1997 did discussions resume on establishing one). A small area of territory changed hands, but the demarcation line still runs quite close to where it did before the war, namely the 38th parallel. The Chinese troops completed their total withdrawal by the end of 1958. The UN troops also withdrew, but a significant number of American troops stayed on, and remain there at the time of writing.

The overall impact of the Korean War was completely devastating, both for Korea and the world at large. Casualties were horrendous, with millions killed, and much of the country destroyed. The division of Korea was set in stone for a long time, the country remaining divided as of the late 1990s. China's relations with most Western countries, especially the USA, were so seriously damaged that they did not recover until the early 1970s, with the fear of China now a major factor in Asia-Pacific security politics. The intensity of American paranoia concerning communism in general, and

UN and North Korean delegates exchange documents at the opening session of the Military Armistice Commission, 28 July 1953

Asian communism in particular, took a dangerous leap forward. The Cold War was as important in Asia as in Europe, probably even more so.

The South-East Asia Treaty Organization

Other than China and Korea, the other country where communism posed the greatest challenge was Vietnam. In January 1946 the French reached an agreement with Ho Chi Minh under which Vietnam would be 'a free state, having its own government, parliament, army and treasury, forming part of the Indochinese Federation and the French Union'. However, this was not nearly enough for the advocates of French grandeur, who moved to re-establish total French control, throwing the country into war by the end of 1946.

The war lasted until 1954. A classic guerrilla war, it saw Ho Chi Minh's revolutionaries, called the Vietminh, occupy the countryside, while the main French military contingent was in the cities. In 1950 the USA began sending military aid to the French, an initial involvement which was to grow enormously in the 1960s and 1970s. In 1953 the French set up a large base in Dien Bien Phu near the border with Laos with the aim of reducing the mobility of the Vietminh troops and preventing them from attacking Laos. As it turned out, however, the Vietminh were able to overrun the base in May 1954, thus inflicting a serious psychological and military defeat on the French.

The seizure of Dien Bien Phu coincided with a conference which the major powers called in Geneva to discuss Korea and Indo-China. Its main achievement was to reach a truce in Vietnam, signed by the French and the Vietminh on 20 July 1954. This agreement declared a 'provisional military demarcation line' along the 17th parallel, to the south of which the French troops would withdraw and the Vietminh to the north. The agreement signalled the end of French military power in South-East Asia. In addition the 'Final Declaration of the Geneva Conference' provided for general elections to be held in May 1956 in order to reunify Vietnam. The USA was unhappy with the agreement because it ceded territory to the communists. However, it did sign a unilateral declaration that it would 'refrain from the threat or the use of force to disturb' the agreements, but 'would view any renewal of the aggression in violation of the aforesaid Agreements with grave concern'; it added that it supported the wish 'to achieve unity through free elections' as long as they were 'conducted fairly' under UN supervision (see Kahin and Lewis, 1967, p.373).

With the end of the Korean War in 1953, and the victory of the left-wing forces in the northern part of Vietnam in 1954, the USA built up its clientele in East Asia to resist communist, and specifically Chinese, 'aggression' in the region. American Secretary of State John Foster Dulles was quite clear that the West must 'face the future opportunity to prevent the loss in northern Vietnam from leading to the extension of communism throughout South-East Asia and the South-West Pacific' (Kahin and Lewis, 1967, p.61). The result was the South-East Asia Collective Defence Treaty, signed in Manila on 8 September 1954. The signatories of this Treaty were the USA, Britain, France, Australia, New Zealand, Pakistan, Thailand, and the Philippines, making up the South-East Asia Treaty Organization (SEATO).

The USA followed this Treaty with the Sino-American Mutual Defence Treaty, signed with Taiwan in December 1954. The aim was to protect Taiwan from any attempts from the Chinese mainland to attack it or to incorporate it into the PRC. So by the end of 1954 the USA had developed a large array of anti-communist, and especially anti-PRC, treaties to contain communism in Asia.

The Sino-Soviet split

When Mao Zedong declared the existence of the People's Republic of China on 1 October 1949, the Soviet Union was the first country to recognize the new state. Mao had declared earlier the same year that China would 'lean to one side, that of the Soviet Union', and the American government declared that China had been reduced to a mere Soviet colony. Shortly after coming to power, Mao Zedong made a long visit to the Soviet Union, for the first of only two trips he made outside China, as a result of which the two countries signed their Treaty of Friendship, Alliance and Mutual Assistance in Moscow on 14 February 1950. The Soviet Union began giving China large amounts of aid. Soviet experts poured into the country showing the Chinese how to organize their economy and to set up large-scale industrial enterprises. The PRC's first Five-Year Plan of 1953 to 1957 followed Soviet models very closely.

However, although the relationship appeared very close in the early 1950s, quite serious disagreements quickly began to emerge. Chinese leaders disagreed with the emphasis on peaceful coexistence with the West which emerged from Soviet leader Nikita Khrushchev's report to the Twentieth Congress of the Communist Party of the Soviet Union in February 1956, thinking it a sell-out to imperialism. In addition, they did not approve of the process of de-Stalinization which followed the Congress.

Mao revisited Moscow in November 1957 and declared that 'the East wind is prevailing over the West wind'. The specific reference was to the Soviet Union's launching of the first space satellite – the Sputnik – the preceding month. But Mao also meant that the socialist system was beginning to triumph over capitalism.

Although this seemed to signal an improvement in relations, in fact things worsened very rapidly and drastically after that. In 1958, when the Chinese made a concerted attempt to seize the island of Quemoy – although close to the mainland it was still held by the Nationalist Party – the Soviet Union failed to support them, and apparently regarded the attempt as dangerous and adventurist. Even more seriously, Mao Zedong was extremely keen that the Soviet Union should share its nuclear defence capability with China. But the Soviet Union, having made a tentative agreement, went back on this nuclear sharing, a very clear sign to the

Chinese leaders that they did not enjoy the trust of their Soviet counterparts.

On 16 April 1960 China's ideological journal *Red Flag* printed a long
article exposing major disagreements between the Chinese and Soviet
Communist Parties, thus beginning public and serious polemics over the
nature of policy and socialism. In the summer of 1960 the Soviet Union
withdrew all its experts and economic aid from China. The point of no
return in Sino-Soviet relations had been reached.

The Cultural Revolution from 1966 to 1976 merely served to make
matters worse. Mao Zedong adopted an obsessive hostility to the Soviet
Union's more liberal version of communism, which he believed would
undermine the revolution and lead back to capitalism. China's former
President and Mao's main enemy in the Cultural Revolution Liu Shaoqi was
labelled 'China's Khrushchev'.

When the Soviet Union invaded Czechoslovakia in 1968 China's
denunciations of the action were every bit as strong as those of the West. In
1969 people were actually killed in border clashes between the two
countries. China had come to regard the Soviet Union as a more dangerous
enemy than the USA. Sino-Soviet relations had reached their worst point of
hostility. This was diametrically opposite to what had been the case when
the PRC was established. Although both parties still claimed to adhere to
Marxism–Leninism, each was charging the other with ideological crimes
even worse than the American imperialism which both were in theory
committed to oppose.

Indonesia and the non-aligned movement

With much of the world divided into American or Soviet client states,
many countries in Asia chose a third, 'neutralist' path, which tended,
however, to be bitterly anti-American with a strongly anti-imperialist
rhetoric. Among these the most important was Indonesia.

Indonesia found far more support from the Soviet bloc for its
revolution than from the USA. Yet by the time it actually achieved
independence in 1949, the USA had swung against the Dutch and was
actively courting the new regime. The Indonesian leadership could see that
what each of the two superpowers wanted was benefit for itself, rather than
for the Indonesians, and was consequently very suspicious. It also believed
that Cold War politics was likely to distract attention from issues they
regarded as much more important, such as to end colonialism, and even
had the potential for a third world war.

In April 1955 the Indonesian town of Bandung hosted a major world
conference which gave meaning and focus to the non-aligned movement.
Twenty-nine countries, mostly African and Asian, sent senior representatives to the Bandung Conference, including Nehru of India, Zhou Enlai of
China, Tito of Yugoslavia, Nasser of Egypt and, of course, Sukarno of
Indonesia. The 29 were countries of diverse cultures, histories and
experiences, but were united by their common hostility to imperialism

and colonialism, and their wish to preserve some semblance of independence from the Cold War imperatives dividing the two superpowers.

In the early 1960s, Sukarno and his policy of 'guided democracy' took Indonesia further to the left, especially in foreign affairs. In August 1963, Sukarno delivered a speech in which he enunciated 'his bipolar view of the world as a radical alternative to the policy of non-alignment' (Leifer, 1995, p.172). It posed 'new emerging forces' against 'old established forces', the former including 'the Asian Nations, the Latin American Nations, the Nations of the Socialist countries, the progressive groups in the capitalist countries'.

Even before the formation of the Federation of Malaysia on 16 September 1963 Sukarno had launched a campaign called 'Confrontation' aimed at 'crushing Malaysia' as an 'imperialist plot' and representative of the old established forces. He found support from the PRC, relations with which warmed very distinctly at that time. However, his attempt to convene an international conference in support of his campaign failed. Moreover, his authority was crucially undermined by a *coup d'état* in October 1965, which lurched Indonesia to the right and brought General Suharto to power as Acting President in March 1967 (with confirmation in that position in March 1968).

In August 1967, the Association of South-East Asian Nations (ASEAN) was formed, linking Indonesia, Thailand, the Philippines, Singapore and Malaysia. Its aims were to solve regional strategic problems and to form a basis for better economic integration within the region. Although Indonesia retained some ambivalence about great power rivalry, the texture was totally different from the neutralism of Sukarno. ASEAN was very much more sympathetic to the American cause and more suspicious of the Soviet Union than non-aligned predecessors had been. Thailand, for instance, was closely involved in the American anti-communist struggle in Vietnam, while the Philippines retained major US bases.

The cause of neutralism was spawned by the Cold War and the ideological division which characterized it. It reached its height during the decade from 1955 to 1965, from the Bandung Conference to the eve of the fall of Sukarno in Indonesia. A comparatively moderate and appealing force in the mid 1950s it tended to move left as it matured, being focused on the relationship between Indonesia and China. It weakened as a force in East Asia with the coup in Indonesia and the turning inwards of China when the Cultural Revolution began. In its place, the more pro-American ASEAN regional grouping evolved.

2.5 The rise of Japan as an economic power

Although defeated and occupied by the USA, Japan re-emerged in the 1960s as a major economic power, experiencing sustained growth over several decades to become, in the late 1990s, the most powerful economy in the world after the USA itself. Actually Japan's economic growth began more or less immediately after its defeat. Other than its Security Treaty with the USA, Japan's post-war diplomacy rested on the so-called Yoshida Doctrine, named after Yoshida Shigeru, during whose terms as Prime Minister (1946–47 and 1948–54) the principles came to fruition. The main aims of the Yoshida Doctrine were:

- all available resources should be devoted to economic development; and

- in defence and foreign policy, Japan should rely entirely on the USA, avoiding the unnecessary drain of an active defence programme.

The major implication of the Yoshida Doctrine, which was for several decades central to Japan's polity, was that politics should be separated from economics. The economy should develop as quickly as possible without any interference from political considerations. Of course, the Security Treaty with the USA meant that Japan remained anti-communist, but that did not stop it carrying on profitable trade with communist countries.

One major illustration of this policy was the document signed between China's Liao Chengzhi and Japan's Takasaki Tatsunosuke in November 1962, the so-called Liao–Takasaki memorandum. This allowed for a 'long-term, comprehensive trade by exchange of goods' between Japan and China. Under the memorandum, Japan became China's largest trading partner, even though there was a momentary decline during the most radical phase of the Cultural Revolution, the lack of diplomatic relations not being an obstacle to trade.

The Security Treaty with the USA had aroused considerable opposition within Japan itself. For instance, in mid 1960 prolonged rioting and demonstrations took place on the streets of Tokyo in a vain attempt to prevent its renewal. Nevertheless, Japan allowed the stationing of American troops on its soil. When American President Richard Nixon agreed in November 1969 to hand back to Japan the island of Okinawa, which the USA had taken over through a three-month campaign towards the end of the Second World War, he did so on the assumption that American bases and troops would continue to be stationed there. In addition, the Japanese government accepted the American nuclear umbrella and resisted periodic pressures from within the country to develop its own nuclear capabilities.

The return of Okinawa and the nuclear question suggest that in fact it has not been easy to maintain Japanese dependence on the USA or the total separation of economics from politics. By 1967 Japan's meteoric rise had made its economy the third largest in the world, behind only the USA and the Soviet Union, and subsequently it overtook the latter as well. During the 1960s pressures began to build up for Japan to assert itself more strongly against the USA and even to develop more extensive self-defence forces – armed forces being outlawed by the American-inspired constitution. In July 1969, American President Richard Nixon enunciated his so-called Nixon Doctrine, the essence of which was that the nations of Asia, including Japan, should be more self-reliant in defence.

In economic terms, then, Japan recovered very quickly from the devastation caused by the Second World War and by the 1960s was approaching the status of economic superpower. It based its policy on strong production, both in quantity and quality, with a powerful export and trade orientation. In security terms it followed a strong pro-American line, but the degree of its dependence on the USA began to lessen with time. Its attempts to keep economics and politics totally separate also began to come under pressure.

2.6   The Vietnam War and the Sino-American *détente*

From 1965 to 1973, American and other foreign troops were again active in Asia, this time in Vietnam, in an unsuccessful attempt to prevent a communist victory. This war produced a cathartic effect in the West itself, especially the USA, where a large-scale protest movement resulted in long-term changes in the social and intellectual life of the country.

Following the Geneva Conference of July 1954, Ho Chi Minh took control of Vietnam north of the 17th parallel, while an American protégé called Ngo Dinh Diem took power in the south in what was a divided country. Ho Chi Minh died in office in 1969 as a national hero, and Diem was assassinated in 1963, being succeeded by a series of weak leaders. The elections of July 1956, which the Geneva Conference had promised in order to reunify Vietnam, did not take place. A few years later guerrilla activity began in the south with the aim of effecting what the electoral process had failed to do.

The Americans and their South Vietnamese clients saw this as aggression from the north, because of the very clear wish to extend the communist control from North Vietnam to the whole country. The argument from Ho Chi Minh's supporters was that the impetus for the guerrilla war had initially come from within the south itself, although by the early to mid 1960s it was receiving substantial help from the north.

In August 1964 the so-called Gulf of Tongking (Tonkin) incident occurred. The Americans alleged that the North Vietnamese had attacked American warships in the Gulf of Tongking on two separate days. In response they bombed North Vietnam and President Johnson secured almost unanimous permission from Congress for a free hand in Vietnam, although no formal declaration of war was made. It later turned out that South Vietnamese naval commandos under American command had raided North Vietnamese islands in the Gulf a few days earlier and that the North Vietnamese response was actually very restrained (see Sheehan *et al.*, 1971, pp.259–70). In other words, the Gulf of Tongking incident was a fraudulent pretext for war.

Early in 1965, the Americans began sustained bombing of North Vietnam and sent troops to counter the communist advance in the south. The number grew over the succeeding years with other countries such as Australia and New Zealand joining in. Beginning on 31 January 1968, New

Year's Day in the lunar calendar, or Tet in Vietnamese, the Vietcong carried out a massive offensive attacking 36 of the 44 provincial capitals and briefly holding many of them. But they were hunted down resulting in enormous casualties, such that militarily the Tet offensive was a failure. But psychologically it was not only successful but decisive. The American Commander in Vietnam William Westmoreland asked the President for over 200,000 more troops, to supplement the existing force of over 540,000 US troops, but for the first time his request was refused. The American commitment, which for so long had been open-ended, was no longer so. In March 1968, the American President Lyndon B. Johnson announced his refusal to stand for a second term in office. The Vietnam War had defeated him.

Johnson's successor Richard Nixon adopted a different policy. He withdrew the large American force by stages, and tried to hand over the fighting to the Vietnamese themselves, a strategy called Vietnamization. From April to May 1970 American troops did, however, invade neighbouring Cambodia (from Vietnam) with the aim of destroying what they believed was the headquarters of the South Vietnamese communists. One of the effects of this action was to inflame the anti-war protest movement in the USA. This had begun several years earlier but now reached an explosive intensity. The reaction to the Tet offensive had turned many influential figures against the war. But in 1970 it was the Americans taking the initiative by sending troops into a neighbouring country. In one protest demonstration, national guardsmen killed four students at Kent State University.

Meanwhile the PRC and the USA saw it as in their interests to move closer together. Both shared a desire to oppose the interests of the Soviet

President Nixon at the Great Wall of China, February 1972

Union and, in addition, each had its own agenda, the Americans believing that they could encourage the PRC to lessen their support for the North Vietnamese. In July 1971, President Nixon's National Security Adviser Henry Kissinger made a secret visit to Beijing and arranged for the President to visit China. Nixon duly made a highly successful visit from 21 to 28 February 1972, claiming it as 'the week that changed the world', because the country which had so recently been America's foremost enemy could now become its friend. The North Vietnamese were secretly furious to see one of their two main allies and supporters welcoming their worst enemy so warmly. However, they could do nothing about it, and maintained public silence.

The strategy of Vietnamization did delay defeat but ultimately it was a failure. In January 1973, the USA signed an agreement in Paris with the North Vietnamese by which American troops would complete their withdrawal but at the same time leave the South Vietnamese client-state intact. However, by the end of April 1975, the North Vietnamese had effected the overthrow of the South Vietnamese government and seized its capital Saigon. In the middle of the following year they formally reunified the country as the Socialist Republic of Vietnam.

2.7   The free-enterprise model gains the upper hand

The period from about 1970 to the early 1980s was one of rapid economic growth in most of East Asia. Although it saw the victory of the communists in Vietnam, it also saw the increasing success of middle class and other entrepreneurial elites in much of the region.

The early 1970s saw further pressures towards greater Japanese independence from the USA, in particular the two 'Nixon shocks'. These were:

- Nixon's announcement of July 1971 that he would visit Beijing, over which he had not consulted Japan; and

- Nixon's announcement of August 1971 that he would impose a 10 per cent surcharge on imports, aimed at halting the declining American balance of trade, especially with respect to Japan.

The result of the first of these was to persuade Japan to establish diplomatic relations with China, which took effect from September of the next year, with Prime Minister Tanaka Kakuei making his own visit to Beijing and meeting with Mao Zedong only seven months after Nixon. This event had major implications because it meant that Japan could maintain good relations with both the USA and the PRC at the same time and no longer needed to regard China as a threat to its security. The Security Treaty which had formed the basis of Japan's foreign relations since its signature in 1951 thus tended to become less important. Within this new context, Japan continued to assert that it would abstain from becoming an autonomous military power and try to promote friendly co-operation with all nations.

Japan reluctantly accepted the second of the 'Nixon shocks', but in fact the 1970s were a period of Japanese protectionism and economic success. Japan became increasingly self-confident, both in economic and political terms. Despite the surcharge it ran large trade surpluses, especially with the USA, and had become the largest, or nearly the largest, trading partner with virtually every country with which it dealt economically. The balance of economic power between Japan and the West, especially that of the USA, had changed in the former's favour since the 1960s. The living standards of the Japanese also rose to become as high, depending on the measurement, as anywhere in the West. In particular, from about 1980, the life expectancy of the Japanese population was the highest, or nearly the highest, in the world. The Japanese experience is the archetypal testimony to the success of capitalism in Asia.

In the PRC, the general direction was similar, although beginning from a very different basis and a much lower level. At the end of 1978, a plenary meeting of the CCP's Central Committee made a basic policy decision for reform. There were two essential aims of the new policy, both of them reflecting the influence of the new era's main architect Deng Xiaoping. These were:

- China would throw all its efforts into economic development and other forms of modernization; and

- China would open itself to the outside world, with the aim of expanding trade, investment, technology transfer, and modern management techniques.

The effect of reform over the following period was dramatic. The Chinese economy began to grow more quickly, with people at large losing an interest in revolution in favour of making money. The rural people's communes were replaced by a contract system based on free enterprise and the efforts of a rural entrepreneurial elite, with the result that production and the standard of living rose enormously. Foreign trade increased, with the Chinese shaking off their previous isolation from foreign, and especially Western, goods, ideas and arts. At the same time, however, inequalities widened in regional, class and gender terms.

Many other places in East Asia experienced rapid economic growth in the 1970s and 1980s. Foremost among them were the four 'little tigers': South Korea, Taiwan, Hong Kong and Singapore. The reasons for their success are still debated but are no doubt a combination which include most or all of the following (see the next chapter):

- sound economic policies;

- geopolitical factors, such as foreign assistance and trade, and the favourable impact of the Vietnam War, especially for South Korea;

- state activism, with the state playing a significant and positive role in all the 'little tiger' economies;

- a significant body of entrepreneurs, such as a middle class; and

- cultural factors, such as Confucianism with its emphasis on education and hierarchy.

South Korea and Taiwan are particularly significant because of the comparisons they enable with the culturally identical North Korea and the PRC. In both cases, the 'free enterprise' model has shown itself decisively more successful economically than the socialist. As far as China is concerned, the PRC has benefited enormously in economic terms from its abandonment of the determinedly socialist model to which Mao Zedong claimed to adhere, and its transfer to Deng Xiaoping's model which allocates far more space to free enterprise, even though Deng claimed his model was socialist.

In summary, the decades preceding the end of the Cold War showed the increasing power of the free enterprise model in East Asia. It saw economic growth on a scale which made the region among the most powerful in the world. Above all, it shifted the economic balance between the West and East Asia decisively towards the latter.

2.8   Summary and conclusion

In the early to mid 1980s, as the Cold War drew to its end, the situation in East Asia was of unparalleled stability and prosperity. There was still war, notably in Cambodia, and still poverty in many places, even extreme poverty. But if the comparison is with any time over the decades discussed in this chapter, then, with hardly any exceptions, the dominant economic situation was positive.

Nationalism was still an important factor in the early to mid 1980s. But it was a very different kind of nationalism from that which had prevailed either during or just after the colonial period. The nationalists of the preceding generation had achieved most of their main aims, they had gained independence or liberation, and the next generation was more intent on economic growth than maintaining a revolutionary momentum. Whether in the PRC or Indonesia, South Korea or even Vietnam, what motivated people was the desire for material or social goods, not any abstract ideas of revolution.

The configuration of power relationships was still tense, but considerably less so than it had been during most of the preceding period. The PRC's relations with Vietnam and the Soviet Union were at a very low ebb, but in the latter case were already beginning to recover, and relations with the USA were as good as they had been since 1949. Japan's political influence was beginning to grow, but the signs of any military resurgence were sparse. It was less dependent on the USA than it had once been, but still maintained very good relations with that superpower. It had given up its fear of China, and the two countries were able to maintain generally friendly relations with each other. Indonesia was keen to get on with its neighbours, with notions of 'Confrontation' in the seemingly distant and traumatic past.

The economic resurgence of the four 'little tigers' was well under way. The PRC had begun its progress on the path of economic modernization. Japan had achieved the status of economic superpower. Even Vietnam, having won its war against the USA, was beginning to choose the path of reform which included rapid economic growth and favourable attention to the private sector. There was extreme irony in the fact that the Americans could lose the war in Vietnam, at enormous cost to themselves, and yet still see the economic system which they advocated move towards triumph in North-East and South-East Asia, even in countries such as China and Vietnam which had once opposed them with all the revolutionary fervour at their command.

It is of great importance to note that the countries within East Asia had come to assert the primary role in determining their own future. Although the USA was certainly not irrelevant, it was no longer the decisive factor it had once been in shaping the balance of power in the region. The once powerful Soviet Union no longer played a decisive role in the region. For the first time since before the colonial era, the Asian countries could exercise their due power in their own region, free of subjection to Western interests.

References

Behr, E. (1987) *The Last Emperor*, London, Macdonald.

Kahin, G. and Lewis, J.W. (1967) *The United States in Vietnam*, New York, Dial Press.

Kinder, H. and Hilgemann, W. (1978) *The Penguin Atlas of World History, Vol.II: From the French Revolution to the Present*, Harmondsworth, Penguin.

Lach, D.F. and Wehrle, E.S. (1975) *International Politics in East Asia Since World War II*, New York, Praeger.

Leifer, M. (1995) *Dictionary of the Modern Politics of South-East Asia*, London, Routledge.

Moore, R.I. (ed.) (1983) *The Newnes Historical Atlas*, Feltham, Newnes.

Sheehan, N. *et al.* (1971) *The Pentagon Papers*, Toronto, Bantam.

Tsunoda, R., de Bary, W.T. and Keene, D. (1958) *Sources of Japanese Tradition*, New York, Columbia University Press.

Further reading

Blum, R.M. (1982) *Drawing the Line: the Origin of the American Containment Policy in East Asia*, New York, Norton.

Cumings, B. (1981, 1991) *The Origins of the Korean War*, 2 vols, Princeton, Princeton University Press.

Dittmer, L. (1992) *Sino-Soviet Normalization and its International Implications, 1945–1990*, Seattle, University of Washington Press.

Horowitz, D. (1969) *From Yalta to Vietnam: American Foreign Policy in the Cold War*, rev. edn, Harmondsworth, Penguin.

Howe, K.R., Kiste, R.C. and Lal, B.V. (1994) *Tides of History: the Pacific Islands in the Twentieth Century*, Honolulu, University of Hawaii Press.

Iriye, A. (1974) *The Cold War in Asia: a Historical Introduction*, Englewood Cliffs, Prentice Hall.

Islam, I. (1995) 'The rise of the East Asian NIEs: theory and evidence' in Mackerras, C. (ed.) *Eastern Asia: an Introductory Survey*, 2nd rev. edn, Melbourne, Longman, pp.400–16.

Karnow, S. (1984) *Vietnam, a History*, Harmondsworth, Penguin.

McWilliams, W.C. and Piotrowski, H. (1990) *The World Since 1945*, 2nd edn, Boulder, Lynne Rienner.

CHAPTER 3

The rise of the Asia-Pacific

Javed Maswood

3.1 Introduction

Throughout the four decades of the Cold War, the countries of East Asia, whether separately or as a grouping, were only marginal players in world affairs. In the early 1950s, most of the countries of the Asia-Pacific were economically and politically insignificant, having either just emerged from a long period of colonial domination (e.g. Indonesia and the Philippines), or were preoccupied with the task of economic reconstruction after the Second World War (e.g. Japan), or were wracked with domestic social and political upheavals (e.g. China and Vietnam). Of the two potentially significant regional powers, China and Japan, the latter appeared to have shed its Asian identity to establish closer links with the USA and the West. It maintained a low international political profile, opting instead to focus on economic objectives. China, on the other hand, following the socialist revolution of 1949, had limited involvement and influence in global affairs. Later in the 1960s, during the Great Proletarian Cultural Revolution, China became even more deeply isolated.

As these two potentially powerful states retreated from international activism, the region failed to develop a sense of cohesive identity. In addition, the end of the Second World War had set in motion intense centrifugal forces and, consequently, the region rarely registered as an important player in world affairs. In contrast, European countries, after the Second World War, had embarked on a process of regional integration through, initially, the European Coal and Steel Community (ECSC) and later, the European Union (EU). However, as we move into the twenty-first century, the situation in the Asia-Pacific appears radically different. Given the region's rapid economic transformation and its consequent collective weight in the global economy, the assumption is that economic power will inevitably translate into greater political influence. Optimists may herald the twenty-first century as the Asia-Pacific Century, but they are not all equally convinced that this is a foregone conclusion. According to Paul Krugman, the Asia-Pacific economic miracle was the result of capital infusion, rather than productivity increases, and that permanent infusion of capital was unlikely to continue to produce high rates of economic growth (Krugman, 1995). He concluded that growth in the region was likely to stall and that the anticipated Asia-Pacific Century, therefore, unlikely to materialize. Most observers acknowledge, however, that the untapped potential of the region is enormous, that China may well surpass the USA in terms of absolute gross national product (GNP) and the collective economic size of the region will cast a long shadow in international politics.

This chapter will examine the rise of the Asia-Pacific countries to global prominence, and their potential global political and economic role in the post-Cold War context. Regional powers have sought to enhance their security or to pursue their national interest either as autonomous units or as members of sub-regional groupings, such as the Association of South-East Asian Nations (ASEAN). But the region as a whole is too diverse, incorporating countries at vastly different levels of economic development, to suggest any possibility of region-wide political integration. Moreover, the key regional powers like Japan have sought an extra-regional political and economic orientation and so limited their regional engagement. This has important implications for the cohesiveness of the region as a political force in global politics. The notion of the Asia-Pacific Century may therefore be more political hubris than potential fact.

3.2 The economic resurgence of the Asia-Pacific

As the previous chapter noted, Japan was the first Asian country to realize rapid economic growth in the post-Second World War period. Japanese economic recovery was assisted by a number of external factors, such as American procurements in Japan during the Korean War, but in general was the result of a particular model of economic growth and development that emphasized state direction, active industrial policy and an export oriented growth pattern. The Japanese model is variously termed as 'neo-mercantilist', where the state intervened to expand exports and limit imports, or as the 'developmental state' model, where the state intervened in the economy by targeting certain industries for development and by offering economic incentives and assistance, but without seriously distorting market signals and the market mechanism.

The success of Japan is best exemplified by the ten year income doubling plan that was adopted in the early 1960s. At the time the plan was regarded as excessively ambitious but in the end proved to be overly conservative because the target was achieved in only seven years. For other countries Japan became an exemplar, a model to follow. Indeed, Korea and Taiwan replicated the Japanese experience and achieved their own economic miracles, as shown in Table 3.1.

The success of these North-East Asian economies with export oriented development came at a time when many other developing countries pursued an inward looking development strategy. In Latin America and much of the 'Third World', for example, the dominant economic strategy

Table 3.1 *Annual growth rate of GNP (percentages)*

	1950–60	1960–70	1970–77	1977–86
Japan	9.3	10.2	4.3	4.0
South Korea	4.6	8.1	9.9	6.6
Taiwan	7.6	9.5	9.1	7.0

Source: Garnaut (1989, p.36)

was one of minimizing trade links with the rest of the world. Dependency theorists argued that trade was a process through which the developed countries exploited the developing countries and that development was impossible in the latter group of countries until they delinked their economies from the world system. Governments in North-East Asia, however, offered specific incentives to manufacturers to expand exports and become internationally competitive rather than shelter behind high protectionist barriers. Manufacturers were protected from competition from imported products but the implementation of export promotion ensured that emergent industries would become internationally viable rather than remain inefficient, as had happened in other economies that relied more on protecting the domestic market. Export promotion took many forms, including, for example, cheaper interest rates if investment loans were repaid in foreign, rather than domestic, currency. Overall, state direction was a major factor in the economic success of North-East Asia. Governments ensured that economic fundamentals were right, especially in maintaining a high rate of domestic savings for investment purposes. Between 1960 and 1985, the North-East Asian economies increased their real income per capita more than four times (World Bank, 1993, p.2).

Some South-East Asian countries also introduced aspects of the Japanese model and achieved rapid economic growth by taking full advantage of export opportunities and by integrating their economies into the global economy. The Malaysian government, for example, introduced a 'Look East' policy in the 1980s to encourage learning from Japan and the North-East Asian example. Where the South-East Asian growth experience differed from that of North-East Asia was in the greater openness to foreign investment and multinational corporations. Whilst the North-East Asian economies relied mainly on local capital for their industrialization drive, sustained and rapid growth in South-East Asia was achieved largely after a transition to a more open and liberal foreign investment regime. The flow of foreign investment, primarily from North-East Asian economies was, as discussed below, critical to the rapid growth of countries like Malaysia, Indonesia, and Thailand. China too, which had isolated itself from international linkages opened up its economy in the late 1970s and liberalization and export promotion laid the basis for rapid economic progress. Between 1978 and 1986, Chinese GDP growth increased at more than 10 per cent a year and its foreign trade dependence also increased dramatically.

By the 1980s the Asia-Pacific had become the most dynamic economic region in the world and its collective GNP was a substantial proportion of global GNP (see Table 3.2). The main export destination for regional countries and their manufactured exports was the USA. Japan, which had already emerged as a large consumer economy allowed little opportunities for regional countries to penetrate its domestic market. Yet, a common bond that brought the countries together was their reliance on trade to generate growth. According to J.M. Roberts, 'By 1985 the whole of east and south-east Asia constituted a single trading zone of unprecedented potential' (Roberts, 1992, p.1066).

Table 3.2 *Shifting economic power in Asia, Europe and North America*

	Asia	Europe	North America
GNP (US$ billion, constant 1987 prices)			
1972	1,871	3,591	3,350
1992	4,511	5,583	5,323
% change	141	55	59
Per capita GNP (US$)			
1972	922	8,674	11,627
1992	1,539	12,140	14,481
% change	67	40	25
Population (millions)			
1972	2,029	414	288
1992	2,930	459	367
% change	44	11	27

Source: World Bank (1994)

In the mid 1980s, however, currency adjustments became an important stimulus to a horizontal economic division of labour in the region. Through the 1980s, exchange rates had become increasingly separated from economic fundamentals. Thus, the dollar appreciated while the Japanese Yen depreciated and this contributed to growing trade imbalances between the two countries. In order to stem this imbalance and contain the protectionist sentiments within the USA, the Plaza Accord among the G-5 countries, of September 1985, resulted in a revaluation of the Japanese Yen. The Japanese government supported this realignment as a proper step in preventing protectionism and a deterioration of the Japanese export climate but it also heightened fears, among sectors of Japanese industry, that the country would lose its international competitiveness. To avert this, Japanese firms began earnestly to invest in other Asian countries to obtain cost advantages and retain international competitiveness. Within Japan this led to much exaggerated fears of a 'hollowing out' of Japanese industry as a result of industrial relocation to cheaper production bases in South-East Asia.

While these fears were exaggerated, the flow of foreign investment to other South-East Asian countries helped create a greater degree of intra-regional economic linkage. Interestingly, however, Japan was not the only source of foreign investment in the region since countries like South Korea and Taiwan, which had substantial foreign exchange reserves and large trade surpluses, also invested abroad. South-East Asian countries were also in the middle of rapid economic growth and maintained an investment climate conducive to foreign direct investment. The complementarity of these two forces produced growing regional integration through investment flows.

The Asia-Pacific's collective GNP, its share of world trade and growing regional interdependence have convinced observers that the region is destined to play a much larger role in international affairs. This is notwithstanding the poor performance of the Japanese economy in the 1990s following the collapse of the 'bubble economy' of the late 1980s.

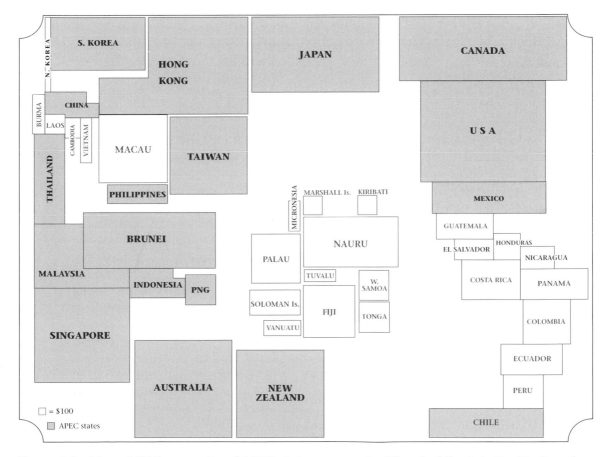

Figure 3.1 *Map of GDP per capita of APEC states compared with rest of the Asia-Pacific, based on purchasing power parity GDP and calculated in US$ (1991–93)*

3.3   Asia-Pacific in the post-Cold War era

In the post-Cold War system, the USA has emerged as the only remaining superpower as Russia tries to rebuild its shattered economy. In this new era, the role and importance of the strategic nuclear balance has also diminished. As elsewhere, the end of the Cold War has lessened tension in one respect but in the Asia-Pacific it has also brought regional conflicts to a higher relief.

There are numerous unresolved political issues in this region, such as the Spratly Islands dispute in the South China Sea involving a number of East Asian countries, the Northern Islands dispute between Japan and Russia, and the continuing conflict on the Korean peninsula. Of these the main challenge to peace and security has been assumed to be the unpredictability of the North Korean regime as it increasingly becomes isolated politically and impoverished economically. The North Korean economy has been devastated by a series of natural disasters which has rendered tenuous the hold of the communist regime. Its primary political ally has been the PRC but China may no longer be in a position to offer it unconditional support on the international stage. Since China began liberalizing its economy in the late 1970s/early 1980s, it has also emphasized better relations with Western countries, including South Korea. South Korea has become commercially important to China and this limits the capacity of the North Korean regime to demand total Chinese support in its struggle with South Korea.

In the case of China, if ever there was a 'China card' during the Cold War which the USA could use against the Soviet Union and which, consequently, gave the Chinese some influence in world affairs, this no longer exists in the post-Cold War period. The end of the Cold War, however, has been generally advantageous to China because it, for instance, no longer has to be concerned with perceived Soviet hegemonic designs in the Asia-Pacific region. With the end of the Cold War, the importance and significance of economic power has increased and the Chinese government is in a better position to pursue an economic modernization strategy. China began to shift its emphasis to economic development and modernization in the late 1970s and in the post-Cold War environment this has assumed greater significance. The Chinese government has pursued normalization of relations with most countries of East Asia, and greater integration in the global economy.

Apart from East Asian economic achievements which have boosted regional confidence, the end of the Cold War has created more room for political manoeuvring. In these circumstances, it is not surprising that there has emerged a drive to realize an East Asian identity and some form of regional integration (see the following chapter). The drive toward regional integration has also been influenced by regionalism in other parts of the world. It was assumed that in the absence of a strong collective voice, the Asia-Pacific would fail to realize its full potential as an important and influential international actor. Various proposals were put forward by different countries, but it is clear that if the Asia-Pacific Century is to

A farming community in 1980 Shenzhen, which lies close to Hong Kong in Guangdong Province, is now a bustling city

become a reality, it can not be narrowly identified with the East Asian countries. In the most prominent and successful efforts to promote regional integration, the East Asian countries have emphasized the importance of incorporating the USA and the western hemisphere in a structure of 'open regionalism'.

An Asia-Pacific century dominated by the countries of East Asia can only become a reality if China achieves a level of development similar to Japan. This is unlikely in the near future. In terms of its gross domestic product (GDP), China is minuscule compared to Japan and it also lags far behind in terms of per capita GDP (see Figure 3.1). In 1991, China's absolute GDP was only a tenth of that of Japan and its per capita GNP a mere US$370. Since the late 1970s, China has made remarkable economic progress which should continue despite the leadership transition in early 1997. However, it began its modernization drive from a very low base and is unlikely to emerge as an economic powerhouse in the near future. The potential, however, is unmistakable and with a population base of more than one billion people its future role in international affairs cannot be easily dismissed.

For the foreseeable future, Japan is the only East Asian country with a potential to emerge as an influential international actor. Its total GDP (US$3.362 trillion in 1991) is more than twice the collective GDP of all the other East Asian economies combined. The post-Cold War era also provides greater opportunities for Japan to play a role more independent of the USA. Moreover, while there is no immediate suggestion on either side of the Pacific to downgrade the Security Treaty that links the two countries, divergent interests might encourage Japan to assume greater foreign policy autonomy. One area of policy divergence is Russia. The West is keen to assist in the Russian transition to capitalism and democracy whereas Japan, despite similar interests in Russian transformation, sees no clear reason for extending large scale financial assistance without prior Russian concessions on the Northern Islands dispute.

The East Asian countries have become less apprehensive of Japan although some hostility remains because of unfinished issues arising from the Second World War, such as a Japanese apology and compensation for 'comfort women'. They would nonetheless prefer the continuation of the US–Japan Security Treaty as an insurance against a completely autonomous and vastly increased Japanese regional role. With all the lingering concerns and doubts, Japan has also become an economic model for some East Asian countries. In the early 1980s, the Malaysian prime minister urged Malaysians to 'Look East', to learn from Japan and replicate the Japanese economic success. South-East Asian countries were also more receptive to Japanese influence because of a continuing need for Japanese investment funds in order to supplement scarce domestic capital. Indonesia, for example, suffered a significant loss of export revenue as oil prices declined in 1983. With the help of Japanese aid and investment, and a more open and deregulated economy, Indonesia began promoting non-oil exports. Its success can be measured by the 26 per cent a year growth of non oil exports since 1983. Other South-East Asian countries, too, have benefited from capital inflows from Japan and other North-East Asian economies.

Other explanations for diminished hostility toward Japan might be developments outside the region, such as the spread of regionalism. On one hand the fear of protectionism, prompted by delays in finalizing the Uruguay Round of the GATT trade liberalization agreement, and the growing significance of the EU and NAFTA on the other, shifted attention away from the Japan problem in the early 1990s. Moreover, there was also a recognition that if the region was to become an important global player, Japanese leadership was essential. As Dobbs-Higginson argues, Japan '... is the only Asia-Pacific country with the economic credibility and strength to negotiate with the rest of the world. The other countries of the region should harness this power for the collective good of the whole' (Dobbs-Higginson, 1993, p.xxiv). As a leading economic power, Japan has the potential to play a more active role but economic power has, thus far, not translated into enhanced political influence.

There are nonetheless strong expectations within many Asia-Pacific countries that Japan should adopt a more active international role. In the automobile dispute with the USA which flared up in 1995, for example, many South-East Asian countries too had a significant stake in the final outcome and feared that if Japan capitulated to US demands, the USA would be encouraged to apply similar pressures on them which they could not possibly resist. As such, countries like Malaysia and South Korea urged Japan to stand firm against US demands for quantitative import targets. Apart from international support, the Japanese government, for its own national interest, rejected US demands. This was an important occasion when Japan forced the USA to drop its harshest demands and might be a harbinger for a more constructive Japanese international role.

Economic issues take precedence in this region despite the fact that there remain a number of unresolved political and territorial disputes with a potential to destabilize the region. At the same time, there appears to be a tacit understanding not to push political tensions too far and instead to concentrate on economic issues on which there is ready agreement. Countries in the region seem to agree that the best way to advance settlement of political conflicts and to promote co-operation is through economic linkages and engagement. Japan was the first country to reinstate aid to China after the Tiananmen Square incident (1989) and it also provided aid and investment to Vietnam despite a US embargo.

Foreign aid has been important in establishing Japan's regional credentials. In the early 1990s, Japan became the leading provider of Official Development Assistance (ODA) and the South-East Asian countries plus China are the main recipients of Japanese aid. Foreign aid is the least controversial and most welcome form of Japanese involvement in regional affairs. However, there have been questions raised about the quality of Japanese aid, specifically that Japanese aid strategy is designed mainly to benefit Japanese industry and that Japan is guilty of 'aid mercantilism'. Shafiqul Islam refutes these charges saying that Japanese aid is less tied than other Western aid or in comparison to the USA. He argues that 'in 1987 the share of fully and partially tied aid in bilateral ODA was 48 per cent for Japan and was over 90 per cent for the United States. On procurement ... about 60 per cent of Japanese bilateral ODA was spent on Japanese goods and services, while the US ratio was about 70 per cent' (Islam, 1993, p.346).

In the late 1980s, Japan also helped to shape the Brady Plan which offered debt relief for the Third World debtor countries. Prior to the announcement of the Brady Plan in 1989, Japan had already offered to write off US$8 billion of debt owed to it by the least developed countries. According to Susan Pharr, the Japanese input into the Brady Plan was 'a good example of the change in Japanese approach, from a passive acceptance of the leadership of other countries to efforts to seize the initiative in international development problem-solving' (Pharr, 1994, p.163).

3.4   Conclusion

The Asia-Pacific has transformed itself in the post-Second World War period from economic stagnation to a potential global economic 'power house'. There remain pockets of continuing backwardness but more than any other region in the world, the Asia-Pacific is characterized as one which is dynamic and rapidly ascending the economic ladder. Politically, however, the Asia-Pacific has lacked an organizing structure or an identity although there is some expectation of an emerging Asia-Pacific Century based on the economic successes of East Asia and, in particular, that of Japan. It would be erroneous, however, to assume that this would mean a global hegemony by countries of the Asia-Pacific. The economic achievements of these economies have been achieved through international trade and export led development strategies in which the USA played a key role by providing a market for their exports. The East Asian economies, not surprisingly, have not demonstrated any readiness to develop an exclusive East Asian regional bloc. Instead, as the next chapter argues, they have sought to foster cooperative and consultative behaviour among the countries of the region, and their main trading partners, in order to maintain their outward looking growth and development strategies.

References

Dobbs-Higginson, M.S. (1993) *Asia Pacific: Its Role in the New World Disorder*, London, Heinemann.

Frankel, J.A. and Kahler, M. (eds) (1993) *Regionalism and Rivalry: Japan and the United States in the Pacific Asia*, Chicago, The University of Chicago Press.

Garby, C.C. and Bullock, M.B. (eds) (1994) *Japan: a New Kind of Superpower?*, Baltimore, Johns Hopkins Press.

Garnaut, R. (1989) *Australia and the Northeast Asian Ascendancy*, Canberra, Australian Government Publishing Service.

Islam, S. (1993) 'Foreign aid and burden sharing: is Japan free riding to a coprosperity sphere in Asia?' in Frankel, J.A. and Kahler, M. (eds).

Krugman, P. (1995) 'Asia's growth: miracle or myth?', *Foreign Affairs*, vol.73, no.6.

Pharr, S.J. (1994) 'Japanese aid in the New World Order' in Garby, C.C. and Bullock, M.B. (eds).

Rix, A. (1988) 'Australia and Japan: the reality of the "special relationship"' in Mediansky, F.A. and Palfreeman, A.C. (eds) *In Pursuit of National Interests: Australian Foreign Policy in the 1990s*, Sydney, Pergamon Press.

Roberts, J.M. (1992) *The Penguin History of the World*, London, Penguin Books.

Wijkman, P.M. (1993) 'The existing bloc expanded? The European Community, EFTA, and eastern Europe' in Bergsten, C.F. and Noland, M. (eds) *Pacific Dynamism and the International Economic System*, Washington, D.C., Institute for International Economics.

World Bank (1993) *The East Asian Miracle: Economic Growth and Public Policy*, A World Bank Policy Research Report, New York, Oxford University Press.

Yahuda, M. (1978) *China's Role in World Affairs*, New York, St Martin's Press.

Further reading

Berger, M. and Borer, D. (eds) (1997) *The Rise of East Asia*, London, Routledge.

Clark, C. and Chan, S. (1992) *The Evolving Pacific Basin*, Boulder, Lynne Rienner.

Godement, F. (1997) *The New Asian Renaissance*, London, Routledge.

Shibusawa, M., Ahmed, Z.H. and Bridges, B. (1992) *Pacific Asia in the 1990s*, London, Routledge.

PART 2

The New Regional Order

CHAPTER 4

The Asia-Pacific: what sort of region in what sort of world?

Barry Buzan

4.1   Introduction

This chapter is concerned with the question, what kind of region is the Asia-Pacific and in what kind of world is it located? The chapter argues that the rhetoric underlying a regional perspective on the Asia-Pacific tells us less about the international relations of this area than a perspective that sees the USA as an outside player in an East Asian region. Section 4.2 explores the concept of region in international relations theory, noting the essential criteria and the diversity of interpretations that they can produce. The next section uses these criteria to examine the case for thinking of the Asia-Pacific as a distinct region, arguing that while there is a case, it is rather weak. Then Section 4.4 applies the same criteria and finds a considerably stronger case for seeing East Asia as the principal regional phenomenon. In this perspective the USA is a global great power player with engagements in several regions, and Asia-Pacific rhetoric one of several anti-regional devices for maintaining US global access and influence.

4.2   The concept of region

The concept of region is widely used, but seldom very clearly defined. The media mostly use it simply to designate where something is happening: the Gulf, Europe, Central Africa. In discussions of politics, region usually refers to a sub-unit of the state: Bavaria, the Midwest, Wales, Siberia. In international relations, region usually refers to something bigger than a state. It should properly be known as an international region, and may be composed of several states and/or parts of states. But if the concept of region is to have any analytical power, one has to specify the reasons that justify separating out one part of the international system from the rest. What are the necessary and sufficient conditions that justify designating something as a region in international relations? Unfortunately there is no clear answer to this question – or rather there are many answers, all based on different mixtures of criteria and so identifying different phenomena. Neither political scientists (Thompson, 1973) nor economists (Grant *et al.*, 1993, pp.48–9) have succeeded in building a consensus on what they mean by region, and this lack of agreement on the concept makes comparisons between different studies tricky. The one major attempt to construct international regions as a general category failed to catch on because of its excessive complexity (Cantori and Spiegel, 1972). But there are, neverthe-less, some ideas that can serve as the basis for analysis, and before I try to assess the status of the Asia-Pacific as an international region, it is worth reflecting on them in some detail.

The most basic requirement for a region is that it be less than the whole international system of which it is a part. A region is thus a species of subsystem, but it is not just any subsystem. One would not identify the members of the Organization for Economic Co-operation and Develop-ment (OECD), or the British Commonwealth, or the Landlocked and Geographically Disadvantaged States group, as composing a region. If writers about regions agree on nothing else, there is a firm consensus that regions are a specific type of subsystem marked by the geographical adjacency and contiguity of their component parts. The USA and Canada can form a region in a way that the USA and India cannot. This geographical requirement seems clear, but on closer scrutiny turns out to conceal ambiguities of its own. There is no problem when the component parts of a region are all territorially connected, as in the case of South America or Southern Africa. There is usually no problem if parts of a region are separated by narrow bodies of water. Sri Lanka is part of South Asia despite the Palk Strait, and Indonesia and the Philippines are part of South-East Asia despite their separation from the mainland by the South China Sea. Britain is part of Europe, though the potential political significance of even narrow bodies of water will be apparent to anyone who has followed the British debates about European integration. There is usually no problem in conceptualizing an international region around a sea. The Black Sea states, the Baltic states and the Mediterranean states have all constructed themselves as regions for certain purposes (most obviously pollution control), and in principle the same could be done with the Caribbean and the Sea of Japan. Defining regions around oceans would seem to stretch the criteria for geographical adjacency and contiguity almost beyond breaking point, but is none the less done. The North Atlantic is quite commonly referred to as a region, and for a time there was a fashion for thinking about the Indian Ocean in this way (the proposal for the Indian Ocean as a Zone of Peace).

The notion of the Asia-Pacific as a region is the most ambitious of these proposals, seeking to connect three continents by stretching the idea of regionness across the widest ocean on the planet. If we are to consider this huge expanse as a region, then we must identify what ties it together sufficiently to justify differentiating it from the rest of the international system. All regions have to be more than just a geographical subsystem. One cannot simply take any collection of adjacent states and label them a region. That 'more' can be provided in any of three ways: by shared characteristics, by patterned interactions, and by shared perception.

Shared characteristics

Shared characteristics is the simplest, but also least interesting, of these criteria. A region might be identified on the basis of many sorts of shared characteristics: a river basin (Nile, Tigris-Euphrates, Mekong); a language or culture (the Arab world); a particular form of government such as democracy (Western Europe) or communism (the former Soviet empire); the range of a particular disease or pest (malaria, the African bee); and suchlike. Mostly this approach does not take us far in understanding international regions, though it may be an important component of them. It is not clear that one would learn anything much about the Asia-Pacific by looking for shared characteristics.

Patterned interactions

More interesting, but more complicated, is how regions are defined by interactions amongst their component parts. Interaction is usually the key to identifying what distinguishes an international region from the rest of the international system. To count as a region, it needs to display an intensity of interaction sufficient to mark it out as a distinctive subsystem in some significant way. This is where the richness and complexity of international regions come into play, for there are many different forms and types of interaction that might define regionness. To understand the linkage between interaction and regionness it is helpful to think about four things: the type of interaction, the attitudes that go along with it, its intensity, and the boundaries that contain it (or which it defines).

First is the type(s) of interaction involved. Is the region defined by military interaction, where a pattern of war, or an interlocking set of alliances and antagonisms, identifies a particular set of states? Pre-1945 Europe, and the contemporary Middle East and South Asia exemplify this pattern. Or is the region defined by economic patterns, where the patterns of trade, investment and technology transfer grow more rapidly within a region than between it and the rest of the world? This is often argued for Europe, and to a lesser extent for North America and East Asia. Or is the region defined in more cultural terms, by the movement of people, the interplay of literature and ideas, or the networks of religious organization, as might be said of the Arab world? Nothing prevents regions from displaying more than one of these types of interaction. Both North Atlantic and trans-Pacific relations, for example, mix economic and politico-military qualities.

A second aspect of interaction is the attitude that accompanies or underlies it. By and large regions have to have some attitudinal angle on them, whether integrationist or conflictual. Interaction is a neutral term, and its contents can range from friendly and co-operative, through neutral and competitive, to hostile and conflictual. There is nothing intrinsically good (or bad) about international regions. They can be either positive or negative (or anything in between). Much of the early writing about international regions came from those interested in the processes and possibilities of integration. This interest was largely inspired by the development of the European Economic Community (later European Union, EU), and its many imitators. There is still some tendency in the literature to associate regions and regionness with processes of integration. But regions can also be formed by conflict or insecurity. It is possible to identify regional *security complexes* as sets of states whose national securities are sufficiently interdependent that it is impossible to consider them separately (Buzan, 1991; Buzan *et al.*, 1997). Israel and its neighbours constitute such a set, as do the countries of South Asia. In such cases the quality of regionness is defined by the relative intensity of security interdependence amongst the actors within the region as compared with their relations with actors outside the region. There have been several intense and large-scale conflicts within the Gulf, South Asia and South-East Asia, but relatively little spillover from any of these into the adjacent regions. A *regional security complex* does not have to be defined by the negative interdependence of a *conflict formation* (where security interdependence arises from fear and mutual perceptions of threat). It can also exist in the more positive forms of a *security regime* (where states have made reassurance arrangements to moderate the threats they pose to each other) or a *pluralist security community* (where states no longer expect or prepare to use force in their relations with each other).

The third feature of interaction is its intensity: how much of it is there both in an absolute sense and relative to what is happening in the rest of the system? Intensity of interaction is what makes regions interesting (or not) as a level of analysis. How much of what is going on can be understood by focusing on the regional level as opposed to the global level on one side, and the national and sub-national levels on the other? During the Cold War there was a fashion for global level explanations (bipolarity and all that). Post-Cold War, regions have come more into fashion as the favoured level of explanation, though there are still many who focus on the processes of globalization. In absolute terms there has to be some interaction to define the region, which otherwise would just be a random collection of geographically adjacent states. In principle any level of interaction could be used to designate a region, but in practice the higher the intensity, the more credible the claim to regionness. Under contemporary conditions of globalization, where highest levels of interaction are the norm world-wide, a relatively high intensity of interaction is usually necessary to distinguish a region from the surrounding system. In other words, the fact that a neighbouring group of countries do 30 per cent of their trade with each other diminishes in significance if most of them are doing similar levels of trade with others outside the region.

One indicator of intensity might be whether a region is institutionalized or not, but this can be deceiving. In a case like the EU, the great range and depth of institutions does indeed signify high levels of interaction in many areas. But an organization such as the South Asian Association for Regional Co-operation (SAARC) signifies little other than the existence of a regional forum in which a limited number of issues might get discussed. Some regions in which a good case can be made for the significance of the regional level are relatively poorly endowed with institutions. East Asia is the most obvious example, where many voices can be heard explicitly rejecting the institution-heavy European approach to regionalism. Where the impulse to regionalism is essentially friendly and co-operative, institutions might be expected to cover the whole region, as the Southern African Development Community does and the EU might eventually do. But where it is conflictual, one would expect institutions to cover only part of the region, as the Gulf Co-operation Council does, and as ASEAN did before its recent expansions.

Finally there is the issue of what boundaries contain, or are defined by, the regional pattern of interaction. In principle, regions could exist with firm boundaries that set them off clearly from other parts of the international system. Occasionally they do, but mostly regions are a matter of relative intensity of interaction within as opposed to without. Few regions approach any sort of self-contained quality, and there may well be problems even in deciding how to put boundaries around a region. Take, for example, the regional security complex in South Asia. This has traditionally been defined around the long rivalry between India and Pakistan, with the smaller states caught up in this pattern. But the question of China remains awkward. China has also fought a war with India, and much of India's military and nuclear policy is justified with reference to China. Should China therefore not be counted as part of the South Asian region? The case against doing so is that China is an intruding power rather than part of the region. Although China may be a principal threat for India, the reverse is not true. India is a relatively marginal matter for China. While India plays its role largely within South Asia, China plays in several regions. China thus has to be seen either as a member of several regions (which would play havoc with the concept) or as an outside power that intrudes into several regions but is a member of only one.

What this case raises is the difficult question of how to classify the membership (or not) of any given region. Just because a power is an active participant in the affairs of a region does not necessarily make it part of that region. The USA, for example, is an active player in the Middle East, but its lack of adjacency means that it cannot be considered part of the region. The case of China and South Asia is more awkward because China does share a long border with the region, and therefore could be counted in under the adjacency principle. But once it is accepted that regions are only one tier in a set of levels (global, regional, state, sub-state), then it becomes clear that account needs to be taken of the penetrative effect of higher levels (globally or super-regionally operating great powers) into regions. Major powers like the USA, China and Russia may well intervene in several regions, but it would be a category error to count them as members of such regions.

Where the intervening great power is geographically remote from the region this distinction between member and outside player is easy to make. But where it is adjacent, the distinction can be difficult. The key is found in the relative weight of engagement in the defining interactions of the region. Intruding great powers, even if adjacent, will normally have equal or greater engagements elsewhere. The USA may be adjacent to, and engaged in Latin America, but its principal engagements are elsewhere. The trick here is first to distinguish between the dynamic of regional-level interactions, and those of global (and other) levels, and then to see how the different levels interact. It usually gives a clearer picture to see super powers on the global level rather than as members of local regions. Security complex theory, for example, predicts that global level, great power actors will tend to penetrate into regional conflict formations by taking sides in the regional antagonism. Thus during the Cold War, the USA and China lined up with Pakistan, and the Soviet Union with India in South Asia, while in the Middle East, the USA sided with Israel and the Soviet Union with several of the Arab states. As you will see below, this issue of how to distinguish between intervening great powers and members of the region is crucial in considering the regional status of the Asia-Pacific.

Shared perception

In addition to shared characteristics and varying types and degrees of interaction, regions can also be defined by perception. If people think that a region exists, and talk about it as if it did, then in a sense it does. Talking about a region may well be the first step in a political strategy to bring it into being. Some argue that a shared perception of regionness is a necessary condition for a region to exist (Thompson, 1973). But I argue that if this applies at all, it applies only to regions based on co-operative and integrative interactions. Conflict-based regions, like balances of power, can exist without the participants recognizing that they form a region. They may, of course, recognize that their relationship forms a regional subsystem, and it might be argued that it would be a useful thing if they did. But each actor may also just see itself as engaged in a set of bilateral relationships without seeing the larger pattern that ties them together. One also needs to look at the balance between the rhetoric of regionalism and the reality in terms of actual patterns of interaction. The two may line up comfortably, as they mostly do in Europe. But they may not. Rhetoric is more visible than substance in the Organization of African Unity, the Arab League, and also traditionally in many of the sub-regional organizations in Latin America. Is this the case for Asia-Pacific, whose main institution, Asia-Pacific Economic Co-operation (APEC), is often accused of being little more than hot air? If so, what is one to make of 'regions' that are more apparent than real?

The next section will apply these criteria to the Asia-Pacific to see how well its claim to regionness stands up. Section 4.4 will look at the case that the Asia-Pacific is less than the sum of its parts, and that a better understanding of it can be gained by seeing East Asia as a region, and the USA as a penetrating outside power.

4.3 First view: the Asia-Pacific as an international region

The Asia-Pacific can meet the criteria of being a geographically defined subsystem, but its vast size puts it at the very outer limit of what might reasonably be thought of as a region. Its ocean-centredness might seem problematic to some, but provided other criteria are met so that the ocean is seen to unite more than it divides, it does provide a version of adjacency and contiguity. Any attempt to define a region larger than this would begin to overlap with the global level.

In a 'region' of this size, it is hardly surprising that shared characteristics, other than bordering on the same ocean, are hard to find. There is little conspicuous in terms of shared culture, geography or suchlike that makes this a region. A claim to shared history might be built on the Pacific part of the Second World War and its antecedents, in which a Japanese–American rivalry became the main axis of international relations in the Pacific. But this was part of a much larger global pattern and is not usually thought of in regional terms. The main claim of the Asia-Pacific thus hangs on more contemporary interaction and perception. There are two types of interaction on which to base a claim for an Asia-Pacific region: politico-military and economic.

In terms of politico-military links, the first thing to say is that the Asia-Pacific is not a security complex in the traditional sense. It is not a conflict formation because there are no central antagonisms that define the region and differentiate it from surrounding areas. It could only become one if the USA and one of the major East Asian powers (China or Japan) fell into military rivalry. It is not impossible to imagine this happening with China in the not too distant future, but it has not happened yet, and if it did happen would have repercussions well beyond the Asia-Pacific. A revival of Japanese militarism and rivalry with the USA is sometimes talked about, but is nowhere on the horizon as a real possibility.

At the other end of the spectrum, the Asia-Pacific is not a pluralist security community. Several of its members, most notably China and Taiwan, and the two Koreas, are prepared to use force against each other, and the USA appears prepared to intervene if conflict breaks out.

There are a couple of elements of a case for seeing the Asia-Pacific as a security regime, but the arguments are not very convincing. The first element is the series of mostly bilateral security treaties that the USA has with a variety of East Asian states: most notably Japan and South Korea, but also Thailand, the Philippines, Australia and New Zealand (ANZUS), and arguably Taiwan. The problem with these is that they do not cover the whole region, and they are mostly one-way guarantees by the USA to protect its clients rather than mutual guarantees. Since the USA has many

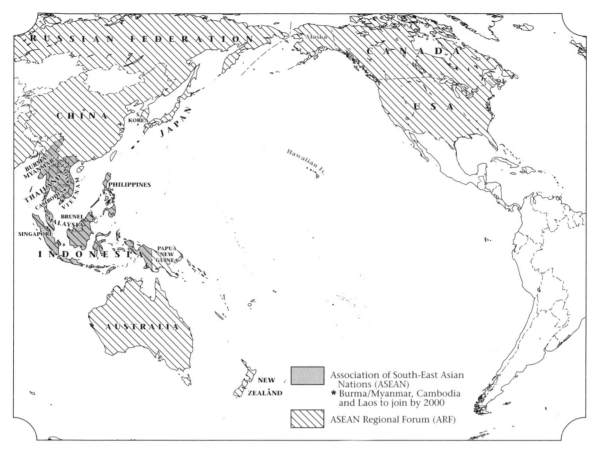

Figure 4.1 *Membership of ASEAN and the ASEAN Regional Forum. The EU is also a member of the ARF. (See also Chapter 12, Table 12.1)*

such arrangements world-wide, it is not clear how this set of relationships can be used to differentiate the Asia-Pacific from other parts of the world.

The second element of a possible security regime is the ASEAN Regional Forum (ARF), but this too is problematic. ASEAN (Association of South-East Asian Nations) is a long-standing sub-regional organization composed of middle and small powers (Thailand, Indonesia, Malaysia, Singapore, Brunei, the Philippines). It has been highly successful in creating a security regime amongst its members, and during the Cold War it also had some standing as a common bulwark against Vietnamese communist expansion. Since the Cold War it has been busy expanding to incorporate its former rivals, with Vietnam joining in 1995, and Burma/Myanmar, Cambodia and Laos expected to join by the end of the century. It has also attempted to construct a wider security framework by drawing its so-called 'dialogue partners' into the ARF, a process backed by Japan (Foot, 1995, p.242). As Leifer (1996, pp.26, 46) argues, post-Cold War ASEAN has been forced to see itself as part of a bigger security picture, no longer confined just to South-East Asia. The not so hidden agenda of the ARF is to engage China, which ASEAN does not want to do by itself, nor in East Asia alone, but in a Pacific and even global context. As Leifer put it (1996, p.55), 'The undeclared aim of the ARF is to defuse and control regional tensions by generating and sustaining a network of dialogues within the over-arching framework of its annual meetings, while the nexus of economic incentive works on governments irrevocably committed to market-based economic develop-ment'. The diplomatic level of the ARF is accompanied by the 'track two' arrangements of CSCAP (the Council for Security Co-operation in the Asia Pacific) which brings together academics and policy analysts from the various countries. The ARF does include most of the Asia-Pacific states (notably excepting North Korea and Taiwan), which potentially gives it standing as the basis for a loose Asia-Pacific security regime. But it also includes India and the European Union, which takes it well out of area (notwithstanding residual British and French colonial leftovers in Pacific Asia). This problem of out of area involvement is also evident in the Five Power Defence Arrangement which involves Australia, New Zealand, Singapore, Malaysia and the UK. The ARF's much touted commitment to 'open regionalism' makes it difficult to see the ARF as a specifically Asia-Pacific phenomenon. It does incorporate much of the Asia-Pacific, but by engaging India and the EU it is effectively bidding for global status.

Thus while there are significant military-political interactions within the Asia-Pacific, they are not strong enough, comprehensive enough, balanced enough, or exclusive enough to differentiate the Asia-Pacific from other parts of the international system.

What about economic interaction? Here the case looks more promising. Although there is no consensus on the necessary and sufficient conditions for an economic region the game is to look at patterns of trade and patterns of foreign direct investment (FDI) with a view both to the relative levels within the region and the rest of the world, and the direction in which the proportions are moving. In both trade and FDI there is evidence for an Asia-Pacific region. Grant *et al.* (1993, p.53) argue that: 'Within-region trade is ... greater within the Asia-Pacific region than within either of the "formal" regions at opposite ends of the Pacific Basin (North America and the hypothetical East Asia)'. This view is shared by Hessler (1994), who uses trade statistics to show how Asia-Pacific trade grew much more strongly than intra-regional trade in either NAFTA (North American Free Trade Agreement) or East Asia between 1960 and 1988. The percentage trade figures are also impressive (see Table 4.1).

Table 4.1 *Asia-Pacific trade as a percentage of total trade*

	1980	1985	1991
North America with East Asia	19%	26%	27%
East Asia with North America	22%	29%	23%

Source: Wyatt-Walter (1995, p.99)

Wyatt-Walter (1995, p.104) argues that East Asia's regional trade bias actually fell over the 1980s. Even those who disagree with these figures, such as Katzenstein (1996, p.135), still see heavy East Asian trade dependence on the US market and no tendency for a division into East Asian versus NAFTA economic regions. FDI flows also show strong tendencies to cross oceans rather than remain centred in any given continent. Hessler (1994, p.6), suggests that: '*inter*regional transatlantic and transpacific investment is much more important than regional flows'. Wyatt-Walter (1995, p.105) notes a strong concentration of Japanese FDI in North America, rising from 34 per cent to 50 per cent of total FDI during 1980–89, about four times the figure for its investment in Asia. Comparable US figures support the trans-oceanic hypothesis, but show a heavy concentration in Europe (around 50 per cent, more than four times the figure for East Asia).

These trans-Pacific economic links, and to a lesser extent the military security ones, have given rise to a great deal of Asia-Pacific rhetoric, and also to an institution, the Asia-Pacific Economic Co-operation (APEC), whose oddly worded name almost suggests a desire to avoid taking an institutional form. The existence of APEC and all of its accompanying Asia-Pacific talk suggests that whatever the realities or shortcomings of trans-Pacific interaction, there is no problem about the Asia-Pacific being

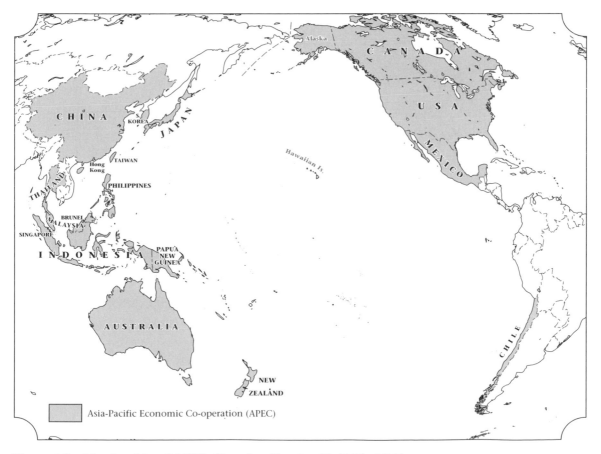

Figure 4.2 *Membership of APEC. (See also Chapter 12, Table 12.1)*

perceived as a region. In part this rhetoric reflects the enhanced wealth and status of East Asia in the global economy, and the desire to project a new Pacific image as the wave of the future in contrast to the Atlantic as the old focus of global power (Mahbubani, 1995). But as Higgott (1994, p.66) points out, much of this rhetoric and its supporting literature is heavily prescriptive and exhortatory, creating the danger of the perception of the region outrunning its rather modest reality. Some voices have been particularly loud, most notably that of Australia. Canberra has promoted Asia-Pacific perspectives in part because it fears finding itself in an East Asian region detached from North America. And there are dissenting voices, most robustly from Malaysia and Singapore, which seek to promote an East Asian region against the Asia-Pacific view. Partly because the USA favoured bilateralism in Asia (as opposed to the multilateralism it fostered in Europe) East Asia and the Asia-Pacific have been notably weak in the development of formal institutions (Katzenstein, 1996, p.141). Like the ARF, APEC is of recent, post-Cold War origin, and not yet deeply rooted. Although both are welcome as overdue starting points for regional institution-building, it is not yet clear whether either of them will become influential in the affairs of their members or whether they will remain largely symbolic.

APEC meeting in Bogor, Indonesia: leaders from the member countries at the presidential palace, 15 November 1994

But while APEC and the Asia-Pacific rhetoric provide firm perceptual evidence in support of an Asia-Pacific region, the attitudes underlying Asia-Pacific interaction are decidedly mixed. While military interactions can be either positive or negative, one cannot make the assumption that economic interactions are necessarily friendly. Trade and investment may also be sources of hostility. Harris (1993, p.15), for example, sees American Japan-bashing as an example of economics as the continuation of war by other means – i.e. a trans-Pacific conflict dynamic. And while liberals will tend to concentrate on the joint gains from economic exchange, there is an underlying linkage between the economic and military patterns in the Asia-Pacific that carries somewhat more sinister overtones. American statements at APEC summits in 1993 and 1994 made it clear that the US links the costs of its regional leadership role and military presence in Asia to continued access to the Asian economy (Stuart and Tow, 1995, p.48; Simon, 1994, p.1051). Public connections of military and economic relations in this way are not just a means of bringing American pressure to bear against the East Asian enthusiasts for a more specifically East Asian bloc. They are also a way of underlining the unequal quality of trans-Pacific relations, and the dependence of the East Asians' political and military security on the US presence.

To sum up, a case can be made for the existence of an Asia-Pacific international region, but not a very strong one. It mostly rests on a rising pattern of reciprocal trans-Pacific trade, on a more lopsided pattern of investment, and on the existence of a wealth of Asia-Pacific rhetoric and a new and still quite superficial regional organization. The question is whether more is gained or lost in terms of understanding international relations in this area by adopting an Asia-Pacific regional perspective? Does the self-promoting Asia-Pacific dialogue reflect an emerging reality, or does it mask a set of relationships more usefully seen in other terms?

4.4   Second view: the Asia-Pacific as an element of the new global structure

The alternative to seeing the Asia-Pacific as an international region, is to see it as one element in the emergent structure of the post-Cold War global political economy. In this rather wider view the central phenomenon is the USA, now beginning to find its feet in the new role of sole superpower, but not unipolar world hegemon. The key regions are East Asia, Europe, North America and South America. The central issue is how the USA relates to this set of regions, in the middle of which it conveniently sits. It is beyond the remit of this chapter to explore all of these regions, but to set up this view one must look at East Asia as a region, and at the special qualities of the USA that make it stand outside, and in some important senses above, the regional level. The key to this view is the argument in Section 4.2 that playing a major role in a region does not necessarily make a power a member of that region. From this perspective, the American role in East Asia is comparable to its role in the Middle East or Europe – an outside great power penetrating into the affairs of a region.

It is not at all unusual for either analysts or practitioners to see East Asia as a region in its own right. Indeed, it is almost standard procedure for political-economy-based regional analysts, particularly in comparative mode, to start with East Asia, NAFTA and the EU (Helleiner, 1994; Hessler, 1994). This might be explained in part by the tendency of regional analysts to give priority to more 'normal' continental, land-linked regions defined by the strong element of shared territorial geography. Pursuit of this approach constructs a two-region logic – East Asia and NAFTA – in opposition to the Asia-Pacific view. This argument needs to be taken into account, but the case to be made in this section places much more weight on the special position and role of the USA as a player operating above the regional level, than on the North American region. To begin with, we need to establish the standing of East Asia (and North America) as regions.

Shared characteristics tell us more about East Asia and North America than they do about the Asia-Pacific. In North America, there is quite a bit of cultural coherence, and a lot of shared history. In East Asia, there is not much cultural coherence: Buddhism, Confucianism, Christianity, Islam and Shinto divide more than they unite. But there is a significant shared history built around several millennia of the waxing and waning of Chinese suzerainty over much of the region. Korea, Taiwan and parts of South-East Asia were regularly within the Chinese empire, and Japan, Burma and parts of Indonesia were within the zone of Chinese trade and cultural influence. Vietnam, Thailand, Malaysia, Burma and Indonesia all have significant Chinese minorities, and Singapore is mostly Chinese.

If we look at these two regions in terms of their military-political interactions we see two quite different pictures. North America might be characterized as a security community. The USA accounts for the great bulk of the wealth, population and power in North America and easily dominates the region. The border with Canada has long been demilitarized, and whatever the tensions with Mexico about drugs and migrants there is no thought of war between the two countries.

In East Asia, as elsewhere, the ending of the Cold War has meant the withdrawal of Soviet power from the area, and the ending of US–Soviet rivalry as the dominating security feature of the region. This has meant that the local security dynamics of the region are now much freer to express themselves. As a consequence, we seem to be looking at the emergence of a classical security complex in East Asia. I have made this case in detail elsewhere and will sketch it out here (Buzan and Segal, 1994; Buzan, 1994, 1996). The security complex emerging in East Asia after the Cold War bears some resemblance to that in nineteenth-century Europe. It is composed of more than a dozen states ranging from large, through medium to small powers. These states are in varying stages of industrialization, which means that absolute levels of power are increasing rapidly, and that the distribution of power is unstable as industrialization changes relative capabilities amongst them. Levels of military capability are rising rapidly as expanding GNPs allow many states to upgrade their armed forces even without increasing the percentage of GNP that they spend on them (Dibb, 1995). Most of these states have territorial and/or historical disputes with their neighbours, and particularly in North-East Asia, these are regularly wheeled out and polished. Two unresolved problems of divided countries left over from the Cold War – China–Taiwan and the two Koreas – are the focus of armed confrontations that could easily tip over into war at short notice.

With the winding down of superpower influence in Asia, China is the key to this emerging security complex. Like the Germany of a century ago, it is playing the role of a large, centrally located, rapidly industrializing, authoritarian, and revisionist state that makes all of its neighbours feel insecure. China's role in integrating the security dynamics of North-East and South-East Asia is reinforced both by its many territorial disputes, and by its long historical record as the imperial suzerain in the region. Its neighbours fear that as China regains power it will try to pick up that role once again, possibly exploiting the Chinese diaspora which in some South-East Asian countries is feared as a potential fifth column. As most recently (1996) demonstrated in its reaction to elections in Taiwan, China is quite unrestrained in using military instruments against its neighbours in traditional power politics fashion.

The parallel with nineteenth-century Europe can be extended to Japan. In some ways Japan mirrors Britain as the offshore island and most advanced industrial country in the region, trying to follow a policy of splendid isolation that detaches it from its region and projects it on to the world stage. But, unlike Britain, Japan is disqualified from playing the role of regional leader, or even balancer. Its unresolved historical legacies from the Second World War and earlier make such a great power role unacceptable both to the Japanese and to most of their neighbours (Buzan, 1988). Anti-militarism remains very strong in the Japanese population and elite, and China and the two Koreas, and to a lesser extent countries in South-East Asia, make a point of cultivating memories of Japanese imperialism and its atrocities.

Japan's exceptionalism hobbles the working of normal balance of power mechanisms, and this fact goes a long way towards explaining the peculiarities of East Asian military-political security dynamics. Most peculiar is the role of ASEAN, particularly the ARF. The credit for ASEAN's impressively successful self-construction of a sub-regional security regime in South-East Asia is largely due to its member countries themselves. But its attempt to construct the ARF as a security forum for East Asia reflects Japan's inability to play a leadership role in military-political relations. This creates the odd sight of a collection of small and medium powers attempting to provide military-political security leadership in a region dominated by two great powers. Their obvious inability and unwillingness to balance China leaves them with only the 'dialogue' strategy of trying to engage China in an ongoing diplomatic process of conflict avoidance and, hopefully, resolution. Because Japan cannot do it, military-political counterweight has to be provided from outside the region, and the ARF's inclusion of the USA is a recognition of this need. The USA, with its network of alliances and commitments in the region left over from the Second World War and the Cold War is ideally placed to hold the ring for East Asian military-political security. The USA is not part of the East Asian complex, but because of the peculiarities of relations within East Asia, plays a major role within it. Most East Asian states, with the notable exception of China, trust the USA more than they trust each other. Again there are parallels with Europe, where the USA also plays a major role from outside the region, but in East Asia the levels of distrust and fear amongst the major powers within the region are much higher than they are in contemporary Europe.

An equally substantial case can be made for North American and East Asian regions in terms of economic interactions (see Table 4.2). Foot (1995, pp.244–5) notes that levels of intra-regional trade in East Asia rose steadily to reach 45 per cent in 1994. She also argues, as does Aho (1993, pp.34–5), that Japanese investment in East Asia during the 1980s created a pyramid of FDI and technological dependence with Japan at the top, then the newly-industrialized countries (NICs), then the rest of ASEAN, then China, Vietnam and Burma. This is the much commented on 'flying geese' image of East Asia as a group of states all committed to development goals, and linked in a hierarchy to Japan. A variant on this picture is provided by Yu (1995), who sets out the case that the 'greater China' of ethnic Chinese outside the mainland has recently become a major element in regional integration through FDI. He argues that since the late 1980s this Chinese diaspora has begun taking over from Japan as the key to future informal integration in the region.

Table 4.2   *Intra-regional trade as a percentage of total trade*

	1980	*1985*	*1991*
East Asia	35%	38%	45%
North America	33%	38%	38%
European Union	52%	54%	60%

Source: Wyatt-Walter (1995, p.99); see also similar figures in Srinivasan *et al.* (1993, p.61)

The informal quality of East Asian regionalism is important, because the area lacks the institutions that mark out North American and European economic regions. As Helleiner (1994) argues, there are distinctly different styles of regionalization in North America, East Asia and Europe. In Europe, the style is characterized by high levels of institutionalization (the EU), strong commitment to the social market and the principle of equalization, and also strong commitment to the creation of a genuine single market including general factor mobility. In North America, the level of institutionalization is relatively low (NAFTA). Regionalization is defined mostly by neo-liberal rules, and there is no commitment to equalization or factor mobility for labour. In East Asia, there is almost no institutionalization and low factor mobility. The 'flying geese' formation is largely created by private capital. The only sign of a regional economic institution is the East Asian Economic Caucus (EAEC), comprising the eleven Asian members of APEC. This is a weaker version of a proposed East

Asian Economic Grouping (EAEG). Because of US opposition and Japanese hesitation it has become a subgroup of APEC rather than an alternative to it (Katzenstein, 1996, pp.139–40).

A reasonably strong case can thus be made for both East Asian and North American regions. In North America, the security community and the free trade area line up in complementary style, and the existence of NAFTA indicates a substantial shared perception of regionness. The East Asian case is much more complicated. There is good evidence for significant regionalization in both military-political terms and economic ones, but these do not line up. Whereas economic interaction tends to unite East Asia, military-political interaction is more divisive, potentially catastrophically so. As Dibb (1995, p.47) argues, 'There appears to be a lack of synergy between economic and military security in Asia, and most of all there is a total absence of any effective formulation of economic and security regionalism'. Within the region this disjuncture creates a strong dilemma about how to relate to China between liberal impulses (trade and invest for profit and to create interdependence) and realist ones (avoid strengthening authoritarian, revisionist states who might use their power against you). As things stand, Asian (and Western) traders and investors face this liberal–realist dilemma in acute form in China. By engaging with the Chinese economy they enrich themselves and China, and hopefully entangle Beijing in the liberal incentive scheme of joint gains requiring peaceful relations. But by enriching a still authoritarian China they also make it more powerful, increasing its means to make trouble should its leaders want to go in that direction. For individual companies or states to try to restrict economic interaction with China would simply leave the field open to competitors and create direct hostility with Beijing. The question is whether the liberal mechanisms of peace-making economic-entanglement work faster or slower than the realist ones of military and political power increasing on the back of an expanding economy? No country faces this dilemma more strongly than Taiwan, which is both a leading investor in China and the principal target of Chinese military threats, though the same logic also operates less acutely for Japan.

In part because of this dilemma, East Asia appears, in terms of perception, to be almost in denial about its regionness. Whereas there is much that is attractive about both North American and European regionalism, in East Asia both of its forms are unpalatable to most of the actors within the region. Few states in East Asia want to be reminded – or face – the fact that their economic boom sits on top of a potentially nasty pattern of politico-military fear, hostility and conflict that embraces the whole region. The region may be a conflict-formation security complex, but that image does not sit well with its pretensions to be the new world centre of economic and cultural dynamism. The pattern of economic integration is also unpleasant to contemplate. The 'flying geese' model is an uncomfortable reminder of Japanese hegemony, echoing the much reviled Japanese-run Greater East Asia Co-Prosperity Sphere built up during Japan's imperial phase. The 'Greater China' model is almost equally aversive, linking to older fears of Chinese hegemonism. Thus while the reality of an East Asian region is quite strong in terms of interactions, acknowledgement of this reality within the region is, with one or two exceptions, notably subdued. The negative qualities of East Asian regionalism go a long way towards explaining both the weakness of its supporting rhetoric and institutions, and the willingness of East Asians to cultivate security dependence on the USA, and the accompanying development of the Asia-Pacific rhetoric and institutions.

More important than the two regions (East Asia and North America) versus the Asia-Pacific view, is the larger position of the USA in relation to regionalism generally. From this perspective, East Asia is only one of the regions in which the USA plays a major role as an outside power. The others are Europe, the western hemisphere (the Americas) and the Middle East. Of these, Europe and the Americas are the most important because, like East Asia (and unlike the Middle East) they offer the prospect of Pacific-Rim-like super-regional integration projects incorporating the USA. Indeed, like the Asia-Pacific, all of these projects already exist in some form. Across the North Atlantic, NATO represents a long-standing and very substantial military-political linkage, and the mooted North Atlantic Free Trade Area would be a way of extending this super-region. Similarly, the Americas have for long been linked in a military-political sense by the Monroe Doctrine and the Organization of American States. The proposed extension of NAFTA into a Free Trade Area of the Americas would be a way of consolidating this super-region.

Looked at in this way, the Asia-Pacific becomes simply one part of a wider pattern that defines the post-Cold War power structure of the international political economy. In this larger picture, the USA occupies a unique position. It is the last superpower in being the only full-spectrum, globally operating power, but it is neither capable of, nor willing to establish a unipolar structure. Instead the USA operates as a kind of 'swing power', solidly embedded in these three key regions, and able to move its attention and favour amongst them. One could see this as the USA finally learning to play a traditional, calculating, balance of power game, rather than swinging between extremes of isolationism and crusade. The object of this exercise is not for the USA to choose one of these regions over the others, but to use the possibility of such choice to maintain its leverage in all of them. From this point of view, the Asia-Pacific, the North Atlantic, and the western hemisphere might all be seen more as kinds of 'anti-region' than as regions. Their purpose is to preserve American influence and leverage, and to ensure that any local regionalism remains open. These anti-regions are designed to prevent the consolidation of East Asian and European regions that might shut the USA out, or even develop as global power rivals to it.

The Americas occupy a slightly different role in this picture because they serve as a last fallback for the USA should the world political economy once again fall into serious closed regionalism. If East Asian and European blocs emerged, then a fortress western hemisphere remains the ultimate fallback option for the USA. This is an option that the USA has to keep open, but one that it does not favour because it would end up tied to the relatively weak economies of Latin America, rather than the strong ones in Europe and East Asia. Hurrell (1995, pp.83–97) also notes the tactical quality of the USA's shift from globalism to regionalism, seeing it as an attempt to gain more leverage over the EU and East Asia during the GATT/WTO negotiations. Since East Asia would be the biggest loser in any move towards closed economic blocs, NAFTA provides the USA with an effective threat (Aho, 1993, pp.23–4, 31). From this perspective, both APEC and American rhetoric about western hemisphere developments can be seen as expressions of the USA's swing strategy in action.

There is every reason to expect that this pattern will continue for the short- and medium-term future. American policy will be anti-regionalism, using super-regional proposals (APEC, Atlantic FTA, NAFTA and FTA of the Americas), to reinforce its presence and undermine any serious local moves towards 'fortress' economic regionalisms, especially in Europe and Asia. This might be seen simply as global multilateralism, but it is more than that. By working on the regional and super-regional level, the USA can increase its leverage by dividing up the world into separate groups, within each of which it is much the biggest player. Since each of these regions is dependent on the USA in important ways, it is not impossible to imagine a kind of bidding war amongst Europe, Latin America and East Asia to engage US attention and commitment. Mahbubani's (1995) polemic in favour of a new and rising 'Pacific impulse', as against an old and declining Atlantic one, might be seen as an example of just this kind of wooing. Seen in this light, Simon's (1994, p.1063) argument that the USA is becoming a 'normal state' in the Asia-Pacific community, 'neither its hegemon nor its guarantor', is almost wholly wrong. While the USA may be becoming more normal in playing traditional foreign policy games of balance, its overall position is highly exceptional. It is the key partner for many other states both economically and military-politically, so much so that it is able to use super-regional ideas as an anti-regionalist policy on several fronts.

4.5   Summary and conclusion

I return to the opening question: what kind of region is the Asia-Pacific, and in what kind of world is it located? By the criteria for regionness set out in Section 4.2, the Asia-Pacific can be seen as a rather weak region sitting at the outer limits of what might reasonably be thought of analytically as a region. It has some economic and institutional substance, but suffers from an excess of rhetoric over reality. One big problem with it is that it cannot claim the exclusive mantle of regionness over the area that it covers. As shown in Section 4.4, much tighter and more substantial regions exist in North America and East Asia, and these would seem to have a better claim for enhancing our understanding of international relations than does the Asia-Pacific. The East Asian region in particular has a strong claim to be seen as the principal regional phenomenon in the area, even though its ratio of rhetoric to substance is the opposite of that for the Asia-Pacific.

A second big problem is that a regional approach to the Asia-Pacific hides more than it reveals about the role of the USA. By including the USA as part of a region, the Asia-Pacific disguises both the global standing of America and its real role in the area. In some senses it also misrepresents the nature of regionness in the Pacific, presenting as a regional development what might better be seen as part of larger anti-regional strategies, both American and East Asian. It seems clear that the Asia-Pacific is not a region in the same sense as East Asia, North America, Europe, or the Middle East. If it is to be compared with other 'regions', its closest companions would be other trans-oceanic super-regions such as the North Atlantic and the Indian Ocean, and possibly also the super-region of the western hemisphere. Much the most obvious comparison is with the North Atlantic, which shares many similarities in economic and military-political interactions and roles, and which embodies the same phenomenon of strong American engagement as an outside power in a region which is itself a major centre of world power.

References

Aho, C.M. (1993) 'America and the Pacific Century: trade conflict or cooperation?', *International Affairs*, vol.69, no.1, pp.19–37.

Buzan, B. (1988) 'Japan's future: old history versus new roles', *International Affairs*, vol.64, no.4, pp.557–73.

Buzan, B. (1991) *People, States and Fear*, London, Harvester Wheatsheaf, Chapter 5.

Buzan, B. (1994) 'The post-Cold War Asia-Pacific security order: conflict or cooperation?' in Mack, A. and Ravenhill, J. (eds), pp.130–51.

Buzan, B. (1996) 'International security in East Asia in the 21st century: options for Japan', *Dokkyo International Review*, vol.9, pp.281–314.

Buzan, B. and Segal, G. (1994) 'Rethinking East Asian security', *Survival*, vol.36, no.2, pp.3–21.

Buzan, B., Wæver, O. and de Wilde, S. (1997) *Security: a Framework for Analysis*, Boulder, Lynne Rienner.

Cantori, L.J. and Spiegel, S.L. (1972) *The International Politics of Regions: a Comparative Approach*, Englewood Cliffs, Prentice Hall.

Dibb, P. (1995) 'Towards a new balance of power in Asia', *Adelphi Paper no.295*, London, International Institute for Strategic Studies.

Fawcett, L. and Hurrell, A. (1995) *Regionalism in World Politics*, Oxford, Oxford University Press.

Foot, R. (1995) 'Pacific Asia: the development of regional dialogue' in Fawcett, L. and Hurrell, A., Chapter 8.

Grant, R., Papadakis, M. and Richardson, J.D. (1993) 'Global trade flows: old structures, new issues, empirical evidence' in Bergsten, C.F. and Noland, M. (eds) *Pacific Dynamism and the International Economic System*, Washington, Institute for International Economics, pp.17–63.

Harris, S. (1993) 'The economic aspects of Pacific security', *Adelphi Paper no.275*, London, International Institute for Strategic Studies.

Helleiner, E. (1994) 'Regionalization in the international political economy: a comparative perspective', *East Asian Policy Papers No.3*, University of Toronto–University of York Joint Centre for Asia-Pacific Studies.

Hessler, S. (1994) 'Regionalization of the world economy: fact or fiction?', paper presented to ISA Conference, Washington, 24 March.

Higgott, R. (1994) 'APEC – a sceptical view' in Mack, A. and Ravenhill, J. (eds), pp.66–97.

Hurrell, A. (1995) 'Regionalism in theoretical perspective' in Fawcett, L. and Hurrell, A., Chapter 3.

Katzenstein, P.J. (1996) 'Regionalism in comparative perspective', *Cooperation and Conflict*, vol.31, no.2, pp.123–59.

Leifer, M. (1996) 'The ASEAN Regional Forum', *Adelphi Paper no.302*, London, International Institute for Strategic Studies.

Mack, A. and Ravenhill, J. (eds) (1994) *Pacific Cooperation: Building Economic and Security Regimes in the Asia-Pacific Region*, St. Leonards, Allen and Unwin.

Mahbubani, Kishore (1995) 'The Pacific impulse', *Survival*, vol.37, no.1, pp.105–20.

Simon, S.W. (1994) 'East Asian security: the playing field has changed', *Asian Survey*, vol.34, no.12, pp.1047–63.

Srinivasan, T.N., Walley, J. and Wooton, I. (1993) 'Measuring the effects of regionalism on trade and welfare' in Anderson, K. and Blackhurst, R. (eds) *Regional Integration and the Global Trading System*, Hemel Hempstead, Harvester Wheatsheaf.

Stuart, D.T. and Tow, W.T. (1995) 'A US strategy for the Asia-Pacific', *Adelphi Paper no.299*, London, International Institute for Strategic Studies.

Thompson, W.R. (1973) 'The regional subsystem: a conceptual explication and a propositional inventory', *International Studies Quarterly*, vol.17, no.1, pp.89–117.

Wyatt-Walter, A. (1995) 'Regionalism, globalism and world economic order' in Fawcett, L. and Hurrell, A., Chapter 4.

Yu, C. (1995) 'Unification of the Asian economies and Japan: with a special look at the role by the ethnic Chinese economies', presented to Dokkyo University International Forum, Tokyo.

Further reading

Dibb, P. (1995) 'Towards a new balance of power in Asia', *Adelphi Paper no.295*, London, International Institute for Strategic Studies.

Fawcett, L. and Hurrell, A. (1995) *Regionalism in World Politics*, Oxford, Oxford University Press.

Mack, A. and Ravenhill, J. (eds) (1994) *Pacific Cooperation: Building Economic and Security Regimes in the Asia-Pacific Region*, St. Leonards, Allen and Unwin.

Stuart, D.T. and Tow, W.T. (1995) 'A US strategy for the Asia-Pacific', *Adelphi Paper no.299*, London, International Institute for Strategic Studies.

CHAPTER 5

The Asia-Pacific security order
J.N. Mak

5.1 Introduction

This chapter examines the strategic and military dimension of the Asia-Pacific by looking at the complex relations between the three-and-a-half major military powers of the region. These powers are the USA, Russia and China. The half power is Japan because it is still an incomplete military power. It is only by looking at the complex web of relations between these major powers on the one hand, and those between each of these powers and the rest of the Asia-Pacific on the other, that we can understand the tensions in the region, and the prospects for peace and stability.

The organizing framework of this chapter assumes that the basis of Asia-Pacific security revolves round these major actors and that every development and security issue 'hangs' onto this web of relations. What comes out clearly is that North-East Asian states tend to be 'realist' in nature, in contrast with the more co-operative and 'neoliberal-institutionalist' South-East Asia. What is also clear is that while the Cold War was an era of USA–Soviet confrontation, the post-Cold War period is likely to be marked by USA–China tensions.

Russia, which borders the Asia-Pacific is not discussed here in detail because its regional activity is currently insignificant although it may emerge as a major player in the future. The end of the Cold War and the break-up of the Soviet Union has removed the threat of an all-out nuclear war between the USA and the Soviet Union. This has made limited conflicts between states in the region seem more possible because regional conflicts are now not automatically linked with superpower confrontation. The withdrawal of the Soviet Union has therefore brought more uncertainty to the Asia-Pacific because of the presence of historical tensions in North-East Asia. The inability of Russia to play a significant role in the near future means that the Asia-Pacific is left with just one military superpower, the USA, although the USA has been described as a power in relative decline. Many states in the region also fear that should the USA withdraw from the region, a 'power vacuum' would be created which other regional powers, notably China and Japan, might fill. The USA's allies such as Japan, South

Korea, and Australia, therefore, believe that a strong US military presence is necessary for peace in the Asia-Pacific. They are not certain, however, whether the USA will remain committed to maintaining a presence in the region.

China, the most populous nation in the world, will indisputably play a key role in the region in future. It is a power on the ascendant because of its fast-growing economic strength and its military potential. Its armed forces, the largest in the world, will become stronger as the country becomes richer. China too, is an 'unsatisfied power' because it feels deeply wronged by Japan and the West for dismembering China at the turn of the twentieth century. China today fears US dominance in the region. Because of differences in ideology, history and political organization between the USA and China, many analysts regard a USA–China confrontation as the region's greatest potential threat. Some South-East Asian nations also see the revival of the China threat as almost inevitable given China's history of fermenting revolutions in South-East Asia. The question of whether China will use force to reunite Taiwan with the mainland is another issue which creates uncertainties in the region.

Japan, the half-power, is likely to become a full military power if the USA decides to withdraw. There are signs that Japan is already trying to find a more dominant role for itself in the post-Cold War world. Japan's assertiveness is worrying to China, South Korea and the South-East Asian countries which have not forgotten Japan's expansionist policy and militarism of the 1930s and 1940s. Consequently, there is a very real fear of Japan, already the most economically powerful nation in Asia, rearming and playing a significant security role.

The North-East Asian sub-region is, therefore, the key to stability in the Asia-Pacific. The concentration of military power in North-East Asia, the prospects of a potential power 'vacuum', and the presence of historical animosities all make up a potentially explosive cocktail which could burst into open conflict if inter-state tensions are not managed. Unfortunately, North-East Asia still lacks comprehensive confidence-building measures (CBMs) in the form of multilateral institutions or structures. State relations are generally conducted on a bilateral basis, with no real forum for discussing issues of common North-East Asian concern.

It is telling that the only multilateral forum involving all the North-East Asian nations is the ASEAN Regional Forum (ARF). The Association of South-East Asian Nations (ASEAN) constitutes the core of the ARF. South-East Asia is important because it has great economic potential. Militarily, it is still a lightweight. Nevertheless, South-East Asia – in particular the core grouping of what used to be known as non-Communist South-East Asia – appears to be spearheading the only meaningful security forum in the Asia-Pacific. Although inter-state tensions are present in this sub-region, conflict is unlikely because of the existence of the 'ASEAN way' of security co-operation which stresses consultation, consensus building and co-operation rather than confrontation. South-East Asia is therefore more stable than North-East Asia. It appears, at first glance, that South-East Asia's framework for security co-operation can provide an ideal model for North-East Asia. Unfortunately, South-East Asia's different historical experiences and political culture raises doubts as to whether the ASEAN experience can be applied to North-East Asia.

The Asia-Pacific region, therefore, faces 'interesting times', and uncertainty for the forseeable future. The issues and relationships highlighted above will affect the new security structure of the Asia-Pacific. They will determine whether the region remains unipolar, i.e., dominated by a single power, becomes multipolar, or whether a new bipolar (or tripolar) balance of power will be achieved.

5.2 Neo-realism, neoliberal-institutionalism and strategic culture

The Asia-Pacific is not one homogenous region. Using *strategic culture* as an analytical tool, we can divide the Asia-Pacific into two core sub-regions – North-East Asia and South-East Asia – plus Russia bordering the northern periphery, the USA on the eastern rim and Australia and New Zealand in the south. North-East Asia comprises Japan, North Korea, South Korea, the People's Republic of China, Hong Kong and Taiwan. The ten South-East Asian states are Brunei, Burma/Myanmar, Cambodia, Indonesia, Laos, Malaysia, Philippines, Singapore, Thailand and Vietnam.

Traditional theories of international relations are in contention over the future of the Asia-Pacific. Neo-realists believe that conflict is inevitable. This *balance of power* school argues that states want to maximize and amass power for themselves. This is because the world is in a state of anarchy with no higher authority to impose order. Two attempts at creating such an authority – the League of Nations after the First World War and the United Nations after the end of the Second World War – failed to maintain world peace. Thus, states are convinced that they must look after their own security. The neoliberal-institutionalists, or school of co-operation, on the other hand, believe that as modern communications make the world 'smaller', and as nations become more economically interdependent, they co-operate more and more because it is to their mutual benefit. Neoliberal-institutionalists think that the Asia-Pacific region will become more stable as a result of this interdependence. Furthermore, the establishment of multilateral institutions in the region such as ASEAN, the Asia-Pacific Economic Co-operation (APEC) forum, and the security-oriented ASEAN Regional Forum (ARF) are positive developments which will contribute towards peace and stability. Finally, the liberals also believe that the growing democratization of the Asia-Pacific nations will contribute to peace since democracies have never fought each other.

Neo-realism and neoliberal-institutionalism are useful analytical tools, within limits, for explaining state behaviour. However, they have their limitations because they assume that all states are *rational actors*. In other words, both theories assume that states are very logical, and cannot act in ways outside the logical dictates of either neoliberal-institutionalism or neo-realism, which is to seek maximum utility. Thus, the 'neo-realist framework discounts the accumulated weight of the past in favour of a forward-looking calculation of expected utility' (Johnston, 1995, p.35). International relations theorists therefore describe both neo-realism and neoliberal-institutionalism as 'overly determined'.

The Asia-Pacific is, however, a complex region, and no one theory can explain everything about it. Nevertheless, theories are useful as frameworks for organizing thoughts and arguments. The theory of *strategic culture* seems to offer a supplementary alternative to either neo-realist or liberal explanations for a state's strategic choices. Early *strategic culture* theories were also overly determined because they assumed that culture resulted in, for example, a distinct US way of war-making which made the USA incapable of thinking that a nuclear war could be won because of the cost in human lives. Later strategic culture theories tend to be less overly determined and imply that strategic culture is a result of historical experience. Different historical and social experiences therefore resulted in the development of different types of strategic cultures between states. *Strategic culture* stresses the importance of ideas and beliefs held by state elites (ideational) rather than states as rational actors which cannot help but seek to maximize utility (gains) for themselves. *Strategic culture* can help to explain military developments in the Asia-Pacific, and why the pessimistic school of the neo-realists will most likely prevail in North-East Asia, but not necessarily in South-East Asia. Explanations based upon *strategic culture*, for the purposes of this chapter, argue that different approaches to war, war-making and the conduct of war, can be linked to culture and the mind-sets which national culture and history engender. *Strategic culture* introduces a historical dimension to international relations theory. This is important because, for instance, it is widely held that history and culture are important features of the Chinese world view. 'China's relationship with South-East Asia goes back almost 2,000 years and the attention paid to the affairs of the region by the rulers of modern China is merely a continuation of a concern which transcends all ideological differences between the old and new China' (Jorgensen-Dahl, 1984, p.4).

Inter-state tensions are very marked in North-East Asia, but less so in South-East Asia. China, which had various parts of its territory annexed by Western powers during the final days of the Qing Dynasty, feels a deep sense of being wronged by Western imperialists. It considers Taiwan to be a legacy of this imperialism, and its duty is therefore to reunite Taiwan, the 'rebel' state, with China. The period of Japanese imperialism in the nineteenth and early twentieth century also left a bitter legacy which is still felt today. The former Japanese colonies suffered greatly at the hands of the Japanese, especially during the Second World War, and they therefore fear that Japan might embark on a new round of colonial and militaristic adventure. All these experiences left deep imprints on the national psyches of North-East Asians. Hence their attitude to military power, and their approaches to conflict-resolution, have been conditioned by their experiences of wars and invasions. This has led to a *strategic culture* which places a premium on the utility of military power, and on the importance of maintaining a power balance.

Strategic culture also accounts for South-East Asia's more co-operative form of inter-state relations. First, their shared historical experiences created an empathy between South-East Asian states and formed the basis of a common understanding. All the South-East Asian states, with the exception of Thailand, experienced colonization at the hands of Western powers such as France, Britain, the USA or the Netherlands. They only gained their independence following the end of the Second World War. During that war, South-East Asia also went through harrowing times as part of the Japanese 'Greater East Asia Co-Prosperity Sphere'. Second, none of the South-East Asian states, with the exception of Cambodia, were invaded by their neighbours, unlike the experience in North-East Asia, although inter-state tensions continue to exist in South-East Asia. Third, since independence the primary concern of most South-East Asian states, especially the ASEAN members, has been with internal consolidation, stability and regime survival. Nearly all of them faced Communist-inspired domestic insurgencies or separatist movements seeking secession. Thus, ASEAN members decided that they could ill-afford to spend their resources and energy fighting each other. Hence, they adopted a strategy of non-interference in the internal affairs of neighbouring states to ensure that they would be able to concentrate on domestic stability and regime survival. They therefore developed a process of consultation, negotiations and bargaining in private with their neighbours to resolve or minimize potential conflicts. This process may be considered part of the ASEAN conflict-resolution process. This process is popularly known as the 'ASEAN way'.

In strategic and military terms, the Asia-Pacific can be treated as two distinct sub-regions (North-East Asia and South-East Asia) each with its own strategic priorities and problems. The behaviour of North-East Asia can be described as neo-realist, while South-East Asian states behave in a more neoliberal-institutionalist manner. Strategic culture can help to explain this difference.

5.3 The end of the Cold War and the new (uncertain) regional order

The Cold War, apart from raising the spectre of nuclear war, provided the Asia-Pacific with strategic balance and predictability. There was bipolar (or sometimes tripolar) stability, with clear areas of Chinese, American and Soviet influence. The ending of the Cold War has resulted in a more unpredictable Asia-Pacific. Depending on their strategic situation and perceptions, some countries see post-Cold War Asia as multipolar or

Table 5.1 *Military expenditure of selected Asia-Pacific nations in 1986, 1990 and 1995 in US$m (constant 1990)*

	1986	1990	1995
USA	335,048	306,170	238,194
Russian Federation[1]	–	–	–
Brunei	140	231	–
China[2]	6,497	6,069	(6,121)
Indonesia	(1,443)	(1,350)	–
Japan	24,811	29,702	30,766
North Korea[3]	–	–	–
South Korea	7,929	9,603	11,763
Malaysia	1,634	1,125	1,794
Burma/Myanmar	580	814	–
Philippines	689	959	–
Singapore	1,528	2,026	2,606
Taiwan	6,270	7,782	10,885
Thailand	1,956	2,169	–
Vietnam[4]	–	781	–
Australia	7,034	6,627	7,106

[1] High inflation, volatile exchange rate and the absence of reliable national statistics for all of the Russian Federation.

[2] Figures reflect official budget figures only. For a discussion of the debate over the true level of Chinese military expenditure, see Bergstrand (1994, pp.441–8).

[3] Figures reflect official figures only and may underestimate North Korea's military expenditure. The lack of reliable economic data makes it difficult to calculate military expenditure in constant US$ and as a proportion of GDP.

[4] Lack of data on inflation makes it impossible to calculate a continuous series in constant 1990 US$. Figures for 1986 are calculated using 1989 as the base year.

Source: SIPRI (1996)

unipolar. China sees the break-up and strategic withdrawal of the Soviet Union as leaving the USA as the *de facto* sole superpower in the region. It sees the USA as domineering and is troubled by the fact that there is no other power which can oppose the USA's tendency of imposing its democratic values and economic agenda on Asia. Other Asia-Pacific states, in contrast to China, feel strongly that the USA must stay in the region. They fear that because there is no longer a need to counter the Soviet Union, there could be a diminished US presence in Asia. A power vacuum could result. Japan is worried that an increasingly strong China might try to fill the vacuum and become the next regional hegemon. China, in turn, fears a remilitarized Japan which might 'go nuclear' (acquire a nuclear weapons capability) without the USA. Unlike during the Cold War era, the situation in the Asia-Pacific today has become more unpredictable and uncertain.

This strategic uncertainty partly accounts for the increases in military expenditure and defence modernization programmes undertaken by nearly all the Asia-Pacific states over the past decade (see Table 5.1). Many states are upgrading their militaries as a strategic hedge, and to acquire a minimal capability to deal with various contingencies (see Table 5.2). They can afford these defence programmes because of their booming economies. The economic success of countries such as the 'economic tigers' of Taiwan, South Korea and Singapore, and most significantly, China, has generated the wealth and foreign exchange needed for the purchase of sophisticated weapons. Force cutbacks in Europe, the Russian Federation and the USA also resulted in surplus arms being offered at cut-rate prices to Asian countries. This new-found wealth has also brought political power and status to Asia. Thus, countries like China have found a new assertiveness as they begin to realize that economic power can often be translated into political and military clout.

The 'arms race' in the Asia-Pacific

Newspapers and magazines often refer to an ongoing *arms race* in the Asia-Pacific at a time when the rest of the world is reducing its military forces. Some conclude that an *arms race* is taking place in the Asia-Pacific. The reasons given for this *arms race* include the fear of a resurgent and militarily powerful China, the fear of a sudden US military withdrawal and all its attendant consequences, the availability of post-Cold War surplus arms at bargain basement prices, or the perceived need to fill a potential power vacuum. However, other more sanguine writers describe the phenomenon as nothing other than a 'normal' force modernization process.

There is no doubt that the Asia-Pacific has witnessed an upsurge in conventional arms acquisitions since the late 1980s. Certainly a mix of all the above reasons account for the present arms acquisitions dynamics. The impact of 'Desert Storm' in Kuwait in 1991 also reinforced the acquisitions process. The USA-led counter-attack showed how sophisticated, hi-tech weaponry could rapidly and effectively neutralize large, well-armed forces equipped with less sophisticated weapons. This made armed forces around the world – including those in the Asia-Pacific – aware that a new age in conventional warfare had arrived.

East Asia's booming economies meant that defence budgets generally grew in real terms despite no significant increases in the percentage of gross domestic product spent on defence. These states could therefore afford to buy more or better arms. To label the phenomenon an *arms race*, is, however, over simplistic. The theory and dynamics of arms races have been well studied. Reasons why states engage in arms races include technological advances, military pressure, action-reaction, technological entrepreneurship, national leadership, military mission and various permutations of these factors (Gleditsch and Njolstad, 1990, pp.4–7). The reasons for arms races are complex, and the models and theories to explain the phenomenon can be even more convoluted. Colin Gray however, has a more straightforward 'test'. An *arms race* must have four characteristics:

1   There must be two or more parties, conscious of their antagonism.

Table 5.2 Military capabilities of selected Asia-Pacific powers (1984 and 1996)

	USA		Japan		China		Taiwan		South Korea		North Korea		Russian Federation	
	1984	1996	1984	1996	1984	1996	1984	1996	1984	1996	1984	1996	1984	1996
Nuclear weapons														
Sea-launched ballistic missiles	592	408	–	–	–	12	–	–	–	–	–	–	981	540
Inter-continental ballistic missiles	1,037	580	–	–	2	17+	–	–	–	–	–	–	1,398	800
Intermediate range ballistic missiles	–	–	–	–	60	70+	–	–	–	–	–	–	596	–
Medium range ballistic missiles	–	–	–	–	50	–	–	–	–	–	–	–	–	–
Nuclear submarines (SSBNs)	35	17	–	–	1	1	–	–	–	–	–	–	79	34
Total armed forces	2,135,900	1,483,800	245,000	235,500	4,000,000	2,935,000	484,000	376,000	622,000	660,000	784,500	1,054,000	5,115,000	1,270,000
Army	780,800	495,000	155,000	148,000	3,160,000	2,200,000	330,000	240,000	540,000	548,000	700,000	923,000	1,840,000	460,000
Main battle tanks (MBT)	11,623	10,497	1,020	1,130	11,450AFV	8,000+	309	630	1,200	2,050	2,675	3,400	51,000	16,800
Navy	564,800	426,700	44,000	43,000	350,000	265,000	38,000	–	49,000	35,000	33,500	46,000	490,000	190,000
Tactical submarines	99	78	14	17	102	63	2	4	–	4	21	25	150	133
Aircraft carriers	14	12	–	–	–	–	–	–	–	–	–	–	–	1
Battleships	2	–	–	–	–	–	–	–	–	–	–	–	–	–
Cruisers	28	31	–	–	–	–	–	–	–	–	–	–	36	24
Destroyers	68	52	32	9	14	18	23	18	11	7	–	–	68	21
Frigates	94	49	18	51	22	36	9	18	8	33	4	3	184	120
Amphibious ships	61	41	6	6	18	55	29	21	33	15	3	–	78	80
Military sealift command ships	68	123	–	–	–	–	–	–	–	–	–	–	–	–
Missile armed attack craft	6	–	–	3	341	185	28	53	2	15(?)	155	46(?)	30	96(?)
Naval combat aircraft	1,450	12 air wings	81	110	800	605	–	31	–	23	–	–	839	396
Helicopters	160	27 sqns	63	99	52	121(?)	–	21	32	47	–	–	265	250
Marine corps	96,600	173,900	NNG	12,000	–	5,000	39,000	30,000	20,000	25,000	–	–	16,000	14,000
Coast guard	38,791	37,300	286	78 coastal	–	–	–	–	–	–	–	–	–	–
Patrol vessels	104	101	42	32	–	–	–	–	–	–	–	–	–	–
Patrol vessels, offshore	45	45	10	–	–	–	–	–	–	–	–	–	–	–
Aircraft	64	73	–	–	–	–	–	–	–	–	–	–	–	–
Helicopters	108	136	5	–	–	–	–	–	–	–	–	–	–	–
Air Force	594,500	388,200	46,000	44,500	490,000	470,000	77,000	68,000	33,000	52,000	51,000	85,000	400,000	145,000
Tactical combat aircraft	3,700	23 air wing	270	379	5,300	5,175(?)	547	392	440	461	740	611	3,260	1,775
Long-range strike aircraft	297	178	–	–	–	–	–	–	–	–	–	–	143	125

Notes: AFV: Armoured Fighting Vehicle, which includes tanks, armoured cars, armoured personnel carriers, and armoured infantry fighting vehicles; NNG: In holdings, but number not given; (?): Total computed from IISS figures of individual types; Sqns: Squadrons. Numbers vary from squadron to squadron, and country to country.

Source: IISS (1995, 1997)

2 They must structure their armed forces with attention to the probable effectiveness of the forces in combat with, or as a deterrent to, the other arms race participants.

3 They must compete in terms of quantity (personnel, weapons) and/or quality (personnel, weapons, organization, doctrine, deployment).

4 There must be rapid increases in quantity and/or improvements in quality.

In East Asia, many countries are very secretive about their military capabilities, acquisitions and defence expenditures. Much data used for comparisons are therefore often just 'best guesses'. For example, analysts still argue about how large China's real defence expenditure is, and whether the official figures should be multiplied by a factor of two, three or four. Even with accurate data and using a constant price index (CPI) comparing defence expenditures is still risky. Simple 'bean counting' is therefore often meaningless. For example, a US-made tank and a Chinese-made tank cannot be compared on a one-to-one basis. The latter tends to be less sophisticated and, other things being equal, less effective than a US tank. Thus, while it is relatively easy to count major platforms, it is difficult to assess what systems are incorporated into them, and how effective they are. Modern systems, such as radar, computers, forward-looking infrared, fire control systems and the software to run them can cost three times more than the platform itself.

In addition, the quality and training standards of personnel, the standard of maintenance and the munitions holdings will all have a direct bearing on capability. Thus, merely counting the paper strength of each country's armed forces often gives a highly distorted picture. This difficulty will increase in the future if, as the Americans believe, the revolution in military affairs (RMA) is inevitable. The RMA bestows a technological edge on countries like the USA through the use of information technology, intelligence, targeting, and the widespread use of dual-use civilian technology such as civilian satellite surveillance systems.

Nevertheless, with these caveats in mind, *arms race* theories are useful because they help explain when a particular arms purchasing cycle becomes potentially destabilizing for a region. They are an important starting point for analysing the prospects for peace and stability in East Asia. There is no doubt that a limited number of reactive arms acquisitions processes are taking place. There is the instance of Taiwan responding to a possible invasion from the People's Republic of China, hence Taipei's decision to procure US F-16 fighters, French Mirage 2000 aircraft and frigates, and submarines from the Netherlands. Similarly, the fear of a Chinese nuclear strike, one which was underscored by China's 'nuclear demonstration' in the Taiwan Straits, is a primary reason why Tokyo is seriously examining the feasibility of a theatre missile defence (TMD) system. The build-up along both sides of the 38th Parallel in the Korean peninsula is attributable to the North Korea–South Korea tensions. These competitive arms acquisitions are confined mainly to North-East Asia, while South-East Asian acquisitions are less reactive and hostile. Moreover, the scale of ASEAN arms acquisitions are fairly insignificant in the context of the wider Asia-Pacific, hence they are potentially less destabilizing.

However, there is no question of a full-blown arms race taking place right across the board. China is not challenging American military superiority at present. Indeed, if we look at the defence modernization taking place in East Asia at the moment, we just cannot ascribe the arms acquisitions dynamics solely to inter-state tensions and rivalries. Armed forces in East Asia, like everywhere else, are designed to fulfil a number of functions.

Generally speaking, defence modernization in East Asia usually reflects both strategic and non-strategic concerns. These include (Mak, 1994):

1   The need to protect and police new ocean space such as exclusive economic zones (EEZs) created as a result of the 1982 Law of the Sea Convention (LOSC).

2   The need to enforce sovereignty *vis-à-vis* disputed maritime claims, again arising out of the ambiguities following the 1982 LOSC.

3   Acquiring defence technology for its spin-off effects on civilian industries.

4   The perceived need to deal with a range of contingencies in the face of a possible US drawdown.

For instance, China's strategic concerns include acquiring the capability to:

1   Defend its declared sovereign territory.

2   Upgrade its defence technology in light of the lessons of the Gulf War.

3   Maintain internal stability, especially with increasing irredentist activities in outlying provinces.

In the case of Taiwan, the threat is very explicit, so military design is largely dictated by the need to defeat any PRC invasion. Japan's immediate strategic goal is to ensure the freedom of the sea lines of communications (SLOC) – out to a theoretical 1,000 nautical miles east and south of Tokyo Bay – on which Japan depends so much for its trade and prosperity. Hence its Maritime Self-Defence Force is structured along anti-submarine warfare (ASW) lines, with air defence capabilities and surface interdiction increasingly becoming more important in the post-Cold War world. America, of course, is still concerned with maintaining military primacy, while the South-East Asian nations are more preoccupied with the protection of (maritime EEZs) and acquiring a limited capability to deal with a variety of contingencies.

A widely-held belief in the West that current Asia-Pacific arms acquisitions have been sparked off by the China 'threat' is not borne out by a US General Accounting Office study. This study concludes that: 'Most regional defense spending and force modernization is not focused on or in direct response to China's current force modernization. In most cases, regional spending and modernization predates or occurs simultaneously with China's recent efforts' (General Accounting Office, 1995, p.7).

Except for China, all the East Asian states have very limited power projection capabilities. They all lack significant amphibious capability and thus their force structures tend to reflect a defensive doctrine. What this means is that the present arms races tend to be strategically defensive in nature, although certain nations such as South Korea may possess great offensive power at the tactical level. Hence, the current arms acquisitions cycle has a limited degree of in-built stability because of its strategically defensive nature.

The current phase of arms acquisitions has also been fuelled by the synergistic effects of the over-supply of arms in the West and Russia following the end of the Cold War, and the availability of funds in East Asia for arms purchases because of its booming economy. In fact, many Asia-Pacific countries feel that they have a right to acquire more weapons or to modernize their arsenals. Many ASEAN countries argue that because their defence forces are presently so weak, the ASEAN defence build-up helps to make them more secure, and that it actually contributes to 'regional resilience', and hence to regional stability. Similarly, China feels that it is more than justified to buy modern arms and equipment since its arsenal comprises mainly obsolete or obsolescent weapons. Hence, from the point of view of many Asian countries, it is preposterous to accuse them of arms racing.

While, in respect of Gray's criteria (see the list above), there is no *arms race* taking place right now, lurking just below the surface is the danger of a highly destabilizing *arms race* breaking out. Despite the unpopularity of the USA with some Asian leaders, there is no doubt that the US military presence has held traditional animosities – and an incipient *arms race* – in check. Looking at Figure 5.1 on Asia-Pacific defence expenditure, it is interesting to note that US defence spending is way above that of the rest of East Asia. America's very high military expenditure of course reflects its global military commitments. Nevertheless, the disparity in expenditure is such that even China would have serious reservations about embarking on an *arms race* against the USA in the short and medium term.

More noteworthy is the 'clustering' of the rest of the Asia-Pacific in Figure 5.1 (Japan, China, Taiwan and South Korea) based on data as interpreted by the Stockholm International Peace Research Institute (SIPRI) using official figures (North Korean expenditures are not available). Here again, the expenditure gap between Japan and China–Taiwan–South Korea seems very large (Figure 5.2). China appears to spend marginally less than South Korea and Taiwan on defence. Thus it would appear that it could also be prohibitively expensive for China to embark on a non co-operative arms acquisitions process against Japan. However, China's official military expenditure apparently does not reflect the true extent of Chinese defence spending. Estimates of real Chinese

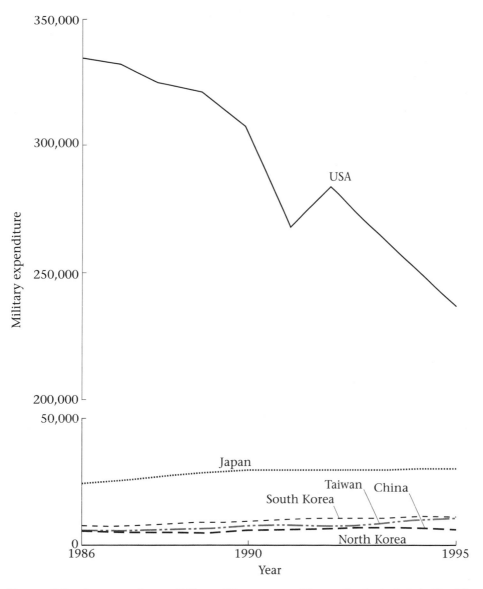

Figure 5.1 *A comparison of the military expenditure of selected Asia-Pacific nations, 1986–95 in US$m at 1990 prices and exchange rates*

Source: SIPRI (1996)

defence expenditure range from two to seventeen times the official figure, with most estimates ranging between two and five times. Thus, if Chinese defence expenditure is multiplied by a factor of three (Figure 5.3), it is apparent that Chinese defence spending ranks next only to that of Japan.

Given the traditional animosities between Japan, China and Korea, an American withdrawal from East Asia might well trigger an *arms race* between these three countries. In view of the fact that the gap, at least in

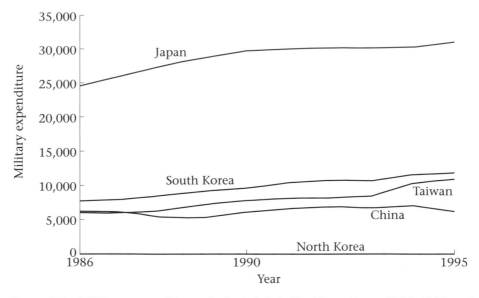

Figure 5.2 *Military expenditure of selected Asia-Pacific nations, 1986, 1990 and 1995 in USm at 1990 prices and exchange rates*

Source: SIPRI (1996)

terms of military expenditure, between Japan and China is quite narrow, arms racing becomes 'thinkable'. As such, any Sino-Japanese *arms race* could be quite intense. Moreover, since Japan has a 'recessed' nuclear capability (capable of going nuclear in a matter of days), a regional nuclear arms race could also be sparked off.

The situation in North-East Asia is therefore potentially highly dangerous. Any sudden USA drawdown could destabilize the region. Thus, while there were a number of somewhat antagonistic arms acquisition processes going on in East Asia over the past decade, this will be nothing compared with the *arms race* that could break out if the USA significantly reduced its military presence. Japan will then surely feel it essential to acquire a more comprehensive defence capability, rather than the somewhat unidimensional defence force that it has at the moment. This in turn could lead to China giving greater priority to arms acquisitions, resulting in a chain reaction which will involve Taiwan and Korea, and probably South-East Asia as well. Hence, while the present situation provides some cause for worry, it is not effectively a 'real arms race'.

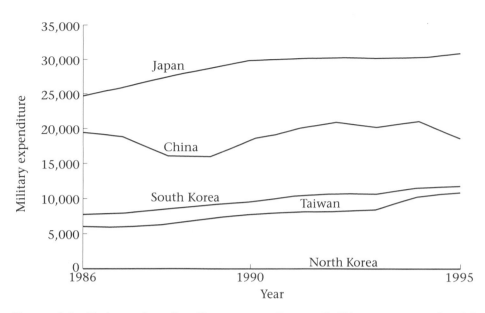

Figure 5.3 *Estimated real military expenditure of Chinese compared with selected Asia-Pacific nations, 1986–95*

Note: expenditure for China is multiplied by a factor of three. Figures are in US$m, at 1990 prices and exchange rates.

Source: SIPRI (1996)

5.4 Regional security: a new balance of power?

The USA: a status quo power

The USA is the linchpin of the Asia-Pacific security structure. In the past, the US presence in the region suppressed historical animosities between Japan, China and the two Koreas. It also maintained stability in the Taiwan Straits and on the Korean Peninsula. The USA–Japan Mutual Security Treaty not only gave Japan a sense of security, but provided the rest of the region with an assurance that Japan would not remilitarize. In South-East Asia, the presence of the US Seventh Fleet gave the sub-region security and stability.

The US presence was, and still is, generally regarded as benign by the non-Communist Asian governments for two reasons. It freed many Asian states from having to worry about defence against external attacks. Second, the US presence, together with the United Kingdom, Australia and New Zealand in the 1950s and 1960s, also checked latent regional animosities by maintaining the status quo.

The end of the Cold War, and the slow growth of its economy led the USA to reconsider its Asia-Pacific strategy. The Defense Department's 1990

East Asia Strategic Initiative (EASI) outlined a plan to cut US forces in Asia from 143,000 in 1990 to less than 100,000 by 1993. The EASI move, together with the rise of a neo-isolationist movement in the USA, made Asia-Pacific states realise that a US military presence could not be taken for granted. It also persuaded otherwise strictly neutral states, such as Indonesia, to adopt a more positive approach to the USA. Engaging and persuading the USA to stay in the Asia-Pacific has therefore become an important strategy for a number of Asia-Pacific states.

The most important question we have to ask today is whether US strategy has changed in the post-Cold War years? The short answer is that it has not. The USA's Asia-Pacific strategy still appears to be based on maintaining the USA's strategic primacy in the region. This is not surprising, since the USA is a *status quo power*. The Asia-Pacific is currently in a state of flux, and a strong US military presence is likely to maintain the USA's hegemonic position. Just as important, the USA's growing economic stakes in the Asia-Pacific means that it must keep open the sea lines of communications (SLOC), which traverse the region, for US trade.

Significantly, given that US security thinking is still premised on US *primacy*, then a USA–China struggle for dominance appears to be inevitable. This is because ascendant or 'fast-rising powers are almost invariably troublemakers, if only because they are reluctant to accept institutions, border divisions, and hierarchies of political prestige put in place when they were comparatively weak ...'.

An air controller on board USS Independence *checks an electronic map of Taiwan and the South China Sea during 'tit for tat' manoeuvres in March 1996*

US officials have constantly reassured their Asian allies that Washington will not back down on its treaty commitments. The USA's response to China's military exercises in the Taiwan Straits in March 1996 is an example of this. China held the exercises, including firing unarmed ballistic missiles, during the build-up to national elections in Taiwan to signal to the islanders that they should not attempt to declare unilateral independence from China. The USA promptly sent two carrier battle-groups into the area, in turn signalling to Beijing that it did not approve of the veiled threats against Taiwan. Although the USA had no direct treaty commitments to Taiwan, it had always been the guarantor of Taiwanese security. Thus, a very strong message was sent not only to China, but also to the rest of the Asia-Pacific that the USA would stand by its friends and allies. In this sense, we can argue that the USA's response was to reassure Japan, too.

Thus, in the medium term, we can expect the USA not to change its Cold War strategy. It will still be at the helm of the strongest network of military alliances in the Asia-Pacific, and will do its best to maintain the status quo. To further ensure that the power balance remains in its favour, the USA is persuading its Asian allies to carry more of the defence burden. South Korea and Japan have been asked to increase their defence spending, to be more self-reliant and to increase their financial contributions as host nations.

The USA's presence is, however, not seen as an unalloyed good. A number of South-East Asian states have rankled at Washington's sometimes brash foreign policy, and the tendency of preaching down to Asia. Even its military presence has aroused hostility in parts of Japan. Yet the USA–Japan Mutual Defense Pact was not merely renewed, but deepened in 1996. This is an indication of how important the USA's presence is to the region. It is not that the USA is particularly loved, but simply that states in the region fear some of their neighbours even more. The fact is that a US military presence continues to be appreciated by virtually every Asia-Pacific state. Even China is sometimes ambivalent about the USA's presence, which it sees as essential for preventing Japan from rearming and going nuclear. While a number of regional elites have expressed their unhappiness with Washington's imposition of its democratic and liberal ideals on the region, they are at the same time not prepared to live without a US military presence.

Some Americans see that the spread of the liberal American norms of democracy, free and fair markets, and human rights as essential for a stable and peaceful Asia-Pacific which will continue to accept American leadership. The downside of this is that if the human rights and democracy initiative is pushed too hard and too fast by Washington, it could alienate those governments which are not yet fully democratic. They might then find common cause with China, which would lead to a drastic change in the power balance. If Washington wants to preserve the status quo without overspending on defence, then the USA must ensure that the region remains sympathetic to the USA's goals and aspirations. The USA is thus caught on the horns of a dilemma.

The central role of China

China plays a key role in the Asia-Pacific security architecture because it is the biggest resident power in Asia, and it has the potential to become the 'next superpower'. Significantly, it is also an unsatisfied power. China's perceptions of the wrongs it had suffered at the hands of outside powers from 1840 to 1949, and the perceived attempts to dismember the country, has made China *neo-realist* in its dealings with the rest of the world. China poses a security 'threat' to the rest of the Asia-Pacific simply because it is almost impossible today to predict how it will behave. Compounding this fear is the fact that China has played a prominent role in nearly all post-Second World War regional conflicts. After the establishment of the Communist government in 1949, China despatched the Chinese Volunteer Army in 1951 to fight in the Korean War. It actively supported the Vietminh and later North Vietnam in the First and Second Indo-China Wars, and propped up the murderous Pol Pot regime in Cambodia. It has also fought border skirmishes with India in 1959 and 1962, and with the Soviet Union along the Issuri River in the Soviet Far East in 1969. In 1973, it wrested the contested Paracel Islands from the then South Vietnamese regime, and attacked its erstwhile ally Vietnam along the China-Vietnam border in 1979. In 1988, the Chinese sank a number of Vietnamese boats in the disputed Spratly Islands area in the South China Sea. In addition, China is remembered for supporting Communist insurgencies in Malaysia and Thailand, while the New People's Army, the armed wing of the Communist Party of the Philippines, drew ideological inspiration from Beijing. Today, China has conflicting maritime claims with Japan, South Korea, Malaysia, Vietnam, Indonesia and the Philippines.

Given China's history of cross-border conflicts, other Asia-Pacific nations have become a little wary of its regional intentions. South-East Asians often refer to China's propensity to use force to settle disputes. Their wariness is compounded by fears that China might use its new-found economic power to become the next military superpower.

In the eyes of Communist China, the USA is still a hegemonic power. With the Soviet threat removed, Chinese security policy is now focused on the USA's Asian policy. Beijing sees the subversion of the world's remaining socialist states, largely through non-military means, as a principal goal of US policy today especially after 1992 when the Clinton Administration adopted a more ideological rather than pragmatic approach to China. Beijing believes that the USA's policy of engagement is really neo-containment in disguise. US engagement or enmeshment of China is to tie Beijing down and to subvert China, including its economic modernization. The real aim of engagement, as such, is to mould China into a shape desired by the West. Some Chinese analysts therefore feel that because the USA is in relative decline, it is attempting to make up for it by leading a coalition of Western-dominated industrialized countries, including Japan, to maintain a unipolar world.

Not surprisingly, China as such feels not only militarily vulnerable, but also threatened by the USA's attempts to impose democratic values on it.

The democratic values expounded by the USA tend to diffuse rather than concentrate power in the hands of ruling elites. Similarly, economic reform can be destabilizing because it tends to distribute wealth away from the centre and into the hands of the masses, thus threatening central authority. This is seen as particularly regime-threatening because Chinese political culture is based on the assumption that the stronger the central authority, the more secure the individual (Wang, 1992, p.6). Washington's emphasis on economic liberalism, human rights and democratic values is therefore seen as an 'invasion' which is more dangerous in the short term than any military threat: 'It has been a widely accepted interpretation in China that foreign invasions, exploitation and *influences* [emphasis added] were the principal cause of the nation's poverty, social ills, demoralization and loss of greatness' (Wang, 1992, p.2).

China has adopted a two-tier military strategy. The first is to upgrade its nuclear capability to deter the big powers, while the second is to acquire sufficient conventional capability to handle regional conflicts (see Table 5.2). Thus *both* nuclear and conventional weapons are considered to be vital and complementary for achieving China's national objectives (Johnston, 1995/96, p.12). This approach to military power was illustrated by Beijing's 'missile demonstration' (read nuclear demonstration) against Taiwan in the Taiwan Straits in March 1996. While ground forces of the People's Liberation Army (PLA) – all units of the Chinese armed forces, not just the ground forces, belong to the PLA – is huge compared with the Taiwanese armed forces, the PLA is incapable of matching Taiwan's sophisticated conventional armed forces. But what Beijing did not lack was a nuclear capability which it did not hesitate to demonstrate, albeit in a rather indirect way.

In contrast to China, one could argue that nuclear weapons have diminished in utility for the USA over the years (see Table 5.2). This is because the USA has developed highly accurate, lethal and effective conventional weapons, as demonstrated during the Desert Storm campaign in the 1991 Gulf War. This conventional superiority explains why the USA is at the forefront of the nuclear counter-proliferation initiative in the Asia-Pacific (Pilat and Kirchner, 1995, pp.153–66; Gebhard, 1995). America's nuclear superiority combined with the effectiveness and versatility of its conventional forces will ensure its military dominance.

China therefore realizes that it needs modern technology to upgrade its armed forces to be *on par* with that of the USA. While the PLA is the largest armed forces in the world, it is still technologically three or even four generations behind those of the West. It is therefore not surprising that China is now paying increasing attention to its conventional forces and emphasizing training and equipment over ideology. In 1996, China announced a 12.7 per cent increase in defence spending from 71.5 billion Yuan to 80.57 billion Yuan despite an overall budget deficit. This was in response to PLA calls for more high-technology arms to 'win regional wars' (Associated Press, 3 March 1997). The modernization of the PLA would give it greater power projection capability. A modern PLA would be a great source of concern to Japan, Taiwan as well as the South-East Asian states. This time round, China is approaching Russia for military technology, purchasing a minimum of US$2.1 billion worth of Russian arms in 1996, or 70 per cent of total Chinese arms procurement from abroad (*Military Technology News*, 1996, p.115). Russia, although still listing China as one of its possible principal enemies, is prepared to sell a range of sophisticated equipment to China because it desperately needs hard currency. This tie-up between China and Russia has been reinforced by Moscow's aim of counterbalancing the USA. Russia has been upset by the USA's insistence on expanding NATO to include former Warsaw Pact members. Chinese access to advanced Russian technology, according to Australian defence advisor Paul Dibb, could 'rapidly undermine the balance of power in the whole region'.

Until its conventional forces are modernized, nuclear weapons represent the great equalizer for China. The attraction of nuclear capability is that it is comparatively cheap, and gives the possessor tremendous political leverage. China is at the moment therefore more concerned about building up nuclear capability rather than building down. Thus in the short and perhaps the medium-term, the Chinese nuclear arsenal is likely to improve both qualitatively and quantitatively. Even if the USA cuts its strategic arsenal to 1,000-deployed warheads, by the year 2003, the PRC is believed to have only between 200–500 strategic nuclear warheads at the moment. China may also develop theatre/tactical nuclear weapons, to make up for its shortcomings in conventional weaponry, to fight 'high-tech limited wars' around China's periphery (Johnston, 1995, p.27). Whether China would really use tactical nuclear weapons in such limited wars is still open to debate. Some analysts see Chinese military power as no threat, since it is merely a reflection of China's new-found status as a great power. Instead, China 'wants to follow its own classic strategist, Sun Tzu, and obtain its goals without actually having to use force' (Kelly, 1995, p.27).

It is likely, however, that China, like the USA, will see the spread of nuclear weapons (or nuclear proliferation) in Asia as a future strategic challenge. With proliferation, China would be literally surrounded by a ring of nuclear-armed states – a unified Korea, Japan, Taiwan, India and Kazakhstan. Many of these powers would be potentially unfriendly to China. The Central Asian republics might support Zingjiang and other Muslim Chinese regions in seceding. Sino-Indian rivalry still exists despite the *rapprochement* between the two countries, a process which began in 1988 with the visit of the then Indian Prime Minister, Rajiv Ghandi, to Beijing. Most of all, China fears a nuclearized Japan because of the latter's technological potential and economic power, and because of the traditional hatred and suspicion which China still feels against Japan. A nuclear-armed Japan might be China's greatest regional rival, and might undertake initiatives detrimental to China's interests, especially if the USA succumbs to one of its periodic isolationist moods.

An understanding of China's long-term and short-term objectives, and its approach to military power in general and nuclear weapons in particular, is therefore critical to any assessment of the prospects of a nuclear arms race in the Asia-Pacific. China appears to still regard nuclear weapons as essential and fundamental to its national power in the immediate years ahead. Yet it seems that China shares the USA's concern over proliferation. This is why China is helping to ensure that North Korea does not acquire nuclear weapons of its own.

Japan: the constrained power

Many people in the Asia-Pacific today still fear a remilitarized Japan. This is because of the region's experience of Japanese aggression and imperialism. Any notion of Japan becoming a 'normal' nation with its own armed forces being responsible for the country's defence is perceived as a potential revival of the Japanese threat. Japanese security today hinges on four factors – a non-threatening, non-nuclear Korea, free access to secure sea lines of communications, a China which is non-threatening, and ultimately, upon a US security guarantee. It is impossible to consider the security role of Japan without taking into account the USA–Japan Security Treaty and the Japanese 'peace Constitution'. Article 9 of the Japanese Constitution renounces war as the sovereign right of the nation 'and the threat or use of force as a means of settling international disputes'. The so-called 'peace Constitution' was imposed by the Americans after the end of the Second World War. The Constitution, in tandem with the USA–Japan Mutual Security Treaty (MST), has served to reassure the rest of the Asia-Pacific that Japan will never be a belligerent nation again.

After the break-up of the Soviet Union, there was some debate in the USA and Japan as to whether the MST was still relevant. At the April 1996 summit between US President Bill Clinton and Japanese Prime Minister Ryutaro Hashimoto, both countries not only reaffirmed their support for the Treaty, but broadened its scope, albeit imprecisely, in the 'Japan–US Joint Declaration on Security–Alliance for the 21st Century'. The reaffirmed Security Treaty moved away from a security focus to a more general focus on 'global issues', including 'environmental preservation, drug trafficking, nuclear non-proliferation, the development of Third World and formerly Socialist nations, the spread of open markets, the fostering of democracy and human rights, and strengthening of UN peacekeeping operations' (Mulgam, 1996, p.5). We can therefore see a move for an enhanced Japanese role in the Asia-Pacific. This represents a new form of burden-sharing for the Japanese, on a global scale. The stress on human rights and democracy, however, must surely be seen as regime-threatening by Beijing and other countries in the region.

The USA–Japan Security Treaty therefore provides an avenue for Japan to move from a diffused, global security role to a more specific regional one in the years to come. Although there are no indications that the 'peace Constitution' will be revised any time soon, Japan is

Japanese Prime Minister Ryutaro Hashimoto meets with US President Bill Clinton prior to the 1996 summit

studying what it can do within the framework of the Constitution to deepen defence co-operation with the USA (Kamiya, 1996, p.17). These moves represent a sea change in Japan's attitude towards regional security. Whether Japan's future role will be positive or negative will depend on its future relations with the USA, and on how it establishes regional alliances and linkages, especially with China and a potentially reunified Korea.

Japan is unlikely to become a direct military threat to the region again because it is a constrained power. Japan is constrained by geography, demography and history. It cannot hope to become an independent security actor in the Asia-Pacific without incurring great political costs. Three factors account for Tokyo's limitations as a potential regional hegemon. The first is that any attempt to dominate the region would trigger off a hostile Chinese reaction. Second, the historical antipathy felt by many countries in the region towards a remilitarized Japan would make any attempt at the unilateral imposition of order by Japan counter-productive. Finally, Japan's post-war 'peace Constitution' also places constraints on any military adventurism. At best, Tokyo can only play the role of balancer.

5.5   Zones of potential conflict

The South China Sea

The history of the South China Sea disputes has been well documented (e.g. Hill, Owen and Roberts, 1991). Essentially, they involve two of the four main archipelagos in the South China Sea. The first is a bilateral dispute between China and Vietnam over the Paracels (650 km south-east of Hainan Island). The second involves overlapping claims over the Spratlys Archipelago which comprises more than 190 islets, reefs and atolls

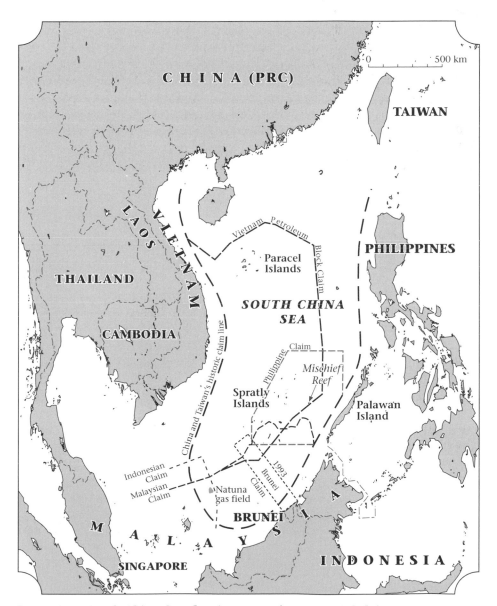

Figure 5.4   *South China Sea showing competing territorial claims*

scattered in a south-western arc across 150,000 square miles of the South China Sea. Whereas China and Taiwan claim all the archipelagos in the South China Sea, the Vietnamese claim the Paracels and the entire Spratlys. Malaysia, the Philippines and Brunei lay claim to various parts of the Spratly Islands (see Figure 5.4).

The competing claims in the South China Sea can be divided into historical claims of sovereignty/colonial heritage and claims based on the extension of coastal jurisdiction as part of the 1982 Law of the Sea Convention (LOSC) process. Only one claimant – the Philippines – bases its claim in part on the principle of *terra nullis*, or discovery and occupation, and proximity to Philippines territory. The Chinese claims were originally based on historical use and administration of the Spratlys and Paracels. Taiwan's claim to the Spratlys is based on the exact same principles as that of the PRC. In 1992, Beijing reiterated its claim to the Spratlys and Paracels by enacting '*The Declaration of the Law of the People's Republic of China on Territorial Sea and Contiguous Zone*', which specifically included the Spratly Islands (Chinese name *Nansha*) the Paracel Islands (*Xisha*) and the Senkaku Islands east of Taiwan, as part of its territory. In 1996 the Chinese reaffirmed their claim to the Spratlys and Paracels when they ratified the 1982 LOSC.

The South China Sea disputes have often been described as a contest for living and non-living resources, especially hydrocarbons. However, no large deposits of gas or oil have been found in the disputed areas so far. Nevertheless, the South China Sea issue is more than a conflict over potential resources. In this respect, China's role is pivotal. This is because the disputes involve more than potential sources of energy, resources and food for Beijing. Analysts have pointed out that Beijing's maritime disputes have important domestic implications.

Besides a sense of historical entitlement, China also fears that any negotiated settlement or compromise in the South China Sea will send the wrong signals to aspiring secessionists in the PRC's outermost provinces of Xinjiang and Tibet and also to Taiwan. At the same time, China is also involved in boundary disputes with Japan, India and Russia. Any resolution of the disputes in the South China Sea will therefore have direct implications for China's other maritime disputes. In short, China stands potentially to lose, or gain, more than any of the South China Sea disputants in any resolution of these disputes. Therefore the tension between China's domestic priorities and its international agenda and ambitions makes it difficult for Beijing to back down or compromise on the Spratlys and Paracels.

Moreover, from the strategic point of view, Beijing views the South China Sea as vital for its survival. It has been the main corridor for China's trade and 'China's principal gateway to the world for some two thousand years' (Samuels, 1982, p.9). Today it still provides access to the economic heartlands of southern China. It is therefore important to understand the place of the South China Sea in China's strategic calculations.

For the majority of the South-East Asian claimants, the South China Sea disputes appear to be the greatest external defence problem they are faced with. While this may be true, it is necessary to put the South China Sea issue into a more balanced perspective. It may be argued that the dispute is not a life-or-death issue for any ASEAN disputant. It does not threaten the sovereign integrity of any state (although it can be argued that it is an extremely vital issue for Vietnam). Neither does it appear to threaten the stability of any regime.

The South China Sea 'threat' therefore involves two elements. The first is the perceived danger from an apparently belligerent China which has not until now renounced the use of force to resolve conflicting claims in the South China Sea. This perception by the ASEAN disputants is reinforced by modern China's record of the use of force to secure disputed border areas. The second threat stems from the fact that the perceived need to cope with a potentially volatile situation in the South China Sea makes it necessary for nearly all the disputants to build up their maritime defence capability. Overall, it appears that the resolution of the South China Sea disputes by peaceful, legal means will be a drawn-out affair because of the general lack of political will and the perception among the disputants that they have more to lose as a consequence of any form of settlement.

The Korean Peninsula and the shadow of nuclear proliferation

The furore over the possible development of nuclear warheads by North Korea in 1994 shows that nuclear proliferation is regarded as a serious threat by the major powers in the Asia-Pacific. The Korean peninsula is crucial for China because it provides a strategic buffer (see Figure 5.5). Beijing's policy is to ensure that it shares borders with friendly or at least neutral states. Japan has historically regarded Korea as a dagger aimed at the Japanese islands, and the peninsula must therefore be controlled by powers friendly to Tokyo. The USA sees the Korean peninsula as a potential arena of conflict between North and South Korea which would destabilize the Asia-Pacific. The greatest danger to stability is posed by the possibility of North Korea being the trigger for Asia-Pacific nuclear proliferation.

Much media attention has been focused on North Korea's alleged nuclear weapons programme. It has been suggested that North Korea's nuclear programme was triggered by South Korea's alleged programme to establish a nuclear weapons infrastructure in the 1970s (Bermudez, 1996, p.5). After the death of Kim Il Sung, and due to the economic problems the regime is reported to be facing, North Korea is apparently using its 'threshold' nuclear capability as a bargaining chip for economic assistance (Garrett and Glaser, 1995, p.529). In this regard, China has consistently denied providing assistance to develop Pyongyang's alleged secret nuclear programme, or to provide it with guided missile technology. This is not surprising since a nuclear North Korea is regarded as the trigger which will put immediate pressure on Japan to go nuclear. Many analysts have asserted that a 'proliferation chain reaction' would result if North Korea were to go nuclear, causing South Korea and then Japan to go nuclear in turn (Caldwell and Lennon, 1995, p.33). Since China is fearful of regional nuclear proliferation, China can be expected to apply pressure and prevent North Korea from developing an effective nuclear weapons programme.

While countries like Japan, South Korea and Taiwan have been described as threshold nuclear states, capable of going nuclear extremely rapidly, it would not be in their interest to do so as long as the USA's nuclear umbrella is available. Indeed, one could argue that these three states would find it a political and strategic liability to acquire nuclear weapons. Why? South Korea, Taiwan and Japan are all relatively small states with the majority of their population concentrated in a number of very large cities. This makes them especially vulnerable to nuclear strikes. Thus, it is unlikely that these states will go nuclear.

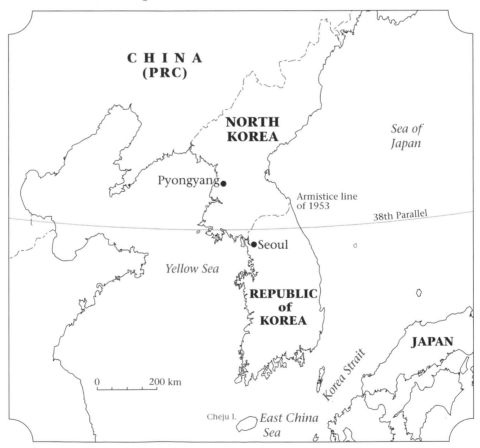

Figure 5.5 *Map of Korea*

5.6   ASEAN and South-East Asia: multilateralism and co-operative security

Although not a military heavyweight, this sub-region has achieved a level of security co-operation which North-East Asia has not. The exceptions are the Indochina states which, in terms of strategic culture, tend to be closer to North-East Asia. Economic realities and political necessity, however, have forced Vietnam and Laos to align themselves with ASEAN today (see Chapter 4, Figure 4.1).

For much of their history, South-East Asian states, especially the non-communist nations, have grappled with serious problems of nation-building and national consolidation. The real fight has been to create nation-states out of a variety of highly diverse ethnic groups contained within very arbitrary state boundaries drawn by former colonisers. ASEAN South-East Asia was therefore more pre-occupied with the process of national consolidation rather than preserving state frontiers against external aggressors. This has made these countries inward-looking in terms of security. Military power is regarded as essential for holding a nation together, not for defeating external enemies. ASEAN's security role is therefore unique. The security dimension of ASEAN is deliberately understated, and ASEAN has never articulated a formal model of regional security (Leifer, 1996, p.4).

ASEAN traditionally relied on a variety of non-military instruments to deal with external threats. These instruments included military alliances and/or alignments, as well as policies of non-alignment and other foreign policy initiatives (Alagappa, 1987, pp.19–28). Thailand and the Philippines, for instance, are US allies under the Manila Pact. The Five-Power Defence Arrangement (FPDA) brings together the United Kingdom, Australia, New Zealand, Malaysia, and Singapore. The FPDA is, however, not a formal defence alliance but an arrangement to consult in the event of aggression against any member. Similarly, the Australian–Indonesian security accord, signed in December 1995, provides for both countries to consult in the event of adverse challenges to either of them.

Non-military initiatives, on balance, have been more important than military alliances for South-East Asian security. This was because regional elites realized that their regimes were highly susceptible to internal subversion and outside meddling in their internal affairs. The Association, through its key principle of 'non-interference in the internal affairs of another state', therefore played a key role in allaying intra-regional tensions.

Ultimately, ASEAN should be seen as an attempt at managing inter-state tensions so that each member could concentrate on domestic consolidation and economic development. This emphasis on the economic dimension of security is reflected in the ASEAN concept of national and regional resilience, which equates economic development directly with stability. ASEAN members are therefore expected to look after their own domestic constituencies by ensuring economic growth and development. The 'ASEAN way' of conflict management and security is unstructured, informal and based on consensus. At the same time, it is an inward-looking, almost cynical way of ensuring the survival of the grouping's ruling elites by emphasizing non-interference and economic progress. The ASEAN principles of national sovereignty and non-interference in the domestic affairs of another state have been described as 'unexceptional norms' (Leifer, 1996, p.11). However, what distinguishes these 'norms' is the zeal with which they are practised. ASEAN made national sovereignty and non-interference the cornerstone of its intra-ASEAN relations, and zealously guarded and practised these core principles within the Association and its immediate environs. ASEAN's preoccupation with 'non-interference' was reflected in the ASEAN stand when Vietnam invaded Cambodia in 1979. Despite the many atrocities of the *Khmer Rouge* regime, the ASEAN states recognized the *Khmer Rouge* as the legitimate government of Cambodia by making it 'abundantly clear their refusal to recognize the transfer of political power within Kampuchea effected through Vietnamese force of arms' (Leifer, 1989, p.94). Similarly, ASEAN is prepared to accept Burma/Myanmar as an ASEAN member despite its poor human rights record because domestic affairs are regarded as the sole prerogative of the Burma/Myanmar regime. However, this principle of 'non-interference' becomes more diluted and less strident the further one moves away from the ASEAN heartland of South-East Asia. Thus, individual ASEAN countries could choose to condemn or ignore South African *apartheid*, atrocities in Bosnia, or the blood bath in Rwanda-Burundi despite these affairs being, strictly speaking, the domestic or 'internal' affairs of the states concerned.

The 'ASEAN way' was effective in managing sub-regional tensions only because there was a security umbrella provided by the USA which looked after the main external threats to the region. In the post-Cold War era, ASEAN leaders are faced with the problem of coping with a more unpredictable world. They have responded by using a twin track approach – contingency planning for defence and the engagement (in dialogue) of potentially hostile neighbours.

ASEAN military planning is not based on threats, but on the health of the economy. Defence spending in ASEAN since 1991 ranges from a low of about 1.5 per cent of gross domestic product (GDP) in Indonesia to a high of six per cent in the case of Singapore. Most countries typically spend three to four per cent of their GDP per annum on defence (see Table 5.3).

The ASEAN Regional Forum

ASEAN has consistently shied away from any suggestion of collective or common defence. The 'ASEAN way' was essentially an intra-ASEAN mechanism for conflict management, or to use the current buzz words, 'preventive diplomacy' which was largely applied within ASEAN itself.

Table 5.3 *Military expenditure of selected Asia-Pacific nations, as percentage of gross domestic product (1986, 1990 and 1994)*

	1986	1990	1994
USA	6.6	5.5	4.3
Russian Federation[1]	–	–	–
Brunei	4.6	6.4	–
Burma/Myanmar	2.9	3.4	[4.2]
People's Republic of China[2]	2.1	1.6	1.3
Indonesia	–1.9	–1.3	–
Japan	1	1	1
Korea, North[3]	–	–	–
Korea, South	4.6	3.8	3.5
Malaysia	5.7	2.6	2.9
Philippines	1.9	2.2	[1.8]
Singapore	6.6	5.5	5.3
Taiwan	5.4	5	5.2
Thailand	3.7	2.5	2.4
Vietnam[4]	–	8.7	–
Australia	2.9	2.4	2.6

[1] High inflation, volatile exchange rate and the absence of reliable national statistics for all the Russian Federation countries make it difficult to calculate military expenditure in constant US$ and as a proportion of GDP.

[2] Figures reflect official budget figures only. For a discussion of the debate over the true level of Chinese military expenditure, see Bergstrand (1994, pp.441–8).

[3] Figures reflect official figures only and may underestimate North Korea's military expenditure for which no official figures are available. The lack of reliable economic data makes it difficult to calculate military expenditure in constant US$ and as a proportion of GDP.

[4] Lack of data on inflation makes it impossible to calculate a continuous series in constant 1990 US$. Figures for 1986 are calculated using 1989 as the base year, and those for 1990 and 1994 using 1990 as the base year.

Source: SIPRI (1996)

However, the changing security environment following the end of the Cold War has forced ASEAN to reconsider its regional role. North-East Asia became a neighbour which could no longer be ignored, especially China which, as the largest resident power, is also a potential superpower. Thus ASEAN was forced to think of a wider regional role for three reasons (Leifer, 1996):

1   To remain relevant in an increasingly globalized and multilateral world.

2   To engage China, which was perceived as a potential regional power. and

3   To maintain the Asia-Pacific *balance of power* or status quo.

Malaysia and Singapore for instance, have invested substantially in China through a process of economic engagement (Wanandi, 1996). This is remarkable because both countries have traditionally been virulently anti-Communist. Until 1991, for instance, Malaysia still considered China to be its main external threat. Indonesia is still wary of Chinese intentions. It restored diplomatic ties with Beijing only in 1990, after they were 'frozen' in 1967. Apart from these individual initiatives, ASEAN members also felt that if the association remained internally focused, its capacity to manage the regional order to its benefit would be severely compromised. ASEAN was in danger of becoming irrelevant with the setting up of other regional organizations and as second-track initiatives began to address wider regional security issues. In response, ASEAN decided in 1992 to discuss security co-operation in the ASEAN-Post Ministerial Conferences (ASEAN-PMC).

ASEAN diplomacy reached a new high in 1994 with the setting up of the ASEAN Regional Forum (ARF). The ARF provides its members, which include the European Union, India and all the Asia-Pacific countries except North Korea and Taiwan, with a venue to discuss security matters. The ARF may be seen as an extension of the ASEAN way of *co-operative security*, or 'ASEAN writ large' (Leifer, 1996, p.25). In the final analysis, the ARF was established as a result of a compromise between China and the USA, with ASEAN in the driver's seat. The forum is therefore unique in that the big powers were prepared to allow a grouping of small-middle powers to be at the head of the regional security initiative.

While this could be attributed to ASEAN diplomatic skill, it also reflected the acceptability to China of the consensual, non-binding approach adapted from the 'ASEAN way'. For the USA the low-risk, snail-pace ARF process appeared to be a low-cost approach to supplementing its bilateral defence arrangements in the Asia-Pacific. A USA-dominated ARF would also have been unacceptable to China, hence both Washington and Beijing were prepared to allow ASEAN to set the pace.

China also possibly agreed to participate in the ARF because it needed, at least in the short-term, to establish its credentials as an internationally responsible actor. Besides, several key ASEAN members were the only countries in the Asia-Pacific which had empathized with China, and which gave moral support to Beijing when the USA accused it of violating human rights, unfair labour practices, and not supporting the principle of free and fair markets. China as such could not afford to ignore this source of international support by refusing to join the ARF. China's membership therefore represented a triumph for the 'ASEAN way'. That China felt that it could not afford to alienate ASEAN was also evident in the ASEAN–China talks on resolving the Spratly Islands disputes. This was a remarkable exception made by China, considering that previously it had always insisted on bilateral negotiations. ASEAN's influence as a grouping, however, should not be over-estimated. The South-East Asian Nuclear Weapons-Free Zone Treaty signed in December 1995 by all ten South-East Asian nations was objected to by both the USA and China. The USA saw the Treaty as constraining the freedom of navigation in the region, while China saw it as likely to undermine its sovereignty claims in the South China Sea. After all, if the South China Sea does belong to China, it has every right to deploy whatever types of weapons it wishes, nuclear or otherwise, in its own seas. Consequently, it is not surprising that while China was talking with ASEAN over ways and means of settling the Spratly Islands issue peacefully at talks in Anhui province, two armed Chinese ships were seen in April 1997, near two islets, Panata and Kota, claimed by both China and the Philippines.

The ARF holds just one ministerial meeting a year. It has therefore been accused of being unstructured, under-institutionalized, and therefore ineffective. Defenders of the ARF point out that it is the only multilateral security forum in the Asia-Pacific, and that the ARF process is more important than the structure. The ARF is regarded as an extension of the 'ASEAN way', and there are hopes that the process of socialization which took place within ASEAN would work for the ARF as well, especially where China is concerned. We have to ask ourselves therefore whether the forum can replicate the success of ASEAN. In this regard, there appear to be many obstacles. The ARF has already grown to be a grouping of 21 disparate countries. The original consensual process worked because the number of actors in ASEAN was limited to five more or less like-minded members for many years. The association was geographically delimited so that members were within easy reach of each other. The original members shared many common values, such as the consensus on the utility of economic over military power, and the role of national and regional resilience in ensuring national security. In contrast, the ARF comprises culturally and economically diverse countries. Any basis for co-operation is also compromised by the fact that the forum contains within it countries with very different agendas, which possess latent hostility towards each other and are potential rivals for power. The consensual, lowest common denominator approach might work for countries with shared values and norms. However, in a grouping which includes countries which still believe in the utility of military power, the consensual approach is less likely to work. The process of socialization itself is problematical because of the many actors in the ARF. Socialization might work over time, but an incremental process such as the 'ASEAN way' may not be able to address immediately pressing issues, such as USA–China tensions.

The 'ASEAN way' is a unique process which involves a great deal of informal diplomatic networking among regional leaders. The 'ASEAN way' is based on person-to-person contact supported by a bureaucracy which holds an average of 300 meetings a year. Key decisions are usually made informally. It is doubtful whether the members of ARF who are not also members of ASEAN share a common social and political background and fully accept a consensus-based process of conflict management. As such, there is the feeling by some ARF members that a more structured institution for conflict management will be needed by the North-East Asian states. As it is, there already exists the second-track North-East Asian security dialogue involving the USA, China, Japan and South Korea. It therefore remains to be seen whether the ARF will abandon the 'ASEAN way' and adopt a more structured approach to regional security. It is unlikely, on balance, that the ARF will simply wither away. It offers a mechanism to supplement bilateral negotiations, and if the Forum is unable to resolve issues, it can at least bring these issues to the notice of all its members. The ARF, in the absence of other alternatives, is a significant step towards Asia-Pacific preventive diplomacy.

5.7 Conclusion

It is difficult to predict the future course of security in the Asia-Pacific because of the complex network of relations and tensions in the region. However, the picture becomes less complicated if we have a theoretical framework to organize our thoughts. The theory of *strategic culture*, despite its shortcomings, provides us with a useful framework to understand that North-East Asia is very different from South-East Asia. *Strategic culture* provides us with a historical perspective which is lacking in the two current mainstream schools of international relations theory – neoliberal-institutionalism and neo-realism. By adapting and using *strategic culture* as one lens to understand why Asia-Pacific states are behaving the way they are, and then using either neoliberal-institutionalism or neo-realism as a second lens to look at their likely action in the future, we can obtain richer insights into regional security developments. Of course, this combination of theories would horrify the purists. Nevertheless, the point to note is that no one theory can explain everything about a situation. It is therefore important to be aware of the range of theories which can be used as analytical tools to enhance our understanding of any complex situation.

The Asia-Pacific is still a region of tension today. From a USA–Soviet Union confrontation during the Cold War, we see the prospects of a clash of wills between China and the USA. China will be one key player in the region. Given the fact that it is an ascendant but unsatisfied power, many states in the region are worried about the prospects of an Asia-Pacific dominated by China. This feeling is not helped by China's record of using force to settle disputes. Overall, China's foreign and domestic policies remain opaque and inscrutable. The world's only military superpower, the USA, may not be able to hold onto its military supremacy forever. The US economy is stronger than many detractors make it out to be, but there is a growing realization in the USA that a strategy of maintaining *primacy* will be extremely costly. In addition, there is an ongoing debate about the optimum foreign and military policy the USA should pursue (see Chapter 8). At present, the USA appears to be pursuing a strategy based largely on maintaining *primacy*, mixed with elements of *co-operative security* and *selective engagement*. This strategy, however, appears to be the result of somewhat indecisive thinking. As such, no one can be sure which way the pendulum will swing next. The key concern of America's allies, particularly Japan, is that the USA can retreat into isolationism if the mood takes it, or if circumstances force it to.

China, unlike the USA, is a resident power which shares common land and maritime borders with nearly all the Asian states. China will therefore not go away. This has made a number of the Asia-Pacific countries realize that it would be far better to engage China rather than confront China. Engaging China has two positive benefits. China's economy is now quite robust and engagement has economic benefits. Engagement would also, at least theoretically, socialize China so that it will become an international good citizen. Containing China in concert with the USA is a risky proposition, simply because the USA is believed to be a power on the decline. Besides, the USA might just one day decide to go back into isolationism. Countries like Malaysia, Singapore and even Japan are therefore investing in China, and attempting to support China in as many international forums as possible.

The Asia-Pacific, therefore, remains a region of tension despite the end of the Cold War. Inter-state relations are complex and multi-faceted, especially in North-East Asia, with the USA and China as the main actors. Japan, the economic superpower, waits in the wings while South-East Asia is attempting to show the way to *co-operative security*. It is unlikely, however, that the South-East Asian model of *multilateralism* can be transplanted into North-East Asia. The USA is still generally viewed as a benign power and necessary for the status quo, and hence for regional stability. States which can afford it, and many of them can, are gradually arming themselves just in case things do go wrong. Although there is not as yet an Asia-Pacific *arms race*, we are currently witnessing a gradual but discernible increase in military capability across the entire region.

References

Alagappa, M. (1987) *The National Security of Developing States: Lessons from Thailand*, Dover, Mass., Auburn House.

Bergstrand, B.G. (1994) 'World military expenditure', *SIPRI Year Book*, Oxford, Oxford University Press.

Bermudez, J.S. Jr (1996) 'North Korea's nuclear arsenal', *Jane's Intelligence Review*, Special Report, no.9.

Caldwell, J. and Lennon, A.T. (1995) 'China's nuclear modernization program', *Strategic Review*, Fall.

Cirincione, J. (1995) 'The non-proliferation treaty and the nuclear balance', *Current History, a Journal of Contemporary World Affairs*, May, p.205.

Department of Defense (US) (1995) Office of International Security Affairs, *United States Security Strategy for the East Asia Region*, Washington, February.

Garrett, B.N. and Glaser, B.S. (1995) 'Looking across the Yalu: Chinese assessments of North Korea', *Asian Survey*, vol.XXXV, no.6.

Gebhard, P.R.S. (1995) 'Not by diplomacy or defense alone: the role of regional security strategies in US proliferation policy', *The Washington Quarterly*, vol.18, no.1.

Hill, R.D., Owen, N.G. and Roberts, E.V. (eds) (1991) *Fishing in Troubled Waters: Proceedings of An Academic Conference on Territorial Claims in the South China Sea*, Hong Kong, Centre of Asian Studies, University of Hong Kong.

Johnston, A.I. (1995) 'Thinking about strategic culture', *International Security,* vol.19, no.4.

Johnston, A.I. (1995/96) 'China's new 'old thinking': the concept of limited deterrence', *International Security*, vol.20, no.3.

Jorgensen-Dahl, A. (1984) *Regional Organization and Order in South-East Asia*, London, Macmillan.

Kamiya, M. (1996) 'Will Japanese security policy change? The significance of the redefinition of the US–Japan alliance', *Pacific Research*, May.

Kelly, J.A. (1995) 'US security policies in East Asia: fighting erosion and finding a new balance', *The Washington Quarterly,* vol.18, no.3.

Leifer, M. (1989) *ASEAN and the Security of South-East Asia*, London, Routledge.

Leifer, M. (1996) 'The ASEAN Regional Forum', *Adelphi Paper no.302*, London, International Institute for Strategic Studies.

Mak, J.N. (1994) 'Armed, but ready?: ASEAN conventional warfare capabilities', *Harvard International Review*, vol.XVI, no.2.

Military Balance 1996–97 (1997) London, International Institute for Strategic Studies.

Military Technology News (1996) 'Russia pushes Chinese defense sales'.

Pilat, J.F. and Kirchner, W.L. (1995) 'The technological promise of counterproliferation', *The Washington Quarterly*, vol.18, no.1.

Samuels, M.S. (1982) *Contest for the South China Sea*, New York, Methuen and Co.

SIPRI (1996) *Year Book of World Armament and Disarmament*, Oxford, Oxford University Press.

Wanandi, J. (1996) 'ASEAN's China strategy: towards deeper engagement' *Survival,* vol.38, no.3.

Wang, J. (1992) *Comparing Chinese and American Conceptions of Security*, North Pacific Cooperative Security Dialogue, Working Paper no.17, Toronto, York University.

Further reading

Calder K. (1996) *Asia's Deadly Triangle*, London, Nicholas Brealey.

Clements, K. (1993) *Peace and Security in the Asian Pacific Region: Post Cold War Problems and Prospects*, Tokyo, Dunmore Press.

Leifer, M. (1996) 'The ASEAN Regional Forum', *Adelphi Paper no.302*, London, International Institute for Strategic Studies.

Yahuda, M. (1996) *The International Politics of Asia-Pacific 1945–1995*, London, Routledge.

CHAPTER 6

Restructuring foreign and defence policy: Japan

Kenneth Pyle

6.1   Introduction

The end of the Cold War has thrust Japan into strikingly new international conditions. Little in Japan's 2,000 year history has prepared it for the challenges of this new era. Despite the recession and the turmoil in its banking system that followed the bursting of a speculative bubble in the 1990s, the fact is that Japan emerged from the end of the Cold War as one of the world's great powers with expectations both at home and abroad that it will have a leadership role in the establishment of a new order in the Asia-Pacific region.

By the 1980s Japan had achieved its century-long national goal of catching up with the world's advanced industrial economies. It became the world's second largest economy, an economic superpower with burgeoning overseas investments and interests. For much of the post-war period the nation had been self-absorbed in its internal development strategies, but now Japan is increasingly aware that its fundamental national interests are at stake in the preservation of a stable and open global trading system. Perhaps no other major power is so dependent on the import of raw materials and the export of finished goods to pay for them. As one economist wrote, 'Of all the industrial countries, Japan has the greatest stake in a smoothly functioning international economic system subject to agreed norms and rules. Its dependence on foreigners for the necessities of life is greater than any other industrial country's' (Frank, 1975, p.13). As Japan's industrialization progressed, its dependence on raw materials grew until it became the world's largest importer of raw materials. Uniquely vulnerable to the closure of markets and disruption of trade and driven by changes in the international economy, Japan increased its investments abroad and many of its major industries moved their production facilities offshore. When the Cold War ended, Japan had perhaps as great an interest in the preservation of a stable international order as any nation. This chapter explores the interplay of domestic and external forces which, in the post-Cold War context, are reshaping Japanese foreign and defence policy.

6.2 Distinctive traits of Japanese foreign policy

If one looks back at the century and a half of modern Japanese diplomacy and foreign relations, certain fundamental interests and continuities persist. From the time Japan entered the international state system in the middle of the nineteenth century, its foreign policy has had several distinctive traits, none of which is conducive to the role of regional and international leadership Japan is now expected to play. First of all, Japan has tended to be *a reactive state* in its foreign relations. In contrast to the common impression shaped by Japanese imperialism, Japan has tended to accommodate itself to each new order formed in the past century and a half. As one of Japan's leading foreign policy analysts observed, the traditional Japanese approach to international norms is passive and situational, a reflection of Japan's particular experience as an island nation:

> Japan is a natural nation-state; the idea that a state is created by common will and contract has not existed in Japan. Japan has existed and will exist, regardless of the will and actions of its people. Hence, norms are considered to be created by nature, not men. The logical conclusion from such a view of the world is that the task for the Japanese is to adapt wisely to the international situation to secure its national interests, and not try to change or create the mysterious framework.

> (Kosaka Masataka quoted in Scalapino, 1977, p.229)

Since the Meiji Restoration of 1868, Japan, as a late developer, has been keenly sensitive to the forces controlling its international environment and has attempted to adapt to them and to use them to its own advantage. The external environment has likewise exercised considerable influence on the shape of the domestic political system. In the middle of the nineteenth century, the Japanese alone among Asian nations quickly adopted Western models and built a modern industrial economy; in the age of imperialism Japan became an imperialist; when the international rules and norms changed after the First World War, the Japanese accepted Wilsonianism. Only once, in the attempt to create their own new order in East Asia before and during the Second World War, did Japan abandon a cautious and circumspect approach, and even then Japanese leaders thought they were acting in accordance with international trends as the great powers were creating their own spheres, Germany seemed about to invade Britain, and fascism appeared to be the wave of the future.

A second and closely related trait is the dominance of *pragmatic nationalism* as the guiding philosophy of Japan's international relations. Rather than any set of fixed principles, an opportunistic adaptation to international conditions in order to enhance the power of the Japanese nation has been characteristic of Japanese foreign policy. While the modern revolutions of other major powers were impelled by rising middle-class demands for political rights, equality, and democracy, the Meiji Restoration – Japan's modern revolution – was above all a nationalist revolution. One of Japan's leading strategic thinkers recently responded to an American journalist's inquiry as to the place of fixed principles in Japanese foreign policy with the riposte that the 'histories of our two countries are different. Your country was built on principles. Japan was built on an archipelago' (Okazaki, 1993, p.61). In other words, the vulnerability of Japan's economy and geopolitical position precludes taking a stand on principle (see Figure 6.1). Japan has had to make its way in the world through a determined pursuit of national self-interest.

Another related trait of modern Japanese diplomacy had been its tendency to view its international relations through the prism of its domestic emphasis on status and hierarchy. Although they have experienced tutelage in democratic values, the Japanese people have never on their own achieved a democratic revolution. The drive for status has powerfully motivated the Japanese nation. It has sought association and alliance with the Western powers (the Anglo–Japanese alliance, 1902–22; the Tripartite Pact, 1940–45; the US–Japan alliance, 1952–present) while shunning identification with the countries of Asia. This drive for status, while a source of national cohesion and purpose, has often handicapped smooth relations with other Asian countries and international leadership. A veteran Japanese diplomat wrote in 1989: 'Japan's sense of superiority toward the rest of Asia is unchanged' (Asai, 1989, p.158).

Finally, Japan has had little experience of leadership in international organizations. Although it held one of five permanent seats on the Council of the League of Nations, it was never active or comfortable with the League's purposes. Following the Japanese 1931 invasion of Manchuria, the League voted overwhelmingly to condemn Japan and it quit the League. In the founding charter of the United Nations, Japan is referred to as an enemy nation. Japan became a member of the UN in 1956 but has yet to

Figure 6.1 *The geo-strategic view from Japan*

play a leading role. As of 1992, although the second largest financial contributor to the UN, Japan was last in terms of personnel contributions to professional UN posts compared to the nineteen other leading donor nations.

6.3   The institutional legacy of Japan's Cold War strategy

Japan had as clearly defined a national strategy as any major power in the Cold War era. In his memoirs, Henry Kissinger concluded that 'Japanese decisions have been the most farsighted and intelligent of any major nation in the post-World War Two era' (Kissinger, 1979, p.324). Japan's Cold War foreign policy manifested and in fact strengthened the deeply rooted characteristics of Japan's traditional approaches to international relations.

The strategy was conceived by Japan's shrewd post-war leader Yoshida Shigeru, who was prime minister during the post-war decade and served concurrently as foreign minister during much of that time. True to tradition, he found a way to accommodate to the new international system by allying with the new world power and at the same time pursuing a pragmatic policy of narrow self-interest. A great admirer of the Japanese imperial institution and of the British empire, Yoshida was a conservative who sought to restore Japan's international status. It was Yoshida who set Japan on a course of economic nationalism and rather than succumb to US pressure to rearm and join the Cold War struggle against the communist bloc, chose instead to accept a subordinate role in the US security system. Although Yoshida agreed to establish lightly armed Self-Defence Forces, he insisted on maintenance of the US-imposed constitution with its Article 9 that pledged Japan not to maintain war potential or to resort to the use of force in settling disputes. Instead, Yoshida proposed that Japan would provide bases for US forces in return for a guarantee of its security. Japan was thereby freed to devote all its energies to building its national economy and gaining parity with the world's leading industrial economies. For this purpose, Japan would abstain from the political-military aspects of international power politics.

To ensure this non-involvement in power politics, Yoshida and his successors devised a set of policies to underwrite what we have come to call 'the Yoshida Doctrine' of exclusive emphasis on economic development while depending on the US security guarantee provided by the US–Japan Mutual Security Treaty of 1951. Let us briefly summarize these policies. First, Japan would trade the right to station US forces in Japan in return for a US guarantee of Japanese security. Second, Yoshida and his successors insisted on an interpretation of the constitution that would not permit the dispatch of Japanese Self-Defence Forces overseas; they could not partici-pate, therefore, in collective security undertakings. In practice, this meant that Japanese forces did not participate in either the Korean or the Vietnamese conflicts. The Japanese economy, however, battened on procurement orders during these conflicts. Third, the Yoshida Doctrine of non-involvement in military strategic affairs was elaborated in 1967 by the enunciation of the Three Non-nuclear Principles which stated that Japan would not produce, possess, or permit the entry of nuclear weapons into Japan. Fourth, at the same time it was determined that Japan would not produce arms for export. Finally, it became a practice in the 1960s to constrain defence spending to less than one per cent of the gross national product.

By the 1980s the Yoshida strategy had become a finely tuned policy for maintaining a strong, domestic consensus on foreign policy. To the conservatives it gave the satisfaction of Japan being squarely on the side of the USA in the Cold War by providing bases for the US army, navy and airforce. To the left wing, which leaned heavily toward pacifism and neutralism, it gave tight limits on Japan's commitments to the US alliance. For the duration of the Cold War it was a brilliant strategy that allowed Japan to concentrate its energies and resources on productive investments and growth strategies, resulting in Japan's recovery from the war and its emergence as an economic superpower.

Nonetheless, the strategy did have an Achilles' heel. In its dependence on the US security guarantee, its acceptance of becoming a military protectorate of the United States, and its required deference to US foreign policy, Japan sacrificed a substantial portion of national pride. Moreover, it left a warped and unbalanced legacy of institutions for the making of foreign policy. The economic ministries (the Ministry of Finance, the Ministry of International Trade and Industry, and the Economic Planning Agency) became the powerful, strategically oriented part of the government, attracting the best and brightest graduates of Japan's intensely competitive education system. Working hand-in-glove with a rejuvenated business elite, the economic bureaucrats formulated policies of economic nationalism that made Japan the prime beneficiary of the international free trade order sponsored by the Pax Americana. In contrast, the political side of foreign policy making was weak and underdeveloped. The Foreign Ministry was compelled to follow in the train of US policy and had limited capacity for creative and autonomous policy making. The Defence Agency, lacking status as a full-fledged ministry, was even less influential in the foreign policy process. Thus, while the Yoshida strategy gave rise to powerful economic institutions in the post-war state, it left an undeveloped political dimension of foreign policy making and a nation unprepared to deal with the political consequences of the economic power it had acquired by the 1990s.

6.4 The Gulf War: Japan's first post-Cold War crisis

The shortcomings of the Yoshida strategy were fully revealed on the international stage when Japan was confronted by the demands for support of the coalition in the Gulf War which broke out in 1991 subsequent to Iraq's invasion of Kuwait. Japan depended on the Persian Gulf for two-thirds of its oil supply. With the Cold War ended and the context of international politics radically altered, the Yoshida strategy had lost its persuasive capabilities, particularly with the USA which was increasingly resentful of Japanese economic policies. The argument that because of constitutional inhibitions Japan could not dispatch its Self-Defence Forces (SDF) abroad to participate in the UN-sanctioned coalition, or provide any personnel support, generated a storm of international criticism that stunned Japan's leadership. Although Japan contributed US$13 billion to support the coalition, it was apparent that Japan could no longer maintain a low profile on strategic issues and that what some critics derided as 'chequebook diplomacy' would not suffice. An influential study group in the ruling Liberal Democratic Party (LDP), where the Yoshida strategy had been the prevailing backbone of foreign policy, recommended a reinterpretation of the constitution. Its report concluded that the changed international system required a change in Japan's policies: 'Japan is being asked to shift from a passive stance of mainly enjoying the benefits of a global system to an active stance of assisting in the building of a new order' (*Asahi Shimbun*, 21 February, 1992).

As a consequence, Japan began to inch away from the Yoshida Doctrine, moving cautiously and deliberately to accommodate the changing order. In 1992, after intense debate, the Diet (parliament), passed the UN Peacekeeping Operations (PKO) Co-operation Bill which ended the ban on dispatching troops abroad but limited deployment to logistical and humanitarian support, monitoring elections, and providing aid to civil administration of UN peacekeeping operations. A section of the bill that

Japanese Self Defence Forces: infantry training

permitted participation in armed UN missions, such as monitoring cease-fires, disarming combatants, and patrolling buffer zones, was frozen for the indefinite future. Despite its very limited nature, the PKO bill survived the die-hard opposition of the left wing and led to the first post-Second World War dispatch of Japanese ground forces to foreign soil.

In the autumn of 1992, the Japanese government dispatched an SDF engineering battalion of about 600 troops to join a UN peacekeeping mission designed to end Cambodia's long civil war. The Japanese effort was tentative and public support fragile. The SDF contingent operated under a bewildering set of rules of engagement. They could use their weapons in self-defence but not to protect non-Japanese because that would constitute collective defence which the government was not yet prepared to sanction. Despite the tentative nature of the effort, the UN Transitional Authority in Cambodia completed its mission under a veteran Japanese diplomat serving the UN, elections were held, and the SDF returned home. Drawing confidence from this first venture Japan sent SDF forces to several other UN peacekeeping efforts and the Foreign Ministry declared Japan's wish to become a permanent member of the UN Security Council. Before this wish could be fulfilled, however, other major powers made it clear that Japan must participate more fully in armed missions such as monitoring cease-fires, disarming combatants, and patrolling buffer zones. Changing the UN charter to accommodate new powers such as Japan and Germany, moreover, would be a difficult and consuming political task.

6.5 Japan's turn toward Asia

For 40 years after the end of the Second World War, Japan's relations with the rest of Asia were distant and largely limited to trade. The era of Japanese imperialism had left a legacy of bitterness towards Japan throughout Asia. Keenly aware of this enmity towards them, the Japanese drew back from close political and cultural ties with other Asian countries and focused their attention on rebuilding their national livelihood. With relentless and single-minded attention, Japan pursued economic growth as a means of catching up with the world's leading industrial countries. By the 1980s it had become an economic superpower whose economy and level of technology had by many measures achieved overall parity with the West.

In the mid 1980s, Japan's aloofness from Asia ended with great suddenness in one of the most momentous changes in modern Japanese history. The defining event was the decision of the Group of Five (G5) industrialized countries meeting at New York's Plaza Hotel to sharply raise the value of the yen by adjusting the exchange rate from 260 to 180 yen to the dollar. Heretofore, Japan had kept its manufacturing base at home and year after year amassed huge trade and current account surpluses. The Plaza Accord, designed to correct this imbalance, made it profitable to shift production and assembly of many Japanese manufactures to other Asian countries which had sharply lower wage levels and where production costs could be controlled. Furthermore, Japan's trade surpluses resulted in savings so great they could not be absorbed at home and had to be exported to the world. Japan had become the 'greatest creditor nation the world had ever known' (Lincoln, 1993, p.59). It was also the largest donor of official development assistance (ODA). In 1970 the cumulative value of Japanese overseas investments was US$3.6 billion, in 1980 US$160 billion, and in 1991 US$2.0 trillion.

The new strength of the yen led to Japan's rapid economic surge into Asia in the late 1980s. By 1991, Japan became the largest foreign investor in Singapore, Hong Kong, the Philippines, and Thailand, and the second largest in Taiwan, Indonesia and Malaysia. The policies and institutions that had promoted Japan's post-war economic development were now turned toward formulation of a regional development strategy. Japan's economic bureaucrats undertook careful studies to determine how the formidable array of economic tools they had at hand might be used to establish leadership of the region's dynamic economies. The Japanese private sector was capable of massive amounts of foreign direct investment (FDI) and the government had immense reserves for official aid. Moreover, Japan had technologies that could be profitably transferred to neighbouring economies. A study by the Economic Planning Agency in 1988 recommended that the Japanese bureaucracy constitute itself as the 'Asian brain' that would mastermind a comprehensive integration of the economies of Asia. Japanese FDI, trade, and ODA should be co-ordinated as a 'trinity' or 'three sides of one body' (Pyle, 1996, p.132–3).

What began to emerge in the 1990s were policies involving close business–government co-operation and the use of private investment and official aid to help Japanese multinationals build vertically integrated production networks throughout Asia. The inter-firm relations that proliferated during Japan's high growth period at home were replicated in Asia. That is, the small and medium-sized firms belonging to vertically integrated *keiretsu* (enterprise groups) domestically followed their parent firms abroad. Japanese majority-owned subsidiaries in Asia as well as local Asian firms were also drawn into these production networks as junior members. Official development assistance was a central element of the Japanese economic strategy. Nearly two-thirds of Japanese aid went to Asia and was carefully co-ordinated to develop structural complementarities with the Japanese economy.

In automobiles, parts, electronics, machinery, and other major industries, these offshore production networks gave Japanese industry great leverage in Asian markets. The networks held the potential for the same kind of exclusionary effects that had made Japan's domestic market so difficult for foreign firms to penetrate. Once established, Japanese companies could pressure their Asian suppliers and distributors to do business only with them and shun contacts with firms not belonging to these networks. Japanese multinational enterprises typically maintain tight control over their network members by developing long-term, multifaceted relationships as the purchaser of the network's manufactures and as the supplier of the network's capital, technology, and managerial guidance. By thus burrowing into the heart of Asian industrial economies the Japanese relieved their concerns over issues of protectionism and trade and investment liberalization in these economies.

6.6   The struggle to define a political strategy for Asia

While Japanese economic policies were fine tuned and well co-ordinated in their approach to Asia, defining a viable post-Cold War political strategy was much more challenging. The Japanese seemed unable to lay to rest the burdens of their imperialist past in Asia. In many countries, particularly China and Korea, nationalism was grounded in anti-Japanese memories. The post-war leadership in Japan avoided issues of responsibility for the disruption and exploitation of other societies. Rather than face such issues forthrightly, post-war conservative politicians laid responsibility for the misdeeds on the errors of military leaders. Prime Minister Yoshida, for example, dismissed the Pacific War as a 'historic stumble'. The effort of the Foreign Ministry bureaucrats to begin a new era of Asian–Japanese relations was repeatedly set back by cabinet ministers arguing that colonization of Korea had been legitimate or that the rape of Nanking was a fabrication, or by education bureaucrats' reluctance to include accounts of Japanese imperialism in school social studies texts. Yasukuni Shrine in Tokyo, the Shinto shrine built by the pre-war government to honour Japan's war dead, was a frequent target of Chinese and Korean protests owing to ceremonies attended by Japanese leaders that seemed to memorialize Japan's imperial heroes. In the same vein, the government was loath to acknowledge that tens of thousands of Asian women had been pressed into providing sexual service to the Japanese army. Conservatives clung to a view of the Pacific War as a campaign to rid Asia of Western colonial intrusion and to liberate Asians from this foreign domination. Unable to reach a consensus on their modern history, the Japanese floundered in their efforts to improve relations with their neighbours. The emperor and successive prime ministers travelled to other parts of Asia on goodwill missions in the 1990s, but their carefully scripted apologies fell flat owing to a series of episodes that demonstrated the persistence of the conservative view. It was often tactfully useful for Asian leaders to keep the Japanese on the defensive about their past, providing pressure in this way for increased Japanese aid and also damping Japanese conservative ambitions for a more assertive foreign policy. On one memorable occasion, in the autumn of 1995, on the eve of the Asia-Pacific Economic Co-operation (APEC) forum meeting in Osaka, the Chinese president and the South Korean president in a joint press conference in Seoul admonished the Japanese to reflect on their past and come to a 'correct' understanding of it.

It was not only the bitter legacies of the Second World War that had to be overcome but also the subsequent policies of economic nationalism. As one former ambassador observed, 'Foreign peoples and governments have no way of knowing whether Japan is really the sane and responsible government it claims to have become until they have had a chance to observe it in action' (Okazaki, 1993, p.61). Because of its adherence to the Yoshida strategy, 'Japan forfeited its chance to build up a record as a country deserving of international trust'. Nor was increased economic aid sufficient to win confidence in Asia because 'the widespread perception of Japan as a country driven purely by economic motives makes this difficult'.

Officials within the Foreign Ministry who favoured a stronger orientation towards Asia emphasized Japan's Asian cultural identity and the germaneness of Japan's modern success in industrializing pointing to the policies and institutions that other Asian countries must adopt. They emphasized the Japan model of economic development because it preserved traditional Asian values. As one high-ranking Ministry official wrote in 1993, 'What Asia has treasured is the view of society and human beings that underlies such areas as Japanese-style management, lifelong education, and family upbringing, and it has also treasured the economic and social systems that are built on this view' (Ogura, 1993, p.41). He also pleaded with Asians to pull together and put the past behind them: 'It will be difficult for Asia to take off and soar again unless it can get over the legacy of ill will caused by past invasion and strife ... Japanese awareness and contrition alone will not suffice ... The countries that were injured will have to refrain from being prisoners of the past and adopt a future-minded position' (ibid.).

Compelled by the burdens of history to move cautiously in shaping a post-Cold War political strategy for Asia that would comport with its vastly augmented economic stake in the region, the Japanese government found a low-key multilaterialism the most compatible policy. Working through multilateral organizations as its political approach to Asia offered many advantages. As I have written elsewhere:

> Japan's economic surge into Asia since 1985 requires more involvement in the region to protect its increased interests. Multilateralism provides some moving away and softening of the dominance of US–Japan relations. While the historic legacy of the Pacific War is still not overcome, multilateralism provides a cover, a quiet approach to the region, one that will help to restore Japan's legitimacy and claim to leadership. Engagement in multilateral organizations not only offers a way to respond to foreign suspicions as well as criticism of its self-absorption, but also a way of overcoming domestic resistance to a more international role. Without question, one of the reasons that Ozawa, Nakasoni and other Japanese advocates of a 'normal country' seek a Japanese permanent seat on the UN Security Council is to wean a substantial portion of the Japanese population of its residual pacifism or what is really isolationism.

> (Pyle, 1996, p.170)

The Japanese government turned its attention to promoting multilateral organizations. Heretofore, the only such organization in which Japan had been active was the Asian Development Bank (ADB). Japan had been the largest contributor to the ADB and provided much of its leadership during the Cold War years. In the same year that the Cold War ended Japan helped bring APEC into being. It suited Japan's political needs. As a forum for discussing trading and financial relationships and principles, APEC is loose, deliberative, and informal by nature. With a small budget and little infrastructure it is unthreatening. It brings the USA into regional issues but in such a way that it cannot impose its own rules of economic behaviour. At the same time Japan resisted a Malaysian proposal for an East Asian Economic Caucus that would exclude the USA, Australia, Canada, and other non-Asian states. Japan therefore could position itself as a bridge between the developing states of Asia and the developed economies of the West. APEC suits Japan's needs because it helps to keep the USA engaged in Asia; it promotes the region's economy; and it may draw China into a more harmonious role in the region. Above all, as two leading Japanese scholars confided:

> APEC will serve as a regional framework for Japan to share a leadership role with the United States. Generally speaking, a hegemonic power like the United States is often reluctant to accept the reality that its hegemonic power has declined and that its leadership role has to be shared with other major powers. A regional framework will serve to make a transfer of a part of the leadership role proceed more smoothly.

(Watanabe and Kikuchi, 1995, p.32)

The ASEAN Regional Forum is another arrangement that Japan was instrumental in establishing in 1994. It has very modest goals of achieving transparency through exchange of information and discussion of confidence-building measures. Like APEC it is committed to gradualism. As the prominent Japanese observers concluded: 'Building a community requires a lengthy process and participation of all Asia-Pacific peoples. For the moment, all we can do is wait for the myriad processes of regional interaction and co-operation to bear fruit' (ibid., p.35).

This slow evolutionary approach to the political issues of regional order is typical of Japan's traditional reactive stance in the international system. Former Japanese Prime Minister Hata Tsutomu approvingly described this approach as 'creeping incremental gradualism by consensus'. Until the outlines of a new regional structure emerge, Japan by inclination and by necessity will move cautiously and with circumspection in the formulation of its political strategy. The domestic political scene very much reflects and contributes to this gradualism in foreign policy.

6.7 The changing political paradigm at home

Modern Japan's political-economic institutions have, to an unusual degree, been influenced by changes in the international system. It should have come as no surprise that Japanese politics, which were critically shaped by the Cold War, should be deeply affected by the changes in the international system that came after 1989. In the summer of 1993 the Liberal Democratic Party for the first time since its founding in 1955 lost the majority of Diet members necessary to form a government. After nearly four decades of one-party rule, unique among the post-war industrial countries, Japanese politics experienced a stunning upheaval.

The post-war political system that collapsed in 1993 had been a product of the radical legacy of the Second World War, the Cold War, and the brilliant strategy of Yoshida and his adherents. The Japanese Socialist Party (JSP), founded in 1955, had brought together progressive forces determined not only to keep Japan neutral in the Cold War; the left wing of the JSP was frequently pro-communist in its sympathies. The JSP opposed the Mutual Security Treaty with the USA, opposed rearmament, and maintained relations with the communist governments in China and North Korea. To prevent the JSP from taking power, conservatives formed the Liberal Democratic Party, and the mainstream of the party pursued the Yoshida strategy of economics first.

The end of the Cold War and the international criticism that was heaped on Japan called into question the foreign policies of both the LDP and the JSP. A growing number of LDP leaders, particularly younger ones such as Ozawa Ichiro, argued that the old Yoshida policies were outmoded and must be replaced by a more activist foreign policy lest the alliance with the USA weaken and leave Japan isolated. Opinion polls for the first time showed a majority – a bare majority to be sure – of the public favouring revision of the no-war constitution. The 1955 system, as it was called, began to buckle. Ozawa, who had played a critical role in the passage of the UN Peacekeeping Operations Co-operation law in 1992, moved to set in motion a fundamental political realignment with the ultimate goal of transforming Japan's foreign policy and international role. In a book published in the spring of 1993 entitled *Blueprint for a New Japan (Nihon kaizo keikaku)*, he advocated a sweeping institutional reform to make Japan 'a normal country'. To facilitate a politically active foreign policy he proposed a new electoral system, a strengthened prime ministership, and a more balanced and equal alliance with the USA. In June 1993 Ozawa's faction joined forces with opposition parties to bring down the LDP government led by Prime Minister Miyazawa Kiichi, a diehard adherent to the Yoshida strategy.

As a consequence, there ensued a succession of coalition governments. The socialists, in ideological confusion, disoriented by the Soviet collapse, allowed their leader Murayama Tomiichi to serve as prime minister in a coalition that held power from 1994 to 1996. For 40 years Murayama and his left-wing socialists had opposed the existence of the Self-Defence Forces, US military bases, the US–Japan alliance, recognition of South Korea, flying the Rising Sun flag, even singing the national anthem. Now in order to take power and hold his coalition with the LDP together he abandoned all these positions. Although this reversal brought them to power for the first time in nearly half a century, the socialists lost their *raison d'être* and a fundamental shift in the political paradigm was underway.

Not only the left-wing foreign policy position was undermined; the Yoshida strategy was now widely questioned. By the late 1990s, despite the return of the LDP to power, formerly taboo issues of constitutional revision, rearmament, dispatch of military forces abroad, and a more independent and activist foreign policy were openly discussed and debated.

6.8 The new context of the US–Japan alliance

As we have seen, the US–Japan alliance was wholly a product of the Cold War. Its unequal and nonreciprocal aspects were overlooked so long as the Cold War continued. The 1960 Treaty of Mutual Security and Co-operation commits the USA to defend Japan, but Japan's contribution to US and regional security does not go beyond providing bases for US forces 'for the purpose of contributing to the security of Japan and the international peace and security in the Far East'. But after 1989 the anomalies of this arrangement could no longer be ignored. In the new context, to have 47,000 US troops still stationed at US bases on Japanese soil and providing a unilateral security guarantee for the Japanese state, which in turn paid 70 per cent of their cost, was a strange relationship. In 1990 the top Marine Corps general in Japan told a *Washington Post* correspondent that US troops must remain in Japan for the foreseeable future because 'no one wants a rearmed, resurgent Japan. So we are a cap in the bottle, if you will' (*Washington Post*, 27 March, 1990). In more measured terms, Harvard professor Joseph Nye, soon to become Assistant Secretary of Defence for International Security Affairs, wrote in a 1993 article entitled 'Coping with Japan' that as a matter of strategy the USA should try to keep Japan as 'a global civilian power' and prevent its rearmament (Nye, 1993, p. 96–115).

Despite the end of the Cold War, East Asia has major residual issues from the past: Korea is still divided; the Taiwan Straits issue is unresolved; China still has a communist government; the dispute with Russia over the Kurile Islands seized by the Soviet Union after the Second World War continues and Russia and Japan have not yet signed a peace treaty. There are, in short, important Cold War issues that help preserve the relevance of the alliance between Japan and the USA, even in its highly asymmetric form (see Figure 6.2).

Looking beyond these residual issues, the leadership of both countries see the alliance as vital to their interests in the future. The Japanese view it as serving their national interest in several respects. Handicapped by the burdens of history which for the time being foreclose an active political-strategic role in the region, Japan needs the US presence because it preserves the regional stability essential to Japan's economic lifeline not only to regional trade and investment but also to its energy needs from the Middle East. It provides assurances that Chinese power and influence will not become destabilizing; that North Korean nuclear weapons and missiles will be dealt with; that Korean unification will be managed in a way that will preserve regional stability. No less important is the fact that domestic stability is bound up with the continuation of the alliance, for the political system, its structure and workings, has been built on the foundations of the alliance. Its termination would necessitate an autonomous defence, with all

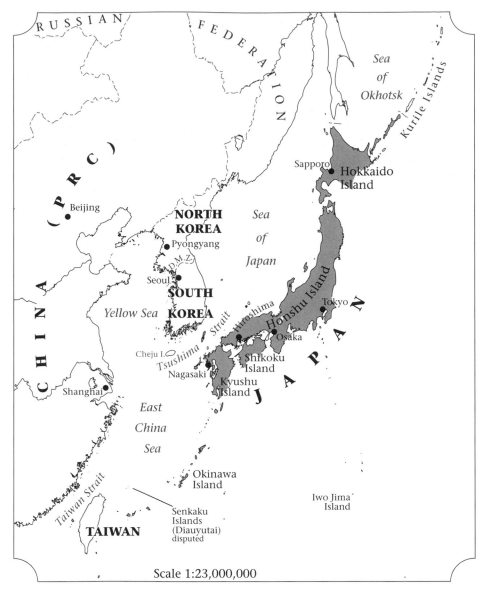

Figure 6.2 *Japan and its near neighbours*

that would entail in terms of institutional upheaval and the confusion of
constitutional revision. It would leave Japan isolated in its international
roles in multilateral organizations. One of Japan's leading strategic thinkers
recently acknowledged that a rift with the USA would undermine Japan's
Asian strategy and result in domestic political turmoil. 'It is vital', he writes,
'not to damage the bedrock of the bilateral alliance on which the fate of
this nation rests' (Okazaki, 1993, p. 61).

The changing Japanese political paradigm described above offers the
possibility of achieving a more forthright consensus on post-Cold War
foreign policy and defence issues. The demise of the left wing with its

divergent policy position provides the possibility of Japanese acceptance of a revised strategic bargain with the USA. There is substantial recognition that the existing asymmetries cannot persist in the post-Cold War era. Two notable developments in 1995–96 are encouraging a cautious rethinking of security arrangements. One is a growing restiveness in Okinawa toward the imposing presence of American bases. Okinawans have borne the burden of the US force presence in Japan and the popular governor of Okinawa Prefecture is pressing for a gradual downsizing of US troop deployment. The other development is the spectre of emergent Chinese power highlighted by its rapid economic growth and its more menacing approach to the Taiwan issue. During the Cold War period, Japan maintained a distant, low profile, largely trade-oriented stance toward China, but recently this conciliatory stance has begun to change. Concern over China's future purpose and goals has been exacerbated by increased Chinese military spending, territorial disputes with its ASEAN neighbours over the Spratly Islands and with Japan over the Senkaku/Diaoyutai Islands, willingness to threaten use of force to settle the Taiwan issue, and recognition of the disruptive potential of Chinese rapid industrialization with all that implies for environmental problems and energy demands. This has engendered a reluctant realism in the Japanese leadership. Optimists in Japan are still hopeful that economic growth will keep Beijing on a peaceful course, that Japanese economic aid and investment can be used to encourage this course, that patience will see China successfully integrated into the regional economy and its multilateral organizations – in short, that a constructive engagement with China will succeed. Reluctant realism, however, requires Tokyo to hedge its bets and quietly seek a tighter security relationship with the USA.

Accordingly, when President Clinton met with Prime Minister Hashimoto in Tokyo in April 1996, they agreed on certain limited concessions to the Okinawans and on a joint review of US–Japan Defence Co-operation Guidelines so that Japan might assume greater supporting roles in a regional contingency. While this meeting indicated a tighter security relationship in the future there was a host of other issues to be addressed before the relationship could be more reciprocal. The Japanese desire much greater joint consultation on foreign and defence issues. The USA wants Japan to share its dual use technology for defence purposes. Japan still interprets its constitution as prohibiting participation in collective defence. Moreover, it is difficult to see the alliance being greatly strengthened without some greater agreement between the two countries which addresses the basis of their persistent trade friction.

Finally, the policies of both countries in the present still unsettled structure of Asia-Pacific politics are likely to continue to be reactive and incremental. The USA has not yet developed a clear strategic vision for the region and is content to extend with modest amendments its Cold War security arrangements. Japan, in keeping with its traditional cautious approach to the international system – particularly given the historical obstacles to a more active policy – will move slowly and with circumspection until the outlines of the future regional order are clear.

References

Asai, Motofumi (1989) *Nihon gaiko hansei to tenkan*, Tokyo, Iwanami.

Frank, I. (ed.) (1975) *The Japanese Economy in International Perspective*, Baltimore, Johns Hopkins University Press.

Kissinger, H. (1979) *White House Years*, Boston, Little, Brown & Co.

Lincoln, E.J. (1993) *Japan's New Global Role*, Washington DC, The Brookings Institution.

Nye, J.S.Jr (1993) 'Coping with Japan', *Foreign Policy*, winter 1992–3.

Ogura, Kazuo (1993) 'A call for a new concept of Asia', *Japan Echo*, vol.20, no.3, pp. 37–44.

Okazaki, Hisahiko (1993) 'Southeast Asia in Japan's national strategy', *Japan Echo*, vol.20 (special issue), pp.52–63.

Pyle, K.B. (1996) *The Japanese Question: Power and Purpose in a New Era*, 2nd edn, Washington DC, The American Enterprise Institute.

Scalapino, R.A. (ed.) (1977) *The Foreign Policy of Modern Japan*, Berkeley, University of California Press.

Watanabe, A. and Kikuchi, T. (1995) 'Japan's perspective on APEC', *NBR Analysis*, vol.6, no.3, pp. 23–36.

Further reading

Funabashi, Yoichi (1995) *Asia Pacific Fusion: Japan's Role in APEC*, Washington DC, Institute for International Economics.

Green, M.J. (1995) *Arming Japan: Defense Production, Alliance Politics, and the Postwar Search for Autonomy*, New York, University of Columbia Press.

Hellman, D.C. and Pyle, K.B. (1997) *From APEC to Xanadu: Building a Viable Community in the Pacific*, New York, M.E. Sharpe Inc.

Pyle, K.B. (1996) *The Japanese Question: Power and Purpose in a New Era*, 2nd edn, Washington DC, The American Enterprise Institute.

Yamamura, Kozo (1996) *Asia in Japan's Embrace: Building a Regional Production Alliance*, Cambridge University Press, Cambridge.

CHAPTER 7

Restructuring foreign and defence policy: the People's Republic of China

Denny Roy

7.1 Introduction

Deng Xiaoping's economic and political reforms which began in 1978 brought historic changes to China, arguably positioning it to regain early in the twenty-first century the greatness Mao Zedong and many other nationalist leaders only dreamed of. Modern China's key deficiency has always been economic development. But with an ongoing economic growth rate close to 10 per cent yearly, China now has the potential to become the world's largest economy in the medium term. With a strong economic and technological base combined with a large population, China could become the strongest power in the region, if not the world. If this occurs, the current international order in the Asia-Pacific will be completely overturned. Anticipating its political ascension, Beijing's foreign and defence policies are changing, and will continue to change, to reflect China's new status in the post-Cold War international and regional distribution of power.

China's current foreign and defence policies reflect both the new strategic environment and also China's anticipation that it will soon assume the status of a major economic, political and military power. This chapter will examine China's foreign policy orientation in the late 1990s and its impact on regional security, then consider the potential ramifications of a future, stronger China.

7.2 China's 'national interest(s)'

'National interest' is a simplistic but convenient way of referring to the rationale that drives a government to select a particular foreign policy option. Two important caveats arise with the use of the term 'national interest'. First, different groups within the policy-making elite may have different ideas of which national goals have the highest priority, and of which policy options best serve these goals. Thus, beyond its most basic formulation, the national interest is not a monolithic, objective concept, but rather a dynamic and unsettled one, subject to constant debate and various interpretations. Second, powerful groups and individuals are subject to self-interested behaviour, and may support the policy option they calculate will enhance their own power and prestige, even if it is not necessarily the best option for the nation as a whole – a phenomenon known as 'sub-optimality'. Practitioners of sub-optimality must of course conceal their narrow motives by arguing that their position serves broader, nobler goals. Thus, the concept of national interest is a useful way to conceptualize China's most basic objectives, but anything beyond this quickly becomes problematic.

In the specific case of China, ultimate foreign policy decision making rests with the paramount civilian leadership (usually the president, premier, or Communist Party chief, depending on the political stature of the individual[s] holding these positions), but two other groups, the Ministry of Foreign Affairs (MFA) and the People's Liberation Army (PLA), which includes the Chinese air force, navy and marines as well as the ground forces, are influential sources of input. Each of these two groups has a distinct foreign policy agenda based on its organizational interests: the MFA generally seeks to avoid tensions with the other major powers, while the PLA is highly sensitive to perceived affronts to Chinese 'sovereignty' and argues that the People's Republic of China (PRC) must turn such challenges back even at the risk of offending powerful foreign governments. In this light, Chinese foreign policy may be seen to be the result of an ongoing debate between self-interested groups or factions arbitrated by a paramount leader who may be swayed toward one viewpoint or another on a given issue.

Much of China's national interest involves basic values and objectives that are common to all states. Stated in general terms, these basic objectives include national survival, wealth and power (i.e. the ability to get other governments to conform to one's wishes). In the service of these objectives, all states seek to protect their populations, territory and assets from seizure or molestation by foreigners; shape the external environment (the international system, and the policies of neighbouring countries) in ways that will increase national influence and opportunities; and enhance national prestige.

China's national interest also has an idiosyncratic aspect that arises from China's unique history, political system and geography. For most of its long history China was the political and cultural centre of the known world. Convinced theirs was the most advanced civilization on earth, Chinese rulers were often complacent as well as arrogant, assuming that the outside world had nothing useful to offer and that foreign peoples could never seriously threaten Chinese society. The Chinese government was more concerned about maintaining unity within its own empire, which was a continual problem. This attitude persisted even after the first contacts with the technologically superior Europeans. Largely as a result of the Qing

Dynasty (1644–1911) regime's failure to undertake meaningful reform or modernization, China found itself a semi-colony of the great powers by the end of the nineteenth century. The foreigners had won several key military victories, each time demanding further concessions – control of key territories, extraterritoriality, reparation payments, and economic privileges – that the Chinese had no choice but to deliver. More hardships were to follow: the revolution of 1911, which swept away the Qing Dynasty and established a republic the following year; the division of the country into fiefdoms ruled by warlords; the corrupt and often brutal leadership of Chiang Kai-shek's Kuomintang (Nationalist Party); and the Japanese invasion, with its countless atrocities. Throughout this period, which later came to be known as the 'Century of Shame' (from the Opium War of 1842 to Mao's Chinese Civil War victory in 1949), most Chinese lived out their years in poverty, bedevilled not only by war but also by natural disasters and the avarice of their various rulers.

The new Chinese Communist Party (CCP) leadership instituted a Marxist world view which affirmed that hostility to the outside world, but from a new angle: the capitalist states saw the new socialist states as a mortal threat and were determined to smother them by any available means. The CCP also promised to overcome the legacy of the Century of Shame and transform China from the 'sick man of Asia' into a prosperous and respected world power. The Party stakes its legitimacy on its ability to raise living standards and recover 'lost' Chinese territory. Finally, the CCP regime presides over an authoritarian system that, in contrast to democratic systems, allows the leadership to dominate political discourse within China and to take foreign policy decisions without direct accountability to the Chinese public.

In sum, China's national interest includes the common objectives of enhancing wealth and relative power, but with a few additional emphases that are peculiar to the PRC: avenging the perceived wrongs of the other major powers against China; economically developing China and 'catching up' with the richer nations; re-establishing Beijing's control over all territory the Chinese consider to be rightfully theirs; and guarding against suspected attempts by the other major powers to divide, conquer and exploit China. Briefly stated, China seeks to return to a status in the modern world similar to the one it enjoyed in the pre-modern world. Furthermore, China seems prone to engendering tense relations with the democratic states, whose policies toward China spring as much from domestic public opinion as from the *realpolitik* of their leaders, a circumstance many Chinese elites fail to comprehend.

7.3   Changes in China's external environment

Chinese analysts generally view the transformation in the international distribution of power from bipolarity to multipolarity as a positive development. For several reasons, the post-Cold War strategic environment provides China with new opportunities to improve its position in the international political system. First, China and the other Asian states are no longer locked into the rigid alignments based on the US–Soviet confrontation. Beijing is now freer to establish diplomatic and economic relationships with whomever it pleases, regardless of ideological connotations. Second, the military and political influence of both the Cold War superpowers in Asia has receded – through break-up in the case of the Soviet Union and retrenchment in the case of the USA. The result is what many analysts have prematurely labelled a 'power vacuum', giving China greater, if not complete, freedom of action. Most importantly, the relatively low level of great power tensions and broad political common ground frees China from the burden of maintaining readiness for imminent major war, providing a breathing space for economic development and military renovation.

The end of the Cold War is not the only reason the USA is retrenching. If Chinese elites no longer see communism as the wave of the future, many believe Asia is on the rise, while the West is in decline. Taking a cyclical view of the great powers, the Chinese see the USA as a dynasty past its prime, a suspicion seemingly confirmed by its host of social pathologies. Thus the USA, as one Chinese scholar puts it, 'still cherishes the ambition to rule the world, but its ability is not equal to its ambition' (Ji, 1994, p.21). The Chinese interpret many Sino-US political and economic disputes within the context of their assumption that Washington is committed to maintaining (if not extending) its hegemony over East Asia. In Beijing's view, the USA's ultimate goal has been to control and exploit China; with the USA's relative strength ebbing this goal may be out of reach, but it still seeks to weaken the PRC to prevent the Chinese from challenging US dominance.

Most Chinese also continue to regard Japan as a potentially dangerous state. Many Chinese analysts believe Japan's vast economic activities throughout the region create pressures for Tokyo to expand its relatively weak military and political power. Redressing these weaknesses would position Japan to dominate the region. Japan's aggressive past makes this prospect even more ominous for the Chinese, who suffered terribly under Japanese bombs, guns and bayonets during the Second World War. The occasional comments from right-wing Japanese public figures justifying Japan's behaviour during the Pacific War or denying that Japanese forces committed atrocities heighten Chinese suspicions that Japan is not honestly confronting its history and that a vestige of militarism persists.

7.4 Foreign policy as an extension of domestic politics

From Beijing's point of view, domestic problems and foreign policy problems have always been closely connected – an outlook captured in the aphorism, 'disorder within, danger without' (*nei luan, wai huan*). The internal–external linkage takes several forms. Chinese elites blame

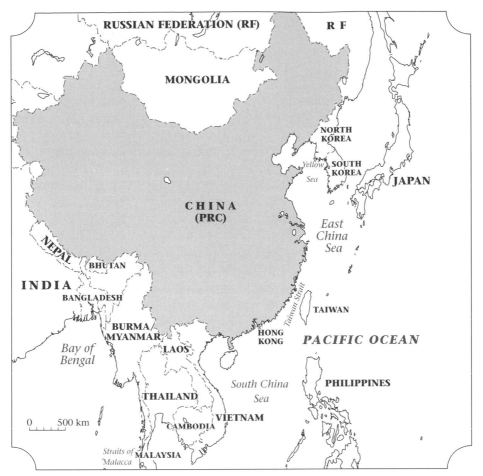

Figure 7.1 *The People's Republic of China and its East Asian neighbours*

foreigners for causing or exacerbating many of China's internal difficulties, sometimes intentionally. The US government and many private Western organizations are believed to engage in 'peaceful evolution' (a term derived from speeches by John Foster Dulles, US Secretary of State during the Eisenhower Administration), which amounts to encouraging Chinese dissidents to overthrow the rule of the CCP. Taiwan is also accused of infiltrating subversive agents onto the mainland. Chinese leaders blamed the Tiananmen Square demonstrations of 1989 largely on foreign influence. The CCP also says foreign encouragement is a major source of separatist sentiment among Chinese minorities, particularly Tibetans and Mongolians. Less purposeful but also harmful, the smuggling of narcotics and pornography into China from foreign countries contributes to 'spiritual pollution' and the breakdown of social order. The strong economic links between Chinese provinces and particular foreign countries (Shandong–South Korea, Guangdong–Hong Kong, Fujian–Taiwan) promote (internal) regionalism, tempting provincial governments to look out for their own interests instead of following Beijing's instructions.

If the activities of foreigners can affect China's domestic affairs, internal conditions may also shape Chinese foreign policy. Despite China's often-criticized 'one-child policy', its population is still growing by some 20 million per year. At the same time, arable land is decreasing. The need for new sources of food, energy and 'living space' is a potential argument for those Chinese elites who favour a more assertive foreign policy in the South China Sea and elsewhere. While Deng's reforms have brought China rapid economic growth since the early 1980s, they have worsened several serious domestic social and political problems, including official corruption, the income gap between the coastal boomtowns and the rural interior, massive and uncontrolled internal migration, rising crime and insurrection, weakened central government control over the provinces, and the hollowing out of public virtue caused by the state-sanctioned fixation on getting rich. Rapid economic growth is also creating pressure for improved living standards that will require China to make unprecedented (and, in some cases, perhaps insatiable) demands on the world market. If internal discontent worsens, the regime might seek to manufacture a crisis abroad to distract the public from problems at home. Alternatively, China might be enfeebled from within, deflecting it from a strong foreign policy, or even leaving it unable to maintain territorial integrity.

Finally, the succession crisis affects China's foreign relations. All of the factions and individuals contending for control of the state in the post-Deng era must take a hard line on foreign policy issues that appear to involve Chinese sovereignty (e.g. Taiwanese independence, the South China Sea islands) lest they leave themselves vulnerable to criticism by their domestic enemies. The intensity of this intra-Party contest is heightened by the fact that the Party itself is fighting to maintain its singular authority within China, its legitimacy having been damaged by the ideological excesses of the Cultural Revolution, post-Mao reforms that have steadily eroded both the institutions and values of Marxism-Leninism, and the violent suppression of the Tiananmen demonstrations in 1989.

7.5 Beijing restructures its foreign and defence policies

The PRC's recent foreign relations indicate that, just as Chinese officials and scholars have insisted for over a decade, China's current focus is on economic development and catching up with the developed world. While the end of the Cold War created new opportunities for China to benefit from foreign markets and suppliers, more significant was China's own shift in developmental strategy a decade earlier. Since the CCP's takeover, China has vacillated in its orientation toward the world capitalist economy. Mao deeply feared that foreigners, especially those in the hostile capitalist nations, would use economic links to weaken and exploit China. Beijing therefore initially favoured joining with the Soviet Union and other socialist states in a separate, alternative international economy. In the 1960s, however, the Soviet Union's 'revisionism' and interest in 'peaceful coexistence' with the USA convinced Mao that the Soviets had drifted into the capitalist system and that a separate socialist economy was no longer viable. China therefore embarked on a policy of autarky, or economic self-sufficiency, still eschewing the capitalist world economy. The results were poor, convincing pragmatists such as Deng that the benefits of international economic links outweigh the dangers. After Mao died and the dust from the ensuing succession crisis settled, Deng moved to hitch China firmly to the capitalist global economy, proclaiming that 'China has opened its door, and will never close it again' (Cumings, 1989, pp.206–7). Trafficking through this open door soon grew heavy. In 1950 China's foreign trade was worth a little over one billion US dollars. In 1978, at the threshold of the Deng Xiaoping 'open door' era, it was US$200 billion. All the important factions in the Chinese leadership now appear committed to keeping the door open, although there is debate over the degree to which Chinese autonomy should be sacrificed to maintain cordial economic relations with the West.

Foreign policy

In Beijing's diplomacy, Deng's pragmatism has been similarly liberating, clearing the way for an omni-directional foreign policy that maximizes Chinese influence, keeps potential tensions at a minimum during this crucial rebuilding period, and provides a hedge against poor relations with Washington. In 1992 China recognized Israel, which went against the grain of decades of support for the Arab nations, and South Korea, which represented a bitter betrayal of its communist neighbour and ally North Korea. China now has relations with all East Asian states except Taiwan. China attended its first meeting of the Non-Aligned Movement in 1992 and championed the Third World's rights to development. The Chinese have also sought, largely successfully, to settle their outstanding border disputes with Russia and India. China and Mongolia signed a Treaty of Friendship in 1994. Chinese relations with Vietnam, which China invaded in 1979, have been normalized, clearing the way for many new political, economic and scientific agreements, including a promise between the two heads of state to shelve their Spratly Islands dispute.

Most of the South-East Asian nations have ethnic Chinese minority populations who are disproportionately wealthy, creating resentment among the indigenous majority peoples. Ethnic Chinese were also sometimes suspected of acting as fifth columnists for communist insurgency campaigns the PRC sponsored in the region in the 1950s and 1960s. China's re-establishment of diplomatic relations with Indonesia in 1990, and with Singapore and Brunei following shortly thereafter, was therefore an important milestone in China's efforts to improve its relations with ASEAN (the Association of South-East Asian Nations).

On several common political issues, China and ASEAN have formed a natural partnership. Semi-authoritarian South-East Asian statesmen such as Malaysia's Mahathir Mohamed and Singapore's Lee Kuan Yew have publicly defended China against proponents of 'containment' and, even more frequently, against Western criticisms of China's human rights record. Many East Asian governments consider Western human rights pressure on China wholly misguided. First, many of these governments are themselves authoritarian and under threat by demands for political liberalization. They therefore sympathize with the CCP's need to protect itself from its domestic enemies. Second, many Asians reject the premises of Western human rights activists, believing instead that social stability and economic growth are worth sacrificing a few civil liberties for, that less developed countries should not be expected to implement the full range of political rights until they become wealthy and educated, and that each country's human rights situation is its own internal affair and ought not to be publicly criticized by foreigners. Third, Asian governments generally believe such criticisms of China only worsen Chinese–Western relations, with serious economic and diplomatic consequences for the entire region, while producing little or no benefit for the Chinese people. Some ASEAN states, in particular, have been important Chinese allies on the human rights issue, calling the West hypocritical and imploring the US government not to let human rights concerns disrupt business as usual.

Defence policy

As China builds up its economic infrastructure, the PLA is preparing to field a military force capable of protecting (or, less optimistically, enlarging) China's new wealth and prestige. Mao's basic military strategy, known as the 'people's war', was inherently defensive. It envisioned mobilizing the entire population for war and employing an indirect strategy based on Mao's adaptations of Sun Tzu's military classic *Art of War*. Serious counter attacks would begin only after the enemy had penetrated deep into Chinese territory, their troops deployed thinly on the ground and with long supply lines.

In the mid 1980s, the CCP Central Military Commission (CMC) announced a fundamental change in Chinese defence policy. Previously, the central mission of the PLA had been to prepare to defend China from an all-out attack by the Soviet Union, including both invasion and nuclear bombardment. By 1985, however, a consensus had emerged that this was no longer the most likely form of conflict in China's future. Instead, the PLA should prepare for a limited war on or just beyond one of China's borders. Subsequent events have affirmed the CMC's judgement. The dissolution of the Soviet Union left in its wake a Russia preoccupied with internal problems and removed the threat of an invasion from the north in the near term. At the same time, the South China Sea and the Taiwan Strait emerged as potential flash points.

The new defence strategy brought a major reorganization of the PLA. China's eleven military regions were reduced to seven (see Figure 7.2). The PLA's 35 field armies were converted to 24 group armies that would combine infantry and armoured units under a single command. The overall size of the PLA has decreased by over a million troops. 'The strength of an army', said PLA Chief of Staff Yang Dezhi, 'is not determined by the number of troops, but by the quality of its commanders and fighters, the quality of its arms, and the degree of rationality of its systems and foundations'. The PLA, in other words, was to become a modern military force.

While 'people's war' was a strategy of the weak, the new 'active defence' strategy is designed to keep the fighting outside of China's borders. Any invaders are to be ejected as quickly as possible. This approach is inherently offensive, implying power projection as well as modernized equipment and tactics. Along with the overall downsizing, the PLA has put more effort into creating and training small rapid reaction forces, known as 'fist' units. And there is an overwhelming new emphasis in the writings and speeches of PLA officers on the importance of advanced technology. Jiang Zemin reflected this consensus when he told a group of PLA commanders after the Gulf War, 'The practice of every limited local war, especially the most recent war, tells us that modern warfare has become high-tech warfare. It is a multi-dimensional war, electronic war, missile war. The backward one is beaten' (Chu, 1994, p.189). To prepare to wage 'high-tech warfare', the PLA has relied heavily on importing advanced foreign technology. Post-

Figure 7.2 *PRC military regions*

Tiananmen sanctions severely disrupted supplies of military technology from the West, but new opportunities followed soon after with a glut of Russian-made weapons systems at low prices.

The PLA navy is shifting its basic strategy from coastal defence to offshore defence, with the objective of building by early next century a 'blue water' navy capable of operating in distant oceans for long periods of time. The Chinese navy scrapped about half of its older ships in the decade to 1997, introducing more advanced classes of destroyers, frigates and submarines and implementing new systems based on imported technology in the remaining vessels. China is also increasing its inventory of support ships designed to replenish warships at sea and building amphibious assault ships capable of carrying infantry and their equipment to the South China Sea islands. Beijing is clearly interested in eventually acquiring two or three aircraft carriers, whether domestically produced or purchased from abroad, but the difficulties of protecting and effectively operating a carrier convince most observers that this capability is at least a decade away.

China's nuclear weapons forces are also being modernized. Chinese engineers are working to improve the range and accuracy of their missiles and to convert them to solid instead of liquid fuel, which would greatly reduce the time needed to prepare them for launching. The next generation of missiles will be mobile, increasing their survivability. China is also developing multiple independently-targeted re-entry vehicles (MIRVs), which allow a single missile to carry several warheads to different targets.

One important effect of China's economic reforms on the PLA has been an explosion of military entrepreneurship. As many as half the PLA's personnel may be engaged in strictly commercial activities. While this would seem to have the positive effect of rendering the PLA less capable of carrying out conquest or coercion in the region, the negative side of PLA entrepreneurship is that Chinese arms sales are now beyond the control of the Ministry of Foreign Affairs. One doubts whether provincial PLA commanders who stand to make huge profits from the sale of missiles or other highly dangerous weapons are seriously deterred by the possibility that their actions might lead to instability in some far-flung region such as the Middle East.

7.6 China's post-Cold War regional engagement

China's current interest in facilitating its own economic development through extroverted trade and investment policies and by fostering, where possible, a co-operative and conciliatory image has generally contributed to the optimism of observers who claim modern norms have triumphed and the use of force has become obsolete in the Asia-Pacific region. Nevertheless, Chinese foreign policy remains obstinate and even assertive in areas where China's 'sovereignty' is at stake or where its interests otherwise differ from those of its neighbours, perhaps offering insight into what life will be like with the potentially stronger China of the near future.

The Spratly Islands dispute is a case in point. Premier Li Peng announced in 1990 that China was prepared to 'shelve' the issue of ownership of the islands and engage in joint development projects with the other claimants. This conciliatory gesture, however, has been accompanied by Beijing's consistent opposition to multilateral discussions of the South China Sea issue (see Chapter 5, Figure 5.4). In 1992, Beijing announced a 'law' that suggested it claimed nearly the entire South China Sea as Chinese territorial waters. It has yet to publicly clarify its claims, and it has signed but not ratified the Law of the Sea Convention. Indonesia considered itself a disinterested party in the Spratly Islands dispute until Chinese delegates to a 1993 workshop in Surabaya, Indonesia unveiled a map showing that the Chinese claim even encompassed Indonesia's Natuna natural gas field. In February 1995, the Philippines announced that Chinese-built structures had been discovered on Mischief Reef, which lies well within the area claimed by the Philippines and is only 170 kilometres off the coast of the Philippine island of Palawan. Nine PLA navy vessels had reportedly sailed the previous month to the reef, where Chinese soldiers arrested Philippine fishermen, built the structures and left guards. Perhaps unwilling and certainly unable to directly retaliate, the Filipinos vented their frustration by destroying Chinese territorial marks on other (unguarded) islands and arresting Chinese fishermen near Mischief Reef. The act was full of ominous overtones. This was the first Chinese action against an ASEAN member (Chinese forces clashed with Vietnamese units in 1974 and 1988, before Vietnam became a member of ASEAN). It also violated a 1992 ASEAN agreement, which the Chinese seemed to accept, that none of the Spratly Islands' claimants would take disputed territory by force. Some observers also saw significance in the fact that the Philippines had recently evicted US military personnel from what had been their only sizeable base in South-East Asia.

For Beijing, the South China Sea islands issue inevitably falls into the context of the 'Century of Shame'. The CCP has publicly adopted the line that Chinese ownership of the islands dates from ancient times, and that this went unchallenged until the 1970s. The issue is thus interpreted as another case of opportunistic foreigners exploiting China's weakness to commit violations of Chinese sovereignty.

In more practical terms, the South China Sea represents a potential source of increasingly scarce resources. Citing the continuing growth in China's population and food and energy needs against a continuous decrease in arable land, a PLA officer wrote in a recent book entitled *A New Scramble for Soft Borders* that 'Our area for survival is shrinking. Therefore, where will our new borderland be? Actually [we have to] reclaim sovereignty and sovereign interests in the oceans – territorial sea, continental shelf and exclusive economic zones' (Chen, 1995, p.28).

While Jiang Zemin, Qian Qichen and other high Chinese officials have been touring the region assuring their hosts that 'China will never seek hegemony' even if it achieves its superpower potential, China's recently upgraded relations with Burma/Myanmar are consistent with suspicions that the Chinese are preparing for hegemony. Fellow authoritarian states, both China and Burma have suffered severe international criticism for their suppression of dissidents (Burma's crackdown was in 1990). Chinese economic and military assistance have been vitally important to the survival of the State Law and Order Restoration Council (SLORC) regime in Burma. Chinese engineers and soldiers are reportedly helping the Burmese renovate infrastructure and military facilities in exchange for basing rights on the Bay of Bengal coast. Many analysts have speculated that this proves Beijing's interest in eventually projecting Chinese naval power into the Indian Ocean, placing China in a position to control both ends of the strategically important Strait of Malacca and to check India's potential military influence. J. Mohan Malik concludes, '[a]rms transfers and economic ties have dramatically increased China's influence within Burma' and 'have turned the non-aligned state of Burma into China's client state' – ironically, 'an objective which three decades of Beijing-supported insurgency and the Burmese Communist Party's armed struggle failed to achieve' (Malik, 1995).

Although Beijing has (somewhat reluctantly) joined the ASEAN Regional Forum (ARF) and the Council for Security Co-operation in the Asia Pacific, the Chinese have distinguished themselves by their lack of enthusiasm for multilateral security co-operation in the Asia-Pacific region. 'We should not be in a hurry to define a multilateral security mechanism. We should let this evolve', said a Ministry of Foreign Affairs official recently (Garrett and Glaser, 1994, p.18). Beijing is reticent about multilateral

Two Chinese men manning the octagonal structures on Mischief Reef at the disputed Spratlys group of islands use binoculars to monitor the Philippine Air Force helicopters ferrying Filipino and foreign journalists for a closer look in May 1995

security frameworks for two main reasons. First, as a large state, China would prefer to negotiate one-on-one with its invariably smaller neighbours over disputes such as the ownership of the Spratly Islands rather than allowing them to gang up on China in a collective forum. More generally, any multilateral security organization has the potential to become an anti-China alliance. Second, China fears that 'internal' matters – such as the Taiwan question, Chinese military modernization, or China's lack of military transparency – might be placed on the agenda of a multilateral security organization, allowing foreigners to erode Chinese sovereignty. Yet China cannot openly oppose the principle of multilateral security discussion and co-operation for fear of being left out or of being viewed as obstructionist. Forced to participate, Beijing must block or reshape some aspects of the multilateral process, a task made easier by the region's recognition that no regional security framework is viable without China's blessing.

Although the blame does not lie entirely with Beijing, China's rising power is, on balance, raising tensions in the region. The stability of the Sino-Japanese relationship, for example, is clearly threatened by China's growing strength. Tokyo is currently content to maintain undersized armed forces and to rely on the USA for its military protection. This, in turn, precludes the re-emergence of a militaristic Japan, which would poison the relaxed political environment that now sustains the economic exchange through which so many Asia-Pacific states prosper. But increased Chinese assertiveness combined with declining confidence in the US defence commitment would leave Japan no choice but to expand its own military capabilities, including the deployment of a Japanese nuclear arsenal.

Apparently out of concern over China's growing power and assertiveness, the usually passive and reticent Japanese government has recently become more outspoken in its criticism of disruptive Chinese behaviour. Tokyo reduced its economic aid to China as a symbolic protest when the Chinese conducted a nuclear weapons test in May 1995 shortly after the Nuclear Nonproliferation Treaty was renewed. Tokyo also does not appreciate Chinese criticism of what the Japanese consider to be purely defensive measures, such as the proposed theatre missile defence system and the restructured US–Japan defence treaty (the Chinese dislike the former because it might negate their nuclear deterrent; of the latter, Beijing says the revised treaty makes it easier for Japan to take on a stronger military role in the region). Regional security would be well served if the Chinese made it a high priority to avoid behaviour that frightened the Japanese. But the Chinese, who see themselves as under-compensated victims of Japanese aggression, feel it is Tokyo that must be sensitive to China's feelings rather than the reverse.

In the USA's eyes, China has gone from quasi-ally to quasi-enemy in the last decade. In the 1980s, Americans were pleased to see China abandoning communism; democracy seemed sure to follow, and China would finally become a responsible, pro-US country (and an economic wonderland for US business). Tiananmen, however, changed all this; thereafter Americans viewed the CCP regime as an evil anachronism standing in the way of liberal progress. The end of the Cold War also ended the special exemption from human rights criticism that China had enjoyed as a prospective US ally against the Soviet Union. Finally, China's rapid growth in the early 1990s fuelled projections that the PRC would soon challenge the USA as the world's strongest economic power. Many US commentators began to call China America's next major security challenge and well-publicized Pentagon war games with China as the hypothetical foe showed the US government was thinking along the same lines. Clashes on a variety of issues, including human rights, intellectual property rights, Chinese missile sales, and China's pressure on Taiwan have recently strained US–China relations, but China's increasing strength is a major, if sometimes unspoken, undercurrent of these strains.

Many Australian officials have argued openly that China should be considered a potential threat to East Asian security. Paul Dibb, one of the country's most influential strategists, calls China the country 'most likely to upset the power equilibrium' in post-Cold War Asia (Dibb, 1995). In the debate over which multilateral economic organization South-East Asia should support, Australian strategists argue that the Malaysian-proposed East-Asian Economic Caucus (which would exclude the 'white' countries of North America, Australia and New Zealand) would leave the region more subject to Chinese dominance than the more expansive APEC. Australia's 1995 security treaty with Indonesia, the first commitment of its kind for Jakarta, is clearly intended at least in part to lay the groundwork for co-operation against Chinese aggression if this proves necessary.

A stronger PRC has unfavourable implications for Taiwan. Both domestic politics and strategic considerations impel the PRC to re-take the island, and the costs of doing so decrease as the PRC's relative power increases. In the medium term, Taiwan is well positioned to defend itself from an invasion by the PLA. Even without direct US intervention, which remains hypothetical, Taiwan's advanced fighter aircraft and airborne warning and command system (AWACS) ensures the attacking PRC forces would be unable to attain control of the air over the Taiwan Strait. Without this, PLA troops travelling by ship over 150 km from the Chinese mainland to Taiwan would be subject to slaughter by Taiwanese aircraft. Taiwan remains vulnerable, however, to a naval blockade by the PRC navy, which has a superiority in submarines Taiwan has been unable to match because of PRC pressure on potential suppliers.

In the long term, Taiwan would find it increasingly difficult to resist the influence and perquisites of a burgeoning PRC. If the PRC becomes the region's new hegemonic power, it will *ipso facto* have attained the military capability to reclaim the island. By then, however, the PRC's economic and diplomatic power would probably have increased enough for it to achieve its goal without an invasion.

7.7 The future: is China a threat to regional security?

History demonstrates that not all powerful countries behave exactly alike. The post-war USA's treatment of Latin America has been substantially different from Nazi Germany's treatment of occupied Western and Central Europe. A Chinese hegemony, too, would have its own unique character. If it fulfils its potential, would China be a benign hegemon, enforcing modern international norms such as open and fair trade, the non-violent resolution of disputes, and Beijing's own proclaimed 'Five Principles of Peaceful Co-existence'? Or will it eschew co-operation and consultation, coercing its neighbours into accepting policies that support narrow Chinese interests? Will a stronger China be a threat to Asia-Pacific security? This has, appropriately, become the most important regional security issue of the 1990s. Let us examine the main arguments on both sides of the issue.

A potential threat?

The arguments for viewing China as a threat to regional security begin with the concern that the PRC is engaged in a military build-up. Although the exact figures are disputed and the range of estimates is broad, Chinese defence spending has risen significantly in recent years. The PLA is clearly undergoing a major modernization and rejuvenation. This is taking place in the immediate wake of the collapse of the Soviet empire, which even Chinese analysts say has made China's environment more peaceful and secure than at any other time in the PRC's history. If the military threat to China has decreased, why is so much effort going into increasing Chinese military capabilities? Another worry is that China seems particularly interested in acquiring weapons systems that would enable the PLA to project power beyond China's borders. Finally, many observers have complained about China's lack of transparency in defence-related issues. These factors lead to suspicions that China plans to build a strong military machine to coerce its neighbours into accepting bold new Chinese political demands. In this view, the Chinese military build-up is taken as the empirical evidence of Beijing's hidden intent to launch an aggressive foreign policy.

A second argument supporting the position that China is a potential regional security threat is that the values of the CCP regime are hostile to peace. A large proportion of foreign affairs analysts believe liberal norms and modern technology and lifestyles are fundamentally transforming the international system. Many of the world's governments, particularly those in the democratic states, seem to increasingly recognize and accept principles such as the non-violent resolution of disputes, human rights, international interdependence, and the importance of supporting international law. In this respect, Beijing is often seen as backward; one scholar writes that the Chinese government 'seems locked in pre-Cold War, almost turn-of-the-century modes of quasi-imperial competition for regional hegemony' (Wortzel, 1994, p.157). Segal says, 'in terms of military security, China remains a nineteenth-century power with unsettled territorial claims, willing to use force to settle disputes and re-order the balance of power' (Segal, 1994).

China seems to defy all the modern liberal values: it has an authoritarian government that represses its people's political freedoms; it forcibly maintains an empire of captive peoples even after other empires have broken up; it threatens to retake Taiwan by force and resorts to crude tactics of military intimidation; it demonstrates resistance to multilateralism in security issues; it often breaks agreements designed to control the proliferation of weapons of mass destruction; and in the opinion of many observers, it seeks to enjoy the benefits of the rules of international trade without itself honouring these rules.

Liberal values presumably contribute to peace. In this view, therefore, a Chinese regime that eschews these values is a threat to peace, and a more powerful China an even greater threat to peace.

A third argument for viewing China as a threat is that because of its historical self-image, China aspires to be the dominant power in Asia. For centuries, the Chinese saw their civilization as the undisputed political and cultural centre of the universe. Traditionally, the Chinese did not accept the Westphalian concept of the sovereign equality of states; rather, international relations were understood within the Confucian framework of prescribed conduct between unequals. China saw itself at the top of the hierarchy, and other peoples, including Japanese, Koreans and the Europeans, as inferiors. China's role within this order was to maintain stability, collect tribute from neighbouring states, and promote Chinese learning among those peripheral peoples who could appreciate it. The legacy of this arrangement is a deep-seated belief among Chinese that China is the natural and proper leader of East Asia. Writes Harlan Jencks, 'some mainland Chinese leaders seem to assume that the PRC is the rightful "hegemon" in Asia. That is to say, Peking should have freedom of action in the region without constraint by any countervailing power, while no Asian government should take any action contrary to Chinese interests' (Jencks, 1994). With such a predisposition, the PRC would be prone to pursuing an assertive political agenda and to disregarding the objections of its neighbours.

Finally, it may be argued that all great powers are domineering, and a strong China would be no different. From a simple geopolitical perspective, qualitative changes in Chinese foreign policy should be expected if China grows from a medium-sized power to a superpower. At its present rate of economic growth, China's productive capabilities and total wealth will soon outstrip those of the other Asia-Pacific powers. As a weaker power, China's dependence on the favour of its neighbours has been comparatively high. But increased relative capabilities make it feasible for a rising great power to exert greater control over its surroundings. As a great power, China will behave boldly, more inclined to force its will upon others than to consult with them.

If China fulfils its expected potential, it will soon be a power in the class of nineteenth century Britain, the Soviet Union, Nazi Germany, Pacific War

Japan, and twentieth century USA. Each of those countries used its superior power to establish some form of hegemony to protect and promote its interests. There is no convincing reason to think China as a great power will depart from this pattern. If the opportunity arises to establish a dominant role in the region, China can be expected to seize it. This would not necessarily involve the physical conquest and occupation of neighbouring countries. It would, however, mean the use of various types of coercion to maintain an environment that was favourable to China's interests, and not necessarily to anyone else's.

A benign power?

Several strong arguments can also be made that China does *not* pose a threat to regional security. First, China is constrained from assertive behaviour both externally and internally. For years, China's leaders have emphasized that domestic economic development is their chief concern, and few outsiders doubt that this is true. It is also clear now that China cannot close the gap between itself and the developed countries without accessing their wealth, technology and expertise. China's economic dependence on external markets and suppliers prevents it from pursuing an aggressive, unilateral foreign policy. In general terms, such behaviour would upset the stability of the current political environment that makes it possible to sustain the kind of trade and investment from which China benefits so greatly. The benefits of peaceful economic interchange are also likely to outweigh what China might gain by attempting to seize by force the resources it desires. As some scholars have argued, for example, the information intensity of modern economies makes the capture of territory less economically profitable than it used to be.

More specifically, aggressive Chinese external behaviour risks a cut-off of economic assistance through punitive sanctions by its trading partners. Chinese economic ties with its neighbours would also make military action against them counterproductive.

Internally, China is constrained from an aggressive foreign policy by its poverty. While strategic analysts often view a large population as a strength, there are many in China who consider their huge, impoverished population a strategic liability that will not be overcome in the medium term. Chinese intellectuals often say China needs another 50 years of rapid economic growth just to become a medium-sized developed economy. One Chinese scholar noted bitterly, 'We get criticized for our population control policy, yet at the same time people fear we will send millions of economic refugees into the region'. Building a powerful military force capable of coercing neighbouring states would require a massive commitment of resources that might otherwise go toward alleviating China's domestic problems. An adventurist foreign policy is not possible until China first satisfies the demand at home for improved living standards.

A second argument against the 'China threat' position is that China has a relatively benign foreign policy track record. Many students of Chinese history conclude that even at the height of its power, ancient China showed little interest in territorial conquest, in contrast to the Europeans and the Japanese. One common explanation for this is Chinese culture: not only did ancient Chinese rulers believe the 'inferior' outside world had nothing of value to offer, they were also guided by an ethical code that taught the use of force must have a just purpose. If present and future Chinese rulers are influenced by the same historical and cultural inputs, a stronger China can be trusted not to use its power for ignoble purposes such as selfish economic gain. In a rebuttal to the usual realist arguments about a China threat, Bruce Cumings writes, 'China is different: its history has been singular, confining its expansion to its near reaches and constraining its choice of means. When China has used force since 1949, it has done so only within its historic region, and, more often than not, judiciously and effectively' (Cumings, 1989). (I'm not sure Cumings' point about Chinese use of force being 'judicious and effective' is all that reassuring.) The Communist Party leadership insists theirs is a proven peace-loving regime that doesn't attack its neighbours and doesn't coerce smaller countries. China has distinguished itself from the other major powers by renouncing 'power politics', promoting the Five Principles of Peaceful Coexistence, and promising that it will never be the first to use nuclear weapons (except possibly against Taiwan, as a Chinese official recently said). The Chinese side can justify the occasions when it has used force. Chinese intervention in the Korean War was to rescue an ally North Korea from US aggression. Hostilities with Vietnam in the Paracel Islands in 1974 and against India in 1962 were to defend Chinese territory and sovereignty from foreign encroachment, and China took military action only after many unheeded warnings. The 1979 war against Vietnam was to help Cambodia. This argument suggests that even a very powerful China will remain a benign and principled actor, a force for peace rather than an avaricious bully.

Third, it might be argued that China's current military renovation is limited, reasonable and is not indicative of any hegemonic aspirations. Chinese military spending is low compared with that of many other countries, including the USA and even the supposedly 'demilitarized' Japan. Increases in Chinese defence spending have mostly gone toward operating costs, such as living expenses for personnel, and the increases have merely paralleled, or perhaps even fallen short of, the rise in overall prices in China during the same period. Chinese officials say there is actually very little money available to purchase high-tech weapons. China has vast territory and borders to defend, and for years its armed forces have put up with obsolete equipment. Deng Xiaoping gave military modernization a low priority during the 1980s, and now that Deng's economic reforms are bearing fruit, the leadership is allowing the PLA to carry out improvements that have been long overdue. The same trend is evident in South-East Asian countries no one sees as a 'threat': military modernization immediately follows strong economic growth, because more money is available. If measured per capita, the approach Chinese analysts prefer for an obvious reason, Chinese defence spending is minuscule; if measured per soldier, it is also low, around one-thirtieth the amount the USA spends per soldier. In an interesting twist, one Chinese scholar even blames the West for China's increased military spending in the early 1990s: 'Due to ... the sanctions that Western countries have imposed on China since 1989, the nation's weapons systems, including its jet fighters, are mostly backward and outdated', he said, necessitating a spending spurt to get the armed forces back up to their appropriate strength (Chen, 1993, p.246). Overall, China's armed forces pose little threat to the region. Indeed, China has reduced the size of its armed forces by over a million men in the last decade. Foreign complaints about insufficient 'transparency' should have been silenced by Beijing's publication in 1995 of its first white paper on defence.

A final note here is that military modernization in China may serve domestic political objectives rather than foreign policy goals. Jiang Zemin attempted to persuade top military leaders to support him in his bid to be appointed successor to Deng Xiaoping by increasing their funding. The party leaders also owe the PLA a few favours after the armed forces did a dirty job for them in and around Tiananmen Square in 1989. Thus, the military build-up may not necessarily stem from the intention to undertake an aggressive foreign policy.

There is still reason to hold open a wide range of possibilities for China's future impact on the region. Both China and the region are entering unexplored territory: China has never been a modern great power in a global international system, and China and Japan have never been great powers simultaneously. The emergence of a new great power is generally an event fraught with tension, as other states see their share of international political power diminished. In this case, historical legacies and the demands of domestic politics may heighten those tensions. Managing China's growth into a benevolent superpower will surely tax the wisdom and skills of statesmen and stateswomen both in China and in the other Asia-Pacific countries.

7.8   Conclusion

China's circumstances have dramatically changed since the establishment of communist rule. The PRC has gone from an underdeveloped, externally insecure revolutionary state into a semi-industrialized nuclear power that has no proximate military threats, finds that many aspects of the international system support its interests, and stands poised to become the world's most powerful national economy. China's defence strategy has evolved from mobilizing the nation for protracted guerrilla warfare to stopping the enemy at the borders or even beyond with modern, elite forces. With its rapid economic growth fuelled by the free flow of goods and capital throughout the region, China appears keen to sustain the political stability upon which this trade is based, rather than challenge the international order as CCP leaders did during the PRC's early decades.

What persists are China's *internal* insecurity and its Century of Shame mindset. China thus remains half in and half out of the 'new world order' – striving to maintain the image of a responsible and progressive power through its omnidirectional foreign policy and its support for some international agreements and institutions, but unable to release its historical baggage (e.g. an archaic notion of 'sovereignty', an overwhelming fear of challenges to the exclusive rule of the Communist Party, insistence on PRC ownership of Taiwan) or to accept the more liberal norms of most of the other major powers. How this contradictory stance plays itself out constitutes a variable of immense importance to the future of not only China, but the entire Asia-Pacific region.

References

Chen, Cui Yu, Lt. Col. (1995) *A New Scramble for Soft Borders,* quoted in 'Soft borders, soft wars', *Far Eastern Economic Review*, April 13, p.28.

Chen, Q. (1993) 'New approaches in China's foreign policy', *Asian Survey*, vol.33, no.3, p.246.

Chu, S. (1994) 'The PRC girds for limited, high-tech war', *Orbis*, vol.38, no.2, p.189.

Cumings, B. (1989) 'The political economy of China's turn outward' in Kim, S.S. (ed.) *China and the World: New Directions in Chinese Foreign Relations*, 2nd edn, Boulder, CO, Westview Press, especially pp.206–7.

Cumings, B. (1996) 'The world shakes China', *The National Interest*, no.43, p.40.

Dibb, P. (1995a) 'The Cold War may be over but friction remains in Asia', *The Australian*, 6 June, p.17.

Dibb, P. (1995b) 'Towards a new balance of power in Asia', *Adelphi Paper no. 295*, London, International Institute for Strategic Studies.

Garrett, B., and Glaser, B. (1994) 'Multilateral security in the Asia-Pacific Region and its impact on Chinese interests: views from Beijing', *Contemporary Southeast Asia*, vol.16, no.1, p.18.

Jencks, H.W. (1994) 'The PRC's military and security policy in the post-Cold War era', *Issues and Studies*, vol.30, no.11, p.68.

Ji, G. (1994) 'The multilateralisation of Pacific Asia: a Chinese perspective', *Asian Defence Journal*, July, p.21.

Jiefangjun Bao, March 20, 1991

Malik, J.M. (1995) 'China–India relations in the post-Soviet era: the continuing rivalry', *China Quarterly*, no.142, pp.340–1.

Segal, G. (1994) 'China changes shape: regionalism and foreign policy', *Adelphi Paper no. 287*, London, International Institute for Strategic Studies, p.34.

Valencia, M.J. 'Conflicting claims and potential solutions in the South China Sea', *Adelphi Paper no.298*, London, International Institute for Strategic Studies.

Wortzel, L.M. (1994) 'China pursues traditional great-power status', *Orbis*, vol.38, no.2, p.157.

Further reading

Garver, J.W. (1993) *Foreign Relations of the People's Republic of China*, Englewood Cliffs, NJ, Prentice Hall.

Goodman, D. and Segal, G. (eds) (1994) *China Deconstructs: Politics, Trade and Regionalism*, London, Routledge.

Goodman, D. and Segal, G. (eds) (1997) *China Rising – Nationalism and Interdependence*, London, Routledge.

Kim, S.S. (ed.) (1994) *China and the World: Chinese Foreign Relations in the Post-Cold War Era*, 3rd edn, Boulder, CO, Westview Press.

Robinson, T.W. and Shambaugh, D. (eds) (1994) *Chinese Foreign Policy: Theory and Practice*, Oxford, Clarendon Press.

Shinn, J. (ed.) (1996) *Weaving the Net: Conditional Engagement with China*, New York, Council on Foreign Relations Press.

CHAPTER 8

Restructuring foreign and defence policy: the USA

Anthony McGrew

8.1   Introduction

'European thought, European commerce, and European enterprise, although actually gaining in force ... will nevertheless relatively sink in importance in the future, while the Pacific Ocean, its shores, its islands, and adjacent territories will become the chief theater of human events and activities in the world's great hereafter' so uttered William Seward, the architect of America's initial Pacific expansion (quoted in Korhonen, 1996). Seward, Secretary of State to Abraham Lincoln, perceived the Asia-Pacific as the Republic's historic 'prize', an 'empire of the seas' (Lafeber, 1993, p.9). Manifestations of Seward's vision are detectable in today's foreign policy rhetoric and the shifting priorities of successive post-Cold War US administrations. As Madeline Albright, the first woman to be appointed Secretary of State, has declared, 'America is, and will remain, an Asia-Pacific power'(Albright, 1997).

But constructing and pursuing a coherent and consistent post-Cold War Asia-Pacific strategy has proved, and continues to prove, a complex and delicate exercise in balancing domestic politics with regional, as well as global, interests and commitments. Although the demise of bipolarity has not diminished significantly the USA's vital interests, or presence, in the Asia-Pacific region it has provoked, for the third time this century, a historic 'revisioning' of the USA's power and purpose. Relations with the Asia-Pacific have thus become entangled in a maturing national debate about the nation's global role into the twenty-first century.

This chapter explores how this debate has shaped, and continues to influence, the re-construction and conduct of the USA's evolving Asia-Pacific policies, together with its role and perceptions of its vital interests, in the region. For in key respects, the Asia-Pacific has become the 'laboratory' for the USA's post-Cold War foreign and national security strategy. The Asia-Pacific, notes Betts, constitutes 'the most fertile ground for adjusting and reinventing ... [the USA's] ... strategic concepts in the post-Cold War era' (Betts, 1993). Furthermore, the chapter seeks to describe and explain the complex configuration of domestic forces and institutional politics which condition, and constrain, the nation's Asia-Pacific posture. In doing so particular attention will be devoted to the core issues which dominate the contemporary policy agenda: security and trade.

No longer the hegemonic power in the region the USA is today having to adapt to the realities of a more assertive Japan, and an increasingly powerful China. This 'multipolar' regional order confronts the USA with new challenges and opportunities as it seeks to devise an appropriate strategy and mechanisms to enhance regional stability and prosperity. In this respect the USA, as Albright's remarks imply, has increasingly sought to identify with its historic role as a 'Pacific power' as opposed to its Cold War role as a 'power in the Pacific'. But in so doing it has been forced to recognize the limits to unilateralism and the reach of its power.

Soldiers of the People's Liberation Army arrive at Hong Kong's border checkpoint of Lok Ma Chau hours prior to the former British colony reverting back to Chinese rule at midnight on 30 June 1997

In seeking to explain the USA's continuing engagement with the Asia-Pacific this chapter will assess critically: the changing structure, form and dynamics of US Asia-Pacific relations; the global, regional and domestic forces shaping its regional posture; the primary challenges and key policy dilemmas which confront US policy makers in their attempts to fashion a coherent and consistent national strategy towards the region; and the USA's role as a key architect of the evolving Asia-Pacific regional order. In short, the chapter is concerned with two broad questions: first, how do we account for the fact that, despite the demise of the Cold War, the 'USA remains politically and strategically omnipresent' in the Asia-Pacific (Camillerri, 1994); and second, what kind of order is the USA seeking to construct in the Asia-Pacific?

8.2 America's Pacific ties

Well before the official conclusion to the Cold War, affirmed in the Charter of Paris (November, 1990), the structure of trans-Pacific relations was experiencing a transition. Whereas for much of the Cold War era the 'US vision of the Pacific as an "American Lake" was more true than ever before' by the mid 1980s the economic ascendancy of East Asia, and the growing military power of China, presented an irresistible force for change in the underlying structure of Asia-Pacific relations (Segal 1990, p.374). The demise of the Cold War, the growing emphasis upon geo-economic competition, and the collapse of the Soviet Union, merely accelerated this process of change.

In the absence of a Soviet threat tacit co-operation between the USA and China, to contain Soviet influence in the region, became superfluous. The original containment rationale for the extensive US military presence in the region was signally undermined. Many of the USA's traditional allies were now amongst its fiercest economic competitors. These developments created an entirely novel set of circumstances for the guardians of US interests. For despite the preponderance of US military power, the demise of superpower rivalry confirmed a growing awareness, amongst the nations' political and military elites, that the region was rapidly becoming 'too powerful to be either contained or controlled by the USA' (Stuart and Tow, 1995, p.17). During the post-war era the relative position of the USA in the Asia-Pacific has been transformed from hegemon to power balancer, exporter to importer, creditor to debtor (Ahn, 1996).

Within the security domain the USA remains deeply enmeshed in the region's military affairs and power politics. Through the 'San Francisco system' of bilateral (and multilateral) security treaties, including the Mutual Security Treaty with Japan and ANZUS, the USA continues to provide security guarantees to its major allies, South Korea and Japan. In addition it has a series of bilateral defence agreements with Singapore, Malaysia, Thailand and Brunei. This security system is underwritten by a huge and permanent military presence which, whilst subject to some phased reductions, will soon equal, if not marginally exceed, the US military presence in Europe (Stuart and Tow, 1995, p.16) (see Table 8.1). In 1994 the USA spent US$44 billion sustaining its Pacific military presence, some 18 per cent of its defence budget, making it the largest (or second largest depending upon how one calculates Chinese defence expenditure) defence spender in the region (Stuart and Tow, 1995, p.16).

Table 8.1 *Phased US troop reductions in the Asia-Pacific in the 1990s*

COUNTRY Service	1990 starting strength	Phase 1 reductions 1990–92	Philippines withdrawal	1993 strength	Phase II reductions 1992–95	1995 strength (approx.)
JAPAN	50,000	4,773	–	45,227	700	44,527
Army personnel	2,000	22	–	1,978	–	1,978
Navy shore-based	7,000	502	–	6,498	–	–
Marines	25,000	3,489	–	21,511	–	21,511
Air Force	16,000	560	–	15,440	700	14,740
Joint billets	–	200	–	–	–	–
KOREA	44,400	6,987	–	37,413	6,500[1]	30,913[1]
Army personnel	32,000	5,000	–	27,000	–	27,000
Navy shore-based	400	–	–	400	–	400
Marines	500	–	–	500	–	500
Air Force	11,500	1,987	–	9,513	–	9,513
PHILIPPINES	14,800	3,490	11,310	–	–	–
Army personnel	200	–	200	relocated	–	–
Navy shore-based	5,000	–	4,328	elsewhere	–	–
Marines	900	672	900	in region	–	–
Air Force	8,700	2,818	5,882	–	–	–
				1,000[2]	–	1,000[2]
Sub-total	**109,200**	**15,250**	**11,310**	**83,640**	**7,200**	**76,440**
'Afloat or otherwise forward deployed'	**25,800**			**25,800**		**25,800**
TOTAL	**135,000**			**109,440**		**102,240**

Note:

The IISS is aware that the figures in this table do not tally, but they are the official figures provided by the Department of Defense.

[1]Korean troop reductions deferred in light of North Korean threat.

[2]Estimated relocations to Japan, Korea and Singapore. Does not include Guam.

Source: Stuart and Tow (1995, p.9)

Buttressing this military presence the USA remains a major arms supplier to the region and a critical source of advanced weapons systems and arms production technology. But as the potential Chinese military threat continues to grow, and Japan shoulders an increasing share (some 70 per cent) of the costs of the USA's forward military presence (Vogel, 1997, p.207), the San Francisco system is entering a transitional phase. Stuart and Tow argue that it constitutes the security architecture of the era of containment rather than a security design for the post-Cold War world (Stuart and Tow, 1995). For this 'hub and spokes' system remains essentially a unilateral enterprise in an era in which 'a unilateralist regional security strategy is not a viable American option' (Pollack, 1996, p.123). Quite simply even though the USA remains the sole military superpower it cannot project that power independently in the Asia-Pacific without the co-operation of its allies upon whom it relies to provide bases or other support (Betts, 1993).

Trade, to paraphrase Clausewitz, is becoming the continuation of war by other means (Huntington, 1993). In 1982 US trade with the Pacific nations overtook that with Europe signalling a significant shift in the global balance of economic power (Linder, 1986, p.16) (see Figure 8.1). Since then East Asia and the Pacific have become the USA's largest regional trading partner such that in 1995 the value of US trade with the Asia-Pacific was 70 per cent greater than its trade with the EU. Trade flows across the Pacific accounted for over 40 per cent of US total trade in 1994 and are predicted to double in value by 2000 (Taylor, 1996, p.17; Department of State, 1997a). In 1995 Singapore, Malaysia and South Korea imported more from the USA than Saudi Arabia, Brazil and France respectively (Department of State, 1997b). Alongside this explosion in trans-Pacific trade there has been a dramatic expansion of foreign direct investment (FDI) flows. Between 1989 and 1993 FDI by APEC member countries in the USA increased by over 40 per cent, to almost US$150 billion, whilst US FDI in APEC states increased by an equivalent percentage to reach almost US$180 billion (Department of State, 1997a). In comparison APEC countries accounted for 18 per cent of total US outward FDI in 1995 whilst US total FDI in Hong Kong alone stood at some US$13 billion.

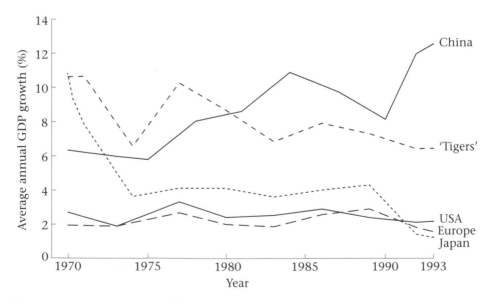

Figure 8.1 *The economic challenge: Asia and the West*

Source: Huntington (1993, p.104)

For the USA, the Asia-Pacific has become the most potentially lucrative regional market for traded goods and services, and according to some estimates, accounts for some three million jobs in the most advanced sectors of the economy. Whilst the 'sun-belt' states of the West and South have benefited most from the growth of trans-Pacific trade and investment, Pacific rim economies have become increasingly critical to the vitality of the entire US economy. As Joan Spero (Under Secretary of State for Economic Affairs in the Clinton Administration) observed, 'In this context, there is no region more important to the US than the Pacific Rim' (US Congress, 1993, p.4).

Yet equally the pattern of trade and investment relations constitute a major competitive challenge to sectors of the US economy as is evident from the massive trade deficit (see Figure 8.2). Although not the only measure of its competitive position the trade deficit with East Asia nevertheless has become an important rallying cry for those industries and communities most vulnerable to foreign economic competition. The trade imbalance with China and Japan especially, which together account

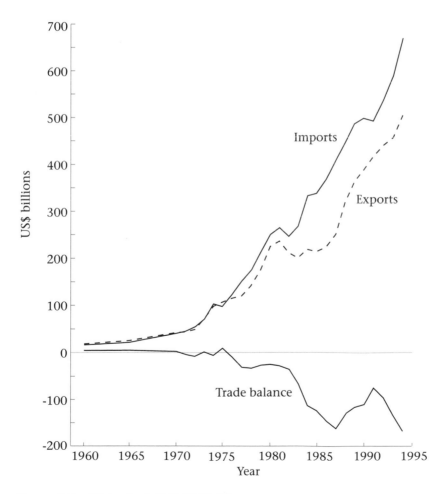

Figure 8.2 *US trade deficit 1960–94*

for some 75 per cent of the entire US trade deficit (see Figure 8.3 and Table 8.2), has provoked a vigorous domestic protectionist response and an increasingly aggressive unilateral US trade diplomacy. Whilst this has brought some positive results, in as much as both deficits have begun to

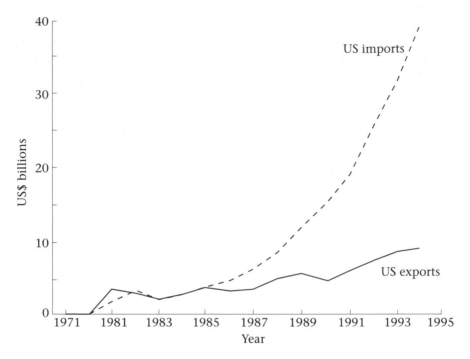

Figure 8.3 *US–Chinese trade (in US$bn)*

Source: Cohen *et al.* (1996, p.232)

Table 8.2 *Bilateral US-Japanese trade balances (in US$bn)*

	US bilateral deficit	US imports from Japan	US exports to Japan	US exports to Japan as a percentage of US imports from Japan
1970	1.2	5.9	4.7	80
1980	9.9	30.7	20.8	68
1986	55.0	81.9	26.9	33
1987	56.3	84.6	28.3	33
1988	51.8	89.5	37.7	42
1989	49.0	93.6	44.6	48
1990	41.1	89.7	48.6	54
1991	43.4	91.6	48.2	53
1992	49.4	97.2	47.8	49
1993	59.3	107.3	47.9	45
1994	65.6	118.8	53.3	45

Source: Cohen *et al.* (1996, p.177)

stabilize, to many observers it is symptomatic of a more profound shift in the balance of global economic power and an intensifying geo-economic rivalry between the USA and its East Asian economic competitors. Indeed for Luttwak it is this (geo-economic) struggle for economic supremacy which is central to understanding the USA's contemporary economic relationship with the Asia-Pacific (Luttwak, 1993).

But the consequences of the growing enmeshment of the US economy with the economies of its East Asian competitors are not fully appreciated by those advocating a geo-economic analysis. For, as Reich argues, the globalization of the US economy erodes the boundary between the foreign and the domestic, such that it is no longer clear 'who is us' (Reich, 1991). This is signally illustrated, in relation to the Asia-Pacific, by the fascinating case of the US subsidiary of a Japanese company – manufacturing typewriters in Tennessee – which brought a legal action against its US competitor which was importing typewriters made in its offshore pro-duction facilities in Singapore and Indonesia, accusing the US company of unfair trade practices (Ruggie, 1996, p.152). Not only is the USA having to adjust to a new balance of economic power with its Pacific neighbours but, in addition, this complex pattern of trans-Pacific economic enmeshment undermines both the possibility of a coherent 'national economic interest' and the rationality of unilateral strategies for managing an increasingly critical trade relationship. For the complexity of trans-Pacific economic networks makes it almost impossible to assess whether the domestic gains from an aggressively unilateralist approach to trade will outweigh the domestic costs.

If goods and services increasingly flow across the Pacific so too do peoples, ideas and cultures. Over the decade to 1997, immigration to the USA from the Asia-Pacific increased dramatically well in excess of that from Europe or elsewhere. During the 1980s, 27 per cent of all legal Asian migrants settled largely in the West (Sassen, 1996, p.79). In reverse, Hong Kong is home to over 40,000 US citizens, one of the largest ex-patriate communities of Americans. The USA has become the primary destination for the majority of Korean, Filipino, Vietnamese and Taiwanese immi-grants. In the mid 1990s over eight million American-Asians resided in the sun-belt and Pacific coastal states creating their own 'Little Koreas' and 'Little Vietnams' to complement the established Chinatowns and Little Tokyos. These Asian diasporas generate strong cultural, economic and political ties between some of the most economically dynamic and politically important states, like California, and their Asia-Pacific neigh-bours. As Segal observes 'the Pacific part of the US has established an increasingly important orientation Westward to Asia' (Segal, 1990, p.138). It should therefore be no surprise to learn that by the mid 1990s trans-Pacific air traffic had overtaken trans-Atlantic air traffic and is forecast to account for almost 50 per cent of global air travel by 2000 (State, 1997b).

This flow of people is also juxtaposed with the spread of US popular culture manufactured in the 'dream factories' of Hollywood and diffused through the information circuits of today's global society. As a result

English is now the principal language of Pacific elites despite the fact that more people in the region speak Chinese dialects. Indeed in China and Japan English is the principal foreign language taught in schools. There is also a 'growing body of Chinese students in the US, especially the children and grandchildren of the leadership' and 'cadres of Chinese business managers, technicians, and administrators' undergoing professional training (Shinn, 1996, p.59).

As economic and cultural connections multiply, so too do transnational political connections. There is an extensive web of associations and links between US non-governmental citizen groups or social movements and their counterparts in the Asia-Pacific. This multiplicity of relations embraces the environmental, human rights, gender, business and professional domains generating a civil society counterpart to formal diplomatic relations. In addition, notwithstanding the well documented financial contributions of Chinese and Taiwanese 'businessmen' to Bill Clinton's 1996 re-election campaign, the visible presence of 'Asia first' lobbyists on Capitol Hill is undoubtedly politically significant. In 1992 of 850 officially recognized foreign pressure groups and lobbyists 145 were Japanese, 37 South Korean and 22 Taiwanese (Valladao, 1996, p.109). On a whole raft of issues, domestic and foreign, this lobbying connects politics within Washington DC to politics across the Pacific, to the interests and political priorities of elites in the boardrooms and departments of state in Tokyo, Seoul, Beijing and Taipei. Sometimes this produces curious political developments such as the case of the Japanese SEGA games company which, through its US subsidiary, lobbied the powerful Office of the US Trade Representative to enlist the support of the Chinese government in preventing the illegal copying of its software in southern China (Shinn 1996, p.82).

Four general points can be distilled from this synoptic overview of the USA's 'Pacific ties':

- First, the end of the Cold War and the economic ascendancy of the Asia-Pacific, have elevated the economic and strategic importance of this region to the USA. As Clinton's first Secretary of State, Warren Christopher, exclaimed, the USA 'has placed Asia at the core of its long term foreign policy strategy' (quoted in Ahn, 1996, p.194). This is not a temporary development since, even disregarding diplomatic rhetoric, the Asia-Pacific's 'importance in American grand strategy is on the increase' (Roy, 1995).

- Second, the intensification of trans-Pacific ties has multiplied the potential sources of conflict and the collision of interests, values and priorities between the USA and its Pacific neighbours. East Asia is simultaneously a direct economic challenge to the USA and its largest export market. Given the USA's trade deficit the potential for 'trade wars' is ever present. In addition the growth of Chinese military power, along with the numerous unresolved conflicts within the region, constitute serious sources of regional instability which present direct threats to US national security (see Chapter 5). As Calder remarks, 'In the post-Cold War world [the Asia-Pacific] has eclipsed the Middle East as the most deadly long-term regional security challenge that the US faces today' (Calder, 1996, p.3).

- Third, the complex structure of trans-Pacific relations is best described as multipolar, multi-layered and multi-dimensional. Put simply, there are: three key powers, the USA, the PRC and Japan; a multiplicity of channels (governmental and non-governmental) of communication and contact between the USA and its Asia-Pacific partners; and a diverse agenda of issue-areas, from the economic to the environmental.

- Fourth, the relative power of the USA has been eroded by the ascendancy of Japan and the PRC such that, as Higgott observes, 'there exists a disjuncture ... between ... America's continuing "hegemonic mentality" and its current practice, ... "hegemonic defection"'(Higgott, 1994). Notwithstanding this, as the largest Pacific economy, the dominant military power in the region, combined with its dominance of global information and knowledge networks, the USA retains considerable *structural power*. By *structural power* is meant the capacity to initiate, promote, organize, or block changes to, the norms and rules which regulate trans-Pacific relations. Thus, for instance, the USA has exploited the export dependence of East Asian states upon the US domestic market as a means to promote the liberalization of these economies. In Rapkin's view the USA may no longer be able to perform the role of a hegemonic (predominant) power in Asia-Pacific but its *structural power* 'continues to be substantial, especially if the military-strategic backdrop to economic relations is factored into the equation' (Rapkin, 1994).

The demise of the Cold War, alongside the spectacular economic ascendance of East Asia, have triggered a *transformation* of the structure and dynamics of trans-Pacific relations. This presents the architects of the USA's post-Cold War foreign policy with a clear invitation to adjust and redefine the nation's Asia-Pacific strategy to reflect more closely the contemporary configuration of power in the region and the political consequences of the dense web of multiplying ties across the Pacific. But responding to that invitation continues to depend upon the prior articulation of a coherent rationale for the USA's post-Cold War global role.

8.3 Forging a new covenant with power

In a moment of exasperation with his foreign policy advisors President Clinton was overhead to remark 'Gosh, I miss the Cold War' (quoted in Lieber, 1997, p.20). Through its crude division of the world into rival camps the 'Great Contest' provided unequivocal answers to the fundamental questions of US foreign policy: 'What should the US be?' and 'What should the US do?' (Chace, 1992, p.7). 'Containment', first enunciated by George Kennan in his 'Long Telegram of 1946' and elaborated in the now historic

National Security Council memorandum number 68 (NSC-68) (1950), had offered a coherent rationale for the USA's post-war global role; a role defined in terms of containing, by military and political means, the expansion of Soviet power and the spread of communism. But with the collapse of Soviet power and communist systems in Europe the rationale for containment evaporated.

With 'no clear and present danger' a new rationalization of the USA's global role, not to mention a defence expenditure which consumes some 5 per cent of GNP, is demanded. Moreover, the removal of the Soviet threat lessens the reliance of the USA's European and Asian allies on its military power. Its greatest asset, as the world's only military superpower, therefore no longer appears to translate directly into global political influence. Even the Gulf War of 1991 did not fundamentally alter the fact that economic power, rather than military power, is emerging as the key currency of international politics. In this respect the USA, although the world's largest economy, confronts the rising economic power of Japan and Germany. To the citizens of Little Rock, Arkansas, it becomes harder to comprehend why, given the end of the Cold War, their taxes continue to underwrite the defence of their European or Asia-Pacific economic competitors. Furthermore, intensifying economic globalization has increased considerably the vulnerability of US society to foreign economic competition. This was evidenced in the dramatic decline, in the 1980s, of the 'rustbelt' industries of the North-East and experienced most visibly in the automobile industry, that icon of US post-war prosperity. Fears about economic decline have encouraged a renewed isolationist sentiment which, in conjunction with the end of the Cold War, set the political context in the early 1990s for the most significant national debate about foreign policy since the Vietnam war.

Reinventing foreign policy

It is important to understand that the contemporary debate about foreign policy is not solely a technocratic exercise. On the contrary, even though the main protagonists may be confined to Washington circles the growing intermeshing of foreign and domestic politics has meant that attempts to reconstruct a coherent vision of the USA's global role reach deep into US society. It is no accident that, on her appointment to office, Secretary of State Madeline Albright initiated a series of 'town meetings' across the USA to establish a dialogue with the American people concerning the conduct of foreign relations.

Foreign policy, even at the height of the 'Imperial Presidency' during the Cold War, has never been the sole preserve of the incumbents of Pennsylvania Avenue, the State Department and the Pentagon. Today foreign policy makers confront an increasingly active Congress and a raft of lobbyists, pressure groups and citizen's organizations all seeking to influence the conduct of the nation's foreign affairs. Moreover, foreign policy has always been inflected with an ideology of exceptionalism, what

Thomas Jefferson referred to as America's civil religion, which historically has shaped a sense of national identity and purpose. In this respect the contemporary debate about the USA's global role is as much about constructing a renewed sense of national identity and national solidarity as it is about the principles which should inform the nation's foreign policy posture. As President Clinton declared: 'We need a New Covenant for American Security after the Cold War, a set of rights and responsibilities that will challenge America's people, leaders and allies to work together to build a safer, more prosperous and more democratic world' (quoted in Valladao, 1996, p.98).

In constructing this 'covenant with power' four contrasting visions of US power and purpose have dominated the political discourse. Each of these visions expresses the interests, values, concerns and aspirations of a distinctive coalition of social forces: political, military, business and labour elites, alongside citizen groups. Each too reflects a distinctive reading of the contemporary global condition. Although all share a common commitment to the promotion of basic American values, such as liberty, democracy, and enterprise nevertheless they offer contrasting prescriptions for how these are best preserved and advanced in the contemporary world. Rosen and Ross identify these four visions as: *primacy*; *neo-isolationism*; *selective engagement*; and *co-operative security* (Rosen and Ross, 1996).

For the proponents of *primacy* the objective of US foreign policy 'is not merely to preserve peace ... but to preserve US supremacy by politically, economically, and militarily outdistancing any global challengers' (Rosen and Ross, 1996). Preserving US primacy, as Huntington argues, is crucial to the USA's long-term prospects since whosoever attains primacy acquires the power 'to insure their security, promote their interest, and shape the international environment in ways that will reflect their interests and values' (Huntington, 1993). This is a *realist* view of world order stressing the struggle for power between states. In advocating *primacy*, however, the 'preponderants' consider that the USA's best interests are served not by engaging in a *balance of power* politics with its potential rivals but rather in seeking to sustain, in both the economic and military domains, clear superiority over them. This, as Tucker and Hendrickson note, is barely indistinguishable from the Cold War strategy of containment, except that in the 1990s its objects are the new potential global rivals: Japan, the PRC, and possibly Germany (Tucker and Hendrickson, 1992). In this regard it is instructive to note that in the conclusion to a recent treatise Huntington asks 'how might war between the US and China develop?' (Huntington 1996, p.313).

Neo-isolationists, by contrast, seek a significant US disengagement from international politics. Pat Buchanan, a one-time leading conservative politician, encapsulated the *neo-isolationist* view in three words 'Come home, America' (quoted in Harries, 1993). In the *neo-isolationist* view the USA has never before in its history been as secure from external threat than it is today. In comparison with the Cold War era it confronts no power or powers capable of inflicting unacceptable damage on its people or territory.

Its *strategic invulnerability* undermines any rationale for extensive foreign military engagements or commitments such that neo-isolationists prescribe withdrawal from NATO and other entangling alliances. A major reduction in US military capabilities is considered desirable since it would free resources which could be redirected to domestic social and economic needs to boost the nation's global economic competitiveness (Nordlinger, 1995). The *neo-isolationist* vision combines a realist view of America's unassailable power and strategic invulnerability with an emphasis upon unilateralism and national autonomy. Yet it also reflects a moralist or idealist impulse in as much as it considers a managed disengagement from the world as vital to the maintenance and rejuvenation of the traditional 'American way of life'.

By comparison proponents of *selective engagement* justify a continuing global role for the USA only where its vital interests are at stake. In Goldberg's view *selective engagement* reflects the pragmatic tradition in US foreign policy; a tradition which informed the foreign policy of the Republic during its first 100 years (Goldberg, 1992). Advocates of this pragmatic strategy eschew any grand plans for the creation of a US inspired 'new world order' or US primacy, which is conceived as profoundly mistaken in its assumption that, in the transformed world of the 1990s, hegemony can purchase a stable or peaceful world order. In this respect the emphasis is upon recognizing the limits to US power in a *multipolar* world whilst advocating a US role in acting to prevent significant shifts in the existing *balance of power* in Europe and Asia. Rather than seek a hegemonic role the USA should therefore act as an 'offshore balancer', ensuring global security through regional but *selective engagement* (Layne, 1993).

Finally, advocates of *co-operative security* promote a more expansive vision of the USA's global role. Based upon a liberal rather than a realist conception of international politics this vision asserts that globalization, the spread of democracy and the diffusion of economic and military power are fundamentally transforming the nature of world order. In this new 'post-international' era the tired old prescriptions of realists, whether couched in the language of primacy or isolationism, are considered dangerous illusions; illusions more relevant to the industrial than the post-industrial age. Indeed the intensification of global interdependence (globalization), which erodes the boundaries between the foreign and the domestic spheres, means that the prosperity of the USA is intimately connected to the dynamics of the global economy. Effectively therefore there can be no real alternative to global engagement although there remain important choices to be made about the form and modalities of that engagement. In these respects the proponents of *co-operative security* stress the centrality of international co-operation, multilateralism (institutionalized co-operation amongst three or more states), collective defence (co-operation against a common enemy), and mechanisms of global and regional governance to the reconstruction of US foreign policy (McGrew, 1994, pp.231–3). But in advocating *co-operative security* they are careful to avoid any suggestion of resurrecting President Woodrow Wilson's project of global collective security, as expressed in the failed League of Nations. On the contrary *co-operative security* is conceived in more fluid, less formal, terms as a strategy which lies between the extremes of a crude *balance of power* (a mechanism by which the Great Powers prevent the dominance of one over the others) and *collective security* ('one for all and all for one'), instead relying upon 'joint means by which potential adversaries prevent, resolve, reduce, contain, or counter threats that could lead to war among them' (Ruggie, 1996, p.80). Such joint means can involve a variety of institutional arrangements from the *security community* of NATO to more informal and limited mechanisms of security and defence co-operation. In essence the advocates of *co-operative security*, 'require the US to abandon any pretence to being the only superpower, yet it would preclude a withdrawal into ourselves' (Chace, 1992, p.192).

Reconstructing foreign and defence policy

These competing conceptions of 'grand strategy' have constituted the discourse from within which successive administrations have sought to construct, and to legitimate, a coherent foreign and defence policy for the post-Cold War era. In this sense the continuing debate about grand strategy has been inseparable from the day to day politics of reconstructing defence and foreign policy. But unlike the Cold War era when one single strategy – containment – acquired an intellectual and political hegemony there is a sense that today the complexity of global politics means that no single 'overarching framework equivalent to the Cold War is likely to reappear in the foreseeable future ... and attempts to define one in the abstract are destined to prove futile' (Ruggie, 1996, p.6). This has significant consequences for the coherence and consistency of US foreign policy. Indeed it is possible to identify all four strategies simultaneously in the conduct of contemporary foreign and defence policy. Where these strategies appear mutually supportive this has been of no great import, other than an irritating intellectual untidiness, but where they contradict one another the consequences, as will later become clear in the case of US relations with its Asia-Pacific neighbours, have proved potentially dangerous.

During the Bush administration the foreign and defence policy establishment clung to a strategy of *primacy* as articulated in the vision of a 'new world order'. Although there were on-going reviews of foreign and defence policy, largely prompted by congressional demands for 'a peace dividend' following the end of the Cold War, it remained effectively business as usual legitimized in part by the Gulf War. Some significant reductions in military capabilities and deployments were initiated, especially in Europe and the Pacific, and a shift from planning for global war to regional conflicts was agreed. Secretary of State Baker called for 'collective engagement' mirroring a recognition of the importance of *co-operative security* in the context of the Gulf War (Callahan, 1994, p.65). But the underlying logic of the *New Regional Defence Strategy* and the *Base Force* plan (approved in 1990) was unashamedly geared to re-affirming US *primacy* and to 'containing' potential rivals. This became even more transparent when extracts from a supposedly secret Department of Defense document, *Defence Planning Guidance 1994–1999*, were leaked in early 1992. The document affirmed that:

> Our first objective is to prevent the re-emergence of a new military rival ... This is a dominant consideration underlying the new regional defense strategy that we endeavour to prevent any hostile power from dominating a region whose resources would ... be sufficient to generate global power. These regions include Western Europe, East Asia, the territory of the former Soviet Union and South West Asia.

(quoted in Klare, 1995, p.100)

During the 1992 US Presidential election campaign, Bill Clinton sought to distance himself from the Bush vision of primacy and a 'new world order' by stressing the signal importance of the domestic economy and *co-operative security*. But in office the Clinton Administration had to address the legacy of Cold War commitments and the inherited plans and military programmes of the Bush/Reagan era. The consequence has been an evolving strategy which, in its attempts to appeal to many different domestic and foreign constituencies, has proved an 'uneasy amalgam of selective engagement, co-operative security, and primacy' (Rosen and Ross, 1996). This is most explicit in the official 'bible' of its foreign and defence strategy, *A National Security Strategy of Engagement and Enlargement* (White House, 1996). As a coherent statement of national purpose it is unparalleled but in replacing the logic of 'containment' with that of 'engagement and enlargement' it shifts readily between the language of *primacy, selective engagement* and *co-operative security*.

For Anthony Lake (Clinton's first National Security Advisor and Chief of the White House National Security staff), the architect of this new strategy, 'engagement' was central to re-building the domestic consensus supporting the USA's global role. Growing strategic and economic interdependence has replaced the Soviet threat as the prime rationale for a continuing US global role. As the national strategy document notes: 'clear distinctions between threats to our nation's security from beyond our borders and the challenges to our security from within our borders are being blurred; ... the separation between international problems and domestic ones is evaporating; and ... the line between domestic and foreign policy is eroding' (White House, 1996, pp.1–2). Ensuring domestic prosperity and national security is thus conceived as indivisible from a strategy of continuing global 'engagement'. Additionally since democracies are considered as inherently peaceful the 'enlargement' of the community of democratic nations is regarded as vital to enhancing both global and US security. 'Engagement and enlargement' thus define the twin pillars of the 'Clinton doctrine' which is to be realized through: '(1) our efforts to enhance our security by maintaining a strong defense capability and employing effective diplomacy to promote co-operative security measures; (2) our work to open foreign markets and spur global economic growth; and (3) our promotion of democracy abroad' (White House, 1996, p.3).

A restructuring and retrenchment of military capabilities has been associated with this strategy of 'engagement and enlargement'. Defence spending plans have been trimmed, force levels reduced and forces re-deployed, and procurement programmes cut. In accelerating the reshaping of the USA's fighting machine the *Bottom up Review* (September 1993) (BUR) and the *Quadrennial Defence Review* (May 1997) (QDR) have laid the foundations of a leaner, meaner, more globally mobile military capability. Central to these reviews has been the aim to ensure that the USA continues to retain its global military primacy and its strategic edge in the on-going military-technological revolution brought about by the information age. Moreover, critical to the sizing, deployment and restructuring of its global military capabilities is the plan to be able to deter, but if necessary to fight and win, two 'major regional conflicts' (nearly) simultaneously. Both the BUR and QDR are based upon the scenario of near simultaneous regional conflict with Iraq and North Korea (Klare, 1995, p.112). As the official military doctrine states: 'The focus of our planning for major theater conflict is on deterring and, if necessary, fighting and defeating aggression by potentially hostile regional powers, such as North Korea, Iran or Iraq' (White House, 1996, p.14). This anxiety with what Klare labels 'rogue states' has significant implications for US military policy in East Asia.

In many respects the Asia-Pacific has become the 'laboratory' for this 'Clinton doctrine' of 'engagement and enlargement'. As the new national strategy confirms: 'East Asia is a region of growing importance for US security and prosperity; nowhere are the strands of our three-pronged strategy more intertwined nor is the need for continued US engagement more evident. Now more than ever, security, open markets and democracy go hand in hand in our approach to this dynamic region' (White House, 1996, p.39). What factors have shaped the implementation of this strategy?

8.4   America's Pacific impulse: contemporary policy towards the Asia-Pacific

'The American people don't give two hoots in a rain barrel who controls North China' railed the editorial in the *Philadelphia Record* at the height of the 1930s Manchurian crisis (Ruggie, 1996, p.16). Today an isolationist posture towards the Asia-Pacific, although perhaps a populist policy, is no longer a rational option for the guardians of the USA's national interest. Indeed, as the evidence so far suggests, the Asia-Pacific has become a focal point of the USA's post-Cold War energies and interests. This will become more evident through an examination of evolving US policy towards the Asia-Pacific embracing: the policy process; the conduct of Asia-Pacific policy; and the dilemmas and contradictions of the USA's contemporary Asia-Pacific strategy.

Process

Since the close of the Second World War, argues Yahuda, 'American policy towards East Asia has been characterised by contradictions and inconsistencies' (Yahuda, 1996, p.110). In part, this is a product of the structure of the US political system, and in part its pluralistic political culture, which together ensure that the making and conduct of foreign policy is highly politicized. In the case of Asia-Pacific relations where, as the discussion of Pacific ties indicates (Section 8.2), there no longer exists a clear distinction between what is foreign and what is domestic – evidenced in the rise of 'intermestic' issues – such politicization is further exaggerated. Asia-Pacific policy is therefore subject to intense bureaucratic rivalries, institutional struggles between Congress and the Presidency, and interest group politics.

Within the executive branch, although the President is formally responsible for foreign and national security policy, the process of policy making is fragmented between many different agencies. Whilst the Departments of State and Defense take the lead they share the stage with many other agencies and departments. The consequence is often a bureaucratic 'struggle for the turf' as bureaucratic interests vie to promote and protect their own domestic (and sometimes foreign) constituencies. The case of trade policy towards Japan is instructive in this respect since Defense Department (DOD) and State Department (DOS) officials have often been marginalized in the determination of policy by the economic agencies, such as Commerce, the Treasury and National Economic Council. On a number of occasions throughout the early 1990s this gave the dangerous impression to outsiders that the USA was willing to jeopardize the stability of its military alliance with Japan simply in order 'to achieve a breakthrough in trade talks' (Vogel, 1997, p.206).

This kind of *bureaucratic politics* is nested within the more permanent institutional struggle between President and Congress, bequeathed by the constitutional separation of powers, or more accurately the division and sharing of powers over foreign policy. With the rise of 'intermestic issues' and the collapse of the Cold War consensus on foreign policy, Congress has adopted a much more assertive role in the determination, and sometimes conduct, of policy towards the Asia-Pacific. This kind of 'micro-managing' of foreign and defence policy matters is often the source of considerable conflict with the White House. In this context much of the energy of the White House is expended in mobilizing its potential allies inside and outside Congress in support of the President's policy initiatives. One of the consequences of this 'perpetual invitation to struggle' can often be an inconsistency and incoherence in Asia-Pacific policy. This is perhaps nowhere so evident as in US relations with China. The Congress has tended to adopt a consistently hostile approach to the PRC complicating the conduct of the USA–China policy. A good illustration of this occurred in 1995 when House Speaker Newt Gingrich mischievously proposed that the Clinton Administration officially recognize Taiwan, despite the long standing US policy not to do so (Ahn, 1996). As Shinn observes, 'Under the system of the division of powers, the US is likely to have two China policies for some time to come, even if the same party controls Congress and the White House' (Shinn, 1996, p.88).

This *bureaucratic* and *institutional politics* is further complicated by *interest group politics*. Organized interests, embracing amongst others labour, business, Churches, women's rights, human rights and environmental groups, seek to influence both the substance and the conduct of Asia-Pacific relations. Through lobbyists, political action committees, the mobilization of public opinion and other means, 'special interests' pressure the Congress, government departments and agencies, and the White House in the pursuit of their interests. Some, like the National Association of Manufacturers or the Business Coalition for USA-China Trade, acquire privileged access to decision makers whilst others remain 'outsiders'. During the renewal of China's most 'favoured nation' trade (MFN) status in 1994, which required Congressional approval, a titanic struggle ensued between the Business Coalition for USA–China Trade, which supported renewal, and a coalition of human rights, Church, women's and environmental groups, and labour organizations which sought to prevent renewal. In this respect policy towards the Asia-Pacific, on key issues, is always subject to a multiplicity of conflicting domestic political pressures and interests.

Conduct

Given the complexity of the USA's foreign policy process it is perhaps not surprising that consistency and coherence are not the epithets most frequently used to describe the conduct of US relations with the Asia-Pacific. Yet in many respects there are important continuities between current policy and that of the Cold War era. Perhaps this is only to be expected given the web of historic commitments and ties, along with the inertia of vital interests, which together tend to limit the prospects for radical shifts in policy direction. Despite the rhetoric, current policy towards the Asia-Pacific, in the realms of security, economics, and politics, does not denote as radical a break with the past as some might desire.

Military security policy
For the last 46 years US soldiers have mounted daily patrols of the Korean DMZ whilst their Air Force colleagues from the Kadena USAF base on Okinawa remain in constant readiness to defend Taiwan, less than an hour's flying time away. Whilst the USA's massive military presence in the Pacific remains only marginally diminished in comparison with the Cold War era, the security challenges it confronts are somewhat different. In seeking to re-fashion the Asia-Pacific security order one key challenge facing the USA arises from its desire to ensure both a regional balance of power without at the same time appearing to be engaged in the containment of China. A second challenge is balancing the desire to shift more of the burden of defence onto its allies, most especially Japan, without simultaneously triggering fears of US decommitment, or Japanese

hegemony, which would fundamentally weaken regional security. Concerns about the regional balance of power and alliance transition therefore have been central to recent US policy initiatives.

To ensure a *balance of power* in the region the USA has sought to retain its major military presence and to reinvigorate the 'San Francisco system'. Following the end of the Cold War significant reductions were planned by the Bush administration in US Pacific force deployments (see Table 8.1). But in the second *East Asia Strategic Initiative review* (July 1992) (EASI-II) a revised ceiling was placed on force reductions. In EASI-III (February 1995) the Clinton Administration reaffirmed that there would be no further reductions to those already planned (Department of Defense, 1995, p.16).

Central to these EASI reviews has been the notion of the US role as a *regional balancer* working to deter the potential expansionist aspirations of other powers in the region, namely China and North Korea (Yahuda, 1996, p.143). But whilst the rhetoric reflects the language of the balance of power, the conduct of US policy could equally well be interpreted as a policy of containment, hegemony, or military primacy. For a *balance of power* assumes the maintenance of an approximate equality between protagonists and the possibility of shifting alliance ties. Yet neither of these conditions appears to hold in the region. In particular not only do most analysts agree that 'the US will remain the strongest military power in the Asia-Pacific region for the near term' but also that its 'permanent' alliance ties with Japan make any shift in alignments appear decidedly implausible (Roy, 1995). Under these conditions US policy appears to reflect a residual attachment to primacy in so far as its role as *regional balancer* is primarily directed at containing China whilst the US military presence in the region also acts as a mechanism for containing Japan too. In this regard it is instructive to note that the leaked *Defense Planning Guidance* document, referred to earlier, prescribes that the USA seeks to remain 'a military power of the first magnitude in the area' (quoted in Callahan, 1994, p.91).

Revitalizing its bilateral alliance relations is central to US security strategy in the region. Amongst these, the USA–Japan Mutual Security Treaty is the most critical to maintaining regional stability and security. In renewing and strengthening it, in early 1996, the USA has sought to expand the agenda of security co-operation and to encourage a more active Japanese role in the regional security order. This is one aspect of a policy to share the burdens and costs of leadership. Alongside this a strengthening of bilateral arrangements and co-operation agreements has been negotiated with its other allies in the region (Stuart and Tow, 1995). Overall since the end of the Cold War there has been a growing intensity of defence and security co-operation between the USA and its regional partners.

In a radical break with past policy the USA has also sought to promote regional dialogue on security issues through the ASEAN Regional Forum (ARF) – (see Chapter 5). During the Cold War the USA eschewed *multilateralism* in favour of *bilateralism*. Indeed the Bush administration greeted Australian proposals for a multilateral security dialogue similar to the Organization for Security Co-operation in Europe '... with open hostility ... out of the fear that it would undercut existing US bilateral arrangements in the region' (Acharya, 1996). But in what is referred to as the 'New Asia Doctrine' speech in Seoul 1993, President Clinton acknowledged the role of multilateralism and co-operation in the security domain (Higgott, 1994). This followed US support for the establishment of the ARF reflecting the administration's general commitment to *co-operative security*. As Callahan argues this acceptance of regional dialogue 'constituted an important, even historic, development' (Callahan, 1994, p.90). But whilst the USA has promoted the further expansion and strengthening of the ARF process it has also tempered this with a cautionary note. As Joseph Nye, one of the architects of the policy, asserts 'while we are indeed stressing the increased importance of multilateral institutions, it is not at the cost of our primary attention to reinforcing the traditional security alliances we have in the region but rather as a complement to them' (quoted in Acharya, 1996). *Multilateralism* constitutes a mechanism for smoothing the path for burden sharing and a larger Japanese role in regional security affairs whilst at the same time engaging China in a security dialogue and reducing its perceived fears of hostile encirclement or containment.

This emphasis upon building *co-operative security* in the region is also reflected in US initiatives to establish a bilateral dialogue between the Pentagon and its PLA counterparts. In 1994 a Joint Commission on Defence Conversion was established whilst a number of bilateral official visits and high level discussions have occurred on a range of issues (Gill and Kim, 1995, p.76). In a historic encounter the Chinese navy too made its first official visit to the USA in March 1997. Additionally, the USA has sought to engage China and others in the region in global arms control regimes and support for concerted policies to limit the proliferation of nuclear and advanced weapons technology. Indeed preventing nuclear proliferation in the region has become one of the primary concerns of the Clinton Administration particularly given China's sales of sensitive nuclear and advanced military technology to Pakistan, Iraq and other states. In responding to the alleged North Korean nuclear weapons programme in 1993 the USA moved rapidly to defuse a potentially lethal crisis and in resolving it through diplomatic, rather than military, means reinforced both its regional counter-proliferation strategy and regional security.

All these confidence building measures, along with the emphasis upon multilateral dialogue, are indicative of a concerted attempt to construct a system of *co-operative security* in the region. In this regard US policy is not simply concerned with ensuring a regional *balance of power* but also can be interpreted as an attempt to attenuate potential rivalries, conflicts and tensions, admittedly to advance its own security interests. For instance in early 1997 it initiated four power talks with the two Koreas, and the PRC in an attempt to create a dialogue on 'resolving' the Korean issue. But the development of a 'security community' NATO style, as Ruggie suggests, is unlikely to be realized although 'strengthening the elements of co-operative security within this fragile balance will not in itself solve outstanding security problems, it may help shape how states decide to solve them' (Ruggie, 1996, p.105).

Promoting *co-operative security*, however, does not mean that the USA conceives its military power to be of declining significance to regional security. On the contrary, as demonstrated during the Taiwan Straits crisis of 1996 – the largest deployment of US naval power in the region since the Vietnam war – its willingness to deter aggression and to defend its allies appears undimmed. In Korea the 'tripwire ' of American troops remains critical to the military security of the South. However, there is a recognition that neither military *primacy* nor the *balance of power* by themselves can ensure regional stability and, as a consequence, significant emphasis is now placed on constructing mechanisms of *co-operative security*. For the USA the stakes are potentially enormous since it is in East Asia that the Cold War twice turned into Hot War.

Constructing a domestic consensus to underpin this evolving strategy, however, remains fraught with political difficulties. For the White House, the Pentagon and State Department confront a Congress and public opinion which is extremely sceptical about, and resistant to, entangling commitments and the burdens of leadership in the Asia-Pacific. More so too because the region is home to its most 'aggressive' economic competitors. Given that in 1996 over 50 per cent of the members of Congress took office after the fall of the Berlin Wall there is a strong Congressional voice for a 'post-imperial' US role in the region (Lieber, 1997, p.17). Amongst the American public, less than 45 per cent now support the use of US troops to defend South Korea whilst public support for Japan has declined precipitately from 87 per cent in 1985 to 50 per cent in 1993 (Shinn, 1996, p.73; Huntington, 1996, p.222). In these respects the attitudes of foreign policy, military and economic elites are at distinct odds with the trend in popular opinion. Politically the strategy of *co-operative security* and the stress upon burden sharing, can be viewed, in part, as an attempt to assuage domestic concerns and to generate a new domestic consensus in support of the USA's continuing Asia-Pacific engagement. For diffusing the political burdens and economic costs of leadership through regional dialogue and burden sharing fits with the more sceptical mood of the American nation. Domestically, as Ruggie observes, seeking to legitimate US engagement with *balance of power* rhetoric is 'rarely a persuasive discourse for the American public outside the Cold War context' such that the most viable domestic political strategy today is promoting *co-operative security* and 'encouraging regional security organizations' (Ruggie, 1996, pp.171–2). This is especially so given the growing East Asian economic challenge.

Economic and trade policy
In responding to this economic challenge US officials regularly reiterate that, as President Clinton put it, the USA does 'not intend to bear the cost of [its] military presence in Asia, and the burdens of regional leadership, only to be shut out of the growth that stability brings' (Clinton quoted in

Stuart and Tow, 1995 p.48). But there is a fundamental contradiction at the heart of US economic and trade policy towards the Asia-Pacific: for whilst globally it champions multilateralism and a liberal trading order in its dealings with this region, unilateralism and managed trade frequently are the order of the day. Indeed in its relations with Japan 'trade wars' and 'trade brinkmanship' are more apt descriptors. Central to understanding US economic relations with its Pacific neighbours is the trade deficit and US attempts to minimize the domestic economic adjustment necessary to reduce it by promoting instead 'managed trade' or 'open regionalism'. In this context the politics of foreign and domestic economic policy have become indivisible.

Trade relations and diplomacy dominate US economic relations with its Pacific neighbours whilst Japan and China are its primary targets. Since the end of the Cold War the USA has conducted an increasingly unilateral and aggressive trade diplomacy towards Japan and China. Driven by a combination of domestic pressures and geo-economic considerations US policy, in the early 1990s, has come close to precipitating 'trade wars'. In response to the huge trade deficit with both these states (see Tables 8.2 and Figure 8.3, earlier in this chapter), and their trade practices, the USA has championed 'managed trade' and 'economic liberalization'. These goals have been promoted through a combination of unilateral, bilateral, and multilateral means.

In the case of Japan, the US policy of 'managed trade' and 'economic liberalization' have been in evidence since the 1980s when Reagan sought to reduce the burgeoning bilateral trade deficit using market sharing agreements (MOSS) and the Structural Impediments Initiative to set limits on Japanese exports to the USA. Paradoxically these measures stimulated Japanese FDI in the USA as a means to circumvent numerical and other controls. Nevertheless in the 1990s the Clinton Administration has sought further 'managed trade' arrangements to restrict Japanese imports in those economic sectors considered essential to US domestic prosperity. In April 1993 the 'US–Japan Framework for a New Economic Partnership' was inaugurated by which means the twin US objectives of 'managed trade' and 'economic liberalization' have been pursued. But very quickly the 'new partnership' was transformed into the 'new trade war' as the USA in 1994 and 1995 threatened unilateral trade sanctions against Japan unless it acceded to US demands. This precipitated a major 'crisis' in US–Japanese bilateral relations, which a summit meeting of both heads of state failed to resolve, but which culminated finally in a compromise agreement (Vogel, 1997). Domestic political pressures have encouraged this policy of 'trade brinkmanship' irrespective of its damaging consequences for alliance relations. As Luttwak comments, in geo-economic terms, 'Japan's misfortune is that it is now the only possible candidate for the role of America's Chief Enemy' (Luttwak, 1993, p.60).

Similarly in respect of China, with whom the USA has a huge trade deficit, aggressive unilateralism has become a means to extract economic advantage. Yet in some respects the USA 'still tends to treat China as a special case' (Wang, 1996). In part this is due to the incredibly powerful 'New China lobby' which, according to Destler, is 'perhaps the most formidable, pro-trade coalition ever sustained by US business on its own initiative' (Destler, 1995, p.234). This was most evident during the debates on the renewal of China's MFN status in the early 1990s when this coalition organized 298 of America's largest companies, 37 trade associations, and even footwear retailers who 'flooded the White House with letters from thousands of shoe store managers,' to support renewal of China's MFN status in order to protect US jobs and access to its fastest growing export market (Destler, 1995, p.234).

Rather than seeking a 'managed trade' policy the USA has tended to reserve its 'aggressive unilateralism' to achieve the 'economic liberalization' of China, the extension of US trade opportunities, and China's adherence to the rules of multilateral trade. Thus in the 1995 dispute over the pirating of US software by Chinese companies, the USA threatened punitive trade sanctions unless the PRC implemented World Trade Organization (WTO) rules on intellectual property rights (Friedman, 1997, p.234). In exchange for vital US support for its membership of the WTO, the PRC reluctantly agreed to US demands, and in a stage managed operation, sent in the local police to close down a number of pirating enterprises whilst CNN and the world's media looked on.

Chinese police gather confiscated pirated music and software CDs and movie cassettes for destruction at a police depot in Miyun near Beijing

In its trade diplomacy with China and Japan the USA has been forced to come to terms with two features of the transformed global economy. First, the changing balance of economic power between the Western and Eastern edges of the Pacific Rim. This is cogently summarized by the brutal fact that whereas in 1950 the US economy was 26 times greater than that of Japan by 1994 it was only 1.4 times as large (Vogel, 1997, p.193). Whilst aggressive unilateralism may produce short-term economic benefits for the USA, it fails to confront the trend in economic power relations responsible for the discordant trade relationships (Huntington, 1996, p.226). Second, the interdependencies created by trans-Pacific economic ties, underscored by intensifying globalization, seriously complicates the pursuit of aggressive unilateralism since any domestic economic gains may be outweighed by the domestic losses as a result of trade opportunities forfeited and the adverse economic impacts on domestic industry and businesses dependent on the import of manufactured goods from the Asia-Pacific. Both these factors have contributed to an evolving US interest in regional economic co-operation. As Camilleri suggests, 'in spite of, perhaps because of, rising economic friction, both the US and Japan are becoming increasingly open to ... new forms of multilateral co-operation. For the US this may be a less costly or painful way of protecting its interests'(Camillerri, 1994).

'APEC is another way for us to engage in the region and promote, not necessarily trade negotiations in the classical sense, but trade facilitation and the removal of barriers' explained Joan Spero in her testimony before Congress in late 1993 just before the historic APEC Seattle Summit (US Congress, 1993, p.5). Called at President Clinton's request the Seattle Summit of APEC leaders was part of a US initiative to accelerate regional economic co-operation but on an agenda which reflected US priorities and interests. Building a new Asia-Pacific Community is a mechanism for assuaging protectionist impulses at home and furthering the neo-liberal economic agenda abroad. Regional economic co-operation provides a vehicle for advancing US interests through initiatives to establish 'common rules on investment, trade, financial services and the protection of international property rights' – what Cohen refers to as a process of 'liberalization by agreement' or more impolitely 'economic acupuncture' (Yahuda, 1996 p.280; Cohen, 1997, p.83). Furthermore it offers a framework for further engaging China in regional affairs and encouraging its 'socialization' within a (US) regime of free trade and an evolving regional structure of 'economic co-operation'. APEC in this 'socializing' sense 'is at the heart of USA–China policy' (Friedman, 1997, p.241).

In this regard the USA's desire for a robust APEC issues more from a drive to anchor China, Japan and ASEAN in a 'liberal' regional trading order than a motivation to prevent the potential emergence of an East Asian trading bloc (see Chapter 4). For the latter seems highly improbable given the export dependence of East-Asia on the US market. By seeking to ensure APEC's agenda reflects its neo-liberal instincts, as is evident from APEC's many official Declarations (Bogor, Osaka and Manila), the USA acquires a significant purchase on the strategic direction of regional economic co-operation and the rules, norms and values which eventually may regulate trans-Pacific economic interdependence. Underlying this too is a strong liberal belief that growing economic interdependence, facilitated by APEC,

Philippines President Fidel Ramos, on right, and US President Bill Clinton wave to the press before the start of the APEC summit, Subic Bay, November 1996

will spill over into the security domain making conflict less likely and the use of military force an 'irrational' instrument for resolving international disputes in the region.

As in the security domain this 'regional turn' in US foreign policy does not supplant but rather supplements existing global, bilateral, and unilateral policy instruments. Even a leading sceptic of the APEC process recognizes that, 'Notwithstanding the important domestic political dimensions of ... [its] ... current foreign economic policy towards the Asia-Pacific, APEC does signal a shift in US policy away from the heavy bilateralism of the Bush administration towards a more multilateral strategy' (Higgott, 1994).

Political relations

The third pillar of US strategy towards the Asia-Pacific is the political: support for democratization, the promotion of civil and political rights, and the construction of a Pacific 'community of nations'. According to

Winston Lord, Assistant Secretary for East Asian and Pacific Affairs in the early 1990s, the USA seeks the 'creation of a community of nations built on shared strength, prosperity and commitment to democratic values as well as regional approaches to global problems' (US Congress, 1993, p.7).

But the desire to 'enlarge' the community of democratic states in the Asia-Pacific sits uneasy alongside the continuing existence of a diversity of state forms embracing 'Communist', authoritarian or partially democratic polities. Attempts to encourage democratization and adherence to universal human rights therefore have been inconsistent and contradictory. In the case of China, engagement and enlargement has involved giving priority to economic and security interests over democracy and human rights. By contrast in the case of Burma/Myanmar, where few economic and strategic interests are at stake, the USA has adopted an assertive policy including economic sanctions. In general, the fact that within the region 'enlargement' has been 'widely interpreted as a campaign of interference and cultural imperialism', not to mention the material interests at stake in pursuing a moral approach, has tempered greatly the US enthusiasm for this political project (Stuart and Tow, 1995 p.12). Moreover, it has stimulated considerable political friction by encouraging those social forces on both sides of the Pacific who consider global politics is entering a stage of inter-civilization rivalry and conflict (Mahbubani 1995; Huntington 1996). By championing 'Western political values' over 'Asian values' the policy also appears to fatally weaken the cultivation of an Asia-Pacific 'community of nations'.

The tensions and dilemmas of US Asia-Pacific policy

'What we see in [the Asia-Pacific] today is not a clash of civilizations, but a test of civilization' suggests Madeline Albright (Albright, 1997). But the real test may be of US civilization since what is at stake is its post-Cold War Asia-Pacific policy and ultimately the doctrine of 'engagement and enlargement' from which it derives. In reflecting critically upon the nature and conduct of that strategy it transpires that rather than one coherent policy towards the Asia-Pacific the USA pursues a plurality of policies through a plurality of means, namely, 'Multilateralism where feasible, regionalism where necessary, and unilateralism only as a last resort' (Cohen, 1997, p.93). Moreover these policies reflect, as does the strategy itself, elements of primacy, selective engagement, and co-operative security. It is therefore not surprising that US policy towards the Asia-Pacific has been described as having 'lost its way 'or more uncharitably as 'incoherent, reactive, and occasionally waffling' (Ahn, 1996; Pollack, 1996).

But such incoherence reflects the serious policy dilemmas confronting the White House and State Department in their attempts to pursue a robust and consistent strategy towards the Asia-Pacific region. In many respects these arise from the particularities of the region itself and its recent economic ascendancy. Amongst the most significant policy dilemmas are:

- The problematic relationship between the USA's geo-political role in the region and its geo-economic role. This arises because the USA is the linchpin of the region's security yet at the same time East Asia's chief economic competitor. In the case of relations with Japan these roles often conflict with the USA simultaneously pursuing policies to enhance the bilateral security relationship whilst threatening a 'trade war'. Attempts to resolve the dilemma created by these sometimes conflicting roles are subject to very powerful, but often irreconcilable, domestic political pressures and interests.

- A dilemma concerning the modalities through which US objectives and interests are most effectively realized or promoted. In utilizing unilateral or bilateral diplomacy the USA risks undermining the fragile mechanisms of regional co-operation. Yet in pursuing regionalism and multilateralism it becomes subject to collective policies which may potentially limit the scope for autonomous action in the pursuit of the national interest. Thus the primacy attached to unilateralism and bilateralism in managing trade relations with Japan and China sits uneasily alongside the desire for a larger APEC role in trade and economic matters, and vice versa.

- The conduct of China policy which gives the appearance of shifting between (unconditional) engagement and conditional engagement reflecting a continuing dilemma as to whether containment or engagement should form the proper basis of US policy.

- The pursuit of military security in the region which confronts US policy makers with a security dilemma. By pursuing a tacit policy of military primacy the potential exists for undermining co-operative security measures whilst the pursuit of co-operative security measures, in the absence of US military superiority, lacks credibility amongst its regional allies.

- A collision between regional and global interests. On issues from human rights to trade policy the conduct of US policy in the Asia-Pacific often undermines its global policy (e.g. managed trade versus free trade). The dilemma for policy makers arises out of a desire to balance often conflicting regional and global interests. By giving priority to regional interests over global interests the latter may be significantly damaged and vice versa.

As the 'laboratory' for US post-Cold War 'grand strategy' the Asia-Pacific presents a daunting challenge to the aspirations of American policy makers seeking to craft a coherent and consistent set of policies. But given the nature of US domestic politics, and the complexities of trans-Pacific relations, the substance and conduct of the nation's Asia-Pacific policies will continue to be marred by inconsistency and contradiction until a crisis demands a choice between the underlying visions of primacy, selective engagement and co-operative security. Until that occurs the alternative is simply 'muddling through'.

8.5   A Pacific power or a power in the Pacific?: US Asia-Pacific policy into the twenty-first century

'The United States is a Pacific nation. We have fought three wars there in this century' (White House, 1996, p.40). To some degree the architects of contemporary policy towards the Asia-Pacific are rediscovering and reinventing that deeply rooted Pacific impulse which, from the era of William Seward and Westward expansion, has animated the American political imagination (Korhonen, 1996). To account for the USA's continuing 'omnipresence' in the Asia-Pacific, despite the end of the Cold War, requires more than a rational assessment of the balance sheet of Pacific ties, interests and commitments but also an acknowledgement of the ideological strand in US foreign policy which, for policy makers and the public alike, imparts meaning on those very material relations. The idea of the USA as a Pacific power has been inflected in US political and military discourse since the turn of the century but it is primarily in the post-Cold War era that the USA 'has become proud of its status as a Pacific power' (Valladao, 1996, p.175). With the historic traumas of isolationism, the Pacific war, and the conflicts of the Asian-Pacific Cold War firmly in the past, the USA may, as a result, increasingly come to perceive its future in Asia-Pacific terms; although not exclusively so. But this is not certain for, as Huntington argues, irrespective of the 'economic connections which may exist between them, the fundamental cultural gap between Asian and American societies precludes their joining together in a common home' (Huntington, 1996, p.307). Nevertheless, it is evident that the Pacific impulse remains a powerful historical narrative which, along with the growing intensity of its contemporary Pacific ties, constitutes the USA today as a Pacific power rather than simply a power in the Pacific.

For the foreseeable future the USA also 'remains by far the most dominant power in the region' (Yahuda, 1996, p.259). As the earlier discussion has argued, US strategy in the region is an expression of its enormous *structural power,* most visible in its attempt to define the nature of, and the values which inform, the evolving international order of the Asia–Pacific. In this respect its strategy is not motivated, as Buzan suggests, by an 'anti-regionalism' (see Chapter 4); on the contrary regionalism is conceived, however mistakenly, as 'complementing components of an effective global policy' (Cohen, 1997, p.94). Despite the inconsistencies and contradictions in its Asia-Pacific policy, US interests in the region have continued to remain 'remarkably consistent over the past two centuries: peace and security; commercial access to the region; freedom of navigation; and the prevention of the rise of any hegemonic power or coalition' (Department of Defense, 1995, p.5). In response to the question what kind of order the USA desires in the Asia-Pacific, it is clearly one which, as the earlier discussion has confirmed, is consonant with its core values, aspirations, and beliefs. As to whether the grand rhetoric of an 'Asia-Pacific community' will ever be realized, the historical evidence so far suggests the sceptics have the edge. The only certainty is that the USA will continue to remain deeply engaged in constructing the future of the Asia-Pacific region.

References

Acharya, A. (1996) 'ASEAN and conditional engagement' in Shinn, J. (ed.).

Ahn, B.J. (1996) 'The US in Asia: searching for a new role' in Shinn, J. (ed.).

Albright, M. (1997) 'American principle and purpose in East Asia', Forrestal Lecture.

Betts, R.K. (1993) 'Wealth, power, and instability – East Asia and the United States after the Cold War', *International Security,* vol.18, no.3, pp.34–77.

Calder, K. (1996) *Asia's Deadly Triangle,* London, Nicholas Brealey.

Callahan, D. (1994) *Between Two Worlds – Realism, Idealism and American Foreign Policy after the Cold War,* New York, HarperCollins.

Camillerri, J. (1994) 'The Asia-Pacific in the post-hegomonic world' in Mack, A. and Ravenhill, J. (eds).

Chace, J. (1992) *The Consequences of the Peace,* New York, Oxford University Press.

Cohen, B.J. (1997) 'Return to normalcy? Global political economy at the end of the century' in Lieber, R.J. (ed.).

Cohen, S.D., Paul, J.R. and Blecker, R.A. (eds) (1996) *Fundamentals of US Foreign Trade Policies,* Boulder CO, Westview Press.

Department of Defense (1995) *US Security Strategy for the East-Asia/Pacific Region,* Office of International Security Affairs, Washington DC, US Government Printing Office.

Department of State (1997a) *Fact Sheet: APEC/US Economic Data,* available from http://www.usia.gov/regional/ea/apec/apec.htm

Department of State (1997b) *Fact Sheet: US Economic Relations with East Asia and the Pacific,* available from http://www.usia.gov/regional/ea.htm

Destler, I.M. (1995) *American Trade Politics,* Washington DC, International Institute of Economics.

Friedman, E. (1997) 'The challenge of a rising China: another Germany?' in Lieber, R.J. (ed.).

Gill, B. and Kim, T. (1995) *China's Arms Acquisitions from Abroad,* Oxford, SIPRI/ Oxford University Press.

Goldberg, A.C. (1992) 'Selective engagement: US national security policy in the 1990s', *The Washington Quarterly,* Summer, pp.15–24.

Harries, O. (1993) 'The collapse of the West', *Foreign Affairs,* vol.72, September, pp.41–53.

Higgott, R. (1994) 'APEC – a sceptical view' in Mack, A. and Ravenhill, J. (eds).

Huntington, S.P. (1993). 'Why international primacy matters', *International Security,* vol.17, no.4, pp.68–83.

Huntington, S.P. (1996) *The Clash of Civilizations and the Remaking of World Order,* New York, Simon and Schuster.

Klare, M. (1995) *Rogue States and Nuclear Outlaws – America's Search for a New Foreign Policy,* New York, Hill and Wang.

Korhonen, P. (1996) 'The Pacific age in world history', *Journal of World History,* vol.7, no.1, pp.41–70.

Lafeber, W. (1993) *The American Search for Opportunity 1865–1913*, Cambridge, Cambridge University Press.

Layne, C. (1993) 'The unipolar illusion', *International Security,* vol.17, no.4, pp.5–51.

Lieber, R.J. (1997) 'Introduction' in Lieber, R.J. (ed.).

Lieber, R.J. (ed.) (1997) *Eagle without a Cause*, New York, Longman.

Linder, S.B. (1986) *The Pacific Century*, Stanford, Stanford University Press.

Luttwak, E.N. (1993) *The Endangered American Dream*, New York, Simon and Schuster.

Mack, A. and Ravenhill, J. (eds) (1994) *Pacific Cooperation*, St Leonards, Allen and Unwin Australia.

McGrew, A. (1994) 'The end of the American Century? The United States and the New World Order' in McGrew, A. (ed.) *Empire: The United States in the Twentieth Century*, London, Hodder and Stoughton in association with The Open University.

Mahbubani, K. (1995) 'The Pacific impulse', *Survival*, vol.37, no.1, pp.105–21.

Nordlinger, E.A. (1995) *Isolationism Reconfigured*, Princeton, Princeton University Press.

Pollack, J.D. (1996) 'Designing a new American security strategy for Asia' in Shinn, J. (ed).

Rapkin, D.P. (1994) 'Leadership and cooperative institutions in the Asia-Pacific' in Mack, A. and Ravenhill, J. (eds), pp.98–129.

Reich, R. (1991) *The Work of Nations*, New York, Simon and Schuster.

Rosen, B.P. and Ross, A.L. (1996) 'Competing visions for a US grand strategy', *International Security,* vol.21, no.3, pp.5–53.

Roy, D. (1995) 'Assessing the Asia-Pacific power vacuum', *Survival*, vol.37, no.3, pp.45–60.

Ruggie, J.G. (1996) *Winning the Peace – America and World Order in the New Era*, New York, Columbia University Press.

Sassen, S. (1996) *Losing Control? Sovereignty in an Age of Globalization*, New York, Columbia University Press.

Segal, G. (1990) *Rethinking the Pacific*, Oxford, Oxford University Press.

Shinn, J. (1996) 'Conditional engagement with China' in Shinn, J. (ed.).

Shinn, J. (ed.) (1996) *Weaving the Net – Conditional Engagement with China*, New York, Council on Foreign Relations.

Stuart, D.T. and Tow, W.T. (1995) 'A US strategy for the Asia-Pacific', *Adelphi Paper no.299*, London, International Institute for Strategic Studies.

Taylor, R. (1996) *Greater China and Japan*, London, Routledge.

Tucker, R.W. and Hendrickson, D.C. (1992) *The Imperial Temptation*, New York, Council on Foreign Relations.

US Congress (1993) *APEC and US Policy Towards Asia,* Hearings, House Committee on Foreign Affairs, Washington DC, US Government Printing Office.

Valladao, A.G.A. (1996) *The Twenty First Century will be American,* London, Verso.

Vogel, S.K. (1997) 'The inverse relationship: the US and Japan at the end of the Century' in Lieber, R.J. (ed.).

Wang, J. (1996) 'Coping with China as a rising power' in Shinn, J. (ed.).

White House, The (1996) *A National Security Strategy of Engagement and Enlargement*, Washington DC, US Government Printing Office.

Yahuda, M. (1996) *The International Politics of the Asia-Pacific 1945–1995*, London, Routledge.

Further reading

Callahan, D. (1994) *Between Two Worlds – Realism, Idealism and American Foreign Policy after the Cold War*, New York, HarperCollins.

Huntington, S.P. (1996) *The Clash of Civilizations and the Remaking of World Order*, New York, Simon and Schuster.

Klare, M. (1995) *Rogue States and Nuclear Outlaws – America's Search for a New Foreign Policy*, New York, Hill and Wang.

Ruggie, J.G. (1996) *Winning the Peace – America and World Order in the New Era*, New York, Columbia University Press.

Shinn, J. (ed.) (1996) *Weaving the Net – Conditional Engagement with China*, New York, Council on Foreign Relations.

Stuart, D.T. and Tow, W.T. (1995) 'A US strategy for the Asia-Pacific', *Adelphi Paper no.299*, London, International Institute for Strategic Studies.

Valladao, A.G.A. (1996) *The Twenty First Century will be American*, London, Verso.

CHAPTER 9

Restructuring foreign and defence policy: strategic uncertainty and the Asia-Pacific middle powers

Nikki Baker

9.1   Introduction

If there is one concept that is ubiquitous in the Asia-Pacific security literature of the 1990s it is *strategic uncertainty*. This concept had its genesis in the immediate aftermath of the Cold War when strategic analysts, turning their attention to this previously peripheral and now economically dynamic region, found in the Asia-Pacific the seeds of conflict being nurtured by rapid change, the increasing complexity of security concerns, and great uncertainty.

Among the contributory factors identified were: the region's economic dynamism; the Russian naval withdrawal; the decline of US military presence; the concomitant rise to prominence of the region's major powers; regional arms modernization; and the increased salience of economic and environmental issues. Pre-existing, and as yet unresolved, causes for concern, including outstanding territorial disputes and lingering ethnic and religious tensions, were soon added to the list. But as the list expanded, so the tendency to disaggregation increased. 'Change', 'complexity' and 'uncertainty', and all their contributory factors, have been conflated into *strategic uncertainty*.

It will be immediately obvious to those who have read the chapters on China and Japan in this book that *strategic uncertainty* does not have the same resonance everywhere in the Asia-Pacific. However, it is not the great powers, or even the micro-states, that are assumed to be concerned by *strategic uncertainty*. The former are the referent objects of security concern while the latter are strategically isolated. Rather it is the Asia-Pacific middle powers which are assumed to be most animated by the effects of *strategic uncertainty*.

This chapter examines the recent evolution of foreign and defence policy in three of the regional middle powers: Indonesia, Australia and Singapore. Although there are more geographically disparate combinations of Asia-Pacific middle powers, I have settled on three countries that inhabit (some might say border in the case of Australia) the same sub-region in order to demonstrate that the diversity of strategic interpretation and response is not attributable only to distance. The focus is on interpretations of *strategic uncertainty* and on attitudes towards defence self-reliance, alignment, and multilateral and bilateral security co-operation.

9.2   What is a 'middle power'?

There is no commonly accepted definition of a *middle power*. Even a cursory examination of the literature shows that the indicators have a habit of changing with the perspective of the writer. Strategic analysts, who measure power by military capability, would define as middle powers those states which cannot afford the large and flexible force structures of the major powers but which have attained a credible minimum level of defence self-sufficiency (Dibb, 1995, pp. 58–9). Foreign policy analysts would emphasize a softer definition of power with the stress on a measure of creative diplomatic potential (Evans and Grant, 1991, p.344). For the purposes of this chapter the term is used of those small and medium-sized states which perceive a strong correlation between their national well-being and the maintenance of regional (or global) order, and which also have the capacity and the commitment to pursue a measure of defence policy independence and foreign policy influence.

With the breakdown of the bipolar system and the diffusion of capitalist modernization, the number of states which fall into this category of middle power has increased. Moreover a high proportion of them are in the economically dynamic Asia-Pacific region: the two Koreas, Taiwan, Indonesia, the Philippines, Vietnam, Thailand, Malaysia, Singapore, Australia and New Zealand.

Middle powers can enhance their security in a number of ways. If they are concerned about being the targets of military aggression or being drawn into armed conflict they can strengthen their capacity to defend themselves by increasing their defence self-reliance and/or by participating in collective or co-operative security arrangements with their neighbours or other powers. Collective security involves preparing a collective response to aggression while co-operative security stops short of such a commitment but involves multilateral or bilateral confidence-building and capability-strengthening security co-operation (see Chapter 8).

Alternatively middle powers might align themselves with a great power or coalition of powers, or minimize the likelihood of being drawn into others' disputes and maximize their freedom of manoeuvre by adopting a non-aligned stance, or encourage a balance between the great powers while maintaining their own equidistance. They might remove sources of tension between themselves and neighbouring states or dampen potentially escalatory third-party disputes through mediation or peacekeeping. They might agitate for a strengthening of the legal and institutional frameworks of international order or encourage the maintenance or extension of what they consider to be peace-promoting conditions such as democracy, economic growth or trade liberalization.

Middle powers concerned about economic, political or cultural threats also have a range of options both in strengthening their internal capacity to resist such threats, and in resisting external pressures. Externally, non-military threats can be moderated bilaterally, through dialogue and engagement, or neutralized by disengagement or sanctions. They can be moderated through multilateral co-operation with like-minded govern-ments, and they can be discouraged by insistence on recognition of non-threatening international or regional norms of behaviour.

The strategies pursued will be contingent on the configuration of the international system and on the level and immediacy of perceived danger. Where a pressing threat has yet to emerge, they will be conditioned by the particular interpretation placed on *strategic uncertainty*. This interpretation will in turn be influenced by a number of objective and subjective factors including geographical position and political traditions (Holbraad, 1984). The Asia-Pacific middle powers are widely dispersed and heterogeneous and their interpretations of their strategic environment are correspondingly diverse.

Middle powers in the Asia-Pacific

There is general concurrence of view between the middle powers of the Asia-Pacific that any significant change in the current security relationship between the USA and Japan would loosen a welcome restraint on Japan and introduce a correspondingly unwelcome level of tension into its relations with its great power neighbour, China. They already share a concern about potential conflict in North-East Asia; at the very least a military confron-tation on the Korean peninsula or across the Taiwan Strait would disturb regional trade and investment flows. All would like China to concentrate on its role as the engine for regional growth and to eschew aggression and uninvited influence.

But there are also differences between them, and these begin with their interpretations of national security. For some states, like the developed antipodean states of Australia and New Zealand, national security is generally interpreted as security from the adverse effects of *external* developments. For others, like Malaysia and Indonesia, which are not as far advanced in the nation-building process, security continues to encompass domestic stability and *internal* security. For states such as these national and regime security has come to be synonymous with economic security. Their governments rely heavily on rapid economic growth and the spread of prosperity to underpin their legitimacy and promote social identification with state goals.

But it would be a mistake to assume a neat divide between the security interpretations of the developing Asian and developed Anglo states. Thailand, for example, is relatively homogeneous, has powerful military interest groups and has fluctuating but ever present external security concerns. And New Zealand, which is far removed from any credible sources of military threat and highly trade dependent, might be externally focused but places greater emphasis on economic security than on military security.

Most of the developing middle powers in the region are still concerned about secessionism and/or the disintegrating effects of ethnic, religious or class tension. Some remain more concerned about subversion than outright aggression and others fear both. This continuing preoccupation with internal stability is often overlooked because of the declining domestic role of many military forces in the Asia-Pacific. But while most governments in the region now rely on other means to maintain internal stability, the need to maintain domestic unity remains a powerful factor in their foreign and defence policy calculations.

The concerns of Indonesia and Malaysia include externally sourced political, religious and cultural threats to domestic stability. These would include Western pressures for economic or political liberalization, for human rights or environmental protection; the more general spread of individualistic Western values; and the influence of radical Islam.

Some regional middle powers form *security communities* with their neighbours (Australia and New Zealand), others are locked in enmity (the two Koreas), and still others keep a cautious eye on old foes (Thailand on Vietnam and Burma; Singapore on Malaysia and Indonesia). Some states like Malaysia are involved in numerous territorial disputes and others, like Australia, in none. Regional territorial disputes vary in intractability and in their potential for escalation.

The upgrading of the military capabilities of some of the regional middle powers has prompted a range of reactions. Many states are ambivalent about the phenomenon as it has the potential to undermine their own security, particularly if it is occurring in a neighbouring state, but can also be seen as contributing to the general security of the region by reducing areas of vulnerability. Whether military modernization is seen in a more positive or negative light will depend on factors such as size, pre-existing threat perceptions, and the centrality of maintaining a techno-logical advantage to defence policy.

Increasing competition for marine resources is a concern for most – but not all – of the maritime middle powers but the level of concern is at its most intense and immediate for Thailand and its neighbours. The likelihood of more general economic competition is of very serious concern to Singapore, which has always relied for its success on staying one step ahead of its neighbours, and to Indonesia, which is still trying to catch up with them.

Nowhere is the range of security concerns so evident as in attitudes towards the rise of China. Although all the regional middle powers are uncertain about its implications, it would be a mistake to assume that all are principally concerned about China's ambitions as a regional power and/ or its increasing military capability. Taiwan does have its heartland directly threatened by China and China's attitude to areas of contested sovereignty is of direct concern to Vietnam, Malaysia, the Philippines and Indonesia, but many regional states, including some of those just named, have more pressing non-military concerns. China's rapid growth has provided greatly increased opportunities for trade and investment but also threatens serious economic competition, particularly for those states which rely on the export of low-cost manufactures. Some regional states are also uncertain about the implications of deepening business ties between mainland China and their own Chinese communities, and some states fear the prospect of a weak China even more than a strong China. Indonesia and Malaysia greatly fear domestic instability in China as the arrival of any significant number of Chinese refugees on their shores would fuel ethnic tensions and undermine their own stability.

These differences are not simply academic. They go a long way towards explaining why the Asia-Pacific middle powers have not formed a security bloc nor developed the kind of formal multilateral security structures that exist in Europe. They also explain why their foreign and defence policy orientations do not always conform to the expectations of Western strategic analysts.

9.3   Indonesia

Indonesia is an archipelagic state of 17,000 islands straddling the equator and some of the world's busiest sea lanes. Although 45 per cent of its population of 195,277,000 is Javanese, there are significant minorities of Sudanese, Madurese and Malays and a large number of smaller ethnic groups. A powerful presidency is buttressed by the support of the Indonesian Armed Forces (ABRI) which has important political and internal security functions. The Indonesian government has begun to liberalize and diversify an economy previously based on the export of oil, and the economy has been growing at between 7 – 8 per cent per annum since 1993.

Internal stability and external 'threats'

In Indonesia, *strategic uncertainty* in the short to medium term relates principally to concerns about internal stability. The military-supported New Order government of President Suharto brought economic recovery, political stability and a greater sense of nationhood but by 1996 it was becoming apparent that 'regional resentment of Java, "excessive" political demands by Muslims, and ethnic tensions, especially those directed at the Chinese – have been merely placed out of sight, not resolved' (Schwarz, 1994, p.47). Indeed these unresolved problems are exacerbated by rapid economic change, and the non-responsiveness of the political system.

Figure 9.1 *Map of Indonesia and its environs*

Low-level insurgencies continue in the provinces of East Timor, Irian
Jaya and Aceh and there has been a serious escalation of civil strife
elsewhere. In Java, the increasing disparity between the Malay majority and
Indonesia's small but economically dominant Chinese minority is becoming the focus of violent protest that is often expressed as Muslim
resentment of Christians and Buddhists. Kalimantan has been troubled
by inter-ethnic strife as indigenous peoples take exception to settlers
relocated under the transmigration programme and popular anger at the
government's efforts to neutralize political opposition has fuelled the worst
riots that Java has seen for decades.

These threats to Indonesia's cohesion and stability are immediate and
pressing. The country is as geographically divided as it is ethnically diverse,
increasing the likelihood of separatism, and the political upheavals, mass
violence and economic disruption that preceded the power transitions in

1996 are fresh in the collective memory of the ruling elite, including the Indonesian armed forces.

The fissures within Indonesian society, coupled with Indonesia's historical experience and its sheer size, combine to make subversion a greater concern than outright aggression. Malaysia, Singapore, the Philippines, the USA and Britain provided assistance to the rebellion in West Sumatra between 1958–61 while China was suspected of supporting the communist party of Indonesia (PKI) in its power struggle against the Indonesian military in Sukarno's later years. The government is also concerned about 'soft' subversion which takes many forms from Western (particularly European and US) support for the cause of East Timorese autonomy in international fora through non-governmental organizations (NGOs) and labour support for opposition political groups and trade unions to the influence of radical Islam and the spread of Western values.

Conversely, Indonesia's size and enormous population allow it to be relatively sanguine about the prospect of conventional attack. It dwarfs its South-East Asian neighbours and could only be seriously threatened by the major powers. Of these, China is the most distrusted but it is believed to lack either the intention or the capability to embark on military expansionism beyond the boundaries of its claimed territories in the foreseeable future.

Indonesia's primary concerns with regard to the region relate to the development of trends which have the potential to undermine stability within Indonesia itself. These include economic competition from its neighbours but most particularly from the vast cheap labour pool of China; regional instability or conflict with the potential to disrupt trade and investment and invite great power intervention; and refugee-generating domestic instability in China.

This is not to say that Indonesia does not have any 'traditional' external security concerns. The border between Kalimantan and neighbouring eastern Malaysia has yet to be definitively decided and sovereignty over the adjacent islands of Sipadan, Ligatan and Sibatik determined. The ownership of Sipadan and Ligatan has been the biggest irritant in Indonesian–Malaysian relations but there have been clashes over border infringements elsewhere in Borneo. The security of the Natuna Islands, which lie in the centre of a planned oil and gas field on Indonesia's western edge, is also a source of concern because of uncertainty about the extent of Chinese territorial claims in the South China Sea (see Chapter 5).

In 1996 Suharto agreed to a personal request from the Malaysian Prime Minister to refer the Sipadan–Ligatan dispute to the International Court of Justice for arbitration. The dispute had been the subject of a series of increasingly elevated bilateral negotiations and Indonesia would have preferred to resort next to the ASEAN High Council. This agreement signalled a new commitment to removing intra-ASEAN sources of friction and attests to the importance Indonesia accords its bilateral relationship with Malaysia. The dispute was constraining the development of this valued relationship and had the potential to divert attention and resources from the priority task of national development, providing yet another potential source of anti-government grievance.

Foreign and defence policy

Indonesia, by virtue of its size and population, is a potentially great power, but underdevelopment and domestic instability have until recently relegated it to the ranks of the less assertive middle powers. With economic growth has come greater self-confidence and a more active foreign policy stance aimed at securing the nation's economic future and maintaining its role as *primus inter pares* in South-East Asia. Indonesia's relatively sanguine assessment of its strategic environment and the continuing prioritization of development constrains defence spending and allows Indonesia to continue to espouse non-alignment and to reject the notion of collective security. It has supplemented a low-frills people's defence strategy with modest improvements in its conventional capability, and the strengthening of bilateral co-operative security arrangements. Indonesia has also placed added emphasis on preventative diplomacy, promoting regional stability through dialogue, mediation and the resolution of territorial disputes.

Indonesia's defence policy rests on the twin pillars of defence self-reliance and stability-in-depth. For Indonesia, defence self-reliance means maintaining an 'active defensive' strategy of deterrence based on guerrilla warfare with limited conventional military capabilities. This strategy of Total People's Defence (*Sishankamrata*) has been in place, with minor variations, since independence and has two major advantages. It is inexpensive compared to a purely conventional military posture and it provides a justification for continuing military participation in all levels of civil administration in every corner of the archipelago. The last major review of Indonesian defence policy was undertaken in the mid 1980s when it was decided to revitalize the guerrilla strategy and to develop the capability to respond to two crises within the archipelago simultaneously. There has been no significant shift since.

As internal security remains Indonesia's highest security priority, the bulk of the defence and security vote continues to go to the territorial forces which are becoming ever more thinly spread as its population grows (see Chapter 5, Table 5.1). Indonesia cannot afford to devote significant resources to strengthening or modernizing the central forces and the modest acquisitions made in recent years still leave it unable to effectively police its extensive maritime exclusive economic zone (EEZ).

Stability-in-depth involves the promotion of internal stability, regional stability and global stability. The key strategies for promoting internal stability are: economic development with an increasing emphasis on redressing the inequalities between eastern and western Indonesia, between the periphery and the centre, and between the rich and poor; insistence on the adherence of all social groups to the secular principles of the state ideology, *pancasila*; and ABRI's continued involvement in politics and the maintenance of public order.

Indonesia's policy makers believe that with a self-reliant defence capability, a sound economy and a cohesive and loyal population, the country will achieve a state of 'national resilience' or invulnerability to serious challenge. Similarly they believe that if each of Indonesia's neighbours concentrates on building sound economies, cohesive societies and strong defence postures, an area of 'regional resilience' will be created. Once a high enough level of 'regional resilience' is achieved, it will be possible to implement Indonesia's ultimate ideal of a South-East Asian zone of peace, freedom and neutrality (ZOPFAN).

Policy makers also stress that regional stability will be enhanced by the development of trust and confidence with neighbouring states, both bilaterally and multilaterally through participation in ASEAN. ASEAN has played an important security function by fostering a sense of solidarity and an ethos of mutual non-interference and conflict avoidance. However, while it was hoped that ASEAN would eventually assume a central role in the management of regional order, collective defence was explicitly ruled out and even official dialogue on security issues was avoided.

The end of the Cold War brought both challenges and opportunities for ASEAN. Shared doubts about Chinese ambitions – particularly in the South China Sea – and about the level of US commitment to the region, propelled the management of regional security rapidly up the association's agenda. The establishment of the ASEAN Regional Forum (ARF) was an acknowledgement both of the extension of ASEAN's strategic interests beyond South-East Asia and the limitations of its ability to secure those interests. Indonesia agreed to its establishment because its structure gave ASEAN a central role in the development of regional security norms and provided a forum for the dissemination of Indonesian security concepts such as national and regional resilience. However it is less keen on the ARF than other ASEAN members because it remains uncomfortable about being committed to a security organization which includes major non-South-East Asian powers (Suryadinata, 1996, p.84).

Alignments

Alignment has always been officially eschewed by Indonesia, not only because it is considered provocative, but also because it could exacerbate domestic political cleavages, and because the role of dependent ally is not one that conforms with its self-image as a natural regional leader. Nevertheless, the Sukarno regime did ally itself rhetorically with the anti-imperialist Third World while its successor regime has been broadly anti-communist and attracted to the West as a source of aid and investment. Because the presence of US forces in the Pacific allowed Indonesia to prioritize national development, US bases in South-East Asia were tolerated by the Suharto government on the understanding that they were temporary and 'not to be used directly or indirectly to subvert the national independence and freedom of states in the area or prejudice the orderly processes of their national development' (Anwar, 1992, p.13) and on the understanding that ASEAN's ultimate goal should be the establishment of ZOPFAN.

Indonesia still considers a US presence important to the maintenance of regional order and was sufficiently concerned by the closure of US bases in the Philippines to offer the use of Surubaya for naval repair and maintenance, albeit on a commercial basis. However, it is anxious that US interests should neither be translated into interference in its domestic affairs, nor into an overt strategy of containment against China.

Indonesia resumed diplomatic ties with China in 1990. China was no longer perceived as harbouring designs on Indonesia and was emerging as an economic and political power that could not be ignored. Indonesia was keen to diversify its trade and investment links and to encourage China to focus its energies on economic development. Indonesia, like many other ASEAN countries, considers China's economic development to be critical to the stability of China and the region. Any significant disruption to the regional growth dynamic would undermine the stability of countries in the region while domestic instability in China could prompt a wave of migration which, if it washed up on Indonesia's shores, would further complicate domestic race relations.

Indonesia opposes placing any pressure on China likely to prejudice the process of economic reform in that country. Confrontation and containment are considered futile, provocative and premature and Indonesia has sought instead to engage China in regional dialogue processes, both to assuage China's insecurities and to persuade it of the benefits of co-operating peacefully with its neighbours in the region. Indonesia is, however, sufficiently wary of China and confident of its own size and weight to temper engagement with assertiveness. Uncertainty over the extent of Chinese claims in the region of the Natuna Islands, for example, has been dealt with by demonstrating Indonesian resolve through military exercises while encouraging China both to clarify its position on its territorial claims in the South China Sea and to be a good international citizen.

After criticizing Australian-sponsored proposals for a region-wide and inclusive liberalization process on the grounds that it would dilute ASEAN, increase great power influence in the region and undermine Indonesia's ability to protect its economy, the Suharto government became a strong supporter of the APEC initiative. This 'about face' was primarily prompted by concerns about economic competition, particularly from the liberalizing economies of Thailand, India and Vietnam, but also by Australia's willingness to make Suharto its regional partner in promoting APEC.

President Suharto also surprised analysts by agreeing to introduce a hitherto unacceptable degree of formality into Indonesia's bilateral relationship with two of its most important neighbours, Australia and Malaysia. In 1995 an Agreement on Maintaining Security (AMT) with Australia was signed, a move that was interpreted as an abnegation of

Indonesia's long-standing policy of avoiding formal treaty entanglements. The president's motivations for agreeing to the AMT are not a matter of public record, but it is widely assumed that he saw it as a means of assuaging Australia's historical fears about an Indonesian threat while weakening the ability of future Australian governments to criticize Indonesia over East Timor and other human rights issues. The Agreement also had the advantage of assuring Indonesia of a secure southern flank and providing a framework for increased defence co-operation between the two countries.

9.4   Australia

For Australia, *strategic uncertainty* is an external condition that is assessed primarily in terms of its potential to lead to inter-state conflict. With no serious communal tensions and with well-established channels for dissent and mechanisms for the transfer of power, Australia has not had to be greatly concerned about internal security or about the possible impact of regional trends on domestic stability. Security denotes security from externally-sourced threats to Australia's territorial integrity or vital national interests. These threats take the form either of direct attacks on Australian territory or assets, or of potentially damaging or escalatory conflict elsewhere in the region. Although Australian policy makers profess concern about the 'new' security problems of economic competition, mass population disturbance, and environmental degradation, much of their concern relates to the potential of these developments to fuel intra-regional tensions.

Since the 1970s Australia has reiterated that it faces no foreseeable threat but has found it difficult to shake its long-held conviction that Asia is unpredictable and volatile and that Australians are a 'remote and vulnerable white enclave' in a region they do not understand. Australian strategic analysts were amongst the first to express pessimism about the regional implications of the end of the Cold War and rapid economic change. Changes in the regional balance of power and in the military capabilities of regional states were considered likely to interact with 'nationalism, state sovereignty, historical antipathies, cultural differences, ideological divisions, religious differences and many outstanding territorial issues' to cause a deterioration in the regional strategic environment (Dibb, 1995). This would induce a deterioration in Australia's ability to influence regional events and to insulate itself from them. Once an important regional agent for the Western alliance, with a regionally formidable defence capability, and one of the strongest economies in the Asia-Pacific, Australia is increasingly concerned about losing its regional relevance and its economic and military edge.

Foreign and defence policy

Australia's defence and foreign policies are both preoccupied and evolving in line with its relegation from one of only a few regional middle powers to one of many. Long-held policy preferences are having to be modified, not only to cope with the new strategic environment, but to accord with new economic realities and with the preferences of its new regional peers.

Originally a British dominion which had no independent foreign policy voice and relied on the British navy to turn back the Japanese at Singapore, and later a partner in the ANZUS Treaty with a policy of joining its Western allies in the 'forward defence' of South-East Asia, Australia had been moving since the 1970s towards achieving a measure of defence self-reliance and an emphasis on the defence of Australia and its immediate approaches.

This objective, and its strategic and force structure implications, were first coherently articulated in the 1986 Dibb Report which, together with a reaffirmation of Australia's commitment to its alliance partners, formed the basis of the watershed 1987 Defence White Paper. Henceforth the Australian Defence Force would be structured for the defence of Australia and its immediate approaches, with emphasis on the sea-air gap to the continent's north through which any attack was expected to come.

Figure 9.2 *The geo-strategic view from Australia*

The publication of the White Paper also marked a 'conceptual watershed' in the evolution of Australian foreign policy. The coherent policy of defence self-reliance that it spelt out and the new confidence that it signalled in the nation's ability to take care of itself in most contingencies, liberated Australian foreign policy. The country had the resources to pursue a wide range of foreign policy interests and much of its ambitious new agenda involved contributing to the resolution of global problems and raising its international profile but it also began to focus more attention on what the White Paper defined as Australia's 'area of primary strategic interest' – South-East Asia and the South-West Pacific. In a 1989 statement on Australia's regional security, the Minister for Foreign Affairs and Trade outlined policies of 'comprehensive engagement' with the countries of South-East Asia and 'constructive commitment' to the island states of the South-West Pacific. Comprehensive engagement aimed to develop multi-dimensional regional linkages – in the military, politico-military, diplomatic, economic and cultural spheres – in the belief that this would gradually lead to greater cohesion and a sense of regional commonality of interests, and thereby contribute to Australia's security.

Comprehensive engagement took on a different dimension with the end of the Cold War. Australian policy makers were increasingly concerned that an unstable multipolar order was emerging and that military capabilities were increasing in an atmosphere of unresolved tension and low transparency and in the absence of what they considered to be vital institutional mechanisms for building confidence or resolving conflict. Australia became a keen advocate of formal regional confidence building measures and in 1990 proposed that the states of the Asia-Pacific develop multilateral processes and institutions similar to those of the then European Conference on Security and Co-operation.

As noted in Chapter 8 the Australian proposal was not well received by the USA, nor by the ASEAN governments who were conscious of the differences between their security preoccupations and those of the European states and reluctant to replace their 'culture of constraint' with legalistic institution-building.

With the failure of the Conference on Security and Co-operation in Asia (CSCA) proposal, foreign policy makers adopted a more modest and sensitive approach, using existing regional fora and supporting the creation of new ones that allowed the airing of proposals for regional confidence and security building measures. Australia was an enthusiastic promoter of regional 'second-track', or non-governmental security discussions, and was an early advocate of the establishment of an ASEAN-centred but region-wide forum for security dialogue (Ball and Kerr, 1996). It also became an increasingly active proponent of regional initiatives for economic liberali-zation and particularly of Asia-Pacific Economic Co-operation (APEC). This new regional economic policy activism aimed principally to secure the economic benefits for Australia of participation in a liberal international economic regime, but it was also motivated by security imperatives.

By 1995 engagement with Asia had become the primary preoccupation of the Labour government. Prime Minister Paul Keating believed that the outcome of Australia's policies for Asian engagement would determine 'the future of this country as we enter the twenty-first century' and worked assiduously to persuade regional governments and the Australian public that it should be regarded as an Asian nation, rather than as an Anglo-Saxon outpost in the Pacific (Ball and Kerr, 1996, p.85).

The ultimate in regional engagement came in 1995 when Australia signed an Agreement on Maintaining Security (AMT) with Indonesia. Keating took advantage of the particularly cordial relationship he enjoyed with Indonesia's President Suharto to negotiate a stabilizing and trust-building formal framework for the bilateral relationship. The AMT had another major advantage for Australia, linking it formally into a region in which its right to a voice was often questioned.

Under the Labour government, the defence establishment had responded to the 'new' strategic uncertainty by retaining the core elements of defence policy – the defence of Australia and the sea-air gap to its north and defence self-reliance within an alliance framework – but by giving a higher profile to engagement with the region (and to a lesser extent, UN peacekeeping). In defence terms, regional engagement meant intelligence exchanges, training, exercises, visits by senior officers and personnel exchanges and all these initiatives gathered momentum after the end of the Cold War. The rationale for the increased engagement was a belief that it would promote greater regional transparency and trust and thereby contribute to the maintenance of a stable regional buffer for Australia.

Although the broad outlines of the defence policy and regional engagement, first formally articulated in the 1994 Defence White Paper, enjoyed bipartisan support, the Liberal/National opposition criticized what it perceived as a 'drift in Australia's alliance with the US and New Zealand, a confused approach to regional engagement' and deficiencies in combat capabilities. When it was returned to power in 1996, after thirteen years in opposition, one of its first actions was to reinvigorate the American leg of the ANZUS alliance. Australia floated proposals for the prepositioning of material and the establishment of a US naval base in northern Australia and agreed to participate in a series of joint exercises with the US Marine Corps and to provide ongoing access to training areas. Joint Australian–US exercises are not new but the scale and the scenario on which they are based, namely 'contingency response operations in the Pacific area', represent a new departure.

The new Minister of Defence hinted at a dilution of the defence of Australia policy and a return to a form of forward defence arguing against a narrow interpretation of security that 'focused solely on continental defence'. This was confirmed by the officer leading the government's strategic review team when he informed a meeting of senior military officials that Australia's future area of military operations would be 'further forward than the sea-air gap'.

In addition to revitalizing the ANZUS alliance, the new government has undertaken a major review of defence spending priorities, and begun to reduce the defence bureaucracy so that it can allocate more resources to the purchase of high-technology defence equipment. The explanation advanced for both these initiatives is that Australia's security environment has become increasingly uncertain and dangerous. The Minister for

Defence argues that Australia is now more likely to be asked to commit troops to a regional conflict (even in North-East Asia), and that regional arms modernization is depriving Australia of the military advantage on which the security previously depended.

Alignments

With a long history of relying for its security on the dominant Western powers, Australia is more comfortable than many of the other regional middle powers with formal alignment. Although alignment is often rationalized in terms of classical balance of power considerations, Australia has a strong ideological preference for US leadership and the maintenance of the status quo. The new government's overtures to the USA suggest that it believes Australia's security will be best secured by a return to its 'traditional' role as loyal ally of the strongest Western power.

This role sits somewhat uncomfortably with Australia's new foreign economic policy. While the Liberal/National coalition was anxious to reassure its constituency that it would correct a perceived over-emphasis on the importance of Australia's relationship with Asia, slow economic growth and high unemployment have if anything increased the importance of strengthening trade and investment links with this dynamic region. However, increasing scepticism about the benefits accruing to Australia from trade liberalization has witnessed a shift in emphasis from the promotion of free trade in multilateral fora to the improvement of key bilateral economic relationships, including that with China.

9.5   Singapore

Singapore is a city-state of 632 square kilometres, linked by causeway to the southern tip of Malaysia, and facing the Indonesian island of Sumatra across the Straits of Malacca (see Figure 9.1). The population of 2,987,000 is predominantly Chinese but there are significant Malay (15 per cent) and Indian (6 per cent) minorities. Singapore is nominally democratic in the Westminster mould but the retention and adaptation of colonial mechanisms of social control means that its political system is more aptly described as 'soft authoritarian'. It is the most trade-dependent country on the Pacific Rim, with a carefully managed and strong economy based on the provision of efficient manufacturing, financial and transhipment facilities. Its economic importance and military capability rank it among the regional middle powers despite its small geographic size and population.

Strategic uncertainty

For Singapore, *strategic uncertainty* has two dimensions. The first of these is concern about the security implications of political transitions in its neighbours, Malaysia and Indonesia. The second is a more generalized concern about the potential of regional developments to undermine regional stability and thereby impact on Singapore's trading environment and economic survival. Both of these concerns have deep roots and relate to its size, location and ethnic composition.

When Singapore was expelled from the Malaysian Federation in 1965, the first challenge facing its leaders was ensuring the economic viability and territorial survival of their resourceless and vulnerable island state. Singapore had no resources other than its population and its location on the most transited sea lane between Europe, the Middle East and the Far East. It was also a tiny and predominantly Chinese state in a predominantly Malay region where relations with minority Chinese communities were uneasy and characterized by periodic outbreaks of conflict. The Singaporean government feared that Malaysia might attempt to reintegrate Singapore by force or take punitive action against it by cutting water supplies to the island. It was also concerned about its even larger neighbour Indonesia, which had a recent history of belligerence. Singapore's worst nightmare was of Indonesian-Malaysian collusion and of becoming 'a Chinese nut in a Malay nut-cracker'.

Singapore currently enjoys reasonably stable relations with Malaysia and has a good relationship with Indonesia. But its policy makers are concerned that these relations may not survive the inevitable passing of the current leaderships in these states. If the process of political transition is not carefully managed, or less secular leaders accede to power, tensions could well increase between Indonesia or Malaysia's Malay majorities and their Chinese minorities. The concern is that predominantly Chinese Singapore would then become the obvious scapegoat.

Any significant slowing of the current high economic growth rates of its neighbours would also increase Singapore's vulnerability. In a region that its Secretary of Foreign Affairs, Kishore Mahbubani, describes as 'the Balkans of Asia', the Singaporean government perceives political tensions, economic inequalities, religious differences, and ethnic conflicts, muted only by rapid economic growth.

Even if Singapore were not directly threatened by serious unrest in neighbouring countries, it could not quarantine its economy from the effects of instability. To maintain its own high levels of economic growth would require an estimated US$7 billion worth of annual manufacturing investments which would not flow inwards if the region was unstable. With such an internationalized economy and such a small population, the island-state would also be particularly vulnerable to capital or population flight.

Instability in Singapore's immediate neighbourhood is not the government's only concern. If conflicts were to develop over the disputed Spratly Islands in the South China Sea, between the two Koreas, or between China and Taiwan they would threaten the stability of the entire region and again, disrupt trade and investment.

High economic growth rates are considered important for the maintenance of Singapore's own cohesion. Although it is a developed country, according to most of the indicators, it shares with its less developed neighbours a strong concern with maintaining internal stability. For it is not a homogeneous society, given its significant minority Malay and Indian communities and with its majority Chinese population divided by dialect and language-preference. Its government believes that inter-communal and intra-communal antipathies make Singapore a 'tinderbox kind of society'.

Internal stability is perceived as critical to Singapore's continued survival. It is a major factor in its attractiveness to foreign investors and to its own population. The Singaporean government is not entirely convinced that Singaporeans have outgrown the migrant mentality of self-interest and little sense of national commitment and doubts continue to exist about their willingness to remain in the event of serious civil strife. Domestic disorder could also provide a justification for intervention by one or both of Singapore's neighbours, particularly if it was threatening Singapore's Malay community.

Foreign and defence policy

Singapore has always placed a heavy emphasis on defence self reliance because of its high level of insecurity, its small size, the proximity of threat and the constraints on alignment and collective security. Its continuing concerns about the stability of its immediate environment have led to the increasing 'externalization' of defence. Added emphasis has been placed both on extending Singapore's military reach and on persuading the regional great powers and extra-regional powers that they have an interest in contributing to the stability of its 'neighbourhood'. Singapore is also weaving itself into a web of multilateral and bilateral co-operative security arrangements and placing increased emphasis on removing sources of friction from its relationships with its neighbours.

Singapore is unique amongst the founding member states of ASEAN in having had, since independence, a conventional defence capability primarily geared towards dealing with external threats. As a city-state, it does not have the strategic depth that would allow for defence based on guerrilla warfare or any kind of defence in depth and it cannot trade space for time and has little choice but to maintain a policy of forward defence. Singapore Armed Forces' (SAF) doctrine, like Israel's, has long been based on *strategic pre-emption* involving offensive counter-air operations and the seizure of neighbouring territory. This defence posture serves a dual purpose by deterring potential aggressors and assuring prospective investors of Singapore's essential security.

Conventional defence self-reliance is, however, only one component of its defence policy. In 1984 the Singaporean government launched its 'total security' policy, outlining three components perceived as critical to the state's security: 'total defence', diplomacy and internal stability. But the 'total security' concept was not in use for long. Reference to the importance of internal stability was dropped in 1991. Defence policy was redefined as 'total defence' and diplomacy, whilst internal stability was subsumed under 'total defence'.

The 'total defence' concept articulated and refined the government's long-standing policy of minimizing domestic sources of disunity and conflict and thereby denying external forces opportunities for intervention. It has five components: psychological defence, social defence, economic defence, civil defence and military defence. Psychological defence inculcates public commitment to, and confidence in, the survival of Singapore; social defence promotes inter- and intra-ethnic and religious harmony; and economic defence encourages economic resilience.

The country's force development has focused principally on the army first and then on the air force, the navy being a low priority for a state that was effectively landlocked by virtue of its proximity to Malaysia and Indonesia and had no EEZ to speak of. Increasing concern about its vulnerability to the disruption of maritime trade has prompted a new emphasis on developing the capability to police its trade lifeline and protect its maritime approaches. The Singaporean surface fleet and its maritime surveillance capability have been expanded and upgraded and a submarine has been purchased for evaluation and training. The SAF have been placing increasing emphasis on acquiring advanced military technologies and force multipliers such as airborne early warning and guided weapons systems to ensure a continuing edge over their regional counterparts and to compensate for Singapore's lack of manpower. To maintain its edge in combat readiness Singapore has widened its search for training space, and negotiated new air force and army training agreements with countries as far away as the USA and New Zealand.

Alignments

The Singaporean government has always tried to give as many countries as possible a stake in Singapore's survival by participating in wide ranging co-operative security arrangements, encouraging international trade and investment, and transforming its port into the region's most efficient transhipment centre. The end of the Cold War and the perceived decline in the USA's commitment to regional security gave this tactic added urgency.

Singapore successfully sought to revitalize the Five Power Defence Arrangements (FPDA) and has widened and deepened its network of defence co-operation, participating in an increasing number of joint exercises with Indonesia, Thailand, the Philippines, Brunei and the USA.

It has consistently remained one of the keenest regional advocates of a US presence in the Pacific but has had to eschew formal alliances, even signing the ZOPFAN Treaty in 1971, for the sake of ASEAN unity. In 1990 it signed a Memorandum of Understanding with the USA on the establishment of a logistics centre to support the US 7th Fleet and the provision of greater US access to Singapore's air and naval facilities. The two countries also initiated formal annual discussions on security matters. Singapore nevertheless hastened to reassure Indonesia and Malaysia that it was not becoming a permanent regional base for the USA.

Singapore has had to be equally circumspect in its dealings with China lest its neighbours categorize it as a Chinese outrider state. The thaw in relations between Indonesia and Malaysia, on the one hand, and China on the other, allowed it to establish relations with Beijing in 1990 and to forge a strong economic relationship and rhetorical alliance. More recently, however, a rise in anti-Chinese sentiment in Indonesia and a more assertive stance *vis-à-vis* China by the Indonesian government have prompted the Singaporean leadership to reassert its multiracial credentials and its independence from Beijing.

Increasingly strong bilateral relations have been forged with Indonesia through deference to Indonesia in regional fora, investment and trade, and joint economic development. Singapore has also been working towards reducing potential sources of conflict with Malaysia, agreeing to refer the Pedra Branca dispute to the International Court of Justice and planning to reduce its dependence on Malaysia for water by accessing alternative sources in Indonesia.

Singapore has also been keen to maintain ASEAN's relevance in the post-Cold War world and to enhance its stature. It is likely that this increased interest is motivated in part by concern that the governments of Indonesia and Malaysia might otherwise outgrow the association. Singapore supported the accession of the Indochinese states to ASEAN membership and the extension of the organization's purview to include security matters. It was also one of the first ASEAN states to advocate the concept of an ASEAN-centred security dialogue, although its motivation in this case was probably in maintaining US interest in the region.

The externalization of Singaporean defence has been accompanied by a regionalization of the Singaporean economy. With no natural resources, finite space, a shrinking population, and facing increasing competition from the more recent Asian boom economies, Singapore began in 1990 to look overseas for new sources of growth. It has invested in growth triangles with both Malaysia and Indonesia, and the government has led an investment push into Vietnam, China, Burma and India. As a natural corollary, it is also taking a more active interest in global and regional trade liberalization initiatives and has become a strong supporter of the WTO and APEC respectively.

9.6 Conclusion

As this comparison of Australia, Indonesia and Singapore demonstrates, there is no consensus between the Asia-Pacific middle powers on what constitutes strategic uncertainty or how best to confront it. This is because changes in the regional security environment are only one factor in policy makers' strategic calculations, with domestic imperatives and ideological preferences colouring their perceptions and influencing their responses.

Each of these middle powers is unique in its ethnic composition, stage of development, political system and world-view, and is further differentiated by size and geo-strategic location.

Although most are participating in a new region-wide security dialogue, it is clear that each hopes to gain something different from the process. The existence of such diversity may constrain the transformation of dialogue into collective action and a complete convergence seems unlikely unless an immediate, definitive and common threat emerges from the dense tangle of regional security concerns.

References

Anwar, D.F. (1992) *Indonesia and the Security of South-East Asia*, Jakarta, Centre for Strategic and International Studies.

Ball, D. and Kerr, P. (1996) *Presumptive Engagement: Australia's Asia-Pacific Security Policy in the 1990s*, St Leonards, Allen and Unwin Australia.

Dibb, P. (1995) 'Towards a new balance of power in Asia', *Adelphi Paper no.295*, London, International Institute for Strategic Studies.

Evans, G. and Grant, B. (1991) *Australia's Foreign Relations in the World of the 1990s*, Melbourne, Melbourne University Press.

Holbraad, C. (1984) *Middle Powers in International Politics*, New York, St Martin's Press.

Suryadinata, L. (1996) *Indonesia's Foreign Policy Under Suharto*, Singapore, Times Academic Press.

Further reading

Anwar, D.F. (1994) *Indonesia in ASEAN: Foreign Policy and Regionalism*, Singapore, Institute of South-East Asian Studies.

Ball, D. and Kerr, P. (1996) *Presumptive Engagement: Australia's Asia-Pacific Security Policy in the 1990s*, St Leonards, Allen and Unwin Australia.

Dibb, P. (1995) 'Towards a new balance of power in Asia', *Adelphi Paper no.295*, London, International Institute for Strategic Studies.

Kwa, C.G. (1995) 'Asia-Pacific security concerns: a Singaporean perspective' in Cossa, R.A. (ed.) *Asia Pacific Confidence and Security Building Measures*, Washington, DC, The Center for Strategic and International Studies.

Leifer, M. (1996) 'The ASEAN Regional Forum', *Adelphi Paper no.302*, London, International Institute for Strategic Studies.

Schwartz, A. (1994) *A Nation in Waiting: Indonesia in the 1990s*, St Leonards, Allen and Unwin Australia.

Restructuring foreign and defence policy: the Pacific Islands

Richard Herr

10.1   Introduction

The islands of the South Pacific have been buffeted by the wave of political change that has swept the globe since the end of the Cold War. For better and for worse, the certainties of the old order have disappeared. On the credit side, the collapse of the Cold War has opened options for relationships that would have been unthinkable in the period of superpower rivalry. Yet these same changes have unleashed nationalistic passions which have proved, in some cases, every bit as dangerous as the tensions of the Cold War. For good or ill, the post-Cold War changes have been not only dramatic but also pervasive, working their way into every corner of the earth including the remotest atolls of the South Pacific.

The empirical reality of a new international order raises questions about its central characteristics and how these impact on the small polities of the South Pacific. In fact, the search for benefits is proving rather more demanding than might be wished by many of the disadvantaged smaller polities of the region. Signs have emerged which suggest that the post-Cold War order is marginalizing further a region already marginalized by its dominant features of insularity, remoteness and, most important, the small size of most of its members. Indeed, a worst case assessment could show that the post-Cold War order offers the South Pacific little more than a thin chance to minimize losses.

Complicating any assessment of the post-Cold War era is the fact that not all of the uncertainties facing the Pacific Islands today are consequences of the collapse of the Cold War. There were changes in train around the globe and across the Pacific which were not directly related to superpower rivalry even during periods of intensity in the Cold War. Two of the more significant of these developments have profoundly affected the Pacific Islands' options in foreign and defence policy – environmentalism and the growth of Asia-Pacific co-operation on a macro-regional scale.

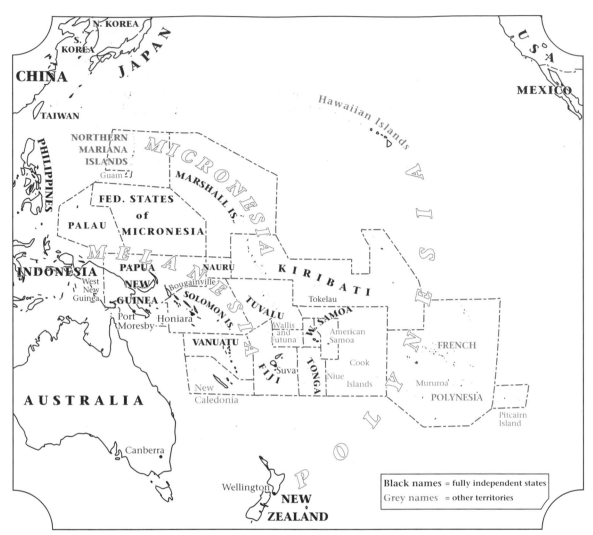

Figure 10.1 *The Pacific Islands*

Adapted from **Eccleston *et al.* (1998)**

Environmental awareness found, perhaps, a much more ready acceptance in the South Pacific than in many other parts of the world. It has become a very substantial part of the contemporary South Pacific's regional approach to foreign policy, ranging from initiatives to protect biodiversity by outlawing pelagic driftnetting to the declaration of a regional nuclear free zone. The emergence of a process of aggregating smaller regional groupings into a broader association ('macro-regionalism') in the Asia-Pacific area has added new challenges to managing the fragile economies of the Pacific Islands with their limited resource bases.

This chapter seeks to reinforce the themes of the search for 'unity in diversity' and the challenge of adaptation to a post-Cold War order in the contemporary Pacific Islands. The first theme will be addressed by identifying the limitations on the tiny states of the South Pacific in exercising sovereignty through the management of their external affairs (both foreign and security policy) and by relating these constraints to the development of regionalism as an appropriate response by the Islands to moderating these limitations. The second theme will emerge through an examination of the pressures for change in the region's external relations since the end of the Cold War. The chapter shows that the range of foreign policy options available to the Islands since the end of the Cold War has almost certainly contracted. Yet, paradoxically in the view of some, the South Pacific's regional system has become more necessary in these circumstances even while the external support on which it depends is jeopardized.

10.2   Diversity in unity?

To outsiders the phrase 'South Pacific' has tended to convey an image of homogeneity; of commonalities based on sun, sand, surf, reefs and coconuts. Such simplifications have always been misplaced, however. The countries and territories of the South Pacific (collectively, 'the Islands') are enormously varied in a number of important respects both natural and social. The physical features of the South Pacific Islands range from low-lying atolls with vast central lagoons such as those typical of Polynesia and Micronesia, through raised atolls with no lagoons such as Nauru and Niue and the volcanic islands of Samoa, to the continental islands with landforms stretching from beaches to glaciated mountains such as New Guinea. While most occur in archipelagoes, three – Guam, Nauru and Niue – are not grouped together either geographically or politically with other islands. Socially, the many thousands of islands in this region are grouped into three broad ethno-geographic areas – Melanesia, Micronesia and Polynesia – and into 22 political entities whose contemporary boundaries were drawn sometimes by tradition but more often by colonial chance (see Figure 10.1).

The pre-colonial diversity of the Pacific was complicated by imperialism, then further extended by decolonization. The Pacific Islands began to rejoin the community of nations from 1962 when the first South Pacific microstate, Western Samoa, reclaimed its sovereignty with the help of the United Nations Trusteeship Council (Herr, 1975). The 'winds of change' arrived in the Pacific somewhat late, due in part to international scepticism at the capacity of non-European microstates to meet the obligations of statehood, yet, ironically, three of the first five states to achieve independence did so with the direct help of the international community through the UN – Western Samoa (1962), Nauru (1968) and Papua New Guinea (1975). Tonga (1970), Fiji (1970), Tuvalu (1978), the Solomon Islands (1978), Kiribati (1979) and Vanuatu (1980) are the remaining countries to have secured full independence in the region. Of these, only Fiji and Papua New Guinea have populations of over half a million.

The Cook Islands was the second colony to grapple with the issue of a post-colonial future, but instead of following Western Samoa into full independence this small territory added a second wrinkle to the region's post-colonial political complexity. In 1965 the Cook Islands eschewed full independence, opting for 'self-government in free association' with New Zealand. This mechanism, a re-invention of the nineteenth-century concept of the 'protected state', involved full internal self-government while accepting external assistance with defence and foreign affairs. It proved to be an attractive mechanism for coping with smallness and was subsequently adopted by Niue (1974), the Federated States of Micronesia (1986), the Marshall Islands (1986) and Palau (1995), albeit with some variations in the agreed constraints on their external relations.

A third element of complexity added by the decolonization process arose from disputes over the validity of colonial boundaries. Generally these involved secessionist demands, but the first actually saw the amalgamation of an autonomous unit into a larger body. West New Guinea (Irian Jaya), a Melanesian territory of the Netherlands, was a full member of the emergent South Pacific regional community and appeared destined for independence until it was absorbed into Indonesia in 1962. Secession has been pursued unsuccessfully (thus far) in a number of areas but most notably and violently in Papua New Guinea and Vanuatu. Secessionist pressures were successful in dividing the Gilbert and Ellice Islands into the independent states of Tuvalu and Kiribati and in separating the Trust Territory of the Pacific Islands into three freely associated states – the Federated States of Micronesia, the Marshalls and Palau – and the Commonwealth of the Northern Marianas Islands.

A fourth post-colonial factor in the contemporary political diversity of the South Pacific has been the continuance of colonial relationships right up to the present day. More than a third of the Islands have some formal dependent relationship with an external power. France has three dependencies – French Polynesia, New Caledonia and Wallis and Futuna; the US also has three – American Samoa, the Commonwealth of the Northern Marianas Islands and Guam; Britain one – the Pitcairn Islands; and New Zealand one – Tokelau. In regional terms this not only complicates the relations between these entities and their independent or self-governing neighbours but also ensures the inclusion of at least one extra-regional power in South Pacific affairs. The relatively high ratio of dependencies to self-governing polities in the contemporary South Pacific is not entirely an accident. It reflects some broader tensions inherent in the South Pacific's decolonizing process since the end of the Second World War concerned with the ability of very small states to function within the international state system, particularly with regard to their defence and security.

10.3   The question of microstate sovereignty

For most of the modern state system's existence there had been a clear if somewhat crudely defined consensus that only those polities with reasonable resources and prospects of protecting their statehood from external threats could claim sovereignty. However, from the First World War the risks to the international community of weak states unable to exercise an adequate level of control over their own territory (internal sovereignty) became increasingly recognized. A new problem for the international community arose as decolonization progressed to liberate ever smaller states. At a certain point the enhanced stability of strong nation-states would be offset by the proliferation of small states unable to meet their external commitments (external sovereignty). The trick would be to know when this threshold was being approached so that 'non-viable' states were not admitted to the comity of nations. Many felt this line was breached when Western Samoa sought independence, but the momentum of decolonization more than carried the day. Even states with far less international capacity were able to secure independence over the next 30 years.

This is not to say that all concerns over the capacity of the small polities of the South Pacific to meet the traditional external obligations of sovereignty were overlooked. The late decolonization of this region and its mixed progress attest to these qualms. Nonetheless, the rivalries of the Cold War and the emergence of a 'third world' combined to work in favour of the international community's general support for decolonization, even if the resultant states could not satisfy all the customary expectations of adequate resources and power. Thus, the Cold War order produced a tacit change in the operation of the states system which relaxed the constraints on the emergence of microstates and temporarily created the appearance of a more formal, if artificial, international equality amongst states of different sizes. On the one hand, there was an implied obligation on the international community to provide for the security of the small states created under these circumstances and, on the other, little was done to make any credible provisions for their defence. In any event, overlooking the matter of the state's obligation to provide for its own security did not alter the South Pacific's geo-political realities.

In the South Pacific, national security capacities were, and are, constrained by three enduring features of the small-scale insularity which beset all the region's states except Fiji and Papua New Guinea. These are:

1   very substantial diseconomies of scale;

2   high levels of vulnerability;

3   the extreme asymmetry of external relations.

The small populations and dispersed geography of most countries in the region not only prevent the achievement of economies of scale, they actually impose diseconomies on these states in seeking to meet the normal claims of the citizens for goods and services. If these diseconomies are not absorbed by the South Pacific microstates, medical services, education, sanitation and the like cannot be provided at the levels that might be expected in larger developing states elsewhere. The same geographic and demographic factors make the South Pacific polities highly vulnerable to natural and man-made disasters. A single cyclone can wreak havoc on one or more national economies in the South Pacific, over-stretching their internal resilience to the extent that only external assistance enables the state to cope. For example, a 1993 cyclone caused an estimated US$130 million in damages to Western Samoa, one of the region's larger microstates, a loss that constituted approximately 150 per cent of the country's expected GDP for that year (see Keith-Reid, 1994). This level of vulnerability is not an inherent characteristic of larger states. Smallness is also a political fact of life for most countries of the region. All their extra-regional relationships are with states that are larger, more powerful and better resourced than they.

Important contextual factors add to the difficulties of these permanent geo-political realities for the individual microstates of the South Pacific. The region is relatively remote from other global centres and markets. Thus while the Caribbean microstates share with the South Pacific the three geo-political factors noted above, these are moderated for the Caribbean countries to some extent by their relative proximity to large population centres and markets in neighbouring North and South America. Only a few of the most westerly of the South Pacific's polities can claim a similar advantage. Moreover, most of the South Pacific suffers from relatively weak economies and poor natural resources. These economic circumstances have promoted a very high dependence on foreign aid and a consequent tendency for the public sector to dominate national economies, with government employment often supplying the bulk of salaried incomes.

While such constraints are naturally of concern to the South Pacific states affected, the disparities of power in such unequal relationships are matters of concern to extra-regional interests as well. Overt charges of 'neo-colonialism' have not enjoyed widespread popular currency in the South Pacific but sensitivities to the inappropriate use of power have never been too far from the surface on either side, but especially in the Islands (see Rokotuivuna *et al.*, 1973). Indeed, recognition of the inherent risks in dealing with the physical and political limitations of the Islands has promoted support for various solutions to meeting the legitimate expectations of sovereign states both within and outside the South Pacific. The two 'local' Western states, Australia and New Zealand (collectively 'the ANZACs'), have enjoyed a close and friendly post-colonial relationship with the Islands based on historical ties, proximity and their international status as middle powers. The two states have invested heavily in a range of mechanisms, both bilateral and multilateral, to secure their aims in the South Pacific without appearing to exploit the asymmetries of their power relationships with the Islands.

More remote external powers may have had more latitude in their strategies for dealing appropriately with these asymmetries of power, since sensitivities to the issue are necessarily less immediate. Some Western countries have been able to rely to some extent on the special relationship the two Australasian countries maintain with the Islands to assist them in managing their unequal relationships with the region. At times, this has involved using the two as intermediaries. Other large powers such as France and the United Kingdom have their own territories in the region and so act in accordance with long-established national interests. Most, but not all, the Western states involved with the South Pacific have maintained some connection with the South Pacific's multilateral system as a means of demonstrating their concern for the problems of asymmetrical power.

10.4   The South Pacific regional system

Although there has been a high degree of agreement between both South Pacific and extra-regional states on the need for multilateral arrangements within the South Pacific to moderate the limitations of microstate sovereignty, the rationale for this need has not been perceived in identical terms. Initially the colonial powers, especially Australia and New Zealand, saw South Pacific regionalism as an efficient administrative device for reconstruction in the Islands following the Second World War. The establishment of the South Pacific Commission (SPC) in 1947 was intended to support the Islands' colonial administrators in achieving economies of scale in various aspects of social and economic (but, importantly, not political) development. Nevertheless, the existence and experience of the SPC promoted a sense of regional identity amongst the Islands which, after independence, became a major factor in the domestic and foreign policies of these polities. The two separate strands of interests wove together to help establish one of the most effective regional systems in the world.

In the years since the establishment of the SPC, a regional system has emerged and diversified remarkably. Although heavily supported by external powers, the Islands are genuinely the architects of this regional network as, except for the SPC, all the current regional inter-governmental organizations were initiated by the Islands themselves. The process began with the creation of a general political association, the South Pacific Forum, which first met in 1971 to circumvent the ban on politics in the SPC. This was a (now annual) meeting of the regional prime ministers and included Australia and New Zealand as foundation members. Although not a formal inter-governmental organization (IGO) in its own right, the Forum has presided over the institutionalization of South Pacific regional co-operation through a number of functionally specialized agencies designed primarily to promote the economic development of the region's independent and self-governing countries.

The first of these was an economic agency with a broad remit founded in 1972 as the South Pacific Bureau for Economic Co-operation (SPEC), but renamed the South Pacific Forum Secretariat (ForSec) in 1988. Its primary role has been to collect and analyse economic data to assist its members' development, but ForSec also administers some aid projects and serves as the Forum's secretariat. The South Pacific Forum Fisheries Agency followed in 1979 to enable the region to win effective returns from its fisheries resources. The South Pacific Applied Geo-Science Commission (SOPAC) was formalized in 1984 to promote the development of the area's marine mineral resources. Despite a somewhat chequered progress, the South Pacific Regional Environment Programme (SPREP) emerged with an independent status in 1991 to research and assist in the management of the region's environmental policies and resources. A Tourism Council of the South Pacific (TCSP), which also had its IGO status confirmed in 1991, was set up to secure multilateral co-operation in the region's most important tertiary industry. In addition, the Islands have pursued regional co-operation at a high level and in important areas through other means such as a regional shipping consortium, the Pacific Forum Line (PFL), and a regional university, the University of the South Pacific (USP). The breadth and general success of these IGOs (including the SPC) has all but obviated the need for formal bilateral relations within the region.

For their own reasons, the non-Islands countries have found the South Pacific regional system equally if not more compelling. There are several indicators of the importance of regionalism to the non-Islands countries. Australia and/or New Zealand have been foundation members of all the region's inter-governmental organizations since the creation of the SPC, a circumstance which speaks volumes for their assessment of the value of these bodies for their relations with the Islands. Another significant indicator of this external interest is the willingness of non-Islands sources to bear the financial burdens of South Pacific regional co-operation: generally over 90 per cent of total expenditure by all the regional organizations. This is not to argue that the region does not pay for regional co-operation. In fact, the members of the various regional organizations do pay for most of their administrative and programme costs. Rather, it is that the overwhelming share of the support of these organizations is borne by the non-Islands members of these bodies – particularly by Australia and New Zealand.

The mutual support for regionalism from both within and outside the South Pacific raises a question as to whether these arrangements exist more to meet the external or internal demands of small state sovereignty. Virtually all the regional organizations claim a paramount responsibility for meeting the internal development needs of their membership. Generally the representational role of these bodies in promoting the external interests of their members is a second order objective if it exists at all. On the other hand, all the South Pacific's regional bodies include non-Islands countries as members. This could be seen as non-Islands' interference or involvement for the protection of outside interests, or it might be interpreted as a prudential effort by the Islands to co-opt support from non-Islands sources for Islands' objectives. Critics of Western interests tended to favour the former explanation, especially during the Cold War.

10.5 The South Pacific's Cold War order

While decolonization in the South Pacific emerged conterminously with the mature phase of the Cold War, this peripheral corner of the global stage appeared at first to have escaped the Cold War's core pressures. Following the Second World War the Islands were entirely under the control or influence of six Western powers, all of which were allied to at least some of the other members of the regional metropolitan powers through such treaties as ANZUS (Australia–New Zealand–United States Treaty), SEATO (Southeast Asia Treaty Organization), NATO (North Atlantic Treaty Organization) and the Five Power Defence Agreement. Western values were therefore fairly evenly distributed across the region. The heavy dependence of most of the Islands on Western foreign aid tended to re-enforce a coincidence of interests between the West and the Islands in the post-colonial period. In short, from the early 1960s to the mid-1970s there appeared to be more continuities than changes in the region's foreign policy and security outlooks.

The first major ripple to disturb the tranquil foreign policy waters of the South Pacific was the establishment of non-resident diplomatic relations between the Kingdom of Tonga and the Soviet Union in April 1976. The symbolic effect of this was probably much more significant than its substantive implications but the symbolism was enough for startled Western states. Despite limited direct evidence of Soviet interest in gaining a substantial foothold in the region, by the end of the 1970s there was a general consensus within the West that Soviet involvement in the South Pacific posed a potential threat that should be opposed. This gave rise to a regional variant of the West's general containment policy known as 'strategic denial' (see Herr, 1986).

Strategic denial embodied a complex of attitudes and policies which were sometimes interpreted differently by the various Western powers concerned as events developed from 1976 to the end of the Cold War in 1989. Broadly, however, this approach had four basic elements. The first was that Western interests were best served by preventing the Soviet Union from gaining direct access to a region from which it had been absent historically. The second held that a collective or regional approach would be the most effective means of discouraging aberrant relationships within an area which was essentially pro-Western in its foreign policy and security orientations. Third, a key mechanism for achieving these aims would be the use of financial assistance to obviate the need for the region to look beyond its traditional friends for help. Fourth, in keeping with the regionalist thrust of strategic denial, Australia and New Zealand were expected (and, indeed, expected themselves) to be the primary interpreters of Western security interests as the regional hegemons.

While the West was pursuing its policy of strategic denial, two important and related issues showed particular dynamism over these years. The first emerged from the global marine enclosure movement incorporated in the United Nations Third Conference on the Law of the Sea (UNCLOS III) in the decade from 1973 through 1982. This general redrafting of marine legal rights greatly extended the jurisdiction over, and thus the potential financial benefits from, marine resources for the Islands which generally enjoyed relatively few land-based natural resources. The 200 nautical miles zones were not an unalloyed benefit for the Islands, however, since the rights to oceanic usufruct had to be purchased by accepting the responsibilities of defending these rights and this demanded a capacity for control at sea that the regional microstates did not have.

In the years from 1978, when extended maritime zones became the norm across the region, the Islands found themselves at the centre of a series of controversies over their rights to exploit the resources of these new zones. The key resource at issue was the vast stocks of highly migratory species of tuna which range widely across the South Pacific, especially in the western half of the region. United States fishing interests moved into the western Pacific in pursuit of these resources. Disputes between the Islands and the USA were to have quite significant foreign policy and security consequences. Less physically threatening than direct challenges to the Islands' jurisdiction over maritime resources, but perhaps no less vital to the economic security of the Islands, was the ensuring of the best financial returns from their new maritime zones. Given the limited capital and expertise to develop these resources themselves, the primary benefit expected initially was through the collection of fees for access to the 200 nautical miles zones. The collective strength to deal with established and powerful distant water fishing nations (DWFNs) over appropriate access terms and conditions (including fee levels) was achieved through the establishment of the South Pacific Forum Fisheries Agency in 1979.

The second significant development in the region's foreign policy environment in the years from 1976 through 1989 concerned a growth in Cold War rivalries intruding into the region, a process intensified by the marine resources issue. Overt Soviet interest in the South Pacific acquired a new intensity, reflected in the *cause célèbre* of Soviet interests in the South Pacific in the later years of the Cold War – the 1985 Kiribati–USSR fishing agreement. This agreement was the culmination to a series of disputes with the United States over coastal state jurisdiction over highly migratory tuna. Annoyance with the US tunaboat owners over access terms and conditions to the Kiribati zone led the government of President Ieremiah Tabai to dust off a circular letter from Moscow offering a fisheries agreement. Despite substantial Western disquiet and rather less but nonetheless real local worries, an arrangement was reached for one year's access. The USSR refused to renew the agreement claiming the initial fees proved too high for the return to Soviet fishermen, but a year later concluded an access agreement with Vanuatu on financial terms similar to those rejected in the failed renewal with Kiribati. Although the Vanuatu agreement included port access (which the Kiribati agreement did not and was, to that extent, more controversial in the West), it too was not renewed after its expiry at the end of the one-year contract. The end of the Cold War interdicted further controversies of a similar nature before they could develop.

10.6 The South Pacific in the post-Cold War international system

The collapse of the Cold War was not entirely an accident although one could scarcely claim it was by design. 'Peristroika', Mikhail Gorbachev's plan for restructuring the Soviet Union, had included a full engagement with global economic and political processes. Nevertheless, his plans for breaking out from more than 40 years of Western containment on terms that the West could accept was scarcely the blueprint for what has emerged as the post-Cold War order. Indeed, there are grounds for believing that the descriptor 'post-Cold War order' focuses undue attention on the short-term dismantling of the superpower rivalries of the Cold War. Patently the Cold War era was not completely static. There were changes in train which would have profoundly influenced global affairs even if the Cold War had continued. These included progress toward the European Union, the emergence of Japan as a claimant to great power status, the growing coherence of the Asia-Pacific as an economic region and the emergence of environmentalism and human rights as important items on the world agenda.

Yet, whatever influence such other developments might have had, the ending of East–West rivalry has defined the core elements of change for international order into the twenty-first century. Indeed, at least four of the five major aspects of the post-Cold War order can be attributed directly to the collapse of the Cold War (see Herr and McDougall, 1993; Herr, 1994). The five key features which characterize the post-Cold War order are:

1   a reassertion of pragmatic national interest as the basis of foreign policy with the end of ideological rivalry;

2   more hierarchically structured international politics with an effective Security Council serving as an arena for a globally co-ordinated concert of powers;

3   increasing multipolarity to replace the bipolarity of the Cold War;

4   the re-emergence of economic advantage as the primary measure of, and motivation for, national interest;

5   the dismantling of Cold War structures such as the Warsaw Pact.

Contrary to the more idealistic hopes of many, the transition to a new international order has not proved peaceful or easy. In some important respects the birth pangs of the new order have been as (if not more) violent as many passages of the old Cold War order. These problems have been most evident in areas closer to the core of Cold War rivalries than in the periphery, but this is not to say that ripples from the new order have not yet lapped the distant shores of the South Pacific. Far from it.

The South Pacific's problems of asymmetrical external relations and diseconomies of scale in coping with the internal burdens of sovereignty have been exacerbated by the ending of the Cold War. Post-Cold War changes in the organization of global politics as well as other changes which have occurred independently with the efflux of time are intensifying some of the pressures on the Islands. Symbolic ideological gains during the Cold War were never fully related to strategic or economic value to the rival camps. Indeed, in the later years of this struggle, incremental ideological success appeared to impose ever higher economic/aid costs on the two superpowers as ever smaller entities were drawn into their rivalry. This was a politically (and prudentially) dangerous game, but it did give the objects of the Cold War rivalry, such as the Islands, disproportionate influence at some level for some period of time. Today, more pragmatic, hard-headed considerations influence the positions of the great powers in regard to their relations with smaller powers.

Post-Cold War economic rationalism has already wrought important changes to external interests in the region and, consequently, to the foreign policy options available to the Islands. The Soviet Union only just secured its long-desired resident representation in the South Pacific in time for a successor state, Russia, to close the mission in Port Moresby, Papua New Guinea, as an economy measure. The American embassy in Honiara, the Solomon Islands, has shut its doors and Washington's aid mission in Suva, Fiji, returned home for the same reason. The United Kingdom also made an economic assessment of its post-Cold War interests in the South Pacific when it decided to withdraw from the SPC, the one regional organization in the South Pacific of which it was a member by right. France has found its interests shifting between its desire to preserve a global position and a need to safeguard its substantial regional interests. The first motivation prompted the Gaullist President, Jacques Chirac, to resume nuclear weapons testing at Mururoa, while the second was responsible for the

Demonstration against French nuclear testing: Papeete, Tahiti, 1995

decision to end it permanently in 1996. China, alone of the great powers, does not appear to have reacted to the changing global environment, perhaps because its level of involvement in the South Pacific has been modest for over 20 years.

Relations between the ANZACs and the Islands

The passing of the Cold War has affected the interests of the two regional middle powers as well. Gordon Bilney, Australia's then Minister for Pacific Islands Affairs and Development Co-operation, gave a clear indication of how far his government's reappraisal of its post-Cold War priorities had shifted in the region at an address to the Foreign Correspondents' Association in June 1994 (Bilney, 1994). In a watershed speech, Bilney detailed how the end of the Cold War had changed Australia's external interests in the South Pacific including its extra-regional perceptions. His expectations that the region should take greater responsibility for its own welfare and well-being would be pursued formally by the Australian Labor Party Government at the Brisbane South Pacific Forum (1994) and the Madang Forum (1995) and carried over by the new Liberal-National Party Coalition Government to the Majuro Forum (1996). New Zealand's attitudes tended to parallel those of Australia in terms of the accommo-dation of post-Cold War trends, although New Zealand appears to have maintained a higher overall priority for the Islands, perhaps because it has fewer other external priorities to juggle with.

The Australian and New Zealand post-Cold War re-evaluation of their South Pacific interests has been informed both by their need to meet the global emphasis on economic rationalism and the realities of their geography. The former factor has increased pressure on the ANZACs to reduce their involvement in the South Pacific (given the relative unim-portance of the Islands' resources to the global economy), while the latter compels the two not to disengage too fully from this region despite new priorities. Charting a sensible passage between economic self-interest and wider strategic interests has been a demanding exercise. Since this process is still in train, it is not possible to pronounce definitively on the final balancing of interests, but present indications are that the Islands have lost substantial ground in their capacities to influence Canberra and Wellington.

Undoubtedly there is a new emphasis on economic responsibility in relations between the ANZACs and the Islands, with the role of aid in the Islands being a central issue. Bilney pointed out in his 1994 address, for example, that the World Bank's 1993 Economic Report on the region estimated average growth rates of the Islands countries at about 0.1 per cent over the previous decade, which compared very unfavourably with the rates of developing island states in the Indian Ocean and the Caribbean (Bilney, 1994). The Islands were on notice, in effect, that the management of aid had to meet certain performance standards if previous levels of support were to be maintained. Related to the implication of mismanagement of aid by the Islands has been an increasingly overt suspicion that corruption is part of the explanation. Fears that corruption might be a significant problem in some parts of the South Pacific have been held for over a decade, but these rarely surfaced in the Cold War era. Today they are an open issue in the media, in part because fear of the political consequences for their relations with the Islands no longer constrains ANZAC authorities (see, for example, North, 1996; Keith-Reid, 1996).

A second theme to emerge from the post-Cold War emphasis on economic responsibility has been a concern for the environment. Ostensibly, this theme is being driven by the global commitment to the environmental value of 'sustainable development'. Both Australia and New Zealand have been anxious that the new demands for economic self-reliance should not force the Islands into short-sighted environmental vandalism at home to meet political pressures for growth. However, critics see another motive in these concerns. Issues surrounding investments in forestry, fisheries and tourism have seemed to focus more on new waves of Asian investment than on the older European (especially ANZAC) invest-ments. Thus, the criticism of some aspects of the Islands' development strategies from Canberra and Wellington have been interpreted as a resistance to the emergence of closer ties with Asia in the post-Cold War order. The two ANZAC powers deny this counter charge through the evidence they have presented at the three Forum meetings detailing the unsustainable rates of resource exploitation, especially in forestry. Given the significant investment made by the Islands over the years in environ-mental protection (for example, the establishment of the South Pacific Regional Environment Programme, the Wellington Convention proscribing the use of long pelagic driftnets, and the South Pacific Nuclear Free Zone Treaty), this issue is probably a trilateral matter between Australia, the individual Islands countries concerned and the specific Asian source countries of the questionable investments. Nevertheless, the use of the regional arenas by Australia in particular seems to be part of an attempt to broaden the impact of warnings on economic responsibility as well as to preserve a somewhat privileged position in the Islands.

10.7   External effects on the Islands' security and foreign policy

Overall, the post-Cold War order appears to be working towards limiting the capacity of the Islands to influence their foreign policy and security environments. Some of the recent marginalization of the Islands would have occurred in any case, of course. The interest of former metropoles in assisting with an orderly and fair transition to independence would have reached a more mature phase of relationships at about the present period regardless of the state of the Cold War. Thus aid based on some notion of distributive justice to compensate for the experience of colonization would have declined at some point. Indeed, if anything, it seems likely that Cold

War rivalries extended the period of Western support longer than it might have been maintained otherwise. Thus, the collapse of the Cold War appears to the region to have had a more dramatic impact on the decline of aid levels than it really has had.

In other areas the post-Cold War order is more evidently and directly undermining the autonomy of the Islands, at least for the present. For example, the post-Cold War order's emphasis on economic regionalism might appear to make an asset of the South Pacific's robust regional system. Yet there are reasons to doubt it will have this effect. Neither collectively nor individually do the Islands control significant global resources. The region's collective resources are essentially the marine environment and its wealth and, while in the case of tuna these are of global scale, they are not the basis of a strategic cartel. Other resources with global or extra-regional significance tend to be located in individual countries: Papua New Guinea's gold and copper, New Caledonia's nickel and Nauru's now depleted store of phosphate. In brief, the region's constituent members are too small in area and their populations too dispersed across the world's largest ocean to create an effective regional market internally or to establish a powerful export cartel.

Nevertheless, the region may well be forced to maintain its regional structures (albeit less lavishly) by the sheer necessity to cope with a more competitive extra-regional environment. Increasing interest by all the South Pacific's extra-regional partners in the Asia-Pacific macro-region is tending to make the South Pacific organizations more of a necessity than an optional extra in their foreign policy armoury. This is particularly evident in the two major associations – the Asia-Pacific Economic Co-operation forum (APEC) and the non-governmental Pacific Economic Co-operation Conference (PECC). The small size of the South Pacific states has worked to deny each Islands country separate membership in these bodies, so involvement in these arenas is largely limited to the membership of Papua New Guinea and such regional organizations as the South Pacific Forum and The South Pacific Forum Fisheries Agency. Given the very limited likelihood that many more South Pacific states will achieve membership in Asia-Pacific fora, it is clear that South Pacific regional organizations rather than national authorities will almost certainly have to bear the representational burden if the South Pacific is to enjoy any influence in these increasingly significant Asia-Pacific processes.

One of the more important factors for the South Pacific in these emergent macro-regional arrangements is the jockeying for influence as the Asia-Pacific hegemon. Japan is seen, and sees itself, as the logical candidate for this status, although the claims of others still have currency. That of the United States will continue to depend in large measure on the outcome of the debate on the geographic scope of this macro-region, while China's claim may be pressed more vigorously in future years as its economic and political influence gathers strength although the Chinese claim is complicated by the Taiwan issue. (This is a dilemma, since Taiwan enjoys important official recognition in some quarters of the South Pacific which could work against the rest of the region if China secures a hegemonic influence within APEC.) Despite its own economic woes, Japan is perhaps the only major power with the political will to pursue the hegemonic role. And if the leadership mantle for the Asia-Pacific macro-region falls clearly to Japan, then management of the political relationship with Japan will continue to assume greater significance for all countries in the South Pacific.

The South Pacific is being affected by Japan's looming emergence as a macro-regional hegemon in two important and related ways. Historically, Tokyo has preferred to maintain its presence in the South Pacific through bilateral mechanisms which, intentionally or unintentionally, tended to accentuate the asymmetries of power between Japan and the Islands. Japanese resistance to recent attempts by some South Pacific states to secure a *de jure* involvement in South Pacific regionalism for Japan through membership of the SPC has tended to reinforce an impression of a preference for maintaining its asymmetrical relations. Nevertheless, Japan has shown some real enthusiasm for joining the The South Pacific Forum Fisheries Agency. In this case, support for regionalism is the other side of the same coin rather than a contradiction. Japan's motive is seen by the South Pacific very much as national self-interest. The FFA has been perhaps the most successful of all the South Pacific's associations in preserving regional control over its area of responsibility. Japanese membership of the FFA thus is interpreted by its members as an attempt to convert it into a broader association which would diminish regional control over fisheries management policy. Consequently, as a leading influence in the increasingly important Asia-Pacific processes, Japan is both more desired and more feared as a participant in the South Pacific region in ways which would not be true of other possible claimants.

10.8   New challenges: the domestic dimension

An important aspect of microstate sovereignty in the post-Cold War order which appears to be constraining the Islands is their capacity to meet changing international obligations as states. The baggage of their own history is an inescapable burden for the microstates of the South Pacific just as it is for any state. Ironically, in the case of the South Pacific, the influence of history may prove a problem for having been too supportive. The relatively benign passage that most of the region had through decolonization has meant that many of the traumas experienced by states elsewhere with this transition were moderated in the South Pacific. Post-colonial aid levels from the former metropoles tended to be relatively high, while the broader political relationships were generally relaxed. Moreover, traditional distinctions between sovereign and non-sovereign polities within the region have been blurred. This has been particularly evident in the general degree of equality amongst independent, self-governing and dependent polities in many of the regional organizations. As a consequence, the need to confront the vicissitudes of statehood directly did not, perhaps, fall as heavily on these microstates as on small states in other parts of the world.

The fact that the post-Cold War international system appears less forgiving of lapses by states (of any size) in meeting the obligations of sovereignty has cast new light on some recent events in the South Pacific. One concerns the crisis of legitimacy which some allege is besetting South Pacific states. This arises from a perception that Western constitutions were forced inappropriately on non-Western societies and therefore do not enjoy substantial legitimacy amongst the populations. As a result, the post-colonial problems that a number of South Pacific states have encountered recently – coups, attempted coups, secessions, attempted secessions and economic failures – could be attributed to the legacy of colonialism rather than to the failings of these states themselves. Whatever the historical validity of the argument, the new international order is exacting costs. Economic aid and investment are being more directly tied to internal stability, economic 'responsibility', human rights and the like than ever before. Thus, the international community is not only demanding that states accept more responsibility for their own affairs but is also defining more completely the international norms which define such 'responsibility'. And historical events do not appear to be acceptable excuses for failing to meet these norms.

Whether grounded in a genuine crisis of legitimacy or not, the past decade has witnessed a number of important challenges to the effectiveness of South Pacific states to meet the internal requirements of sovereignty. Two particular events have dominated external perceptions: the 1987 military coup which overthrew a democratically elected government in Fiji and the long-running secessionist war on Bougainville in Papua New Guinea. The former ultimately resulted in a new constitution which has been widely regarded as racially biased and the latter brought down a national government in March 1997 that sought to use foreign mercenaries against its own population. Less spectacular, but no less important for the states concerned, has been a series of other perceived shortcomings by the South Pacific states in meeting their domestic responsibilities. These have ranged from imprudent use of aid monies, through substantial financial irregularities and other forms of official corruption, to failure to provide effectively for domestic order.

While aspects of this 'crisis of legitimacy' are undoubtedly real, it is likely that in some quarters the problem has been made to look worse than is warranted. The 'rose-tinted glasses' approach of some early appraisals of South Pacific politics may have helped to exaggerate apparent difficulties by making the recent problems of internal stability appear unusually aberrant. Certainly, interpretations of the South Pacific as an 'Eden' or a 'paradise on earth' encouraged the more naive to believe it did not have the same weaknesses as other developing areas and thus worked to intensify disappointment at some recent events. Misguided efforts to make the region appear 'special' by comparison with developing areas in other corners of the globe have now backfired by increasing external impressions that South Pacific states are unusually unstable because they are experiencing some of the same difficulties that states elsewhere have encountered.

Not unrelated to concerns over the internal competence of South Pacific states has been the heightened perception of threats to sovereignty from non-state actors. Arguably this change can be explained primarily by the receding of state-based threats to the South Pacific in the wake of the collapse of the Cold War. Earlier threat assessments tended to play down the existence of non-state threats simply by refusing to acknowledge them as the equivalent of state threats. Post-Cold War concern for the capacity of states to meet their obligations as states; emphasis on the economic viability of states; and sensitivity to the consequences for states of drug trafficking, money laundering and organized crime have combined to give credibility to the issue of non-state threats. It is debatable whether current international fears are fully justified in this area, but the perception that non-state actors pose real threats in the South Pacific has generated a need to respond. Since the core of this issue lies in the expectations of other states, the problem of international crime has to be managed in ways which are acceptable to these third parties. Such factors have worked to make the treatment of international crime a substantial and regular issue for the South Pacific Forum since 1991.

Finally, it is not just the political climate which is changing. Environmental concerns loom large on the region's horizons. Population pressures are severe in some of the smaller atoll states of the region, especially those such as Kiribati and Tuvalu without guaranteed rights of entry to their former metropoles. Problems with securing fresh, clean water and safely disposing of wastes (of all sorts) have been severely intensified by population growth. In turn, meeting these human needs has raised new environmental problems by placing unsustainable demands on the water resources of small islands and threatening the ecology of lagoons upon which subsistence livelihoods depend. Protecting biodiversity, maintaining sustainable development and the like are often regarded as internal problems for the region to be managed by the states concerned and their regional agencies, particularly the South Pacific Regional Environment Programme. However, not all the South Pacific's environmental threats arise from activities within the region. Global warming and the possibility of substantial sea level rise cannot be solved by the region but, if worst case scenarios prove correct, low-lying states in this area may well pay the highest relative price for the atmospheric pollution of other states – their very existence. Determining the possible extent of this problem and developing appropriate adaptive strategies for coping with climatic change have been significant issues for the South Pacific for about a decade.

10.9   Conclusion

The focus of this brief survey has been the challenges and opportunities the emerging post-Cold War order poses for the small states of the South Pacific. On balance, it appears that the challenges are more substantial and menacing than the likely pay-offs in the form of opportunities. The South Pacific was never a central player in Cold War politics but its emergence as an area of microstates coincided with a period when Cold War priorities temporarily gave the region heightened salience. The new post-Cold War priorities are, however, re-establishing patterns of asymmetrical relationships found in other parts of the world in previous eras. Such patterns may not be as supportive in important ways of South Pacific microstates as the external relations of the first few decades of their independence. These changes are compelling the South Pacific states to adjust their foreign affairs and defence policies to a less congenial environment.

The nature of the issues facing the Islands on the threshold of the twenty-first century is encapsulated in the question of South Pacific regional co-operation. South Pacific regionalism has had a chequered career, but has enjoyed substantial support amongst the Islands, the regional middle powers and their extra-regional supporters, as a significant and mutually acceptable mechanism for moderating the unavoidable asymmetries of power. However, regional structures were tied to the concurrence of interests of all parties involved. Since the end of the Cold War maintenance of sufficient commonality of interests has proved something of a problem. Western supporters no longer perceive the same returns from their substantial financial investment in regional agencies, while new Asian actors have yet to discern significant benefits to them in filling the void left by the Western states. For their part, the Islands do not have the resources to maintain the present system without outside assistance, yet the need for some collective means for engaging with their external environment has increased. This need is driven by a variety of state, non-state and environmental risks that are more real than the Cold War threats to the extent that they seem unlikely to challenge the extra-regional powers that might once have kept them in check.

The demands of microstate sovereignty in the post-Cold War order are great, but the challenges are not insurmountable. The reality is that the countries of the South Pacific will continue to want to influence their own destinies as fully as they can. They will continue to want to offer their citizens as many opportunities for prosperity as possible, and they will therefore attempt to be as effective as states as they can manage. And the history of the region over the past 30 years demonstrates that the Islands can overcome obstacles which have often appeared almost impassable.

References

Bilney, G. (1994) 'Australia's relations with the South Pacific: challenge and change', address to Foreign Correspondents' Association, Sydney, 15 June.

Eccleston, B., Dawson, M. and McNamara, D. (1998) *The Asia-Pacific Profile*, **London, Routledge in association with The Open University.**

Herr, R.A. (1975) 'A minor ornament: the diplomatic decisions of Western Samoa at independence', *Australian Outlook*, December, pp. 300–14.

Herr, R.A. (1986) 'Regionalism, strategic denial and South Pacific security', *Journal of Pacific History*, vol.XXI, pp.170–82.

Herr, R.A. (1994) 'Regionalism and nationalism' in Howe, K.R., Kiste, R.C. and Lal, B.V. (eds) *Tides of History: The Pacific Islands in the Twentieth Century*, Sydney, Allen and Unwin.

Herr, R.A. and McDougall, D.J. (1993) 'The South Pacific: retreat from Vladivostock' in Thahur, R. and Thahur, C.A. (eds) *Reshaping Regional Relations: Asia-Pacific and the Former Soviet Union*, Boulder, Westview Press.

Keith-Reid, R. (1994) 'South Pacific' in *Asia Yearbook 1994*, Hong Kong, Far Eastern Economic Review.

Keith-Reid, R. (1996) 'Don't mess with Mrs Clean Up', *Islands Business*, September, pp.16–18.

North, D. (1996) 'Wave of financial "scams" strikes Island countries', *Pacific Islands Monthly*, September, pp.23–5.

Rokotuivuna, A. *et al.* (1973) *Fiji: A Developing Australian Colony?*, North Fitzroy, Victoria, International Development Action.

Further reading

Baker, R.W. (ed.) (1994) *The ANZUS States and Their Region: Regional Policies of Australia, New Zealand and the United States*, Westport, Conn., Praeger.

Hennington, S. (1995) *The Pacific Island States: Security and Sovereignty in the Post-Cold War World*, Basingstoke, MacMillan.

Hoadley, S. (1992) *The South Pacific Foreign Affairs Handbook*, North Sydney, Allen and Unwin.

Howe, K.R., Kiste, R.C., and Lal, B.V. (eds) (1994) *Tides of History: The Pacific Islands in the Twentieth Century*, Sydney, Allen and Unwin.

Lal, B.V. (1992) *Broken Waves: A History of the Fiji Islands in the Twentieth Century*, Honolulu, University of Hawaii Press.

PART 3

A Pacific Community?

CHAPTER 11

Regionalism and globalism

Christopher Brook

11.1   Asia-Pacific integration in a wider setting

That the Asia-Pacific region has become a key arena for economic and diplomatic activity is not in doubt; what is less clear and more debated is the evolving character and geography of these linkages and political collaborations which cross the region and connect it to the wider world. The dramatic economic growth of many Asian states bordering the Pacific has brought increased pressure on local, national and global interests to manage such growth to their advantage. At a security level the end of the Cold War has led to changing relations among Asia-Pacific states as growing power centres like Japan and China attempt to extend regional and global influence and as the military and diplomatic presence of the USA becomes more dispersed. On environmental matters there is a growing awareness of the need to monitor uses and abuses of the Pacific Ocean and to establish fishing and mineral rights at a time of increasing pressure on resources. On all these fronts there is pressure to respond politically to co-ordinate state and other interests in the continual jockeying for position and influence on the regional and world stages.

The main thrust of this chapter is to pull together ideas and debates about the future direction of political arrangements in the region, set within a wider world context. Two images of future world order will be considered, but it should be clear that what is happening does not conform exactly to any one image and that evidence is often conflicting. The Asia-Pacific region is marked by massive inequalities and by a great richness of local cultures and histories. This diversity and its legacy is also reflected in the complex relations between Asia-Pacific communities and between those communities and other local groups across the world. The increasing globalization of affairs brings pressures to extend political relations to manage these forces and support local and national interests. But what is the dominant character of these wider relations?

11.2   Two images of emerging world order

Across the world there is increasing pressure to respond politically to manage the forces of globalization. While nation-states remain key actors in wider governance we are now seeing the development of other forms of political arrangement, producing new ideas of how the world will be ordered and managed in the next millennium. This chapter will focus on two images which have attracted considerable attention and examine whether and how Asia-Pacific development fits these representations.

One image is of regional and global pressures inducing development of powerful regional blocs. Under this image there are strong *regionalization* forces at work, drawing states and groups together on the basis of their proximity both because of transport and information cost advantages and because of shared regional interests and ties. In turn this brings pressure for a level of institutional integration (or *regionalism*) to reflect and manage this regionalization (see Ravenhill in Chapter 12). The development of first the European Union and then the North American Free Trade Agreement (NAFTA) as major economic groupings has brought visions of a world dominated by three 'global regions': the Asia-Pacific, North America and Europe. Various general arguments are used to rationalize such a trend. A regional grouping is often seen to provide more counter-leverage than single states when negotiating with international capital. It is seen as increasing the viability of small states by enhancing their political and market status. It is viewed rightly or wrongly as providing a greater measure of territorial security against outside threat, military or otherwise. It is also argued that a large regional market with progressive liberalization of trade within its borders will expose local businesses to more intense competition, allow them to increase efficiency and perhaps size and thus equip them better to compete in the global market place. *Regionalism is seen then as providing a measure of security against the vagaries of the global economy and a strong base from which to compete within it.*

Regionalism can vary in its character and it is dangerous to assume that what has happened in Europe presents some kind of model for regionalism elsewhere. It is not possible to build a kind of 'regional bloc transition model' with different regional groupings at different stages in a broadly similar trend. There may be common features but each development is a product of a particular combination of local and regional circumstances set within a wider world context. The European Union was established (in 1957 as the EEC) as much for political and security reasons as to energize economic development. A key aim underlying the creation of an economic community was the wish to rebuild relations after the devastation of the Second World War and a key influence was US concern to strengthen western Europe against the perceived threat of the Soviet Union. NAFTA was established in 1993 under a different set of regional circumstances. It was designed as a 'free trade area' rather than a political unit in its own right (as with the EU) though like the EU there is trade discrimination against non-members. Unlike the EU, NAFTA is dominated by the interests of one state, the USA, which has produced a different kind of arrangement and pattern of winners and losers. The reasons underlying the grouping's establishment were again both economic and political. It was seen by US interests as developing a trading counterweight to other core economic powers centred on Europe and Japan and in cementing relations in the 'USA's backyard'. For Canada and Mexico the NAFTA formalized their strong trade links with the USA and provided a 'safe-haven arrangement' in the event of a collapse in multilateral trade and a rise in US protectionism.

So how does the Asia-Pacific fit within this vision of growing regional integration and regionalism? What kind of integration is developing in the Asia-Pacific and to what extent is there support for the argument that the world is being carved up into three powerful regional blocs? Indeed, what scope for regionalism is there in a world that is becoming more interconnected and interdependent? Such questions will be considered in Section 11.3.

A second image sees the emergence of a more *global* politics where states are increasingly required to stretch and share governance with other groups across the world in order to maintain some say over how things develop. It is argued that while states remain important actors in developing a political response to globalizing forces they are increasingly being drawn into what are very fluid and messy arrangements to confront the realities of a world that is shrinking economically and in terms of cultural and environmental impact. Not only has there been a rapid rise in forces which appear outside the control of single states, but also many of these forces appear to cross territorial boundaries with relative freedom. Flows of information and investment can often escape conventional political divisions as states become sites of flows rather than organizers and controllers of flows. In such a world there may be less scope for managing change simply through inter-governmental action or by carving the world into large regional blocs.

These complex political arrangements (or 'international regimes') are sometimes viewed as an early stage in the development of a more global governance. They come in all shapes and sizes, and may include international non-governmental organizations, sub-national groups and various transnational pressure groups as well as intergovernmental arrangements. Many of these arrangements have developed around international organizations while others have come into being through international conference resolutions and specific treaties and are sustained through follow-up meetings and more detailed proposals.

In subsequent chapters discussion of the future direction of governance in the Asia-Pacific includes many references, direct or implied, to these two images, regional and global. Here we want you to give some initial thought to such ideas. In each case we want you to consider the evidence and develop your own thoughts on which image fits best the developments in the Asia-Pacific. Also you need to think whether the two images are necessarily mutually exclusive. Must regionalization always undermines globalization? Could regionalization merely be a stepping-stone to a more globalized world?

11.3   What evidence of Asia-Pacific regional integration?

Most commentators remain cautious on the level of Asia-Pacific regional integration possible or even sought, a view reflected in previous chapters. Various factors underlie such a view. The rapid growth of East Asian economies has been predicated on open access to the markets of Europe as well as North America. In addition the region's rapid industrialization is not matched by local energy supplies where there is comparative insufficiency; regional bloc development would run the risk of increased global division and therefore increased insecurity of external supply.

Another factor is the great diversity of communities found in the Asia-Pacific. Diversity can of course be found almost anywhere but it can be argued that these countries have much less common history than those in Europe say. In East Asia communities are often more aware of the cultures and languages of colonizing societies in the West than of their neighbours (e.g. see Ignoguchi, 1995). As Mak notes (see Chapter 5), in the aftermath of the Cold War there has been some surfacing of local rivalries fuelled by the increasingly competitive environment and a massive arms build-up, though by and large these have been kept in check by the general level of dynamism and economic development across the region. Attempts to increase regional co-operation and integration could bring these differences and rivalries into much sharper relief.

So what kind of regional integration, if any, is developing in the Asia-Pacific? A commonly held view, and one stressed by Buzan in Chapter 4, is that the Asia-Pacific is developing a level of informal integration without being shaped by regional institutions which discriminate against or exclude outside interests (see, for example, Garnaut and Drysdale, 1994). Such 'open integration' is seen as primarily market driven rather than political though it depends also on inter-governmental and other initiatives to set conditions conducive to trade liberalization. One might contrast this with the economic integration between members of the European Union which has been supported by a level of institutional integration, both as a common market and with significant harmonization of national economic policies.

One economic region or many?

Although most economic co-operation within the Asia-Pacific region has been supportive of a market driven integration, the membership and character of these arrangements can vary. In consequence they are likely to shape and support slightly different patterns of integration. In the case of the Asia-Pacific Economic Co-operation (APEC), membership is clearly regional and in that sense supportive of an Asia-Pacific identity. But other arrangements have a membership and focus which are not region-wide. Reference has been made to the impact of NAFTA in extending economic integration across North America, while in Central and South America economic organizations like the Caribbean Common Market and Latin American Integration Association supported by a series of US bilateral trade arrangements have brought visions of a pan-Americas trade focus. On the Asian side of the Pacific an East Asian Economic Caucus (EAEC) was proposed in 1991 linking the Association of South-East Asian Nations (ASEAN) states with China, Japan and South Korea. The proposal was partly in response to fears of greater protectionism from NAFTA and the EU but also had the intention of slowing 'the flow of local Chinese capital back to the mainland by integrating China into a network of economic co-operation' (Hook, 1996, p.194). In 1993 ASEAN heads of state agreed to introduce an ASEAN Free Trade Area in all manufactured and processed agricultural products by 2008 to promote trade between member states and increase competitiveness. To the south east Australia and New Zealand are also linked through a free trade agreement and there have been proposals to extend the 1983 Closer Economic Relations agreement to produce a single market in goods and services with common commodity taxation and a common external tariff.

Nor does integration apply only to groupings of whole states. Regional integration can also develop on a transnational basis to link sub-national as well as national economies. One interesting example is the economic integration linking Hong Kong and Taiwan with the southern provinces of China, particularly Guangdong and increasingly Fujian. The stimulus of a vast developing market in China together with the advantages of geographical proximity and strong cultural links between Chinese business groups has brought an increasing level of market integration across these

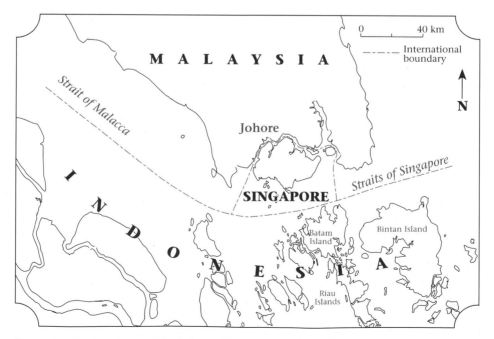

Figure 11.1 *The Singapore–Johore–Riau growth triangle*

territories. A complex network of transnational flows has built up despite there being no formal diplomatic links between China and Taiwan, and despite strict border controls on movements of labour between China and Hong Kong prior to its handover in 1997. A further example where market integration appears to be developing across state borders is in the area linking Singapore with Batam Island in Indonesia and the Johore province of Malaysia (see Figure 11.1). Here the level of integration is evidenced by the fact that Singapore Technologies Industrial Corporation built the Batam Industrial Park. But it is an uneven integration. While the city state of Singapore is keen to build up its global financial and industrial management roles, much of the labour-intensive work within this sub-region is being passed to lower wage locations in nearby provinces of Indonesia and Malaysia.

What of regional defence and security arrangements?

Enmeshed with these uneven regional economic networks is an under-developed defence and security system finding it difficult to shrug off its Cold War legacy. While there has been growing interest in a more collective security system there are uncertainties and tensions over the future role of the USA and its bilateral system of regional security. The most significant recent initiative was the establishment of the ASEAN Regional Forum (ARF), which includes a more global membership including the USA, Russia and the EU. At first sight it seems strange to see a collection of small and medium sized ASEAN powers exercising such a key role in a region containing Japan and the PRC, and over which the USA continues to maintain military security. However, as Buzan (Chapter 4) points out, Japan's leadership role remains in doubt because of the events and legacy of the Second World War; there is also continuing mistrust between the major powers particularly of Chinese ambition.

Across the region views differ on how best to manage future security. A major concern for the US government is to rework its bilateral security arrangements with key East Asian states to reflect post-Cold War realities. For example, some US strategists argue that Japan should now take greater responsibility for conventional defence of its home territories and key sea routes while the USA remains responsible for nuclear defence. There is also US support for multilateral security if the USA is allowed to play an active role in its development, but there is concern that instabilities may be introduced by any unravelling of bilateral relations. Many East Asian states would rather see a multilateral architecture developed that is not US led. The success of the ARF in securing PRC participation has brought optimism that Chinese territorial claims might be restrained through dialogue and that the Forum will build a level of trust across the region. In essence the ARF initiative is attempting to build a level of East Asian regional identity through consultation and preventive diplomacy. While there is a level of agreement on the continued need for a US military presence in East Asia there is less agreement on the level of US participation over matters of general security and economic development (see, for example, Hook, 1996, p.196).

So what kind of region is it?

What does all this add up to? What kind of a region, or regions, is it? The growing levels of trade and investment flows between the Asia-Pacific states and the heavy dependence of East Asian economies on the North American market points to a significant level of regional economic integration, but with integration occurring at different rates in different parts of the region. What we find is a complex of overlapping regional and sub-regional economic networks reflecting the distinctive interests and histories of the different communities and the need to respond in varied ways to the pressures of globalization. On the other hand, regional institutional integration and collective security arrangements remain comparatively weak. There is then an apparent *disjuncture* between the development of the Asia-Pacific as a dynamic economic complex and as a security complex.

In fact the search of regional level integration and identities may oversimplify matters. Buzan (Chapter 4) argues that it is difficult to make a strong case for regions like the Asia-Pacific or East Asia because of '... the larger position of the USA in relation to regionalism generally' (Section 4.4). That is the USA should be seen as acting 'above the regional level' to penetrate all regional developments. Furthermore, the US government may be the single most important player in the global economy today, but it is not the only global player and not all players act at the level of nation-states. This makes it difficult to define regions in a clear-cut way. Connections across the Pacific region and beyond do not map out into sharply defined spheres of influence and interdependence. *Instead regional networks will be uneven, will not necessarily follow the boundaries of whole nations and will be tied to a web of more global dependencies which may loosen that integration.*

What scope for regionalism in a globalizing world?

A common driving force behind regional arrangements is the belief that neighbouring states, by getting together, can strengthen regional well-being and security. There are dangers though in assuming that all regional security issues can be dealt with from within the region. *Put another way, it has become increasingly difficult to draw lines around areas like East Asia or Asia-Pacific and look within them for explanations and solutions to problems found there.* The increasing speed of communication, the global impact of the mass media, the power of world financial markets and the increasing migration and mixing of cultures has produced a world where seemingly everywhere is affected by everywhere else. In East Asia the massive military build-up in recent years has increased pressure for a collective regional security arrangement yet much of the supply of sophisticated weaponry comes from outside the area, from Europe, North America and the Russian Federation.

Figure 11.2 *Headlines providing different images of Asia-Pacific relations*

Issues of economic security are particularly difficult to manage through regional arrangements. While regional groupings may have more leverage than single states in negotiating with multinational corporations, given their increased market status, this impact is undermined by the complex global character of much business and investment activity. Massive investment transfers now take place between corporate divisions of international firms while speculative capital crosses political boundaries with comparative freedom. The argument that regional arrangements can provide a measure of security against wider economic collapse has a certain hollowness when applied to East Asia given that much of the region's economic success is predicated on export penetration of the markets of Europe and North America. Even the notion that regional integration can provide a more competitive base for local businesses to flourish in global markets begs questions about pre-existing patterns of trade and industrial linkage.

A further dimension of regional security is environmental impact. For example it is argued that the Pacific Ocean plays the role of 'environmental commons' where the dumping of toxic waste or over-fishing has a potential regional as well as local impact. However there are also increasing pressures to co-ordinate green policies at a more global level. Physical threats to the environment appear more interconnected across the world. The air pollution found in Tokyo, Manila or Los Angeles seems little different to that found in London or Athens. Connections are made between deforestation in Malaysia and Indonesia, the increasing energy needs of East Asian states and wider issues of 'global warming'. The more polluting activities of multinational businesses are often relocated to developing areas in the Asia-Pacific where jobs are at a premium and environmental safeguards may be less in evidence. The idea of a shared world interest in the environment has become more credible as governments have realized they need to worry about more than their immediate neighbours' policies. So again the notion of regional security soon draws in wider interests and connections.

While regional arrangements and integration may in part be a response to globalization pressures of one kind or another, those very pressures can also act to undermine that integration. *Economic integration across East Asia is incomplete and uneven because states and communities within the region are linked unevenly into the world economic system. The same complex of globalizing forces is both promoting and frustrating regional integration.*

11.4 What signs of global politics?

If signs of an East Asian regional bloc (and certainly a wider Asia-Pacific bloc) are far from clear what signs are there of a more global political response? To what extent are we seeing the development of a more global politics to manage, even police, the globalization apparent in other spheres, economic, cultural and environmental? How do developments in the Asia-Pacific relate to this notion of a more global politics?

Before going further it is useful to distinguish two constructions of world power relations. One account focuses on the persistence of the nation-state as a centre of power and the continued dominance of inter-state relations, whether bilateral, multilateral or regional. Adherents argue that this 'realist' image and the privileging of statehood and state agencies over other actors continue to resonate with what we see happening, even in a world of complex global connections. A second construction argues that globalization has brought about a major change in the world stage across which political actions are played out and that states are no longer able to manage by themselves world affairs in an effective manner. Here it is stressed that the world has become much more fluid and multicentred with power being chipped away from the territorial state to produce a fragmented pattern of authority structures.

Both these constructions have their following and perhaps the most effective image is one which recognizes this duality. Reference is sometimes made to the notion of a 'bifurcated world order' where, for the moment, the two constructions sit uneasily together; a persistent state system on the one hand and the growth of a bewildering array of multicentred arrangements on the other.

Transnational movements – how global are they?

Many commentators point to the development of transnational movements as a sign of a globalizing politics. Such movements bring together local groups at a regional or global level and act outside the interstate system and without a dominant base in one country. Their defining interests can be social, cultural, environmental or political and are seen not only as a response to globalization but also as a part of that process. In Chapter 13 Lawrence Woods looks in some detail at the development of transnational interactions and arrangements within the Asia-Pacific region. Here the focus will be on more general issues and the context more global.

Transnational movements have developed in large part because of the perceived ineffectiveness of states and inter-state arrangements to satisfy peoples' needs and concerns. While some transnational groups act to confront the perceived status quo others seek to establish alternative means of political mobilization. However because of pre-existing inequalities and differences across the Asia-Pacific and around the world the take-up of interest and activity is far from even and some organizations are more powerful than others. Take the case of environmental politics. Because of the transnational, even global, character of many environmental issues there appear limits to what can be achieved through inter-governmental action. Increasingly we see 'communities of interest' developing which span conventional political boundaries. But global penetration of these communities remains incomplete and uneven. Transnational non-governmental organizations (NGOs) like Greenpeace, Friends of the Earth, and the

World Wide Fund for Nature have strong representation in Western societies but for many living in newly developing countries environmentalism may look like the latest in a long line of excuses designed to restrict their sharing in economic growth. In Asia-Pacific, environmental NGO activity appears strongest in North America and Australia/New Zealand. Elsewhere in the region there are increasing numbers of environmental NGOs though their impact and size tend to be more modest. Collaborations between groups take a variety of forms, through informal and formal networks, coalitions and less frequently through permanent alliances (Eccleston, 1996). Eccleston's research which focused mainly on East Asian NGOs highlighted some of the problems and tensions which limit the level of effective global collaboration on environmental issues. Tensions arise not only between Western led groups and those in developing East Asian societies, but also between the local groups themselves. Not only is there fear of losing control to more powerful organizations, but also concern that Western led groups may not be fully aware of the national and local contexts of environmental issues in the developing world.

Although it is tempting to see transnational environmental movements as the beginnings of a globalized green response it is difficult to see them developing a single coherent character. The same goes for other transnational movements with global ambitions, though the actual dynamics and impact will of course vary from case to case. Take the example of Islam. Because Islamic communities play a largely subordinate role in a world development process orchestrated by Western culture, they have been forced to construct their own alternative networks. But talk of these networks amounting to a cohesive transnational movement capable of providing an alternative global politics is difficult to sustain. Islamic communities have great diversity making it difficult to come together as a single united force. They have developed unevenly within the wider international system and have varied relations with Western and other societies. In some countries of the Middle East, north Africa and central Asia, Islam has found direct expression in the politics of states; elsewhere, for example in Indonesia and Malaysia, it plays a more repressed role. There are different sects and sub-divisions within Islam, extreme differences in wealth, and varied complexions of Islamic politics. All these differences are reflected in the varied and uneven character of Islamic networks and undermine notions of Islam as a fully global force.

Although both environmentalism and Islam appear incomplete as global movements they do have the effect of drawing together groups in different regions of the world, *constructing transregional connections and identities which may fragment regional integration*. The main centres of global environmental research and activism are in Western societies (North America, Europe and Australia/New Zealand) and this is reflected in the transnational patterns of scientific collaboration and campaign organization. By comparison it appears more difficult to develop a collective response on environmental issues across a region like Asia-

Pacific where development has been so uneven and where simply trying to define the problems may meet with disagreement. In the case of Islam impact on the Asia-Pacific region is confined largely to Indonesia and Malaysia in South-East Asia and the dominant axis for Muslim networks runs east-west through central Asia and the Middle East to Europe. So in a sense Islamic networks and identities run counter to ASEAN integration, while the development of ASEAN may isolate further Islamic identities in Indonesia and Malaysia.

The complex systems of global governance

The growth of transnational movements and their networks reflects a world which has become more connected, economically and culturally. While it appears futile to search for the emergence of a government and institutions that are truly global, political researchers have drawn attention to an embryonic form of global governance constituted by complex webs of international and transnational political arrangements. These so-called *international regimes* can be found in a wide range of policy sectors, from telecommunications to air transport and from human rights to defence and security (see, for example, Zacher and Sutton, 1996; McGrew, 1995). It is argued that such regimes set the regulatory frameworks to govern our globalizing lives and that world order can only be maintained by countries sharing their roles as governing powers with many other agents.

International regimes are very varied in make-up but generally comprise a range of political groups, governmental and non-governmental. Their spheres of influence and impact will also vary. More global arrangements and conventions may develop alongside, and overlap with, more regional networks of governance and agreement may be frustrated by cultural differences and inequalities. Take the case of international human rights. At the global level a political response is enshrined in the United Nation's Universal Declaration of Human Rights and is supported by non-governmental organizations such as Amnesty International and the League of Human Rights. Yet its impact is far from even and not all governments share the same commitment to human right's legislation. There was hope that the 1993 Vienna World Conference on Human Rights would produce a new post-Cold War consensus on rights abuses, one that would be less distorted by ideological competition. But the conference had limited success and showed the difficulty of seeking a common commitment to a single standard of human rights across such an unequal world. For example it was argued that the West was using 'human rights as a stalking horse, to achieve global economic dominance over the developing and poorer world' (Boyle, 1995, p.84). Some states, notably from East Asia, also argued that the Western world was attempting to impose their ideas and values on parts of the world that were culturally different, and that human rights practices in places like Tibet and East Timor were an internal matter for the state concerned (China and Indonesia respectively).

With some Asian states less ready to endorse human rights legislation, there have been attempts to exert pressure for a region-wide arrangement on human rights. Regional human-rights regimes exist in Europe, the Americas and Africa, with permanent regional organizations (The Council of Europe, Organization of American States, Organization of African Unity) and agreed sets of conventions. One of the recommendations from the Vienna World Conference was the need to establish a similar system for Asia but pressure to date, and development of non-governmental organizations like Law Asia, have had only limited impact. The ASEAN grouping of states has made a tentative commitment to build a regional human-rights mechanism but its development does not appear to have high priority. When pressured by Western led groups ASEAN leaders counter with charges of 'Western arrogance' and interference in internal affairs. Indeed Vietnam, the latest member to join the grouping, has not been asked by ASEAN to establish a commission on human rights (*Far Eastern Economic Review*, 1996).

Some regimes have a more global orientation than others. The regimes for sectors like telecommunications and postal services are highly globalized reflecting the massive build-up in telephonic, telegraphic and mail flows, and in satellite communication. By contrast the regime for international security has a more regional orientation but with considerable overlapping of security arrangements, and a wider role for the USA. International regimes can also be more focused geographically, as in the arrangements and conventions designed to protect Antarctica or North Pacific fisheries (e.g. see Young, 1989). Although there are a large number of international regimes their varied character, memberships and spheres of influence produce a complex and uneven pattern of global political enmeshment. Also most regimes have been Western, and particularly US, led and the political involvement of East Asia within them is comparatively weak. This prompts questions about the stability of existing regimes should US power decline. Will these regimes extend their influence, or even maintain their present status, in a world where power relations are more fluid? To what extent will the rise of China as a world power fragment existing arrangements?

International regimes are not only seen as a response to globalization, they are also part of the globalization process itself. Regimes which allow groups to interact and exchange information globally must be implicated in the general process of making the world a smaller and a more interconnected place. This is perhaps most visible in the development of global financial management and telecommunications regimes but it is also true of human rights and the environment. Furthermore since regimes are uneven in their coverage and impact they are likely to complicate further the patterns of development that they were established to manage.

Does East Asia's increasing influence represent an alternative to Western globalization?

The debate over human rights and cultural distinctiveness between East Asia and the Western world leads to other thoughts. Just how different is the global influence of East Asia in comparison with that of the West? Does the development of the region bring more than an intensification of global competition? Are its characteristics so different that we might see a rejection and replacement of Western led globalization? And even if a Western led globalization continues to dominate is it possible to conceive of Western globalization being undermined and contested by global networks based in East Asia? John Allen in the book *Geographical Worlds* (1994) toys with the possibility of a Chinese led globalization linking its indigenous 1.1 billion people with a vast global network of overseas Chinese, the product of many centuries of voluntary or enforced dispersal. Allen argues that it is not just the scale of these social and economic networks but also their nature which makes the Chinese a potential threat to existing Western led globalization. He notes that 'The Asia-Pacific rim in particular, and Asia itself, is cross-cut by family-based business ties and relationships that do not function along formal, Western lines' (Allen, 1994, p.133). Allen also suggests that any alternative network may be difficult to understand unless you are actually part of it.

Overseas Chinese business networks

Consider a typical tale of Chinese family capitalism. In 1994 Richard Savage, a Singaporean businessman, met some officials from North Korea and passed on these contacts to his brother, Ronald, who works at Loxley, a Thai firm controlled by the Lamsam family. Loxley has a huge range of business interests, from environmental engineering to property and entertainment. In October 1995 senior members of the Lamsam family met various North Korean politicians over diner. Soon afterwards the firm won a contract to build an international telephone system for North Korea's new Rajin Sombong free-trade zone. The company has yet to see a dollar out of North Korea, but thinks that in ten years time Rajin Sombong will be the 'Singapore of the north'.

Such entrepreneurial deal-making is typical of overseas Chinese capitalism, which has its roots in the families that migrated from various mainland provinces – mostly coastal Guangdong, Fujian and Hainan – around 100 years ago.

(*The Economist*, 1996, p.10)

Talk of alternative routes to globalization brings with it concern for future global stability. Samuel Huntington in his influential 1993 paper 'The clash of civilizations?' argues that future global tensions are most likely to occur along 'cultural fault lines' between Western, Islamic and East Asian civilizations. Non-Western societies are no longer seen as targets of Western led globalization but as 'movers and shakers' in their own right.

Huntington's view of a resurgent Chinese-led East Asian civilization finds some support in the stress given to so called 'Asian values' and the 'Asian way' by some East Asian leaders. Others argue, however, that the notion of 'Asian values' is being used more as a smoke screen to diffuse criticism of the human rights record of authoritarian regimes (see, for example, Kim Dae Jung, 1994). The debate is complicated further by talk of 'Asian values', sometimes as a code for Chinese values, sometimes covering a more mixed bag of ideals from a wider grouping of East Asian societies.

It remains unclear whether 'Asianization' would represent a truly alternative route to Western globalization. Are Western and Eastern values somehow exclusive or are they both influenced by the same wider processes of change? Huntington's 'clash of civilizations' thesis suggests the two cultures are separate and impervious. By contrast Robinson (1996) argues that both sets of values are under pressure from wider forces and that each is affecting the impact of the other. He sees it less as a global contest between East and West, more as one between different variants of capitalism – organic-statist, liberal and social democratic. So depending on where you stand in this debate, you could view East Asia's impact on globalization either as contested models of social organization within the broad contours of capitalism or as a more fundamental division between different civilizations and a source of potential global conflict.

11.5   Conclusion

So which of the two images, carving the world into regional blocs or the development of a more global politics, fits best with developments in the Asia-Pacific? Looking at the forgoing discussion the evidence for regionalism appears less than compelling. While there is growing economic interdependence and dynamism across the region the flows and networks remain diverse and uneven with patterns difficult to discern. There is a continuing heavy East Asian dependence on US markets and statistics show that trade between NAFTA and East Asian economies from 1960 to the late 1980s grew faster than within NAFTA and East Asia (see Hessler, 1994). But, as Buzan makes clear in Chapter 4, there is little practical sign of a developing pan-Pacific identity and little common interest in deeper co-operation. East Asia itself is far from having regional coherence; there is an apparent *disjuncture* between growing economic interdependence and the military-political divisions and continuing threat of conflict. In Buzan's view East Asia is a 'classic security complex', and a region only in the more negative sense of there being a high level of potential conflict and common insecurity.

The image of the region, and particularly East Asian states, being drawn into a wider global politics can also be contested. Existing international regimes remain dominated by the USA and other Western states and interests. Within this Western led world order it is perhaps not surprising to find East Asian governments and other groups dragging their heels or seeking change to a system in which they are expected to play a largely subordinate role. The search by Japanese and Chinese governments for a new global role may undermine existing structures and disrupt relations with the West. Reference has already been made to the debate over 'Asian values' and whether there are significant differences, even divisions, between the cultures of East and West. The idea that there could be alternative routes to globalization suggests that developing international regimes will continually be distorted and undermined, or maybe transformed, by movements and networks based outside the West.

Although regional interdependencies have deepened considerably with growing business and other networks linking Asia-Pacific capitals there is also a sense of some parts of the region remaining marginalized or drawing further apart. As well as the prospect of recurring international tensions in the Korean peninsula and around the borders of the PRC, there are local tensions between ethnic groups, between city and countryside, and between haves and have nots generally. While key Pacific Rim states have been drawn into the process of wider governance most Pacific Island communities remain at the sharp end of an externalized decision-making process that brings local economic uncertainty and environmental dangers. The complexity of wider political arrangements and their power structures reflect not only on such differences and inequalities but also on the uneven way the region has been drawn into a more globalized system.

References

Allen, J. (1994) 'Global Worlds' in Allen, J. and Massey, D. (eds) *Geographical Worlds*, Oxford, Oxford University Press.

Boyle, K. (1995) 'Stock-taking on human rights: the World Conference on Human Rights, Vienna 1993', *Political Studies*, vol.XLIII, pp.79–95.

Eccleston, B. (1996) 'Does North-South collaboration enhance NGO influence on deforestation policies in Malaysia and Indonesia?', *Journal of Commonwealth and Comparative Politics*, vol.XXXIV, no.1, pp.66–89.

Far Eastern Economic Review (1996) 'ASEANs unkept promise', 22 August, p.31.

Fu-Chen Lo and Yue-Man Yeung (eds) (1996) *Emerging World Cities in Pacific Asia*, Tokyo, United Nations University Press.

Garnaut, R. and Drysdale, P. (eds) (1994) *Asia-Pacific Regionalism*, Pymble, NSW, HarperCollins.

Hessler, S. (1994) 'Regionalization of the world economy: fact or fiction?' paper presented to the ISA Conference, Washington.

Hook, G. (1996) 'Japan and the construction of Asia-Pacific' in Gamble, A. and Payne, A. (eds) *Regionalism and World Order*, Basingstoke, Macmillan.

Huntington, S. P. (1993) 'The clash of civilizations?', *Foreign Affairs*, vol.72, no.3, pp.22–49.

Inoguchi, T. (1995) 'A view from Pacific Asia' in Holm, H. and Sorensen, G. (eds) *Whose World Order?*, Boulder, CO, Westview Press.

Kim Dae Jung (1994) 'Is culture destiny? The myth of Asia's anti-democratic values', *Foreign Affairs*, vol.73, no.6, pp.189–94.

McGrew, A. (1995) 'World order and political space' in Anderson *et al.* (eds) *A Global World?*, Oxford, Oxford University Press.

Robinson, R. (1996) 'The politics of "Asian values"', *The Pacific Review*, vol.9, no.3, pp.309–27.

The Economist (1993) 'Japan ties up the Asian market', 24 April, pp.79–80.

The Economist (1996) 'Survey: Business in Asia', 9 March, p.10.

Young, O. (1989) *International Regimes*, Ithaca, NY, Cornell University Press.

Zacher, M.W. and Sutton, B.A. (1996) *Governing Global Networks*, Cambridge, Cambridge University Press.

Further reading

Gamble, A. and Payne, A. (eds) (1996) *Regionalism and World Order*, Basingstoke, Macmillan, especially Hook, G., 'Japan and the construction of Asia-Pacific' and Ngai-Ling Sum, 'The NICs and East Asian Regionalism'.

Inoguchi, T. (1995) 'A view from Pacific Asia' in Holm, H. and Sorensen, G. (eds) *Whose World Order?*, Boulder, CO, Westview Press.

Lasater, M. (1996) *The New Pacific Community: US Strategic Options for Asia,* Boulder, CO, Westview Press.

Yunling, Z. (1995) 'China in the post-Cold War era' in Holm, H. and Sorensen, G. (eds) *Whose World Order?*, Boulder, CO, Westview Press.

CHAPTER 12

The growth of intergovernmental collaboration in the Asia-Pacific region

John Ravenhill

12.1   Introduction

The Asia-Pacific region historically has been characterized by an 'institutional deficit', that is, by the absence of region-wide institutions for intergovernmental collaboration. Collaboration among some countries of the region is of long-standing, for instance, the Association of South-East Asian Nations (ASEAN) was formed in 1967. But no institutions linking the western Pacific Rim, Oceania, and the eastern Pacific Rim existed before the establishment of the Asia-Pacific Economic Co-operation grouping in 1989 (see Figures 4.1 and 4.2). In the 1990s, however, proposals for various forms of intergovernmental collaboration in the Asia-Pacific region have proliferated.

This chapter seeks to explain why there was little intergovernmental collaboration in the form of regional institutions in the Asia-Pacific before the mid 1980s and the reasons for the growth of such institutions in subsequent years. It concludes with an assessment of the likely direction of such collaboration in the future.

12.2   The absence of a 'Pacific' tradition

The Pacific Ocean historically has been seen as a dividing rather than a unifying force (Segal, 1990). Even on the western Pacific Rim, the idea that East Asia might constitute an integrated region is of recent origin. Indeed, the term 'East Asia' in contemporary studies is often used to refer only to the countries of North-East Asia (Japan, the two Koreas, and the three Chinas – the People's Republic of China, Hong Kong, and Taiwan) that share a Confucian heritage. In this chapter I use 'East Asia' to refer to both

North-East and South-East Asia. In the many studies of regionalism written in the 1960s and early 1970s, the only part of the Asia-Pacific area regarded as a region in which intergovernmental collaboration took place was South-East Asia.

The reasons for this *institutional deficit* – the absence of institutionalized regional intergovernmental collaboration – are not hard to ascertain. The principal dividing force in the Asia-Pacific after 1945 was the struggle between communist/nationalist regimes and the USA and its allies (see Chapter 2). East Asia was the principal geographical region where the ideological struggles of the Cold War were played out on the battlefield. This ideological divide created significant barriers to region-wide collaboration, as did the preference of some countries, most notably Indonesia, for membership of the non-aligned movement in this era of superpower confrontation.

Unlike Western Europe, where the presence of an extra-regional threat, the Soviet Union, stimulated regional integration, in East Asia the primary security threat for many countries came from other states within the region. Civil wars and anti-colonial wars in the first decade after 1945 left a legacy of divided countries: China–Taiwan; the two Koreas, and North and South Vietnam. Other countries were worried about the support they believed regional neighbours were providing to domestic political movements hostile to the ruling regime. The legacy of Japanese aggression in the 1930s and the Second World War further complicated the security situation. This legacy had dimensions that were both internal and external to Japan. Internally, a substantial political constituency opposed Japanese involvement in any security or peace-keeping arrangements; externally, anti-Japanese feelings were rife (in 1974, the visit of Japanese Prime Minister Tanaka to Indonesia, Malaysia and Thailand prompted anti-Japanese riots).

The consequence of these divisions was that the major post-war security arrangements were not region-wide but largely constructed to provide assurance against the perceived threats from other states from within the region (see Chapter 5). The ANZUS pact, for instance, which linked Australia, New Zealand, and the USA, had its origins in the quest of the two Oceanic countries for assurance that the end of the US occupation of Japan would not lead to a revival of Japanese militarism. The Five Power Defence Agreement between Australia, Malaysia, New Zealand, Singapore and the United Kingdom originated in the Anglo-Malayan Defence Agreement of 1957. The aim was to provide a security guarantee to Malaysia (which included Singapore until its expulsion from the Federation of Malaysia in 1965) against its neighbour, Indonesia, whose hostility came to a head in President Sukarno's policy of *konfrontasi* from 1963 to 1966. In North-East Asia, the bitter memories that the Koreans had of Japanese colonialism, and Taiwan's unwillingness to provoke mainland China by entering into formal security treaties, ensured that no regional security treaty would emerge.

The USA was pivotal to the construction of the Asia-Pacific's post-war security architecture. In Western Europe, the USA had preferred a multi-lateral treaty, the North Atlantic Treaty Organization (NATO), as a means of pressuring the Western Europeans to make a larger contribution to their defence. In Asia, in contrast, the USA feared that a multilateral treaty would do little to enhance joint capabilities while enabling allies to increase demands on its resources (Kahler, 1995, pp.19–20). Washington believed a 'hub and spokes' arrangement of largely bilateral treaties would maximize US influence in the region. Accordingly, the USA negotiated bilateral arrangements with Japan, South Korea, Taiwan, the Philippines, and Thailand as well as the ANZUS alliance with Australia and New Zealand. The major multilateral treaty in the region in which the USA was involved, the South-East Asia Treaty Organization (SEATO), which emerged out of the abortive Geneva settlement of the Vietnam War in 1954, proved an ineffective instrument. This was in large part because of the heterogeneity of its membership (the other members were Australia, France, New Zealand, Pakistan, the Philippines, Thailand, and the UK) (Buszynski, 1983).

If greater control was the original factor underlying Washington's preference for bilateralism in the security realm, it was joined in the 1980s by a fear that a multilateral security conference would offer an opportunity for the Soviet Union to increase its stature in the region. In particular, Washington did not wish to give the Soviet Union an opportunity to place naval arms control on the regional security agenda. The proposal by Soviet leader Mikhail Gorbachev, in a major speech at Vladivostok in 1986, for a Pacific conference similar to the Helsinki conference on security co-operation in Europe was rebuffed by Washington. A similar fate befell a suggestion in the following year by Australian Foreign Minister, Bill Hayden, for the construction of various confidence-building measures among the superpowers and other regional states in the Pacific. Even after the end of the Cold War and the break-up of the Eastern bloc, the American Bush Administration resisted overtures for a regional security dialogue (Kerr et al., 1995).

American policies also provide a significant part of the explanation for the absence of region-wide institutions for economic collaboration (Crone, 1993). Here an explicit linkage with security is evident. The USA was willing to provide largely open access to its market for the exports of its allies in East Asia (on a non-reciprocal basis) because it believed that the promotion of economic prosperity was the best safeguard against 'communist' subversion. For the first four decades after the Second World War, Asian allies of the USA were able to take advantage of the US commitment to trade liberalization under the auspices of the General Agreement on Tariffs and Trade (GATT). US support for the multilateral economic institutions went a substantial way towards compensating for the region's institutional deficit in the economic realm. And the East Asian states had little interest at this time in constructing a regional economic institution – levels of trade with other Asian states were low compared with those with the USA. Issues of sovereignty were also significant. Membership of a formal regional economic institution threatened to bring unwanted scrutiny to the industry and trade policies of Asian states. Some, particularly the recently-independent member states of ASEAN, were hostile to any proposals that limited their sovereignty or had the potential to establish a rival to their own (largely ineffective) form of regional economic collaboration. In the 1960s and 1970s, North–South issues also divided the Asia-Pacific region with the ASEAN countries (sometimes supported by Australia and New Zealand) keen to use multilateral negotiations to attempt to improve the position of economies heavily dependent on earnings from the export of primary commodities.

12.3   The new regionalism in the Asia-Pacific

Given this unpromising history of intergovernmental collaboration in the Asia-Pacific, a central puzzle is why so many proposals for such collaboration were launched in the decade after 1985. What has happened to change the interests of countries towards regional collaboration? Clearly, given the centrality of the Cold War to divisions in the region, its effective termination with the onset of the 1990s was a key factor in permitting enhanced collaboration in the security sphere. But action on proposals for increased collaboration in the economic realm pre-dated the end of the Cold War. Other factors were at work.

Countries enter into regional collaboration for a multitude of reasons. Some relate to the direct benefits that they hope will develop from such co-operation; others from aspirations that collaboration will produce less tangible but none the less significant gains by, for example, enhancing the bargaining position of regional countries as opposed to that of outsiders. To search for a single factor that explains the renewed interest in regionalism in the Asia-Pacific would thus risk a gross over-simplification. A more fruitful approach is to look at various theoretical approaches put forward to explain the growth of interest in regional intergovernmental collaboration in recent years. In this section I examine three theoretical perspectives on the study of collaboration: the first, the mainstream economist's approach to regional collaboration, the other two drawn from the literature of international relations – the neo-institutionalist and neo-realist approaches. But first, a few words on definitions.

In the now voluminous literature on regions, writers have used concepts such as regionalism and regionalization in various ways, often without any consistency. For the purposes of this chapter I will distinguish regionalization from regionalism (borrowing from Hurrell, 1995a, b; and Fishlow and Haggard, 1992). *Regionalization* refers to an economic process in which trade and investment flows among component parts of a region grow more rapidly than such flows with the rest of the world, a process that creates greater economic interdependence within the region. The activities of private actors – firms and individuals – drive regionalization, which does not necessarily depend on the actions of states. *Regionalism*, on the other hand, is shorthand for what I have called regional intergovernmental collaboration – the creation of agreements among governments to manage various regional interactions. Where these agreements are more than *ad hoc* arrangements, they are frequently called 'international regimes'. An 'international regime' is defined by Krasner (1982, p.185) as the 'principles, norms, rules, and decision-making procedures around which actor expectations converge in a given issue-area'. An example would be the global trading regime.

An economic or functionalist perspective

A key issue in the literature on regions is the relationship between the processes of regionalization and regionalism. For most economists, a straightforward relationship exists: regionalization is the motor that drives regionalism. Increased levels of regional economic interactions result from 'natural' economic forces such as the proximity of economies (which facilitates trade and investment because transport and information costs are lower than in relations among more distant economies) and the complementarity of their factor endowments (resources, levels of technology, skilled labour, etc.) (Drysdale, 1988). They are also the product of a convergence of policies and of income levels (Fishlow and Haggard, 1992, p.12). These economic forces drive regionalism: governments increasingly perceive it in their interests to construct governance structures to manage their increasing economic interdependence. The economist's explanation for the growth of regionalism essentially rests on functionalist premises: increased co-operation is necessary to cope with the problems arising from growing trade and investment flows.

Recent developments in trade and investment flows in the Asia-Pacific region certainly provide ammunition for this argument. Trade and investment flows among East Asian economies in particular, and those of the Asia-Pacific region more generally, grew much more rapidly after 1980 than such flows with other countries. In large part, this increase in the share of intra-regional transactions in total flows of trade and investment reflected the rapid growth rates of East Asian economies relative to those of other parts of the world (Frankel, 1991). The share of the total trade of East Asian economies transacted with other East Asian economies rose from 35 per cent in 1980 to close to 50 per cent in 1995. For APEC (see Table 12.1 in Section 12.4), the ratio of intra-regional trade climbed from 57 per cent to 75 per cent in the same period.

Intra-regional investment flows also increased markedly following the negotiation of the Plaza Accord in 1985. This agreement among the Group of 7 industrialized economies led to a significant appreciation of the yen *vis-à-vis* other currencies, and encouraged Japanese companies to relocate some manufacturing activities to other parts of the region – initially ASEAN and, later, China. Although the share of Asian countries in total investments declined (because of the large outflows to North America and Europe), the absolute amounts invested in manufacturing in other Asian countries rose significantly. This outflow of investment was to pave

Leaders of the Group of 7 industrialized economies at the Western Economic Summit, Bonn, 3 May 1985

the way for subsequent 'reverse exports' back to Japan. Following the Plaza Accord, the Korean won and Taiwanese dollar also appreciated against other regional currencies, encouraging flows of investment from these North-East Asian newly-industrialized countries to other parts of the region, most notably Malaysia and Thailand. Regionalized networks of production became increasingly prominent in East Asia; linkages among firms went beyond investment ties to include arrangements for the transfer of managerial and technological expertise (Bernard and Ravenhill, 1995).

The higher level of transactions within the region undoubtedly spurred governments to seek new arrangements to reduce the barriers – whether in the form of tariffs or non-tariff barriers to trade, or the absence of security for foreign investors – to the efficient conduct of business. This response is exactly the outcome that economists would predict. And a major stream of international relations theorizing on regionalism shares this functionalist emphasis.

A neo-institutionalist perspective

Neo-institutionalist approaches to regionalism also give prominence to the role that international regimes can play in reducing transactions costs (i.e. all the costs involved in conducting an exchange, including the costs of acquiring information, of undertaking bargaining, and of enforcing agreements, to which are added the cost – 'opportunity costs' – of the benefits that might otherwise have been generated had these resources been invested in other activities). Neo-institutionalists, however, go beyond a study of economic transactions: their focus is on how regionalism evolves as a political process, and the reasons why institutions are necessary to sustain economic co-operation (Keohane, 1984).

The neo-institutionalist approach assumes that states are rational self-interested actors. They co-operate because they cannot achieve desired outcomes at an acceptable cost through unilateral action alone. States often have common interests, but this in itself does not guarantee successful co-operation. In particular, without a supranational authority to enforce agreements, states will always be tempted to cheat. In international trade, for instance, the potential political response of domestic constituencies that may be hurt by trade liberalization provides governments with powerful incentives to protect them and to not implement trade agreements. International regimes can help states to overcome this dilemma and to achieve joint gains that otherwise would not be realized. Through, for instance, facilitating the monitoring of the behaviour of their partners, international regimes improve the prospects for co-operation. Moreover, as states experience the benefits of co-operative behaviour, regimes themselves change states' perceptions of the possible gains from future co-operation. As interdependence among states has increased, so has the possibility for the creation of international regimes to reach mutually beneficial agreements.

Much of the neo-institutionalist theorizing on regionalism has focused on the European experience. It is often premised on the workings of a pluralist political system. Consequently, some of the most important neo-institutionalist work on regionalism, such as the neo-functionalist approach, which focuses on the interaction between increasing levels of economic interdependence and the transfer of political allegiances to a regional centre, has limited relevance to the Asia-Pacific region. More applicable to this region is a development in neo-institutionalist writing on how interstate collaboration comes about: the focus on *epistemic communities*. The term epistemic community, originally coined by Michel Foucault (1973), was first applied in the literature on international regimes by John Ruggie (1975), and refers to groups of professionals with common political values and a commitment both to a common causal model and to seeing that model translated into public policy (Haas, 1990, p.41). The essence of the argument is that, with the development of transnational communities of professionals with expertise in particular issue areas, members of those communities will pressure their national governments to adopt policy prescriptions that follow from the communities' preferred models.

The *epistemic community* concept appears to be particularly applicable in the Asia-Pacific region to the development of a transnational community of professional economists supportive of trade liberalization. Despite the lack, until recently, of region-wide intergovernmental institutions, the Asia-Pacific has a long experience of institutionalized collaboration among academics, business representatives and public officials (dating back to the Pan-Pacific Union, which was founded in 1917) (Woods, 1993). In the last quarter of a century the principal forums have been PAFTAD (Pacific Trade and Development) conferences (first held in 1968) that bring together academics (predominantly economists) from around the region, the private-sector dominated Pacific Basin Economic Council (PBEC) and, from 1980, the Pacific Economic Co-operation Conference (subsequently Council, PECC), which links academics, business representatives and public officials (who participate in a private capacity) (see Table 12.1). Although it is impossible to demonstrate the exact influence of members of these groupings, it is plausible to argue that, together with pressure from the World Bank, these economists and business people have helped to place economic liberalization high on the agenda of governments of the region. Policies and rhetoric alike have changed markedly from the 1970s when mercantilist ideas and the rhetoric of Southern (Third World) solidarity were prominent in some of the region's less developed states (Harris, 1994).

The epistemic community concept is also relevant in the security sphere where 'second track' diplomacy (institutional linkages and meetings organized under the auspices of non-governmental bodies that, like PECC, sometimes include officials who participate in a private capacity) has gained increasing prominence in the 1990s (Kerr, 1994). One of the most significant of these non-official bodies is the Council for Security Co-operation in the Asia Pacific (CSCAP), established in Kuala Lumpur in June 1993. CSCAP is intended not only to link non-governmental organizations working on regional security questions but also to help these organizations to influence the official regional security co-operation dialogue (Ball and Kerr, 1996, pp.30–2).

A neo-realist perspective

Yet if epistemic communities have played an increasingly important role in promoting intergovernmental collaboration in the Asia-Pacific region in the last decade, this has been possible, many commentators would argue, only because of fundamental changes in the systemic context. For the neo-realist, a growth in regional intergovernmental collaboration has to be understood in the context of changes in the broader international system and the external challenges confronting countries within a region (Hurrell, 1995a, b). ASEAN's history provides several clear examples where closer collaboration in a regional organization in the Asia-Pacific was driven by external developments. Indeed, each of the major stepping stones in ASEAN's institutionalization can be traced to increased concerns about a perceived external threat. The first ASEAN summit in 1976, nine years after the organization's founding, was a response to the fall of Cambodia, Laos and Vietnam to communist regimes. Similarly, the creation of the ASEAN Regional Forum (ARF), discussed later in this chapter, was a response to the perceived risks of the emergence of a regional power vacuum following the end of the Cold War and the desire to foster security co-operation (Leifer, 1996). Some commentators argue that the timing of ASEAN's proposed expansion to ten members (Vietnam joined in 1995; Burma/Myanmar,

Cambodia and Laos are expected to join by the end of the century) was driven in part by concerns about China's growing power. And in the economic realm, the commitment in the early 1990s to the establishment of an ASEAN free trade area was prompted by fears that foreign investment would be lost to China, whose far larger economy was undergoing rapid liberalization (Ravenhill, 1995c).

Two factors are central to a neo-realist explanation of the development of regionalism in the Asia-Pacific: the end of the Cold War, and the changes in the relative power of the USA. One strand of neo-realist theorizing has focused on the supposed relationship between the presence of a hegemonic power and a liberal (open) international system (Kindleberger, 1973; Krasner, 1976). Little empirical support has been found for this relationship, however (Cowhey and Long, 1983; McKeown, 1983; Stein, 1984; Gowa, 1989). Moreover, an equally plausible theoretical argument can be made that it is in the interests of hegemonic powers not to promote a liberal system but to utilize the power asymmetries in bilateral relationships to maximize their gains from regional interactions (Conybeare, 1987; Hirschman, 1945). The experience in the Asia-Pacific region differed markedly between the economic and security realms. In the latter, as noted above, the USA preferred to maintain bilateral relations to maximize its leverage and control over the commitment of its resources. In the economic realm, on the other hand, US support for an open multilateral trading system shaped US economic relations with other regional states.

Relative US economic and military power capabilities have moved in opposite directions. In the military realm, the end of the Cold War left the USA as the world's only superpower, its military ascendancy essentially unchallenged at the systemic level. In contrast, the relative economic strength of the USA has been in decline for several decades, a reflection of the more rapid growth achieved by the East Asian economies. By the early 1980s, the USA was a less enthusiastic supporter of the existing multilateral economic institutions. In particular, Washington increasingly believed that GATT was failing to address the structural barriers in East Asian economies that handicapped US efforts to export to these markets (see, for instance, Krasner, 1987; Lincoln, 1990). To some extent, GATT was a victim of its own success. The reduction in tariffs and official tariff barriers through successive rounds of negotiations under GATT auspices gave greater prominence to the distortions caused by differences in economic structures and national policy regimes.

The end of the Cold War, by enhancing US military superiority, somewhat paradoxically weakened the incentives for the USA to maintain open markets for its East Asian trading partners. In the absence of a security threat emanating from a common global adversary, Washington no longer perceived a need to strengthen its allies through non-reciprocated economic concessions. Changes in the security sphere thus intensified pressures for a renegotiation of the foundations of regional economic relations. Moreover, although the demise of the Soviet bloc left the USA in a position of unprecedented military superiority, it also weakened the incentives for the USA to extend a security guarantee to its regional allies, thereby reinforcing pressures against US military assistance that stemmed from US economic problems.

For regional economic relations, the critical turning point was 1985. Although Washington had previously pursued sporadic protectionist actions in its bilateral relations with East Asian countries (such as the negotiation of 'voluntary' export restraints on Japanese textiles and cars), that year marked the turn to a new aggressiveness in US trade policies. The enormous trade deficits generated by budget deficits and an overvalued dollar in the first Reagan Administration prompted three new trade policy directions. The first was to force a devaluation of the dollar against other currencies, particularly the Japanese yen, through the Plaza Accord. Simultaneously, the Administration announced two other policy changes. One was the adoption of a far more aggressive approach in its efforts to force open foreign markets and to end what it perceived to be 'unfair' trading practices by its partners. The preferred instrument was Section 301 of the US Trade Act. This authorized the President to retaliate against 'unjustifiable, unreasonable, or discriminatory' foreign trade practices (for alternative perspectives on the desirability and success of this policy see Bhagwati and Patrick, 1990; and Bayard and Elliott, 1994). The second change was Washington's new enthusiasm for the negotiation of regional trade agreements.

Although concerns about the security of Western Europe had caused the USA to support the formation of the European Community, for the first four post-war decades it had consistently expressed its preference for multilateralism rather than regionalism in world trade. Growing frustrations with the inability of GATT to tackle the distortions caused by differences in economic structures, and with the growth in the European Community's programme of subsidies for agricultural exports, caused a change of heart. Immediately after the Plaza Accord, the Canadian government approached Washington with a proposal for the negotiation of a free trade area between the two countries (whose commerce constitutes the world's largest single bilateral trade flow). The President was able to use the fast track authorization of the 1984 Trade and Tariffs Act that had permitted the negotiation of a free trade agreement with Israel (Destler, 1992). The Canada–US Free Trade Agreement was concluded in 1988. Two years later, the Bush Administration responded positively to a Mexican request to negotiate a free trade agreement; the eventual outcome in 1992 was the North American Free Trade Agreement (NAFTA). Moreover, in his Enterprise for the Americas initiative of June 1990, President Bush signalled US willingness to negotiate bilateral framework agreements to improve trade relations with other economies of Central and South America.

The attractions of this new regionalist strategy for Washington were obvious. In bilateral negotiations (with much smaller economies) the USA was able to exert its considerable economic muscle. Consequently, it had a far greater likelihood of obtaining its objectives than in global negotiations where it faced resistance from more formidable economic partners such as the European Community. Furthermore, the bilateral negotiations enabled Washington to place on the agenda various issues of 'deeper' integration such as treatment of foreign investment, and labour and environmental standards, whose inclusion in multilateral talks other countries had resisted (Haggard, 1995). The pursuit of bilateral arrangements offered the USA a further advantage; they increased the pressure not only on the European Community but also on other states in the Asia-Pacific region to reach agreement in multilateral trade talks and to accommodate the USA in bilateral negotiations.

The problems the new US stance caused for other Asia-Pacific states are equally obvious. The relatively secure and non-discriminatory access to the US market that they had enjoyed appeared increasingly under threat. A regionalized North American economy might place East Asian and Oceanic exports at a disadvantage in the world's largest market. Investment might also be diverted away from the less developed economies of the western Pacific Rim to Mexico or South American economies if an enlarged North American free trade area imposed restrictive 'rules of origin'. Such rules stipulate the requirements that must be met if a product is to be treated for trade purposes as originating in that country rather than as an extra-regional import; frequently such rules require that a certain share of the overall value of a product must be produced domestically.

The new US policy of 'aggressive bilateralism' added unwelcome pressure for domestic economic policy reform in targeted states. With the European Community committed to both widening (an expansion of its membership) and deepening (through the establishment of the single internal market in 1992), it appeared to the governments of East Asia and Oceania that the new regionalism was being pursued largely at their expense. They looked to the Uruguay Round of GATT negotiations, launched in 1986, as a means of preventing the breakdown of the world trading system into rival regional blocs. But the early negotiations under GATT auspices were unpromising; the mid-round talks in Brussels in 1988 broke down with the parties far apart on key issues.

It was this environment of unfavourable developments in the global system and potential external threats to welfare that provided the context for the new interest in establishing institutions to promote intergovernmental collaboration in the Asia-Pacific, in particular, the launch of the APEC grouping. When Australian Prime Minister, Bob Hawke, proposed in Seoul in January 1989 that a ministerial meeting be held to promote closer economic co-operation in the Asia-Pacific region, unfavourable international developments loomed large in his thinking (Ravenhill, 1998). With the GATT's Uruguay Round apparently floundering, a fallback position was to promote closer regional economic collaboration. Another important factor in APEC's foundation was the hope of other governments that the development of disputes-resolution mechanisms within APEC would constrain US behaviour by thwarting its resort to bilateralism. As Aggarwal (1995) notes, governments negotiate international regimes not just, as some neo-institutionalists argue, because they may reduce transaction costs but also because they believe they can assist in constraining the behaviour of their partner states.

APEC also came to be seen as having the potential to play a positive role in the security sphere. With the end of the Cold War, concern grew that the USA would withdraw its forces from the Asia-Pacific region, a fear heightened by the Bush Administration's decision in November 1991 to close the major naval base at Subic Bay in the Philippines. Other governments aspired to sustain an active US role in regional security matters by increasing the enmeshment of the USA in the regional economy through collaboration under APEC's auspices. APEC itself has not been directly concerned with security issues; Taiwan's membership in APEC is itself sufficient to make an extension of APEC to the security sphere unlikely (given the sensitivity of the People's Republic of China on sovereignty issues). The primary vehicle for intergovernmental collaboration on security issues in the Asia-Pacific has been the ASEAN Regional Forum (ARF).

As with APEC, the establishment of the ARF owed much to changes in the external environment. Although Cold War rivalries had contributed to conflicts in the region, the involvement of superpowers also constrained other regional interstate disputes. The end of the Cold War removed this source of constraint. Other governments feared that should the USA significantly reduce its security involvement, local arms races would be triggered. Moreover, many of the other governments were concerned at China's potential military capabilities and its apparent willingness to resort to force to resolve territorial disputes. It was not just the Cold War, however, that had prevented the establishment of regional intergovernmental collaboration in the security sphere. The other constraining factor was the unwillingness of the USA to participate in a regional security dialogue. The disintegration of the Soviet Union in December 1991 was a critical factor in the change in the US attitude towards a regional security dialogue, evident in the last year of the Bush Administration. The Clinton Administration, which assumed office in January 1993, was far more enthusiastic about a regional security dialogue than its predecessor.

The erosion of US economic hegemony and the ending of the Cold War offered greater scope for smaller powers within the system to take initiatives on regional collaboration (Cooper et al., 1993). An initiative from one or more of the smaller countries was less likely to arouse the suspicions of other states than if it came from Japan or the USA. Australia was well placed to launch the APEC initiative on economic co-operation. In the security realm, ASEAN was to provide an appropriate venue when, with the encouragement of its 'dialogue partners' – especially Australia and the USA – it decided to turn its post-ministerial conference into a forum for the discussion of regional security issues. The ARF, whose first meeting was held in July 1994, was the outcome.

Theoretical perspectives on the growth of regionalism

Which of the three theoretical perspectives – economic functionalism, neo-institutionalism, neo-realism – provides the best explanation for the growth of regionalism in the Asia-Pacific since the end of the 1980s? All three offer some insights into various dimensions of the process. The growth of economic interdependence among regional economies and governments' desires to realize the potential benefits of such interdependence by negotiating collaborative arrangements certainly was an important background factor. The problem with this reasoning, however, is that it ignores the possibility that growing economic interdependence will lead to greater conflict rather than collaboration (as some suggest has occurred between China and the USA). Moreover, it does not specify what levels of interdependence are critical for prompting government interest in concluding regional co-operative arrangements. Does this occur when trade with other economies in the region reaches 30, 40, or 50 per cent of a country's total trade? Why was there no regional agreement between the USA and Canada, the two economies responsible for the world's largest bilateral trade flow, until the late 1980s?

This inability to account for the timing of regional agreements also afflicts approaches that emphasize the role of epistemic communities. As discussed above, the ideas of transnational groupings of economists, through organizations such as PECC, provided the intellectual foundations for APEC. But such groupings were in existence long before 1989: the question that has to be addressed is why were their ideas accepted at that time whereas they had been dismissed before? The answer lies in the changes in governments' perceptions of their interests, and of the utility of regionalism, that flowed from developments in their external environments in the late 1980s – in the economic realm, the stalemate in the Uruguay Round of the GATT talks; in the security realm, the ending of the Cold War.

If the neo-realist emphasis on changing external environments provides a convincing explanation of the timing of the development of APEC and the ARF, it is far less successful in explaining the nature of the arrangements that have been developed, particularly in the security realm. For the ARF has eschewed traditional realist concerns with the establishment of a balance of power. Instead its focus, as Kerr observes, has been on promoting comprehensive security for all states in the region; an approach that is both generally preventive rather than deterrent in its focus (depending, for instance, on an increase in the transparency of military issues among the member states) and constructed upon a more comprehensive definition of security that goes beyond military threats to include economic underdevelopment, environmental concerns, terrorism, and transnational criminal activities (Ball and Kerr, 1996, pp.76–7; Wiseman, 1992).

12.4   An Asia-Pacific way?

Within a decade, the Asia-Pacific region has moved from a situation of an institutional deficit to one where proposals for intergovernmental collaboration have proliferated. New collaborative arrangements have mushroomed across the region, ranging from economic collaboration among parts of different countries in so-called 'growth triangles', to the widening and deepening of existing regional arrangements, such as the ASEAN Free Trade Area (AFTA) and ANZCERTA (Australia–New Zealand Closer Economic Relations Agreement), to the establishment of the transregional groupings of APEC and the ARF (on 'growth triangles' see Chia Siow Yue and Lee Tsao Yuan, 1993; Toh Mun Heng and Low, 1993b; and Lee Tsao Yuan, 1991; on AFTA see Imada and Naya, 1992; and Toh Mun Heng and Low, 1993a; on ANZCERTA see Eichbaum and Gerritsen, 1993; and Woodfield, 1994). Table 12.1 shows the membership of major regional organizations. This section will focus on the characteristics and prospects of APEC and the ARF, which have the most comprehensive membership of all collaborative arrangements in the Asia-Pacific.

Table 12.1   *Major organizations and their membership (1997)*

| | Political/security forums | | | | Economic forums | | |
| | Track I[1] | | Track II[2] | | Track I | | Track II |
	ASEAN[3]	ARF	CSCAP[4]	NEACD	APEC	ASEM[5]	PECC[6]
Asia/Oceania							
Australia		✓	✓		✓		✓
Brunei	✓	✓			✓	✓	✓
Burma/Myanmar		✓					
Cambodia		✓					
China		✓	✓	✓	✓	✓	✓
Hong Kong					✓		✓
India		✓	✓(am)				
Indonesia	✓	✓	✓(fm)		✓	✓	✓
Japan		✓	✓(fm)	✓	✓	✓	✓
North Korea			✓	✓			
South Korea		✓	✓(fm)	✓	✓	✓	✓
Laos		✓					
Malaysia	✓	✓	✓(fm)		✓	✓	✓
Mongolia		✓					
New Zealand		✓	✓		✓		✓
Papua New Guinea		✓			✓		
Philippines	✓	✓	✓(fm)		✓	✓	✓
Russia		✓	✓	✓			✓
Singapore	✓	✓	✓(fm)		✓	✓	✓
Taiwan					✓[7]		✓[7]

Table 12.1 *continued*

	Political/security forums				Economic forums		
	Track I[1]		*Track II[2]*		*Track I*		*Track II*
	ASEAN[3]	ARF	CSCAP[4]	NEACD	APEC	ASEM[5]	PECC[6]
Thailand	✓	✓	✓(fm)		✓	✓	✓
Vietnam	✓	✓	✓			✓	✓
North/South America							
Canada		✓	✓(fm)		✓		✓
Chile					✓		✓
Colombia							✓
Mexico					✓		✓
Peru							✓
USA		✓	✓(fm)	✓	✓		✓
Others		EU	EU (am)			EU	Pacific Is. nations

[1] Track I organizations have 'official' members, i.e. they are intergovernmental organizations.

[2] Track II organizations are 'unofficial' in that their members are generally non-governmental organizations and officials act in a private capacity.

[3] Only ASEAN member states participate in AFTA. Burma, Cambodia, and Laos were unanimously approved in December 1995 for membership in ASEAN. All three states are expected to become full ASEAN members by 2000. Along with China and Russia, India became a full Dialogue Partner of ASEAN in December 1995 and has been invited to join the ARF (currently there is a debate on whether ARF membership should be contingent upon whether a state has signed the Non-Proliferation Treaty). All ASEAN Dialogue Partners and Observers may sit in at ARF and other ASEAN meetings. Pakistan is a Sectoral Partner of ASEAN.

[4] Countries are represented by member committees and/or institutes. (fm) = founding member. (am) = associate member. The terms under which Taiwan may become a member of CSCAP are under consideration. Taiwan scholars and security specialists participate in a private capacity in all working group meetings. The EU is counted here as one member.

[5] Australia, New Zealand, India, Pakistan, and Russia have all expressed interest in participating in the next summit.

[6] Countries are represented by member committees and/or institutes.

[7] Member as 'Chinese Taipei'.

ASEAN: Association of South-East Asian Nations; AFTA: ASEAN Free Trade Area; ARF: ASEAN Regional Forum; CSCAP: Council for Security Co-operation in the Asia Pacific; NEACD: North-East Asia Co-operation Dialogue; APEC: Asia-Pacific Economic Co-operation; ASEM: Asia–Europe Meeting; PECC: Pacific Economic Co-operation Council.

Source: adapted from Stimson Center (1997)

APEC and the ARF

APEC and the ARF have much in common, not surprisingly as the ARF was consciously modelled on APEC. Both have their foundations in the experience of more than a quarter of a century of collaboration within ASEAN. The centrality of ASEAN countries to the ARF is obvious; they have been no less pivotal in APEC. In the Kuching Consensus adopted by their foreign and economic ministers in February 1990, ASEAN member countries stated their primary conditions for participation in APEC – namely that APEC should not adopt mandatory directives for its participants, and that it should not become an inward-looking trade bloc. Subsequently, these have been the guiding principles for APEC.

ASEAN countries entered the 1990s with new confidence. Their organization, the most fully developed collaborative forum in the region, had survived the Cold War, the conflict in Indo-China, and numerous bilateral tensions among its member states. After long being in the shadow of the North-East Asian newly-industrialized countries (Singapore was the exception), ASEAN member states, most notably Indonesia, Malaysia, and Thailand, began to record very high rates of economic growth in the mid 1980s. Meanwhile, the loss of Soviet support in the late 1980s drove Vietnam towards a new accommodation with its South-East Asian neighbours. Not only did ASEAN members aspire to create a free trade area within a decade, but they looked forward to the expansion of the grouping to include all ten South-East Asian states.

ASEAN members believed that the grouping's *modus operandi* offered an appropriate model for regional collaboration in the Asia-Pacific, an assessment accepted by other East Asian states. The essence of the ASEAN model was conflict avoidance rather than conflict resolution or dispute settlement, that is, potentially disruptive issues were put to one side rather than confronted directly. The hope was that these would sink into insignificance when weighed against the risks of disrupting gains from other areas in which co-operation was possible. Collaborative activities

Opening session of the twenty-third meeting of ASEAN, Jakarta, 24 July 1990

took place on the basis of consensus; the sovereignty of all member states was respected. Non-intervention in the internal affairs of other states was enshrined as a cardinal principle – in part a response to the recent experience of colonialism and to the support given, until ASEAN's formation, by some of its member states to anti-government forces in their neighbours. The formal equality of member states was honoured, even though the grouping was characterized by great disparities in economic development, size, and diplomatic capabilities; a majority never sought to prevail over a minority.

In ASEAN, the emphasis was on the diplomatic process rather than on legally-binding treaties or on institutions. Although ASEAN has a central secretariat, it is small (especially in the context of the very large number of meetings of officials held under ASEAN's auspices) and subordinate to the national governments whose officials are responsible for most of the preparatory work for meetings. And within the member states, it is the foreign ministries that play the predominant role on ASEAN issues. The European Union model, with its large and partly autonomous bureaucracy and popularly elected parliament, was consciously eschewed. In ASEAN there would be no question of creating a regional institution to rival the member states.

APEC and the ARF mimic key features of ASEAN's working procedures. In both groupings, the emphasis is on dialogue and the formation of consensus among member states rather than on the adoption of legally-binding treaties or resolutions. Thus in APEC proposals for a trade disputes-settlement procedure focused on mediation rather than the arbitration procedure used by the GATT/WTO: members were not to be placed in a situation where they would appear to lose face. Although the Bogor leaders' meeting in 1994 agreed on deadlines for the liberalization of intra-regional trade, some Asian members declared that these were voluntary targets rather than legally-binding commitments. At the next leaders' meeting in Osaka in 1995, members agreed that trade liberalization would take place through a process of 'concerted unilateralism'; in other words, members would decide for themselves the pace at which liberalization would take place. In the ARF, participants have made no attempt to impose obligations on one another; rather, the emphasis has been on starting a dialogue and on helping parties to gain confidence in one another. At the first meeting, members agreed that 'the ARF process shall move at a pace comfortable to all participants' (quoted in Leifer, 1996, p.42).

Confidence-building measures have been central to both groupings – although some Asian members of the ARF avoid this terminology because they associate confidence-building with attempts to mend relations among adversaries. Efforts to promote greater transparency are a principal means adopted to increase confidence among members. In the economic sphere, the various APEC working groups are responsible for collecting information about government policies on issues ranging from tariffs, competition policy, to energy and telecommunications (for a list of the APEC working groups see Rudner, 1995). In the ARF, an Inter-Sessional Support Group on

Confidence Building Measures was established to promote dialogue on countries' perceptions of the regional security situation, to encourage members to submit an annual defence policy statement to the ARF, and to enhance high-level contacts and exchanges among defence staff colleagues. Members were also encouraged to participate in the United Nations Register of Conventional Arms. An Inter-Sessional Meeting on Peacekeeping Operations promotes an exchange of information on participation in UN Peacekeeping and training of personnel for these operations.

Neither grouping has undergone significant institutionalization. Although APEC has a permanent secretariat based in Singapore, it is very small, and staffed primarily by officials seconded from member states. Member states themselves are responsible for the studies undertaken by the grouping's various working parties; occasionally the grouping commissions studies from the PECC secretariat. The ARF, a more recent creation, has no secretariat. Again it relies primarily on the bureaucracies of its members, supplemented by studies done by the various non-governmental organizations linked through CSCAP. Both groupings place a great deal of faith in the process of economic development helping to overcome existing bilateral tensions.

Neither grouping has sought to discriminate against outsiders. APEC adopted a policy of 'open regionalism', that is, of extending the benefits of trade liberalization that it undertakes on a non-discriminatory basis to non-members of the group. This unconditional extension of 'most favoured nation' treatment is an alternative means of complying with the GATT/WTO norm of non-discrimination rather than the more usual derogation that regional groupings seek under GATT's Article XXIV (which establishes specific criteria for the establishment of preferential economic arrangements on a regional basis). Members of the ARF have emphasized that they are not attempting, in the manner of traditional balance of power politics, to create a conventional security organization against a common enemy. Rather, the intention is to bring all interested parties to particular security problems together in the hope that the pursuit of 'co-operative security' will help resolve tensions. In particular, the ARF has been seen as a way of engaging China in regional security discussions rather than confront it through a policy of containment (see Chapters 5 and 8).

Have APEC and the ARF developed a unique form of multilateralism, an 'Asia-Pacific way'? And, if so, what are the advantages and problems of this particular approach to regional collaboration?

For some observers, the current process of regional dialogue in the Asia-Pacific epitomizes a novel approach to the building of international collaboration, an 'Asian Way' (Mahbubani, 1995). This is said to have its origins in village life in which processes of consultation and consensus-building are prominent, and in the Asian respect for hierarchy and desire to avoid inter-personal conflict in public. Others see nothing unique in the idea that improved inter-personal understanding may facilitate international dialogue (Leifer, 1996).

A contrast *is* evident, however, between the ASEAN approach to multilateralism, with its emphasis on consensus, and that practised among Western countries since 1945 in which treaties have spelled out detailed obligations as, for instance, in GATT and the Treaty of Rome (which established the European Community) or, in the defence sphere, in NATO. It is easy, however, to exaggerate the significance of cultural factors. For instance, governments may wrap themselves in a blanket of cultural excuses in attempting to rationalize the actions or non-actions that they are undertaking for straightforward reasons of perceived national interest. Moreover, explanations of action grounded in culture frequently exaggerate the immutability of national traditions. In reality, 'cultures' are rarely stagnant but continually adapting to the challenges posed by economic, technological and social change (**Maidment and Mackerras, 1998**).

The strongest argument in favour of the ASEAN approach to intergovernmental collaboration is that in many instances it is the only approach that would be acceptable to many of the region's governments. A NAFTA-style treaty, for instance, that not only imposes legally-binding obligations on tariffs but also on some items on the deeper regionalism agenda, such as environmental standards, would simply not attract the support of most East Asian governments. Similarly, in the security sphere, where several regional countries were on different sides of the Cold War divide, no formal treaty is imaginable for the foreseeable future: establishing a mechanism that merely allows for better communication is a major step forward.

The ASEAN approach, sometimes termed 'soft regionalism', is probably the only one that is feasible at the present time. It does, however, have significant weaknesses. The emphasis within both APEC and the ARF on dialogue, as opposed to obligations and sanctions, places a heavy burden on the socializing influences of the two bodies. In the absence of legally-binding commitments and sanctions, the groupings themselves do little else to change the incentives for co-operative behaviour than increase the risk of embarrassment for countries that fail to meet the expectations of their partners (Fane, 1995; Ravenhill, 1995a). A clash of cultures *does* exist between the Asian and especially the North American members of the regional bodies (Ravenhill, 1995b). Washington looks to APEC with an expectation that it will produce results – both in reducing trade barriers and in resolving the difficult issues of market access that have caused irritation in its trade relations with East Asian states in the last two decades. Whether a process of concerted unilateralism in trade liberalization moving towards a non-binding target will exert sufficient pressure on others to satisfy Washington remains to be seen. Certainly APEC has done little so far to preclude the USA resorting to bilateralism in its economic relations with other states of the region or to discourage members from taking trade disputes to the WTO.

The ARF suffers from similar weaknesses. The ARF has adopted an unusual approach to security co-operation that rests overwhelmingly on political dialogue and the encouragement of transparency on security issues. It makes no provision for collective security or for collective defence.

Sources of bilateral tensions are seldom confronted directly in the forum's deliberations, imitating ASEAN's pattern of conflict avoidance. ASEAN was aided, however, in maintaining a certain amount of group solidarity over a quarter of a century by the presence of an external threat – Vietnam, which at one stage enjoyed the support of both the Soviet Union and China. In the context of this external threat, territorial and other disputes among ASEAN's own members shrank into insignificance. Whether an ASEAN-style arrangement can cope with the more severe security problems of the wider Asia-Pacific region, most of which are concentrated in North-East Asia, is questionable. Certainly, the ARF has had no impact to date on the high levels of arms expenditures by most countries of the western Pacific Rim. Moreover, ASEAN's proprietorial attitude towards the ARF has produced tensions with non South-East Asian countries that believe it is not giving sufficient attention to problems outside the ASEAN region (Leifer, 1996).

Proponents of both APEC and the ARF pin their faith on the socializing capabilities of the dialogue process that these groupings have established. Inevitably, confidence building through dialogue takes time. The key question confronting both groupings is whether member states, especially those who wish to see significant change in the regional economic or security regimes, will perceive sufficient short-term benefits from the process to continue to give it their support at the highest levels. Again the USA is the key actor here. The US President is continually under pressure from Congress to produce results. Neither Congress nor the modern presidency have an incentive to adopt a long time horizon. If results are not forthcoming soon, Washington may lose patience with the groupings. The USA may not necessarily withdraw its support; rather it will prefer other (probably bilateral) channels that enable it to mobilize its considerable leverage to attempt to force more rapid movement in its preferred direction.

12.5   Conclusion: towards an Asia-Pacific community?

To write in the mid 1990s of an Asia-Pacific community would seem not premature but entirely fanciful. Even in Western Europe, 40 years of economic and political integration – including the development of a popularly-elected European Parliament – has seen little growth in popular identity with 'Europe' as a political, economic or social construct. In the Asia-Pacific, increasing intergovernmental collaboration has been only weakly institutionalized. Australia's former Minister for Foreign Affairs, Gareth Evans, termed Asia-Pacific Economic Co-operation 'four adjectives in search of a noun'. The expression is still applicable. East Asian countries have resisted attempts from the USA and Canada to inject a greater contractual element into APEC. Asian states even rejected an attempt to change the grouping's name to Asia-Pacific Economic Community at the Seattle leaders' meeting in 1993 because they associated this term with the creation of regional institutions. The meeting adopted the Chinese character for 'family' in preference to that for 'community'.

The region is far from being a 'security community', a phrase applied by Karl Deutsch *et al.* (1957, p.5) to a process of integration that leads not only to a sense of community but also produces 'institutions and practices strong enough and widespread enough to assure, for a "long" time, dependable expectations of "peaceful change" among its population'. The region, as Chapter 5 explained, contains a number of potential military flashpoints. These include the Cold War legacies of conflicts between China and Taiwan, and between North and South Korea. In addition, there are territorial disputes between ASEAN countries and China over the South China Sea, between Japan and China over Senkaku Island in the East China Sea, between Japan and South Korea over the Takeshima or Tak-do island, between the Philippines and Malaysia over the state of Sabah and its territorial waters, and border conflicts between Cambodia and Vietnam. Such sources of dispute pose significant challenges of conflict management for governments in the region (for alternative views of the gravity of the security problems of the contemporary Asia-Pacific region see Buzan and Segal, 1994; Dibb, 1995; and Richardson, 1994/95).

Moreover, the Asia-Pacific contains a particularly heterogeneous group of states. It includes the world's most populous state, China, and the tiny city state of Singapore. Levels of development range from some of the world's highest per capita incomes in North America to some of the lowest in China and Papua New Guinea. Histories and cultures are diverse, even within East Asia itself. Despite the recent popularity of ideas about an 'Asian Way', East Asian countries lack a common cultural heritage. Compare, for instance, the Confucian tradition of Korea with the Islamic heritage of Indonesia and Malaysia. And even where cultural commonalities are present as, for instance, in Japan and Korea, centuries of interstate conflict have generated a climate of deep suspicion between the peoples of the two countries as well as their governments – casting doubt on arguments that the most likely division in post-Cold War politics will be between 'civilizations' (Huntington, 1993).

To conclude: even though intergovernmental collaborative arrangements in the Asia-Pacific region have developed at a rate that few would have thought possible a decade ago, there is still little sense of an Asia-Pacific community. Differences between 'Western' legalistic approaches to economic integration and the consensual model favoured by East Asian governments continue to haunt APEC. And in the security realm, the fledgling ARF has yet to demonstrate that its consensus-oriented approach to security co-operation will be sufficient to defuse the many potential territorial conflicts among East Asian states.

References

Aggarwal, V.K. (1995) 'Comparing regional cooperation efforts in the Asia-Pacific and North America' in Mack, A. and Ravenhill, J. (eds), pp.40–65.

Ball, D. and Kerr, P. (1996) *Presumptive Engagement: Australia's Asia-Pacific Security Policy in the 1990s*, Sydney, Allen and Unwin.

Bayard, T.O. and Elliott, K.A. (1994) *Reciprocity and Retaliation in US Trade Policy*, Washington, Institute for International Economics.

Bernard, M. and Ravenhill, J. (1995) 'Beyond product cycles and flying geese: regionalization, hierarchy, and the industrialization of East Asia', *World Politics*, vol.45, no.2, pp.179–210.

Bhagwati, J. and Patrick, H.T. (eds) (1990) *Aggressive Unilateralism: America's 301 Trade Policy and the World Trading System*, Ann Arbor, University of Michigan Press.

Buszynski, L. (1983) *SEATO: the Failure of an Alliance Strategy*, Singapore, Singapore University Press.

Buzan, B. and Segal, G. (1994) 'Rethinking East Asian security', *Survival* (summer), pp.3–21.

Chia, S.Y. and Lee, T.Y. (1993) 'Subregional economic zones: a new motive force in Asia-Pacific development' in Bergsten, C.F. and Noland, M. (eds) *Pacific Dynamism and the International Economic System*, Washington, Institute for International Economics, pp.225–69.

Conybeare, J.A.C. (1987) *Trade Wars: the Theory and Practice of International Commercial Rivalry*, New York, Columbia University Press.

Cooper, A.F., Higgott, R.A. and Nossal, K.R. (1993) *Relocating Middle Powers: Australia and Canada in a Changing World Order*, Vancouver, University of British Columbia Press.

Cowhey, P.F. and Long, E. (1983) 'Testing theories of regime change: hegemonic decline or surplus capacity?', *International Organization*, vol.37, no.2, pp.157–88.

Crone, D. (1993) 'Does hegemony matter? The reorganization of the Pacific political economy', *World Politics*, vol.45, no.4, pp.501–25.

Destler, I.M. (1992) *American Trade Policies*, 2nd edn, New York, Twentieth Century Fund and Institute for International Economics.

Deutsch, K.W. *et al.* (1957) *Political Community and the North Atlantic Area*, Princeton, Princeton University Press.

Dibb, P. (1995) *Towards a New Balance of Power in Asia*, London, International Institute for Strategic Studies.

Drysdale, P. (1988) *International Economic Pluralism: Economic Policy in East Asia and the Pacific*, Sydney, Allen and Unwin.

Eichbaum, C. and Gerritsen, R. (1993) 'The impossible politics of CER?', *Australian Quarterly*, vol.65, no.1.

Fane, G. (1995) 'APEC: regionalism, globalism, or obfuscation?', *Agenda*, vol.2, no.4, pp.399–409.

Fishlow, A. and Haggard, S. (1992) *The United States and the Regionalization of the World Economy*, Paris, OECD.

Foucault, M. (1973) *The Order of Things*, New York, Vintage.

Frankel, J. (1991) 'Is a yen bloc forming in Pacific Asia?' in O'Brien, R. (ed.) *Finance and the International Economy 5: The AMEX Bank Review Prize Essays*, Oxford, Oxford University Press, pp.5–20.

Gowa, J. (1989) 'Rational hegemons, excludable goods, and small groups: an epitaph for hegemonic stability theory?', *World Politics*, vol.XLI, no.3, pp.307–24.

Haas, E.B. (1990) *When Knowledge is Power: Three Models of Change in International Organizations*, Berkeley, University of California Press.

Haggard, S. (1995) *Developing Nations and the Politics of Global Integration*, Washington, Brookings Institution.

Harris, S. (1994) 'Policy networks and economic cooperation: policy coordination in the Asia-Pacific region', *The Pacific Review*, vol.7, no.4, pp.381–96.

Hirschman, A.O. (1945) *National Power and the Structure of Foreign Trade*, Berkeley, University of California Press.

Huntington, S.P. (1993) 'The clash of civilizations?', *Foreign Affairs*, vol.LXXII, no.3, pp.22–49.

Hurrell, A. (1995a) 'Explaining the resurgence of regionalism in world politics', *Review of International Studies*, no.21, pp.331–58.

Hurrell, A. (1995b) 'Regionalism in theoretical perspective' in Fawcett, L. and Hurrell, A. (eds) *Regionalism in World Politics: Regional Organization and International Order*, Oxford, Oxford University Press, pp.37–73.

Imada, P. and Naya, S. (eds) (1992) *AFTA: the Way Ahead*, Singapore, Institute of South-East Asian Studies.

Kahler, M. (1995) 'Institution-building in the Pacific' in Mack, A. and Ravenhill, J. (eds), pp.16–39.

Keohane, R.O. (1984) *After Hegemony: Cooperation and Discord in the World Political Economy*, Princeton, Princeton University Press.

Kerr, P. (1994) 'The security dialogue in the Asia-Pacific', *Pacific Review*, vol.7, no.4.

Kerr, P., Mack, A. and Evans, P. (1995) 'The evolving security discourse in the Asia-Pacific' in Mack, A. and Ravenhill, J. (eds), pp.233–55.

Kindleberger, C.P. (1973) *The World in Depression 1929–39*, Berkeley, University of California Press.

Krasner, S.D. (1976) 'State power and the structure of international trade', *World Politics*, no.28, pp.317–47.

Krasner, S.D. (1982) 'Structural causes and regime consequences: regimes as intervening variables', *International Organization*, vol.36, no.2, pp.185–205.

Krasner, S.D. (1987) *Asymmetries in Japanese–American Trade: the Case for Specific Reciprocity*, Berkeley, Institute of International Studies, University of California.

Lee, T.Y. (ed.) (1991) *Growth Triangle: The Johor–Singapore–Riau Experience*, Singapore, Institute of South-East Asian Studies.

Leifer, M. (1996) 'The ASEAN Regional Forum', *Adelphi Paper no.302*, London, International Institute for Strategic Studies.

Lincoln, E.J. (1990) *Japan's Unequal Trade*, Washington, Brookings Institution.

Mack, A. and Ravenhill, J. (eds) (1995) *Pacific Cooperation: Building Economic and Security Regimes in the Asia-Pacific Region*, Boulder, Westview Press.

McKeown, T.J. (1983) 'Hegemonic stability theory and nineteenth century tariff levels in Europe', *International Organization*, vol.37, no.1, pp.73–91.

Mahbubani, K. (1995) 'The Pacific impulse', *Survival*, vol.37, no.1, pp.105–20.

Maidment, R. and Mackerras, C. (eds) (1998) *Culture and Society in the Asia-Pacific*, London, Routledge in association with The Open University.

Ravenhill, J. (1995a) 'Bringing politics back in: the political economy of APEC', Seoul, Institute of East and West Studies, Yonsei University, Conference on the Future of APEC, November.

Ravenhill, J. (1995b) 'Competing logics of regionalism in the Asia-Pacific', *Journal of European Integration*, vol.XVIII, no.2–3, pp.179–99.

Ravenhill, J. (1995c) 'Economic cooperation in Southeast Asia: changing incentives', *Asian Survey*, vol.XXXV, no.9, pp.850–66.

Ravenhill, J. (1998) 'Australia' in Aggarwal, V.K. and Morrison, C. (eds) *APEC*, London, Routledge.

Richardson, J.L. (1994/95) 'Asia-Pacific: the case for geopolitical optimism', *The National Interest*, vol.38, pp.28–39.

Rudner, M. (1995) 'APEC: the challenges of Asia Pacific economic cooperation', *Journal of Modern Asian Studies*, vol.29, no.2, pp.403–37.

Ruggie, J.G. (1975) 'International responses to technology: concepts and trends', *International Organization*, vol.29, no.3, pp.557–83.

Segal, G. (1990) *Rethinking the Pacific*, Oxford, Clarendon Press.

Stein, A.A. (1984) 'The hegemon's dilemma: Great Britain, the United States, and the international economic order', *International Organization*, vol.38, no.2, pp.355–86.

Stimson Center (1997) *Confidence Building Measures in the Asia-Pacific*, Washington, Henry L. Stimson Center.

Toh, M.H. and Low, L. (1993a) 'Is the ASEAN Free Trade Area a second best option?', *Asian Economic Journal*, vol.7, no.3, pp.275–98.

Toh, M.H. and Low, L. (eds) (1993b) *Regional Cooperation and Growth Triangles in ASEAN*, Singapore, Times Academic Press.

Wiseman, G. (1992) 'Common security in the Asia-Pacific region', *The Pacific Review*, vol.5, no.1, pp.42–59.

Woodfield, T. (1994) 'A trans-Tasman community?', *New Zealand International Review*, XIX, vol.4.

Woods, L.T. (1993) *Asia-Pacific Diplomacy: Nongovernmental Organizations and International Relations*, Vancouver, University of British Columbia Press.

Further reading

Leifer, M. (1996) 'The ASEAN Regional Forum', *Adelphi Paper no.302*, London, International Institute for Strategic Studies.

Mack, A. and Ravenhill, J. (eds) (1995) *Pacific Cooperation: Building Economic and Security Regimes in the Asia-Pacific Region*, Boulder, Westview Press.

Woods, L.T. (1993) *Asia-Pacific Diplomacy: Nongovernmental Organizations and International Relations*, Vancouver, University of British Columbia Press.

CHAPTER 13

Regional co-operation: the transnational dimension

Lawrence T. Woods

13.1 Introduction: regional co-operation and transnationalism in the Asia-Pacific

Contemporary discussions of Asia-Pacific regionalism tend to share three assumptions: that an historical perspective limited to the period since the mid 1960s, or even since 1989, is sufficient; that the objective is an enhanced and now redefined form of national security; and that this objective is to be achieved through the creation of intergovernmental arrangements shaped by the transnational collaboration of academic, business and government representatives – the tripartite policy network (see, for example, Hellman and Pyle, 1997; Mack and Ravenhill, 1995). After briefly outlining the meaning of *transnationalism* and these three dominant assumptions, this chapter explores an alternative conception of transnationalism in the Asia-Pacific region. The time line is extended back to the 1920s, the conventional analysis of the security being sought is challenged, and the grassroots reaction to the exclusive tripartite policy network approach to regional co-operation is assessed. The argument presented here is that a 'people-centred' transnationalism exists beyond the dominant, narrow depiction of regional co-operation. We need a broader view of the social forces engaged in regional co-operation as well as a multidimensional conception of security.

13.2 Transnationalism defined

The term 'transnational' was popularized in the early 1970s by two American scholars of international relations, Keohane and Nye (1973). Conceding the growing influence of nongovernmental organizations (NGOs) in a variety of policy areas, and the utility of including these actors in the study of international affairs, Keohane and Nye talk of *transnational relations and interactions*. *Transnational relations* are defined as 'contacts, coalitions, and interactions across state boundaries that are not controlled by the central foreign policy organs of governments' (Keohane and Nye, 1973, p.xi). A *transnational interaction*, however, is defined as one involving 'nongovernmental actors – individuals or organizations': it 'may involve governments, but it may not involve only governments' (ibid., 1973, p.xi). To clarify the distinction between these and other forms of international interactions, Keohane and Nye set out a classification scheme composed of three types, the other two being *interstate* – those interactions between states which are formally channelled through and controlled by the foreign offices – and *transgovernmental* – those interactions between states in which government departments other than the foreign office take the lead. The latter category arises in recognition that in many issue areas national bureaucracies have taken to communicating with one another directly; the notion of inter-state relations always going through foreign offices officially designated and designed for this purpose no longer holds. Advances in communications technologies and capabilities have facilitated transnational interactions to the point where they warrant being conceived as a separate category of interaction.

The main point of confusion arising from this analysis is the suggestion that transnational relations may involve governments. Moreover, for Keohane and Nye transnational relations are composed of *transnational* **and** *transgovernmental* interactions. It is important to keep this in mind because in conventional analyses the term *transnational organization* is usually reserved for discussions of for-profit and not-for-profit nongovernmental entities (for example, Amnesty International, the Catholic Church) operating across state boundaries or in issue areas which transcend these boundaries. Similarly, the concept of *transnationalism* is normally used to connote only the nongovernmental aspects of what Keohane and Nye call *transnational relations*.

Keohane and Nye's pathbreaking analysis included a discussion of the ways in which states and governments relate to transnational interactions and organizations. These strategies include: not responding; unilaterally implementing defensive policies to thwart domestic nongovernmental activities; extending the impact of domestic laws beyond state boundaries through controls on transnational flows; pursuing defensive policy co-ordination with other states (possibly through an intergovernmental organization); attempting to co-opt the nongovernmental activities in support of state objectives alone; and pursuing a symbiotic relationship with a nongovernmental actor. Looked at in this context, it is perhaps easier to see how governments can form part of what Keohane and Nye refer to as *transnational relations* or a *transnational interaction*. For neo-realist scholars – who by definition adopt a state-centric model of international relations – it is by provoking state responses that transnational entities enhance their legitimacy as actors worthy of study anyway. Keohane and Nye themselves place great emphasis on the issue of control, in particular the decreasing ability of states to manage nongovernmental actors. One problem with this focus on the state's ability to deal with NGOs is that it leads such scholars to undervalue the need to examine how transnational actors respond to interstate and transgovernmental interactions. It can also blind them to the possibility that those transnational relations which do not involve states or governments may be worthy of study in their own right. The overwhelming emphasis on intergovernmental institutions such as Asia Pacific Economic Co-operation (APEC), with life before APEC sometimes completely absent from the discussion, suggests that these problems have been manifest in the study of Asia-Pacific regionalism.

13.3 Dominant assumptions in Asia-Pacific analyses

A limited historical perspective

Some commentators begin the story of the evolution of trans-Pacific institutions with the creation in 1989 of the first intergovernmental forum dedicated to the promotion of regional economic co-operation. However, that APEC is now commonly referred to pejoratively as 'four adjectives in search of a noun' should alert students of regionalism to the existence of life before APEC. In a very real sense, APEC arose in response to transnational interactions and transnational relations: the activities of NGOs promoting regional co-operation via governmental policy co-ordination and the impact these activities were having on states. Those who appreciate the nongovernmental initiatives which preceded, prodded, provoked and now parallel official diplomatic channels will usually consent to extending their historical perspective back as far as the mid 1960s and the near simultaneous founding of two regional NGOs: the Pacific Trade and Development Conference (PAFTAD) and the Pacific Basin Economic Council (PBEC). These bodies were joined in 1980 by a third NGO, the Pacific Economic Co-operation Council (PECC, formerly Conference), although its nongovernmental credentials are not beyond question (Woods, 1993). As later sections will argue, the focus on this phase and form of Asia-Pacific transnationalism overlooks other past and present initiatives from which important lessons can be learned.

The key aspects of this phase of transnationalism relate to the goals of the nongovernmental actors involved and the nature of their interactions with governments. PAFTAD was formally launched in 1968 in order to create a network in which economists from around the region could discuss ways to facilitate the co-ordination and harmonization of national economic policies. The membership size and geographical scope of this network have seen an impressive level of expansion over time. However, despite claims about harbouring a diversity of viewpoints, it has been noted that neo-liberal economic theory and an emphasis on trade liberalization measures dominate PAFTAD analyses. Generally seen as the academic impetus behind the regional economic co-operation movement, PAFTAD's first conference occurred in the same year as that of PBEC, an association of corporate executives seeking to promote the creation of a policy climate in which free enterprise could thrive. The preferred form of policy co-ordination for PBEC members is thus also that which fosters economic liberalization and allows for the relatively unfettered operation of market forces. Due to differing attitudes towards the role of corporate activity at the national level, the expansion of PBEC's geographical scope has been slower than that of PAFTAD and the Council has struggled to shed its early image as a 'rich man's club' (Palmer, 1991, pp.133–40; Woods, 1993, pp.41–88).

PAFTAD and PBEC directed their efforts to influencing the decisions of state policy-makers, frequently including bureaucrats and legislators (past, present and future) in their activities. The participants in PAFTAD and PBEC meetings have also frequently found themselves being expected by other participants to act as representatives of their governments. Some consider themselves – and are considered by their home governments – to be unofficial diplomats. As such, PAFTAD and PBEC have come to be classified as major players in what is now referred to as 'track two' diplomacy (Volkan *et al.*, 1991; Berman and Johnson, 1977).

The objectives and approaches of these NGOs led to the creation of PECC, a further 'track two' diplomatic channel which brought together representatives of the academic, business and governmental sectors, all of whom are described as acting in their private capacities. Founded in 1980 as a result of discussions between the Japanese and Australian governments (Japanese and Australian interests were also early supporters of the PAFTAD and PBEC initiatives), PECC became the purveyor of what is at best a polite fiction if one ponders the notion of an 'unofficial government official'. Nevertheless, it was the subsequent momentum gained by the PECC process, and its popularity in official circles as a way to shape the regional response to issues arising within the global trading system, that eventually prompted the establishment in 1989 of APEC, again as a result of collaboration between the governments of Australia and Japan (Cooper *et al.*, 1993, pp.50–115; Palmer, 1991, pp.130–94; Woods, 1993, pp.89–148).

Having at the behest of the USA set its sights on achieving free trade amongst all member nations by 2020, APEC was joined on the intergovernmental side by the ASEAN Regional Forum (ARF) in 1994 (Rudner, 1995). ARF has been complemented by a nongovernmental channel, namely the Council for Security Co-operation in the Asia-Pacific (CSCAP). The Council was created by a network of research institutes from around the region, some of which are led by people already engaged in the NGOs active on economic issues. All, however, have close links to their respective governments. Various forms of membership have now been sanctioned, thereby allowing for regional and extra-regional representation (including European). The level of co-operation and competition between these official and unofficial policy networks may well play a role in determining the future course of Asia-Pacific regionalism. CSCAP's arrival should also be seen in the context of a proliferation of informal regional security dialogues in the post-Cold War period (Evans, 1994a, 1996; Kerr *et al.*, 1995).

As Chapter 12 dealt with the aforementioned forms of inter-governmental and nongovernmental collaboration, I will move on to address the transnational dimensions arising from the following questions:

- Will intergovernmental arrangements such as APEC, ARF and CSCAP be able to redefine security in a meaningful way?

- Would their failure to do so provoke transnational reactions from those who feel marginalized by existing track one (official) and track two (unofficial) diplomacy, or feel threatened by the narrow foci of these activities?

Redefining security

In recent decades the field of international studies has been awash with commentaries promoting the redefining security thesis (see, for example, Ullman, 1983; Mathews, 1989). According to this thesis, security should no longer be viewed in strictly military or national *cum* international terms, with the integrity of the nation-state being always the central concern. Instead, it introduces the companion idea of global security, drawing attention to the need to attend to the integrity of the entire globe and all physical features and life forms existing upon it. While this thesis has been challenged in some quarters, and various scholars have forcefully questioned its analytical utility, those who argue that security is being redefined in practice, and that our analytical perspectives must thus by necessity be adjusted to accommodate this change, are essentially claiming that we must have both a multilevel and multidimensional view of the concept (Buzan, 1991; Krause and Williams, 1996). If we do this, distinct policy implications follow.

With this attempt to be inclusive comes the call for discussions of security to involve issues beyond the military/strategic or military/strategic *cum* political realms. State interest in the role of business and finance has made it easy to add matters pertinent to economic security, and Asia-Pacific NGOs such as PAFTAD, PBEC and PECC have been created to make this link. But the proponents of the redefining security thesis have made their most obvious contributions to the debate by drawing attention to environmental and human security. Perhaps the most salient policy implication flowing from the inclusion of these issue areas is the need to democratize the national and international policy-making process so as to include the representation of interests other than those of states and corporations. The main impetus here arises from the observation that states are – in their own eyes and those of their citizens – no longer able to deal effectively with military/strategic, political, economic, environmental and/ or human security concerns by acting unilaterally. Individual, local, national, regional, international and/or global initiatives may be required. We can no longer consider security to refer to the state's military/strategic concerns only, or allow the pursuit of security to be addressed by the state without input from other stakeholders.

The most frequently heard academic criticisms of this redefinition of security are that by broadening the term we render it devoid of any real meaning, or that this thesis merely exacerbates the ambiguity and semantic symbolism which has long plagued the concept. One way of ending the debate might be to throw out the term altogether, but its roots in the field are so deep that this is unlikely to be done. If security is thus destined to live on as a concept used in discussions of international affairs, I favour a usage which exposes its many levels and dimensions. But I also favour an approach which shows an appreciation of its evolution. As the next section will explain, in the Asia-Pacific context this would mean an approach which incorporates an understanding that we are *rediscovering*, not redefining, security.

Nevertheless, in response to an apparent shift in the way people – as opposed to states – view international affairs, APEC and ARF have periodically expressed interest in pursuing concerns pertinent to a broader definition of security, to moving beyond economic and military/strategic issues and addressing the security implications of social and environmental issues. As with many new ideas, resistance has been strong and progress slow. Governmental commitment to acknowledging the relationships between issue areas is questionable. The NGOs that underpin APEC and ARF have also taken tentative steps to broaden their perspectives, with power politics and bureaucratic politics hindering these efforts as well (Harris, 1994; Kerr, 1994; Klare, 1997). The most prominent 'track two' elements of the contemporary regional co-operation movement seem similarly reticent about learning from the past. As a result, those who feel left out are being forced to counterbalance the dominant view by forming networks of their own. In so doing, they begin at a distinct disadvantage in terms of resources. Their main advantage comes from the evident inability of PAFTAD, PBEC, PECC, CSCAP, APEC and ARF to shift gears in a meaningful way.

The tripartite policy network

The third common assumption in analyses of Asia-Pacific regionalism is that the institution-building story is one which involves the evolution of intergovernmental collaboration shaped primarily by academic, business and government interests – the *tripartite policy network*. This view is consonant with the epistemic community approach noted by Ravenhill in Chapter 12, but it also reflects aspects of what in an earlier era of regional integration studies was termed *neo-functionalism* (Haas, 1958, 1964; Palmer, 1991, pp.5–12). Such studies and their attendant theories – pronounced obsolescent long ago – have recently been revived in the form of what Palmer has called *new regionalism* (Palmer, 1991). According to this view the underlying dynamic of regional integration is an exclusive elitism (Higgott, 1994). Regional co-operation is driven by intergovernmental interactions facilitated by corporate and academic elites. In order to acknowledge the contributions of academic ideas and business interests, this 'new regionalism' identifies the ways in which these extra-state players have helped forge an elite consensus. These extra-state players normally have unusually good access to governments, often because the latter have helped initiate or fund the tripartite policy network promoting Asia-Pacific regionalism. Extra-state players would rarely admit to being under the direct influence of governments, but it is clear that their own activities owe much to the privileged access and funding they receive from states, state agencies and allied foundations (Evans, 1994b; Woods, 1993; Yamamoto, 1995).

Reflecting on the state strategies highlighted by Keohane and Nye (see Section 13.2), one wonders whether this is all part of a symbiotic relationship between states and NGOs, a co-optation strategy being implemented by states and/or used by NGOs. Given that interest in, and support for, the NGO components of this network is waning as attention shifts amongst all sectors to the work of APEC and ARF, it would seem that control has also shifted to the intergovernmental fora. The question of who is influencing or controlling whom will require further study, unless we accept the view that the academic, business and government participants in these fora essentially share the same socio-economic backgrounds, educational foundations, ideological perspectives, and/or policy predispositions, that they all believe at some level in the necessity of pursuing what are seen to be the benefits which will accrue to the state as a result of economic and trade liberalization.

13.4   An alternative perspective

An earlier voyage

Let us now explore an alternative view of the regional co-operation story by overturning the dominant assumptions discussed above. On the issue of historical perspective, it must be understood that the promotion of regional co-operation through *transnationalism* in the Asia-Pacific has a continuous and important history which goes back much further than the mid 1960s. As Ravenhill noted in passing (Chapter 12), the Pan-Pacific Union, founded in 1917, has been cited as one of the earliest regional NGOs , the activities of missionary groups having by that time already had a long history of attempting to bridge the Pacific (Hooper, 1988; Davidann, 1995). Although the Union's impetus and utility were questionable through to its collapse in 1934, many other nongovernmental groups arose shortly after its initiation, some of which – such as the Pacific Science Association – are still active (Rehbok, 1988). Numerous pan-Pacific NGOs have also arisen more recently in various sectors beyond those concerned with economic, political or military/strategic security (Yamamoto, 1995).

The period following the First World War was the heyday for the creation of regional NGOs. Arguably the most significant step was the 1925 establishment of the Institute of Pacific Relations (IPR), in that the intellectual roots of many academic institutions round the world pursuing

Asian studies in a concerted way today lie in the IPR. Furthermore, it was the precursor of the 'track two' regional diplomacy outlined above (Hooper, 1988; Woods, 1993). Bringing together multipartite national delegations (each consisting of academics and educators, business people, journalists and editors, philanthropists, service group and church officials, labour leaders, retired politicians, and active diplomats) for thirteen conferences between 1925 and 1958, the IPR engaged participants from eighteen countries and territories (Australia, Burma, Canada, Ceylon, China, France, Great Britain, Hawaii, India, Indonesia, Japan, Korea, the Netherlands, New Zealand, Pakistan, the Philippines, the Soviet Union, and the United States) in its research and dialogue activities. Tarred by the 'guilt by association' brush wielded by anti-communist McCarthyites in the USA during the early 1950s, as they looked for a scapegoat after the 'loss' of China, the Institute eventually succumbed to the wounds inflicted upon its reputation, and ability to attract funding, and was disbanded in 1960 (Stone, 1996, pp.77–8; Thomas, 1974).

Worthy of study because of both its successes and its failures, the Institute lives on today in the form of journals such as *Pacific Affairs* (originally published by the IPR's international secretariat) and *Asian Survey* (originally published by the American council of the IPR). Its legacy is also manifest through the many scholars round the globe who began their careers with IPR support or have benefited from the Institute's impressive research and publication programmes, the many institutions which have built upon the Institute's foresight in promoting the study of Asian languages and cultures, and the many unofficial diplomatic channels which have intentionally or unintentionally taken up variants of the IPR's approach to regional co-operation. In the wake of the disbanding of the IPR in 1960, it was no coincidence that founders of PAFTAD and PBEC drew upon the IPR example when fashioning their organizations. Though sectoral in nature, these bodies were seeking to fill the void left by the IPR in recognition of the continuing utility of 'track two' diplomacy (Hooper, 1995; Woods, 1991, 1995a). Indeed, narrowly-defined sectoral organizations such as PAFTAD and PBEC were created to promote regional co-operation, because support for a new IPR-like body could not be found, and because it had become necessary to narrow the working definition of security in order to conform to the political orthodoxy of the day in the West. Hence, only military/strategic and economic/business issues could be included in the definition of security, the latter underpinning the primacy of the former. Economic matters could be discussed safely by NGOs, regional military/strategic issues being left to bilateral treaties such as that between the USA and Japan or to interstate organizations such as ASEAN.

Rediscovering security

Perhaps an even more telling IPR legacy, therefore, is found in the contemporary effort to redefine security. For when one surveys the range of the societal backgrounds of participants at Institute conferences, the breadth of the topics tackled by their innovative dialogue process, and the scope of their research programme, one begins to see that what is today being called a redefinition should properly be seen as a voyage of rediscovery. In its earliest years the IPR was close to being as inclusive in terms of participation and range of topics as those now promoting the redefinition thesis are arguing for. Immigration policies, cultural relations, the treatment of 'aliens' and native peoples, gender, standards of living, working conditions, population growth, food supply, land utilization, natural resources, foreign investment, trade barriers, economic issues, industrialization, public opinion, international education, the role of the media, diplomatic structures, China, and armaments were all issues explored using the IPR's experimental scientific approach to comparative national studies and the frank discussion of this research by delegates drawn from a wide range of societal backgrounds (Hooper, 1995).

This approach reflected to some extent the many variants of idealist internationalism prominent in the wake of the First World War, which stressed the importance of education and cross-cultural understanding in the promotion of international co-operation, the objective being the enhancement of security for both peoples and states (Long and Wilson, 1995). Getting to know one another better would, in the view of many an Institute proponent, help to prevent international political conflicts. Early leaders disavowed direct connections to, or active roles within, official diplomatic channels. If ideas generated by the IPR found their way into official diplomatic practice, so be it. This result would only confirm their belief in the need for, and effectiveness of, nongovernmental channels such as the IPR, given the relative absence of intergovernmental links in the Asia-Pacific region (Woods, 1993, pp.29–40).

The scope of the Institute's attention admittedly narrowed quickly. By 1933, economic conflict and Japanese expansionism overshadowed other matters. As the Second World War loomed, the IPR could not avoid the vicissitudes of the nationalism and militarism swirling around it. While the Allies utilized its meetings to craft the post-war global and regional order, thereby verifying the Institute's utility as a track two diplomatic channel, the IPR's cable address – INPAREL (pronounced 'in peril') – had proven prophetic, in part precisely because of the way in which official diplomacy and national council connections to national governments had impinged upon the Institute's activities and raised fundamental questions about its nongovernmental credentials.

In form and function, the Council for Security Co-operation in the Asia Pacific (CSCAP) looks like the IPR reincarnated. But is it? Was 1993 the right time – twenty-five years after the creation of PAFTAD and PBEC and thirteen years since the arrival of PECC – for a network of research institutes to move beyond the economic sphere, to take up military/strategic and other security matters in the track two context? The answer to this question seems to be, 'Yes, but … '. This hesitation is prompted by two observations. First, it remains unclear that early CSCAP efforts actually share the same multifaceted view of security as early IPR activities. CSCAP proponents talk a good game, but the military/strategic conception has been dominant from the start. Second, whereas IPR proponents actively eschewed direct ties to governments, CSCAP proponents – following the lead of PAFTAD, PBEC and PECC proponents – actively pursue such ties, to the extent that the overt CSCAP–ARF relationship is a badge of honour (Evans, 1996; Kerr, 1994; Kerr *et al.*, 1995). The development of nongovernmental and intergovernmental institutions intentionally conceived as complementary components of a two track approach to regional diplomacy illustrates a major difference between the IPR and post-IPR phases of transnationalism in the Asia-Pacific.

The IPR's first statement of purpose spoke of its objective as being 'to study the conditions of the Pacific peoples with a view to the improvement of their mutual relations' (Condliffe, 1928, p.607). Given that the transnational dimension as conventionally understood seems to have been given over to the relations between states, one wonders whether we are now having to bring the people back into the analysis. In the post-First World War era, the IPR understood the reasons for the intergovernmental institutional deficit, referred to by Ravenhill in the previous chapter, and chose to facilitate cross-cultural and cross-national understanding by bridging civil societies. In this way, the Institute focused upon a capacity rather than a deficit, our capacity to learn about, learn from, understand and appreciate one another as human beings.

Focusing on governmental linkages and their NGO supports, we may be promoting a reification of the state that overlooks the ties amongst peoples. Will the allegedly ascendant Asian-Pacific 'way' or 'impulse' remain the political, military and corporate way, a symbol of what is acceptable to governments and their well-heeled backers (Mahbubani, 1995a, b)? While Ravenhill correctly observes in Chapter 12 that it is as yet absent in the region, is Karl Deutsch's 'security community' – with its emphasis on building a sense of community and mechanisms for peaceful change amongst peoples – even remotely related to the goals of the governments involved in APEC and ARF or their supporting nongovernmental complements? Does the idea of 'new regionalism' – with its emphasis on consensus decision making, ambiguity and elite NGO participation – address the aspirations of the Pacific's peoples?

The inclusive approach

A central lesson to be learned from the IPR story, as an aspect of the transnational dimension, thus pertains to the question of nongovernmental credentials. For if regional co-operation is about achieving, maintaining or enhancing security, beyond asking, 'What type or types?', we must also ask, 'For whom?' If it is to be the 'open regionalism' championed by APEC, we must ask, 'Open for what and to whom?' (Garnaut, 1996). The creation of APEC could be seen as seizing the opportunity to take the momentum gained by the PAFTAD–PBEC–PECC network to a higher level (as suggested by the symbiotic PECC–APEC relationship), or as an interstate response to the perceived threat of NGO success in hijacking the transnational process (as suggested by the apparent ineffectiveness or failure of the PECC–APEC relationship from the PECC perspective). Either of these scenarios leaves the interests of the Pacific peoples subservient to the interests of academic, corporate and/or state proponents of regional co-operation, with the sometimes very different interests within these sectors playing themselves out as well. As Barry Buzan warned in Chapter 4, while the case of Asia-Pacific regionalism rests on lopsided patterns of trade, investment and rhetoric, it may be that the process itself has now been hijacked by one state, the USA, as part of its anti-regional, anti-social isolationist, global liberalization scheme (see also Chomsky, 1997a).

For many citizens of the states engaged in Asia-Pacific regionalism, this fear provides a definite answer to the question (addressed by Segal in Chapter 15) of whether the Asia-Pacific should be viewed as an emerging threat or a benign challenge. To them, the dominant direction of regionalism today is both a threat and a challenge, the latter being anything but benign (Bello, 1992). The early IPR agenda is out and is not coming back under present intergovernmental conditions, claims about redefining security in the region notwithstanding. Neo-liberalism, with its faith in the market mechanism and its assumption that some people will fall between the cracks, is in (Garnaut, 1994, 1996). The voices and concerns of labour, women, human rights groups and aboriginal peoples, once heard in the IPR context, have been marginalized in favour of the corporate and state agenda (Woods, 1995b).

At the Seattle APEC meeting in November 1993, the US government began its push for the neo-liberal corporate agenda by convening a summit of the leaders of APEC countries. Prior to this point, US administrations had been lukewarm about the APEC initiative. Environmental groups based in the USA, together with local labour councils, took the lead in protesting against the corporate agenda. Environmental sustainability and labour practices were their key concerns. At the 1994 Bogor Summit, NGO attempts to mount protests and press conferences were thwarted by the Indonesian authorities. The following year, as a counter to the APEC gathering in Osaka, a forum involving 100 NGO and trade union representatives was held in Kyoto. The resulting Kyoto Declaration rejected the free market and trade liberalization assumptions of APEC, argued that freedom and democracy were being eroded, urged that human develop-ment be given priority over the blind pursuit of economic growth, and – as in Seattle – offered recommendations for governmental action (Policy Working Group, 1997).

In November 1996, political divisions in the Philippines led to five NGO fora involving 1,000 activists being held in response to the Subic Bay APEC Summit. A demonstration critical of APEC drew 10,000 protestors. Again, repressive actions were taken by the host government. Nonetheless, media coverage of these events increased and the NGO community judged this series of counter conferences to be a success. The Manila People's

Forum on APEC issued a declaration and detailed plan of action, reminding APEC governments of their responsibilities under their existing international commitments. The Asia-Pacific Labour Network released a statement calling for APEC to attend to the protection of working and living conditions, the need for more involvement by trade unions, and the implementation of sustainable development practices. The People's Conference Against Imperialist Globalization, meanwhile, advocated an entirely rejectionist position depicting APEC as part of an elite neo-colonial co-optation strategy, and the International Women's Conference on APEC vowed to oppose the trade liberalization goals which could threaten food security and increase the negative impact market forces are having on women (Policy Working Group, 1997; Enloe, 1989). That the primary intergovernmental and nongovernmental organizations of Asia-Pacific regionalism are dominated by men should not go unnoticed.

Police block demonstrators from marching to the Philippines presidential palace to protest against the 1996 APEC summit

Despite their different points of emphasis, these parallel NGO and labour networks have been consolidated since 1993. As vital representations of civil society, and because of their links with the growing struggles of peoples in the Asia-Pacific for justice, they now co-ordinate and articulate the concerns of hundreds of organizations and millions of people opposed to some or all APEC plans. The APEC refusal to recognize these elements of the NGO community has only served to strengthen these

Students shouting 'Down with APEC' protest against the summit, Manila, 25 November 1996

opposition voices. The most significant differences among them up to this point have arisen over whether or not to try to penetrate APEC structures. For the time being, this issue will probably be resolved on a country-by-country basis and be dependent upon societal circumstances. While there are also tensions between North and South and between differing political experiences, there is a healthy degree of consensus on the 'non-viability of [APEC's neo-liberal] economic agenda and its undemocratic and non-transparent structures' (Policy Working Group, 1997).

The Vancouver APEC Summit in November 1997 was greeted by two complementary counter-conferences: a 'People's Summit', expending about US$1 million provided by labour, churches and United Nations agencies, and a 'No to APEC' gathering, operating on a shoestring budget (Sarti, 1997; Canadian Advisory Board, 1997). Such initiatives prompt several questions. How will APEC respond to the challenges posed by this 'new transnationalism' pursuing 'global social change' (Boulding, 1991)? How concerned should we be about this response? Will APEC respond constructively to the sorts of people-centred security concerns emanating from the grassroots of civil society (Ekins, 1992; Alger, 1990; Kothari, 1989)? Will it respond at all? Or will APEC and ARF alike eventually be overtaken by more holistic governmental or nongovernmental fora pursuing a conception of security akin to that upheld by the early IPR?

13.5 Conclusion: where the (re)action is

This chapter has presented two views of Asia-Pacific transnationalism. The first view holds that a tripartite policy network composed of academics, corporate executives and unofficial government officials has been driving a regional co-operation movement begun in the 1960s. This perspective, in which the nongovernmental organizations involved and their intergovernmental offspring continue to concern themselves primarily with economic and military/strategic aspects of security, is the one which dominates most scholarly, state and journalistic discussions of Asia-Pacific regionalism.

The alternative conception contends that the dominant view conveys but one act within a much longer play, and not even the first act at that. This play opens with the nongovernmental IPR, holding high its multidimensional conception of security and broad membership aspir-ations, quickly taking centre stage in 1925 before being run into the wings and out of the theatre by the violent machinations before, during and after the Second World War. With the blacklisting of the Institute in the early 1950s and its subsequent disappearance in 1960, new but narrower organizations soon filled the vacated role, until in 1989 one finds the emergence and intentional development of complementary official and unofficial diplomatic scripts. However, the continuing narrowness of the conception of security upheld by these entities raises questions about their representative nature, prompting grassroots transnational networks of NGOs and labour groups to emerge in an opposition chorus. It is by considering these different dimensions and paths of Asia-Pacific transnationalism that the spectator comes to appreciate the variety of actors, to grasp where the real action is, and to see where that action is likely to be in the future.

So why then do we not already know more about this opposition chorus? Adopting Noam Chomsky's mode of institutional analysis, I would argue that the answer to this question is directly related to the reason we do not know more about the dominant players: that is, because there are social, economic and political forces – namely those who own, control and/ or benefit from mainstream mass media outlets – who through agenda setting and manipulation seek to control information so as to manufacture consent, to allow one to claim people's 'consent without consent', to divide and conquer (Chomsky, 1997b, p.237; Hindell, 1995).

But just as technology allows these forces to control the messages they want us to absorb about the virtues of open regionalism, deregulation and privatization, so too is this technology enabling a concerned citizenry, spread across great distances, more opportunities to communicate and co-operate with one another in contesting the neo-liberal agenda and state-centred process of regional co-operation across the Pacific. Witness the significant public response to the Multilateral Agreement on Investment once news of the ongoing and behind-the-scenes negotiations (aimed at limiting national abilities to regulate foreign investment and the activities of multinational corporations) came to light via the alternative media and Internet sites such as http://www.citizen.org/gtw. News of the negotiations which led to the signing of the North American Free Trade Agreement garnered the same sorts of opposition as large segments of the populations directly affected responded to word that bureaucrats – again in the name of globalization – were similarly bartering away human and environmental security alongside national sovereignty and cultural identity. So, too, have negotiations on aspects of the World Trade Organization, especially its provisions on labour standards (Chomsky, 1997a). Now it's APEC's turn. In practising 'critical regionalism', one doesn't have to adopt a Marxian analysis (Dirlik, 1993; Palat, 1997). Critics of APEC could be seen as addressing the link between politics and economics – a link often denied by APEC leaders with a neo-functionalist penchant for arguing that they are about business, not politics – by searching out alternative political space (Walker, 1988). As Christopher Brook notes in Chapter 11, we could just as easily speak in terms of a clash of capitalisms, with the opponents of the neo-liberal agenda favouring a form of social democratic capitalism.

Are politicians across the Pacific afraid of informed citizens? The answer, as demonstrated by the response pattern emerging with respect to regional co-operation, appears to be 'Yes'. No longer willing to accept being told, 'If you don't like business you have a problem' (or even worse, 'It's none of your business!'), civil society across the Pacific is beginning to respond in kind. This brings our voyage almost full circle from the time of the early IPR's 'people-centred' approach to security, since to understand the transnational dimension of regional co-operation in the Asia-Pacific today is to understand that one transnational challenge is now being met by another. Students of things Asia-Pacific would therefore be wise to heed the basic advice given to children learning to cross the street: look both ways!

References

Alger, C.F. (1990) 'Grass-roots perspectives on global policies for development', *Journal of Peace Research*, vol.27, no.2, pp.155–68.

Bello, W. (1992) *People and Power in the Pacific: The Struggle for the Post-Cold War Order*, London/San Francisco, Pluto Press/Food First and the Transnational Institute.

Berman, M.R. and Johnson, J.E. (eds) (1977) *Unofficial Diplomats*, New York, Columbia University Press.

Boulding, E. (1991) 'The old and new transnationalism: an evolutionary perspective', *Human Relations*, vol.44, no.8, pp.789–805.

Buzan, B. (1991) *People, States and Fear: An Agenda for International Security Studies in the Post-Cold War Era*, 2nd edn., Boulder, CO, Lynne Rienner.

Canadian Advisory Board to the 1997 People's Summit on APEC (1997) 'Citizen groups want APEC agenda to address human rights and sustainable development', News Release, 25 April.

Chomsky, N. (1997a) 'The passion for free trade: exporting American values through the new World Trade Organization', *Z Magazine*, vol.10, no.5, pp.25–33.

Chomsky, N. (1997b) *Perspectives on Power: Reflections on Human Nature and the Social Order*, Montreal, Black Rose Books.

Condliffe, J.B. (ed.) (1928) *Problems of the Pacific*, Chicago, University of Chicago Press.

Cooper, A.F., Higgott, R.A. and Nossal, K.R. (1993) *Relocating Middle Powers: Australia and Canada in a Changing World Order*, Vancouver, University of British Columbia Press.

Davidann, J.T. (1995) 'The American YMCA in Meiji Japan: God's work gone awry', *Journal of World History*, vol. 6, no.1, pp.107–25.

Dirlik, A. (ed.) (1993) *What Is In a Rim?: Critical Perspectives on the Pacific Region Idea*, Boulder, CO, Westview Press.

Ekins, P. (1992) *A New World Order: Grassroots Movements for Global Change*, London, Routledge.

Enloe, C. (1989) *Bananas, Beaches and Bases*, Berkeley, University of California Press.

Evans, P.M. (1994a) 'Building security: the Council for Security Co-operation in the Asia Pacific (CSCAP)', *The Pacific Review*, vol.7, no.2, pp.125–39.

Evans, P.M. (ed.) (1994b) *Studying Asia Pacific Security: The Future of Research, Training and Dialogue Activities*, Toronto/Kuala Lumpur, University of Toronto–York University Joint Centre for Asia Pacific Studies/Centre for Strategic and International Studies.

Evans, P.M. (1996) 'The prospects for multilateral security co-operation in the Asia/Pacific region' in Ball, D. (ed.) *The Transformation of Security in the Asia/Pacific Region*, London, Frank Cass, pp.201–17.

Garnaut, R. (1994) *Asian Market Economies: Challenges of a Changing International Environment*, Singapore, Institute of Southeast Asian Studies.

Garnaut, R. (1996) *Open Regionalism and Trade Liberalization: An Asia-Pacific Contribution to the World Trade System*, Singapore, Institute of Southeast Asian Studies.

Haas, E.B. (1958) *The Uniting of Europe: Political, Social and Economic Forces, 1950–57*, Stanford, Stanford University Press.

Haas, E.B. (1964) *Beyond the Nation-State: Functionalism and International Organization*, Stanford, Stanford University Press.

Harris, S. (1994) 'Policy networks and economic co-operation: policy co-ordination in the Asia-Pacific', *The Pacific Review*, vol.7, no.4, pp.381–95.

Hellman, D.C. and Pyle, K.B. (eds) (1997) *From APEC to Xanadu: Creating a Viable Community in the Post-Cold War Pacific*, Armonk, NY, M.E. Sharpe.

Higgott, R. (1994) 'Ideas, identity and policy co-ordination in the Asia-Pacific', *The Pacific Review*, vol.7, no.4, pp.367–79.

Hindell, K. (1995) 'The influence of the media on foreign policy', *International Relations*, vol.12, no.4, pp.73–83.

Hooper, P.F. (1988) 'The Institute of Pacific Relations and the origins of Asian and Pacific studies', *Pacific Affairs*, vol.61, no.1, pp.98–121.

Hooper, P.F. (ed.) (1995) *Remembering the Institute of Pacific Relations: The Memoirs of William L. Holland*, Tokyo, Ryukei Shyosha.

Keohane, R.O. and Nye, J.S.Jr (eds) (1973) *Transnational Relations and World Politics*, Cambridge, MA, Harvard University Press.

Kerr, P. (1994) 'The security dialogue in the Asia-Pacific', *The Pacific Review*, vol.7, no.4, pp.397–409.

Kerr, P., Mack, A. and Evans, P. (1995) 'The evolving security discourse in the Asia-Pacific' in Mack, A. and Ravenhill, J. (eds) *Pacific Co-operation: Building Economic and Security Regimes in the Asia-Pacific Region*, Boulder, CO, Westview Press, pp.233–55.

Klare, M. (1997) 'East Asia's arms races', *Bulletin of the Atomic Scientists*, vol.53, no.1, pp.18–19.

Kothari, R. (1989) *Rethinking Development: In Search of Humane Alternatives*, New York, New Horizons Press.

Krause, K. and Williams, M.C. (1996) 'Broadening the agenda of security studies: politics and methods', *Mershon International Studies Review*, vol.40, supp.2, pp.229–54.

Long, D. and Wilson, P. (eds) (1995) *Thinkers of the Twenty Years' Crisis: Inter-War Idealism Reassessed*, Oxford, Clarendon Press.

Mack, A. and Ravenhill, J. (eds) (1995) *Pacific Co-operation: Building Economic and Security Regimes in the Asia-Pacific Region*, Boulder, CO, Westview Press.

Mahbubani, K. (1995a) 'The Pacific impulse', *Survival*, vol.37, no.1, pp.105–20.

Mahbubani, K. (1995b) 'The Pacific way', *Foreign Affairs*, vol.74, no.1, pp.100–11.

Mathews, J.T. (1989) 'Redefining security', *Foreign Affairs*, vol.68, no.2, pp.162–77.

Palat, R.A. (1997) 'Reinscribing the globe – imaginative geographies of the Pacific Rim', *Bulletin of Concerned Asian Scholars*, vol.29, no.1, pp.61–9.

Palmer, N.D. (1991) *The New Regionalism in Asia and the Pacific*, Lexington, MA, Lexington Books.

Policy Working Group (1997) 'Canada and APEC: perspectives from civil society', Canadian Organizing Network for the 1997 People's Summit on APEC, Discussion Paper, First Draft, 22 April.

Rehbok, P.F. (1988) 'Organizing Pacific science: local and international origins of the Pacific Science Association' in MacLeod, R. and Rehbok, P.F. (eds) *Nature in Its Greatest Extent: Western Science in the Pacific*, Honolulu, University of Hawaii Press, pp.195–221.

Rudner, M. (1995) 'APEC: the challenge of Asia Pacific economic co-operation', *Modern Asian Studies*, vol.29, part 2, pp.403–37.

Sarti, R. (1997) 'Two groups plan to protest APEC summit', *Vancouver Sun*, 21 March, p.B3.

Stone, D. (1996) *Capturing the Political Imagination: Think Tanks and the Policy Process*, London, Frank Cass.

Thomas, J.N. (1974) *The Institute of Pacific Relations: Asian Scholars and American Politics*, Seattle, University of Washington Press.

Ullman, R.H. (1983) 'Redefining security', *International Security*, vol.8, no.1, pp.129–53.

Volkan, V.D., Julius, D.A. and Montville, J.V. (eds) (1991) *The Psychodynamics of International Relationships, Vol. II: Unofficial Diplomacy at Work*, Lexington, MA, Lexington Books.

Walker, R.B.J. (1988) *One World, Many Worlds: Struggles for a Just World Peace*, Boulder/London, Lynne Rienner/Zed Books.

Woods, L.T. (1991) 'Non-governmental organizations and Pacific co-operation: back to the future?', *The Pacific Review*, vol.4, no.4, pp.312–21.

Woods, L.T. (1993) *Asia-Pacific Diplomacy: Nongovernmental Organizations and International Relations*, Vancouver, University of British Columbia Press.

Woods, L.T. (1995a) 'Learning from NGO proponents of Asia-Pacific regionalism', *Asian Survey*, vol.35, no.9, pp.812–27.

Woods, L.T. (1995b) 'Economic co-operation and human rights in the Asia-Pacific region: the role of regional institutions' in Tang, J.T.H. (ed.) *Human Rights and International Relations in the Asia-Pacific Region*, London, Pinter, pp.152–66.

Yamamoto, T. (ed.) (1995) *Emerging Civil Society in the Asia Pacific Community: Nongovernmental Underpinnings of the Emerging Asia Pacific Regional Community*, Tokyo/Singapore, Japan Center for International Exchange/Institute of Southeast Asian Studies.

Further reading

Bello, W. (1992) *People and Power in the Pacific: The Struggle for the Post-Cold War Order*, London/San Francisco, Pluto Press/Food First and the Transnational Institute.

Hellman, D.C. and Pyle, K.B. (eds) (1997) *From APEC to Xanadu: Creating a Viable Community in the Post-Cold War Pacific*, Armonk, NY, M.E. Sharpe.

Palmer, N.D. (1991) *The New Regionalism in Asia and the Pacific*, Lexington, MA, Lexington Books.

Woods, L.T. (1993) *Asia-Pacific Diplomacy: Nongovernmental Organizations and International Relations*, Vancouver, University of British Columbia Press.

Yamamoto, T. (ed.) (1995) *Emerging Civil Society in the Asia Pacific Community: Nongovernmental Underpinnings of the Emerging Asia Pacific Regional Community*, Tokyo/Singapore, Japan Center for International Exchange/Institute of Southeast Asian Studies.

CHAPTER 14

The European Union and the Asia-Pacific

Michael Smith

14.1   Context and questions

Earlier chapters in this book have focused on the components and the dynamics of the Asia-Pacific region. This chapter introduces you to a rather different perspective: that of the concerned outsider in the global economy and the world political-security arena. Because of the growth and dynamism of the Asia-Pacific region it is impossible for outsiders to ignore it, whether they see it as a threat or an opportunity. The Asia-Pacific has become a source and a target for trade investment and global competition; it has also become a focus of many of the diverse tensions and risks characterizing the post-Cold War era.

In this chapter, the perspective taken is that of the European Union (EU). The EU is at one and the same time a prime mover in the evolution of the Asia-Pacific and the source of important questions and ambiguities. Historically, many of the present-day members of the EU were significant powers in the Asia-Pacific region, particularly through their imperial and colonial activities; this is true of the British, the French and the Dutch in particular, but the Germans, the Spanish and the Portuguese have also had important involvements. Economically, the EU has vital and growing connections with the Asia-Pacific in the form of trade and foreign direct investment (FDI). More distantly, but none the less importantly, the EU and many Asia-Pacific countries have political and security links which have been challenged but not eliminated by the ending of the Cold War. There is thus an inevitable convergence – or collision – of interests among both Asia-Pacific and EU countries in a number of spheres.

But to state the extent of common – or at least shared – interests is also to uncover significant areas of uncertainty or contradiction. EU member states are historically and in other ways linked to the Asia-Pacific region, but it is only very recently that the EU *per se* has started to develop an Asia-Pacific strategy. The very act of developing this strategy has given rise to important tensions between the EU and some of its member states, and between the EU and Asia-Pacific countries. Central to this set of tensions and uncertainties, and to the EU's slowness in developing a strategy, is the fact that, whatever else it may be, the EU is not a nation-state. As Ravenhill observed (Chapter 12), the international relations of the Asia-Pacific can be fruitfully investigated as a process of *intergovernmental relations,* but the EU does not have the status of 'just another government': rather, as many commentators have pointed out, it is an actor which has some state-like qualities and governmental powers, but which also functions as a complex form of international organization (see also Smith, 1996; Allen and Smith, 1990, 1997a; Hill, 1993). It might be felt that this gives a good basis for analysing EU relations with the Asia-Pacific in terms of *inter-regional relations,* but the two regions concerned are very different both in terms of their geographical and political makeup and in terms of their specifically regional institutions (Smith, 1997). Alternatively, it could be argued that EU–Asia-Pacific relations are best conceived not as *intergovernmental* or *inter-regional* but as part of a *global* set of networks in which private groupings such as large companies are the central actors, but here again the argument comes up against the inherent diversity and fluidity of the relationships in question (Brook, Chapter 11).

It is clear even from this brief sketch that we are confronted with an intriguing phenomenon when we investigate the development of EU strategy towards the Asia-Pacific area. In the spring of 1996, as a major EU initiative in building relations with the Asia-Pacific took place, *The Economist* asked in a feature article 'Has Europe failed in Asia?' (*The Economist,* 1996). It came to the conclusion that, whilst the development of economic relationships with the Asia-Pacific had been relatively successful, there was a series of reasons for the relative failure of the Europeans in the political sphere and the security domain. These will be explored later in this chapter. But another – implicit – conclusion from the article was that a specifically EU strategy for developing and managing these relationships faced significant obstacles, both within the EU itself and in the Asia-Pacific region. It was not simply that a strategy had been tried and had failed; rather it was that the evolution of strategy itself was a major challenge, and that the EU's initiatives were bound to fall short of those already practised by the USA in the Asia-Pacific arena (see Chapter 8).

This chapter thus sets out to analyse and evaluate the process by which the EU has developed an 'Asia-Pacific strategy', and in doing so casts light upon the international relations of the Asia-Pacific from a different angle. I will be seeking to answer four interrelated questions:

- How can we explain the *growth* and the *focus* of relationships between the EU and the Asia-Pacific region?

- How has the *development of a strategy* in the EU towards the Asia-Pacific region taken place, and what tensions and limitations has it uncovered?

- How does the development of this strategy relate to the *broader context* of EU–Asia-Pacific relations? In particular, how does it relate to the accounts of competing blocs, international institutions and globalization you have encountered elsewhere in this book?

THE EUROPEAN UNION AND THE ASIA-PACIFIC

- How can we evaluate the *overall texture* of the relationship, and how can we relate it to central issues raised in, for example, Chapters 11 and 12? In particular, how can we answer questions about 'who is doing what to whom?' – in other words, questions relating to participation, the nature of power and costs and benefits?

14.2   The growth and focus of a relationship

When the European Community (EC), predecessor of the EU, was established in the late 1950s its central focus in terms of external relations was upon two sets of linkages: between Europe and the United States, and between major members of the EC and their ex-colonies. The latter gave the EC an implicit Asian dimension, although this was complicated by the pressures created by the Cold War, and particularly in the 1960s by the war in Vietnam. The British, with their substantial involvement in the Asia-Pacific region, were not to become members of the EC until the early 1970s, by which time their 'retreat from East of Suez' was well underway. At the same time, until the 1970s the EC did not face a substantial economic challenge from the Japanese, let alone the Koreans or other newly industrializing economies. The French President, General de Gaulle, once memorably described the visit of the Japanese Prime Minister as an appointment with a transistor salesman, and although there was some European concern about the success of the Japanese in industries such as shipbuilding or steel, until the mid 1970s this remained a largely peripheral issue (Thomsen, 1991).

From the mid 1970s onwards, though, there was an increasing tendency in the EC to recognize a 'Japanese challenge' where previously the 'American challenge' had predominated. This was felt particularly sharply in a number of sensitive areas, such as automobiles and consumer electronics, which became increasingly politically salient during the early 1980s. Alongside this, from the mid 1970s onwards, there was a more comprehensive and integrated approach to relations with the developing countries of the Asia-Pacific, particularly those that had been dependencies of the British or the French, under the umbrella of the Lomé Conventions (trade agreements with former colonies and Third World states). This approach was strictly limited, however: countries that were too large or too challenging were excluded from the group of so-called ACP (African, Caribbean and Pacific) partners. This meant in particular that the People's Republic of China, with whom official relations were established in 1975, would continue to be dealt with on a bilateral basis, as it was with a trade agreement in 1978 and a trade and co-operation agreement in 1985. By the early 1980s, with the conclusion of a range of partnership and co-operation agreements, the EC had begun to establish a more formal network of partnerships in the Asia-Pacific region; for example, the first agreement with the countries of the Association of South-East Asian Nations (ASEAN) as a group was concluded in 1980 (see Table 14.1). The impression at this stage was that a series of building blocks was being established, but there were important limitations on the extent to which these blocks could be put together or extended into the political rather than the economic sphere (Hine, 1985).

Table 14.1 *The European Union's co-operation and other agreements with the countries of Asia and dates of establishment of EU delegations in Asian countries*

	Framework trade and/or co-operation agreements, declarations, etc.	Sectoral trade agreements	Establishment of delegation
North-East Asia			
Japan	Joint Declaration (1991)	fusion (1989) environment (1989)	1974
South Korea		textiles (1987)	1989
Taiwan			
Hong Kong		textiles (1986)	1993 (office)
Macau	1993	textiles (1987)	
Mongolia	1993		
North Korea			
South-East Asia			
ASEAN	1980		
Brunei			
Indonesia		tapioca (1982) textiles (1987)	1988 (representation)
Malaysia		textiles (1987)	
The Philippines		textiles (1987)	1990
Singapore		textiles (1987)	
Thailand		tapioca (1982) textiles (1987)	1978
Cambodia			
Laos			
Vietnam		textiles (1993)	
Burma			

Source: Commission of the European Communities (CEC) (1994)

By the early 1980s it had become possible to talk in terms of a more generalized EC concern with the Asia-Pacific region. Predominantly, this was an economic concern, either with challenges from Japan or the newly industrializing economies, or with the demand for aid from the less developed countries of the region. In the case of Japan in particular there was increasing anxiety on the part of the EC about the bilateral trade deficit, which by 1985 was registering at around 10 billion ecus (european currency units), or around £8 billion a year in Japan's favour. This deficit rose considerably during the late 1980s and early 1990s to reach a peak of around 35 billion ecus in 1992. It was not simply that there was a deficit; the deficit was concentrated in a number of highly visible areas such as automobiles, consumer electronics and information technology products. During the 1980s the competition from Japan was joined by challenges from Korea and Taiwan, as their export-orientated economic strategies took effect. Figure 14.1 shows trade flows for the years 1989 to 1994.

In the field of aid and development assistance, the ending of the Vietnam war and of subsequent regional conflicts meant a diversification of the targets for EC funding, and this in turn meant that there was a need to reassess the ways in which such funding was made available. Relations with China also underwent a reassessment, particularly after the Tiananmen Square massacre of 1989, and were 'on hold' for at least a couple of years. The nascent inter-regional framework for managing relations between the EC and ASEAN moved relatively slowly, complicated for example by the entry of the Portuguese into the EC in 1986, which injected their disputes with Indonesia about human rights violations in East Timor into the broader picture (Dent, 1996).

At the end of the 1980s, therefore, three distinct patterns could be seen in EC–Asia-Pacific relations. First, there was the predominantly bilateral competition with Japan and the newly industrializing economies, led by the Koreans. Second, there was the aid and development relationship managed partly through the Lomé Conventions but increasingly through bilateral deals with new recipients. Finally, there was the inter-regional relationship, expressed almost entirely through the EC–ASEAN co-operation agreement of 1980. It would be misleading to draw too strong a distinction between these three types of relationship, since the diversity and dynamism of the Asia-Pacific region meant that there was a constant need to review and adapt existing agreements. Nor is the pattern uniform, since the relationship between the EC and China fitted very uncomfortably across a number of categories: neither an aid relationship, nor a competitive one, but an uneasy mixture of these and other features (Grant, 1995). Not only this, but the individual EC member states with strong Asia-Pacific connections continued to make their own arrangements; for example, only around ten per cent of Community aid was actually channelled through Community agencies, with the remainder being dispensed on a bilateral basis, whilst arms sales were dominated by a small number of EC members (particularly Britain and France). In the same way, although there was a 'Community problem' with imports of Japanese cars, or with the impact of foreign direct investment, there were different solutions to this problem on the part of each of the then twelve EC member states (Thomsen, 1991).

In addition to these variations in patterns of relations, two further features should be noted. In the first place, the 'problem' with the Asia-Pacific region at the European level was overwhelmingly seen as an economic one. Partly this reflected the reality that the geo-political distance between the EC and the Asia-Pacific region implied very little direct political or security involvement by the Europeans collectively; partly it reflected the reality in Europe that there was no fully integrated EC foreign or security policy and thus no basis on which to pursue collective

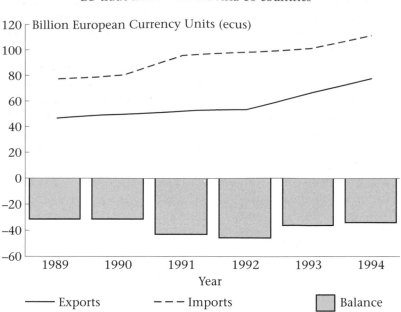

EU trade flows with the Asia 10 countries

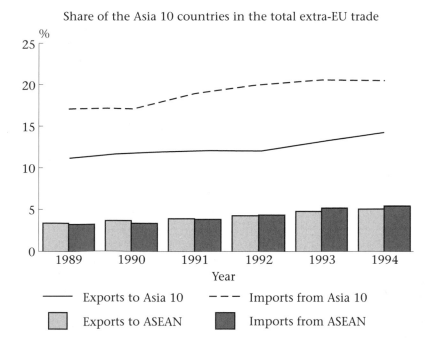

Share of the Asia 10 countries in the total extra-EU trade

Asia 10 = The Association of South-East Asian Nations (ASEAN) countries (Thailand, Vietnam, Indonesia, Malaysia, Brunei, Singapore, The Philippines) plus China, Japan and South Korea

Figure 14.1 *EU trade flows with Asia-Pacific countries*
Source: Eurostat (1996, p.33)

initiatives in the field. Individual members such as Britain or France undoubtedly had important security interests in the Pacific region, not to mention interests in such activities as arms sales which had both commercial and security implications, but their preference was generally to keep these out of the Community orbit. A second feature of the problem was that EC policies were overwhelmingly defensive in nature: there was a perceived 'threat' and a variety of means were used to defend the Europeans and their industries from it. This defensiveness was only slightly modified by the EC's aid and development policies, and it extended from worry about imports of cheap textiles from developing countries to the already noted concerns with cars and consumer electronics.

Patterns of trade, investment and aid

Despite this defensiveness, and despite the EC concern with its trade deficits, economic relations developed rapidly during the late 1980s and early 1990s. In the trade sphere, consistent pressure on Japan to reduce its tariffs and other barriers to trade, combined with the programme to complete the Single European Market (SEM) by 1992, meant that the total volume of exchanges grew from under 60 billion ecus in 1985 to nearly 90 billion in 1995, while at the same time the relative deficit was reduced. The relationship with ASEAN in trade grew from under 20 billion ecus in 1985 to over 60 billion in 1995, and in that year the EU even registered a slight surplus, after consistently running modest deficits. With China, trade grew from around 10 billion ecus in 1985 (with a surplus for the EU) to over 40 billion in 1995, with a major deficit of over 10 billion ecus (Dent, 1996, pp.19–24).

An overview of the general pattern of EU–Asia-Pacific trade relations as they had developed by the mid 1990s is provided in Figures 14.2 and 14.3. These show that the overall patterns described above conceal a number of important variations, both between the Asia-Pacific 'targets' for EU activity and between the 'recipient states' in the EU for Asia-Pacific trade. In trade, there was an inevitable preponderance of Japan in the Asia-Pacific links with the EU, but the ASEAN and Chinese shares were substantial and growing. Germany and Britain together accounted for nearly 50 per cent of total flows into and out of the EU, but other important flows concerned France and the Netherlands, for example. It would be possible to develop this analysis by pointing out the variations between individual EU members in terms of their trade balances with Asia-Pacific countries, and to draw conclusions about where the areas of particular sensitivity and concern might be at any one time. The important point here is that within the EU and the Asia-Pacific region there are certain key 'nodes' of economic linkage and activity, and this is bound to condition EU policies.

Alongside a rapid growth in the trade relationships there was an acceleration of foreign direct investment (FDI) (see Figure 14.4). The EU's stock of total FDI in East Asia rose from under US$5 billion in 1980 to nearly US$30 billion in 1993 (Dent, 1996, pp.30–1); this appeared less impressive than the rise in both Japanese and United States investment

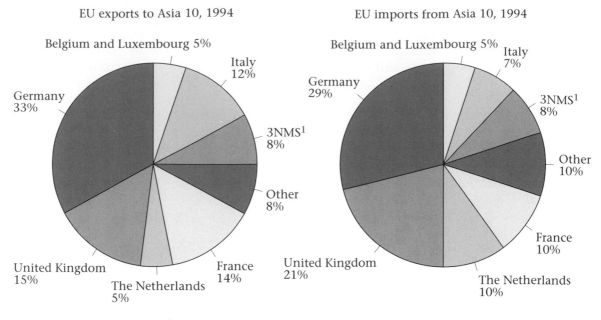

EU exports to Asia 10, 1994

Belgium and Luxembourg 5%
Italy 12%
Germany 33%
3NMS[1] 8%
Other 8%
France 14%
The Netherlands 5%
United Kingdom 15%

EU imports from Asia 10, 1994

Belgium and Luxembourg 5%
Italy 7%
Germany 29%
3NMS[1] 8%
Other 10%
France 10%
The Netherlands 10%
United Kingdom 21%

[1] new member states: Austria, Finland, Sweden

Figure 14.2 *EU trade flows with Asia-Pacific countries by member state*
Source: Eurostat (1996, p.8)

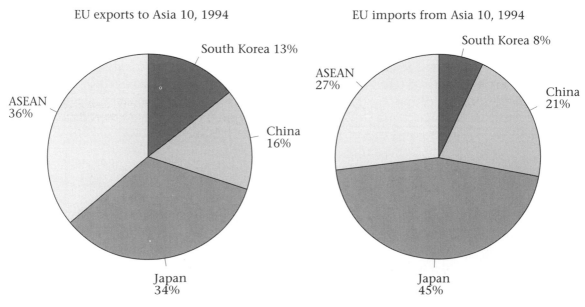

EU exports to Asia 10, 1994

South Korea 13%
ASEAN 36%
China 16%
Japan 34%

EU imports from Asia 10, 1994

South Korea 8%
ASEAN 27%
China 21%
Japan 45%

Figure 14.3 *EU trade flows with Asia-Pacific countries by individual country*
Source: Eurostat (1996, p.9)

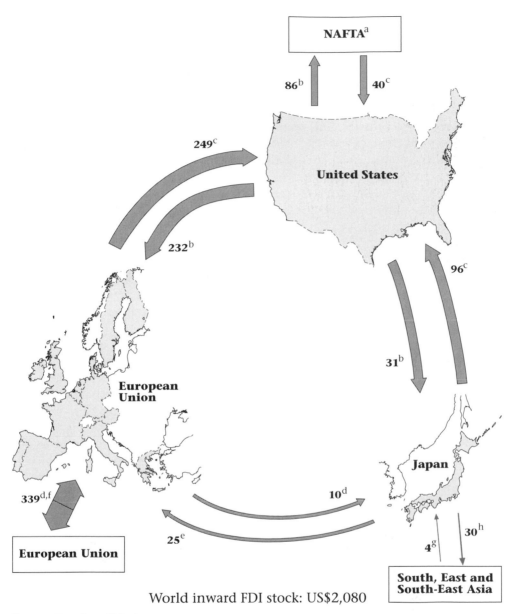

World inward FDI stock: US$2,080

a   Canada and Mexico
b   United States outward FDI stock
c   United States inward FDI stock
d   Outward FDI stock of Austria, Finland, France, Germany, Italy, Netherlands, Sweden and
     the United Kingdom. Data for Austria are for 1991 and data for France and the Netherlands
     are for 1992.
e   Data from inward FDI stock of Austria, France, Germany, Italy, Netherlands and United Kingdom.
     Data for Austria and France are for 1991 and data for Italy and the Netherlands for 1992.
f   For Sweden, the data reflect FDI to and from all European countries. Intra-European Union FDI,
     based on inward stocks, is US$225 billion.
g   Data are based on approvals/notifications and represent those from countries other than those
     in North America and Europe.
h   Estimated by multiplying the values of the cumulative flows to the region according to FDI
     approvals by the ratio of disbursed to approved/notified FDI in developing countries.

Figure 14.4 *Flows of FDI stock among EU–Asia-Pacific–US, 1993*

Source: UNCTAD (1995, p.5)

over the same period. *The Economist,* on the other hand, in the article cited at the beginning of this chapter, noted that for the 1986–94 period, out of a total inflow to East Asia (China, Indonesia, Malaysia, Philippines and Thailand) of US$146 billion, the EU accounted for 10 per cent, compared to 18 per cent for Japan, 11 per cent for the USA and 49 per cent for other newly industrializing economies (*The Economist,* 1996, p.64). Areas of particular strength for EU FDI were to be found in the ASEAN countries, where post-colonial ties undoubtedly played a part. At the same time, especially from the late 1980s, there was a surge first in Japanese investment in Europe and then in investments by other Asian 'tigers', especially Korea and Taiwan. One notable feature of this investment was its concentration particularly in the United Kingdom, which made great play of its ability to attract Asia-Pacific investment projects, thereby setting up tensions with other EU member states which felt less positive about the process (Thomsen, 1991).

Meanwhile, the aid and development relationship was also evolving. Three forms of assistance have been given by the EC and now the EU to developing countries: humanitarian assistance, development assistance and economic co-operation assistance. During the 1970s the first two of these categories accounted for virtually all of the EC's aid expenditure in ASEAN countries, but during the 1980s and 1990s there was a marked swing towards the third category, dealing with economic co-operation. While development assistance accounted for around two-thirds of the total during the 1990–95 period, economic co-operation assistance had risen from zero to around one-fifth of the total, reflecting the shifting balance of EU–ASEAN relations in general. Aid to China has been modest, as has that to Korea, which ended completely in the early 1990s. The pattern of EU aid to Asian countries, as illustrated in Table 14.2, thus shows marked disparities between those countries which receive a significant amount of aid and those which have virtually no such dependence on the EU (but remember, this does not show the variations between EU member states' bilateral aid efforts). In addition to direct financial assistance, the EC operates a Generalized System of Preferences (GSP), giving trade privileges to less developed countries; but during the 1990s, in an increasing number of product areas, Asia-Pacific countries have 'graduated' from the GSP (again, this particularly refers to ASEAN countries).

It is clear from this outline that the growth of the relationship between the EU and the Asia-Pacific region up to the early 1990s falls into several phases. Initially, there was a certain distance, reinforced by the effects of decolonization and by the impact of the Cold War. During the 1970s this changed, with a recognition that in certain areas of trade there was a strong Asia-Pacific (especially Japanese) challenge, this being followed up by the challenge from the Asian 'tigers'. The 1980s, if anything, accentuated this feeling, and implanted it into a growing concern with the competitiveness of the EC in a globalizing economy. Then, during the late 1980s and early 1990s, there was a shift in the balance, first of all to reduce some of the most glaring trade deficits and then to boost direct investment in both

Table 14.2 *EU aid to East-Asian countries in US$ millions (excluding bilateral aid from member states)*

	1991	1992	1993
Brunei	0.00	0.09	0.06
Indonesia	12.02	12.95	13.46
Malaysia	5.05	2.93	0.97
The Philippines	15.97	17.71	20.14
Singapore	0.35	0.17	0.49
Thailand	13.62	21.72	17.46
Vietnam	19.07	20.82	14.25
ASEAN total	66.08	76.39	66.83
China	26.77	31.29	19.51
South Korea	0.02	0.00	0.00

Source: Eurostat (1996)

directions (albeit not to the same extent that investment was boosted either in the EU itself or within the Asia-Pacific region).

These shifts in the economic relationships between the EU and the Asia-Pacific region went alongside a gradual and patchy politicization of the relationship more generally. Partly because of the inherent limitations of the EU itself, and partly because of the diverse ways in which the Asia-Pacific challenge made itself felt, there were no compelling reasons to develop overtly political structures. Political exchanges and political dialogue were not absent, but they were more frequently handled through bilateral channels between EU member states and those of the Asia-Pacific region, or through the broader channels afforded by the United Nations or global economic institutions. Although the relationship had clearly grown, it was not yet clear that it had a focus at the European level which went beyond the purely commercial. It was difficult to discern a European strategy for handling the relationship. During the mid 1990s, this position was transformed, at least on the surface, and this produced a number of intriguing policy dilemmas for both European and Asia-Pacific countries.

14.3   The development of EU strategy

European responses to the development of relations with the Asia-Pacific region up to the 1990s were characterized by unevenness and diversity, reflecting factors internal to the EU as well as the challenges posed by the Asia-Pacific region itself. In this section, I will deal with the ways in which, during the mid 1990s, the EU developed a more pro-active strategy for dealing with the Asia-Pacific region, and with some of the difficulties this has encountered. In particular, I will deal with the following three topics:

- the pressures and constraints operating not only to make a strategy desirable but also to make it difficult to construct;

- the components of the strategy that emerged within the EU, and the ways in which it has been pursued;
- the tensions and contradictions that have emerged from the implementation of the strategy.

Pressures and constraints

Why was there growing pressure in the early 1990s for the development of a comprehensive 'Asia strategy' on the part of the EU? A number of powerful forces came together to create momentum behind the idea, but at the same time these forces also carried with them constraints and limitations.

One set of pressures was to be found in the broader development of the global arena. As noted above, during the 1950s and 1960s the development of EC–Asia-Pacific relations was structured primarily by the Cold War. On the part of the EC, this meant that its role was constrained to that of a 'civilian power', operating within the structure provided by the superpowers and limiting itself to economic concerns (although, as noted earlier, individual EC member states had important political and security links in the region). Paradoxical as it may seem, this was one of the attractions of the EC for some potential partners in the Asia-Pacific region, such as the members of ASEAN: the EC was not a superpower, and thus a relationship with it was less fraught with the possibilities of domination than with the United States (or, for rather different reasons, with a newly powerful Japan). When the attractions of 'civilian power' were added to those of a fast-developing European market, there were distinct incentives for outsiders to want some kind of partnership with the EC.

But these attractions bore within them the seeds of frustration. Simply because the EC was a 'civilian power', with little in the way of a developed foreign policy capacity, it could only play a limited role when the political chips were down. In addition, because it was a 'supermarket' rather than a superpower, it was difficult to trade off economic disputes and tensions against political support, as might happen with the USA. During the late 1980s, though, the waning of the Cold War seemed to increase not only the attractions of the EC as a partner but also (from an EC point of view) the desirability of constructing a new political strategy towards the Asia-Pacific. Two other factors fed into this set of pressures. First, the programme to complete the SEM in 1992 markedly increased the advantages for those who could gain privileged access to it and the penalties for those excluded. Second, the negotiation of the Maastricht Agreements during 1990 and 1991 gave the EU a framework for a common foreign and security policy which seemed to create the basis for a more comprehensive partnership with countries such as those of the Asia-Pacific region.

The general picture was thus one in which 'permissive' factors, such as the end of the Cold War, came together with 'positive' pressures, such as the desire for a more active EU international strategy, to create the demand for a more active Asia-Pacific strategy. In the case of Asia particularly, this was augmented by some very concrete calculations about the growth of markets and the opportunities for exporters and investors. Thus, the demand for an EU strategy was fed by considerations of economic welfare and political/security advantage, and it was promoted by the European Commission, the executive arm of the European Community (now the EU), which could see the strategy as a means of increasing its own influence and leverage. There was a strong feeling that if the opportunity for an active role was not seized, the EU would lose out to both the USA and Japan, and that it would also face a more potent set of Asian competitors without a reliable structure in which to regulate the competition.

The pressures and the incentives from within and outside the EU thus came together. But, as already noted, there were significant constraints operating on the EU. Some of these constraints emerged from the nature of the Asia-Pacific region. The sheer size, diversity and dynamism of the region did not make it easy to create a unified strategy. At the same time, the growing self-confidence and assertiveness of many Asia-Pacific countries meant that EU policy could not simply be 'imposed'; they would wish to be treated on the basis of equality and reciprocity. Not only this, but the variations in historical and current involvement of the EU member states (fifteen in 1997) made for considerable diversity of motive and priorities within the EU itself, as we shall see shortly. Another constraint on EU activism – again, paradoxically the concomitant of one of its perceived advantages – was its distance from the Asia-Pacific arena, which meant that in many of the growing institutions of the region it could claim observer status only at best (this was the case, for example, in APEC). This perception, in fact, only served to increase the desire of many EU member states and officials for their 'own' forum for partnership with Asia-Pacific countries.

The picture emerges of a basis for a strategy which combined potent incentives with powerful constraints. The EU had clear incentives to forge a new strategy, not least the threat of exclusion, but the diversity of motives, priorities and demands meant that such a strategy would be difficult to bring off. This quandary was underlined by the ways in which the strategy had to be developed within the EU. Policy-making in the EU context has inherent complexities, arising out of the existence of a 'negotiated order' with powerful rules and institutions. Thus, there was a need to engage in a highly formalized consideration of member state views and to process the strategy through a variety of institutional channels. The danger was that the strategy that emerged at the end of this process would be full of 'deals' inserted by various groups, and that as a result it would not be flexible enough to meet the needs of a fluid and diverse situation.

The components of a strategy

The framework for the EU's new Asia-Pacific strategy was set out in a communication presented by the Commission to the EU's Council of Ministers in July 1994 (CEC, 1994). Essentially, a communication is a means of initiating the policy formation process where the issues are those of broad strategy rather than specific legislation. In the communication, the Commission set out the following four key objectives for the new line of policy:

- the strengthening of the EU's economic presence in Asia, in order to maintain the Union's leading role in the world economy;
- a contribution to stability in Asia through promotion of international co-operation and understanding;
- promotion of economic development of the less prosperous countries and regions;
- a contribution to the development and consolidation of democracy, the rule of law, human rights and fundamental freedoms.

It must be emphasized here that this was a strategy for the whole of Asia, not simply for the Asia-Pacific region, but it is clear that the policy towards the latter was essentially in conformity with these basic objectives. As we shall see later, there are some inherent tensions between these objectives, particularly when applied in the context of the Asia-Pacific region.

The strategy document also set out the means through which the objectives were to be pursued. Essentially, these were a combination of bilateral agreements, inter-regional channels and multilateral institutions. Thus, framework partnership and co-operation agreements would be pursued with individual Asian countries, and increasingly these would be focused not only on economic co-operation but also on political dialogue. At the same time, there was a desire – important in the context of the discussion here – to pursue and expand the existing inter-regional arrangements, central among them the EU–ASEAN dialogue which during the previous decade and a half had taken the form of annual meetings. This coincided with pressure from members of ASEAN itself to develop a wider forum for EU–Asia-Pacific interchange. To some extent this had been achieved through the use of the ARF and the device of so-called 'dialogue partners' of which the EU was one, but there was a desire on both sides for a grouping that did not include the United States. Multilateral institutions entered the picture in two ways: one, and the most explicit, was the desire on the part of the EU to canvass Asia-Pacific views on the agenda for the newly-established World Trade Organization (WTO), which was expected to have a far-reaching effect on the management of world trade. The other way, particularly for the Asia-Pacific countries, was to mobilize EU support for reform of a number of UN institutions, particularly the Security Council, to reflect global political and economic realities. It must not be forgotten either that these were in a sense only the 'governmental' parts of the strategy: the EU was determined to encourage more active Asia-Pacific engagement by European companies, and to encourage linkages between European and Asia-Pacific firms.

During 1995 the working out of the strategy followed all three of the strands noted above. The Commission produced substantial new documents on relations with Japan and China, aimed at consolidating the progress made in the previous decade and at formulating new frameworks for managing relations, and it also initiated wide-ranging negotiations with Korea, both bilaterally and within the context of the proposed Korean Peninsula Energy Development Organization (KEDO) (CEC, 1995a; 1995b). It also began negotiations for framework and co-operation agreements with a wide range of individual Asia-Pacific countries. At least as important as these initiatives was the second, inter-regional strand which emerged from an EU–ASEAN ministerial meeting in Karlsruhe (Germany) during 1994. This meeting established a number of principles aimed at placing the relationship on a more equal footing and at broadening it to include more explicitly political discussions, as well as working on the implementation of the Uruguay Round of agreements which had set up the WTO and established a new trade policy agenda for the mid 1990s. At a similar EU–ASEAN ministerial meeting in 1995, the Prime Minister of Singapore proposed what was to become a major new initiative: the convening of an Asia–Europe Meeting (ASEM), to include the member states of the EU, the members of ASEAN and, in addition, Japan, China and Korea. At this stage, there was no move to include other major Asian countries such as India, or other Pacific countries such as Australia or New Zealand (CEC, 1996).

In the light of what was said earlier about the ways in which EU policy is a product of a 'negotiated order', one interpretation of this process is that it was essentially a unilateral set of initiatives on the part of the EU: in other words, negotiating with Asia-Pacific countries was something that the EU decided to do for its own purposes, the member states negotiated a strategy within the European context and then the Commission, acting for the member states, implemented it. There is a germ of truth in such an explanation, but it is equally clear that this is only part of the story. One of the notable features of the process that unfolded during 1995 and 1996 is that it was driven both by the EU and by the Asia-Pacific (particularly the ASEAN) countries. It was also undertaken on the basis that this was a relationship of equals, not necessarily at the level of individual states but certainly at the level of the inter-regional groupings. Not all EU leaders found this comfortable: after all, much of the previous negotiation between the EU and Asia-Pacific countries had been carried out on a rather less equal basis, with the exception for the most part of EU–Japan relations (Suthiphand and Erdmann-Keefer, 1996).

The centrepiece of the new EU–Asia-Pacific relationship was thus to be the ASEM, held in March 1996 in Bangkok, and then to be followed up by a range of government and private initiatives. As with all such international meetings, much of the key discussion took place before the formal meeting itself – a process termed 'pre-negotiation' by some analysts, in which the agenda is defined and in which understandings about the acceptable and the unacceptable areas for discussion are developed. This meant that the process from the autumn of 1995 to the spring of 1996 was crucial not only to the success of the meeting itself, but also to the definition of the EU and Asia-Pacific positions on a number of key issues. Significantly, one part of the pre-negotiation phase was the convening of a 'Europe–Asia forum on culture, values and technology' and of a range of other educational and information seminars, which were designed to try to improve mutual understanding about differences on such issues as human rights (Allen and Smith, 1997b). As we shall see, such efforts did not iron out all possible difficulties about issues of values and culture, or about the politics of South-East Asia in particular.

The first Asia–Europe Summit meeting in Bangkok, 1 March 1996

The agenda that emerged from the ASEM was an amalgam of EU and Asia-Pacific (largely ASEAN) preoccupations. As was to be expected, trade was at the centre; but it was clear that while the EU wanted above all to enlist Asia-Pacific support for certain items on the WTO agenda, the Asia-Pacific countries themselves wanted to ensure that the notion of 'open regionalism' got a good airing. This important difference of view did not lead to direct confrontation, but it defined at least some of the parameters for discussion. The EU might see the ASEM as a means of increasing its leverage and recruiting support in the WTO, but the Asia-Pacific countries were equally determined to put forward their apprehensions about potential EU protectionism. Likewise, the EU pressed strongly for progress in defining general rules for investment and the opening of markets, but ASEAN countries in particular were at pains to point out that they would be unable to make progress as rapidly as the EU wished. Nonetheless, on both trade and investment important progress was made and initiatives set in train (Dent, 1996, pp.37–9). In addition, the meeting provided a forum for the raising of bilateral economic issues between EU member states and individual Asia-Pacific countries; perhaps the most important of these was the discussion of EU support for the entry of China into the WTO, but the ASEM also provided the context for signature of an EU–Korea framework trade and co-operation agreement (Wise, 1996; *The Nation*, 1996).

Much more sensitive were issues of political dialogue, regional conflict and human rights. Here, there were clear clashes between the EU view that there were universal standards to be pursued and the Asia-Pacific view that the regional context and cultural factors needed to be taken strongly into account. The central focus for conflict was the case of Burma; indeed, a number of EU heads of government found they had pressing engagements elsewhere and sent their substitutes, at least partly because they knew this issue would come up. A related issue was that of China, and there was for at least some EU leaders a direct link between what was decided on Burma and what might then cause difficulties with Beijing (Wise, 1996). Resistance to EU pressure was stout on the part of ASEAN leaders in particular, and forms of words had to be found for the final communiqué that glossed over the differences. Significantly, though, a number of EU countries made it clear that their priorities lay in trade and investment promotion rather than in punishing the Asians. Within the EU itself, therefore, there were and remain differences of view, and these interacted with a strong Asia-Pacific consciousness of 'the Asian way' to defuse the confrontation, at least temporarily. The ASEM final communiqué on the subject of political dialogue emphasized a position crucial to Asia-Pacific awareness: that political dialogue should be conducted on the basis of 'mutual respect, equality, promotion of fundamental rights, and, in accordance with the rules of international law and obligations, non-intervention, whether direct or indirect, in each other's internal affairs' (Agence Europe, 1996, p.2).

The ASEM was explicitly intended to be the start of an extended process, although not the inception of a formal set of institutions (again, you can see the resistance of Asia-Pacific countries to a reduction of national freedom of action and manoeuvre). A second meeting was scheduled for London in the spring of 1998, and a third for Seoul in Korea during the year 2000. In addition, a range of working groups including the Senior Officials' Meeting on Trade and Investment (SOMTI) and the Asia-Europe Business Forum was set up, and discussions initiated on a range of programmes including trade and investment promotion, educational networks, transportation and the development of the Mekong Delta.

Although the ASEM was clearly the centrepiece of the new EU–Asia-Pacific dialogue, it must not be forgotten that it was implanted in the wider framework of bilateral and multilateral contacts sketched above. It must also not be forgotten that simple dialogue is not necessarily the way to resolve pressing clashes of political interest or values. This was evident in the further development of the tensions over Burma in the months after the ASEM. Continuing suppression of the opposition party led by Aung San Suu Kyi was central to this, but it was given added force by the death in prison of an honorary consul who had represented a number of EU member states in Rangoon, and by the growing evidence of the use of forced labour in Burma, which led to active consideration of sanctions by the EU. This did not prevent the ASEAN leaders at their meeting in mid 1997 from agreeing to the admission of Burma as a member. This was only one of a series of tensions which have not disappeared from EU–Asia-Pacific relations (Allen and Smith, 1997b).

Tensions and contradictions

From what has been said, one can conclude that the definition of a new strategy by the EU, and indeed its implementation, did not resolve some important tensions and contradictions. These tensions and contradictions go to the heart of the ways in which outsiders approach the Asia-Pacific, and also expose some of the important political differences and diversity within the Asia-Pacific region itself. The key areas of tension and contradiction seem to me to be the following:

- The tension between commercial interests and other values. From the EU point of view there is an obvious clash between the desire to promote commerce in its broadest sense and the desire (more deeply felt by some EU members than by others) to uphold what are seen as universal standards of behaviour, particularly on the part of governments. This translates at some points into a generalized EU concern with security and stability in the Asia-Pacific region, which can also be focused by the concerns of individual EU member states. But from the point of view of Asia-Pacific countries, and particularly those fast finding their feet in the world arena, this is at odds with another value at least as vital: the need for autonomy, non-intervention and mutual respect among countries. Such a tension will not disappear easily or soon. In addition to the case of Burma, there is the continuing clash between Portugal and Indonesia over East Timor (partially defused by negotiations on the margins of the ASEM, in fact), and, even more potentially explosive, the likelihood of what EU members will see as human rights abuses in China.

- The tension between 'closed' and 'open' regionalism. This is not a clear-cut and stark distinction in all cases, but it is clear that the EU's highly institutionalized and 'well-armed' version of regionalism is seen as potentially threatening by the Asia-Pacific countries who have espoused the APEC version of 'open regionalism'. This links with another tension, between a preference for supra-national solutions and rules and a preference for intergovernmental co-operation, which in turn links back to the value problems of intervention and non-intervention noted above.

- The related tension between EU desires for institutionalization of the EU–Asia-Pacific relationship and the Asia-Pacific preference for a loose form of dialogue in which the emphasis is on mutual adjustment. This is clearly linked to the issues of rules and 'closed' regionalism outlined above, and cuts across a number of areas of policy, such as that of FDI. What needs to be said in this case, though, is that some of the most powerful institutional arrangements are often those which do not have elaborate formal organizations attached to them. To that extent, both the EU preference for institutions and the Asia-Pacific preference for looser arrangements may miss the point; their regular mutual interaction may well set up powerful informal institutional constraints.

- A tension between the 'public' intergovernmental process of interaction and the 'private' transnational processes set up by the activities either of commercial enterprises or of other non-governmental organizations (NGOs). As noted above, alongside the ASEM governmental meeting went a series of private business meetings, and it is clear that the priorities of many private firms might differ from those of governments, for example over the balance between human rights considerations and investment decisions. The same might be said, in a very different sense, for NGOs in humanitarian and other areas; the ASEM was accompanied by a meeting of NGOs, also in Bangkok, at which issues such as weapons proliferation, nuclear testing, environmental degradation and human rights were understandably more prominent than in the governmental arena.

These are not the only areas of tension and contradiction in the EU–Asia-Pacific relationship, but they do clarify some of the fundamental forces working both to create incentives for co-operation and to make co-operation difficult. It is impossible to avoid the linkages between material economic welfare, assumptions about the role of government and cultural factors, such as those attaching to human rights and the role of the individual, which are central to the study not only of the Asia-Pacific itself, but also of the EU as another very different form of regionalism. This brings me to consideration of the global context for EU–Asia-Pacific relations.

14.4   The EU and the Asia-Pacific in a global context

Implicit in this analysis of EU–Asia-Pacific relations so far has been an awareness of the ways in which they fit within the broader context of the global arena. In this section I briefly explore three aspects of this broader context: the EU–US–Japan 'triangle', the multilateral institutions, and what I will call 'Asia-Pacific in Europe'. Together, these three areas give some impression of the ways in which processes of *multilateralism* and *globalization* shape the EU's search for an Asia-Pacific strategy.

The EU–US–Japan 'triangle'

It is apparent that EU–Asia-Pacific relations must be viewed in the light of the 'triangular' relationship between the EU, the USA and Japan. Indeed, one of the main motivations for EU policy makers in developing their new Asia strategy was the desire to achieve some leverage in an arena where they might be left behind by the other economic superpowers (CEC, 1994). Likewise, for Asia-Pacific participants in the process, a key consideration was the desire to broaden their options in the global political economy beyond those provided by the USA and Japan. The status of the EU as a 'civilian power', as noted earlier, has been important throughout the development of EU–Asia-Pacific relations: the EU is neither the USA nor Japan, and does not have an assertive regional presence in the political and security domains. But this gives the EU both benefits and limitations, narrowing the range over which negotiation can take place and focusing attention on the commercial and the humanitarian in a way which is peculiarly restricted. One way of conceptualizing the EU–Asia-Pacific relationship in the context of the 'triangle' is thus as a means through which both the EU and its Asia-Pacific partners can create some room for manoeuvre and some leverage in respect of their major rivals or patrons. Things are not, unfortunately, always so simple. One major complicating factor, as you will be very well aware, is that both the United States and Japan have strong claims to be considered as integral parts of the Asia-Pacific region. In the case of Japan this goes without saying, and it is interesting to reflect on the ambiguities this injected into the ASEM; in the case of the USA, which could be seen as one implicit 'target' of the ASEM and the EU's Asia strategy, the relationship is less direct, and the USA reacted with a kind of amused detachment to the EU initiatives. Other Asian countries, such as India, pressed very strongly their claims to inclusion in future ASEMs, as did Australia and New Zealand. It could be argued in the light of these ambiguities and 'boundary problems', that the key relationship in ASEM is that between the EU and the ASEAN countries, since these were the sources of the initiative.

While there are many uncertainties in the EU–Asia-Pacific relationship, as conditioned by the EU–US–Japan 'triangle', one feature is central. The EU has been conscious since the early 1980s that successive rounds of confrontation and negotiation between the USA and Japan have the potential to damage European interests severely. This phenomenon, which might be termed 'third-partyism', is a matter of great sensitivity for policy makers in the EU, and they have made consistent efforts since the mid 1980s to get themselves a seat at the table, for example in discussions of deregulation in Japan, or in negotiations about trade in cars and car components or semiconductors. The danger, as seen in Brussels, is that the United States can strong-arm the Japanese into concessions which favour US interests. Although the new Asia strategy, and more particularly the ASEM, are not to be seen simply as a ploy by the Europeans to increase their bargaining power within the 'triangle', this is not to be ignored in considering EU–Asia-Pacific relations. In the same way, ASEAN countries faced with economic threats from Japan or perhaps China, can hope to increase their bargaining power through interaction with the EU. Quite what the impact of such manoeuvres might be has still to be seen.

Global institutions

Just as the EU–Asia-Pacific relationship is inevitably affected by the evolution of EU–US–Japan relations, it can also be seen as part of a 'game' involving global (multilateral) institutions. Indeed, the EU's new Asia strategy and its responses to the ASEM were fundamentally conditioned by the potential benefits to be exploited in the context of the WTO, whilst for Asia-Pacific countries there were also strong links to the broader UN context. In setting out its aims for the ASEM, the EU was sharply aware of the fact that it would precede by a few months the first ministerial meeting of the WTO, to be held in Singapore during December 1996. The Europeans were anxious to gather as much support as possible from the Asia-Pacific for their positions in relation to negotiations on trade in information technology and telecommunications, and they also wanted a forum in which their positions on investment, competition policy and other areas could be given an airing (Islam, 1995–96). While the Asia-Pacific partners, and particularly those in ASEAN, were not unwilling to listen, they were resistant to any EU attempts to recruit them as 'cannon fodder' in the global arena. Thus, there were sharp exchanges over investment policies, and hard bargaining over other items on the agenda. In the end, when it came to the WTO meeting, many Asia-Pacific countries did sign up for agreements also supported by the EU, but it is vital to these countries that they are not perceived simply as stakes in a game played by the larger economic powers. Within the WTO context also, the EU has 'special relationships' with the USA and Japan in what has become known as the 'Quad Group' (Canada is also a member). While this has enabled a number of negotiating log-jams to be cleared in recent years, it can be viewed with some suspicion by the other Asia-Pacific countries. Looming over the WTO in general is the question of Chinese membership, and the terms on which it might be granted. The EU has made a point in the past of distancing itself from US policy on China and the WTO (Acharya, 1995).

This discussion indicates that the structure and politics of global trade governance plays an important part in conditioning the EU–Asia-Pacific relationship, but also that its impact is not always clear-cut. Asia-Pacific countries are relatively recent full members of the international trading system, and in many cases have not yet gained membership of such 'clubs' as the Organization for Economic Co-operation and Development (OECD); indeed, Korea's entry into the OECD, agreed in 1996, caused domestic strife because of the conditions on which it was accepted. This issue of global institutional engagement also extends to the United Nations system, in which many Asia-Pacific countries feel that there are structural barriers to their influence. The demand for reform of the Security Council, for example, causes the EU some difficulties: at present, the Security Council has two European permanent members (France and the UK), and they are resistant to giving their positions up, even to other Europeans, or to a single EU representative. More likely is an enlargement of the Security Council to give new seats (permanent or semi-permanent) to other countries, including some from the Asia-Pacific. When the question is put in those terms, the EU can respond positively to Asia-Pacific pressures, but within strict limits.

It becomes clear from this review that the global institutional structure is both an influence on EU–Asia-Pacific relations and a subject for bargaining between the partners. This bargaining, as in other areas, is no longer asymmetrical: the EU is one of the most powerful and well-organized bargainers in the global arena, but it meets resistance and effective counter-measures from its Asia-Pacific partners when it exceeds the limits of consensus.

The Asia-Pacific in Europe

One of the impacts of globalization in the world political economy, as already pointed out, is the increased interpenetration of what might otherwise be thought of as purely 'national' or 'regional' economies. While the discussion above of EU–US–Japan relations might be seen as encouraging a 'competitive bloc' model of relations between the participants, with Asia-Pacific regional concerns seen as a function of the global contest, it is possible to take a very different view based on interpenetration and the difficulties of knowing 'who is us'. In relations between the EU and the Asia-Pacific, this growth of transnational networks and interpenetration has had important but asymmetrical effects. The most obvious area in which the EU has been 'penetrated' by Asia-Pacific forces is that of Japanese investment within Europe, a phenomenon which increased rapidly in the late 1980s and which triggered discussion of threats to European economic management (Thomsen, 1991; Mason and Encarnation, 1994). Less well developed, but gaining momentum in the 1990s, was the Korean 'invasion', which like the Japanese was focused particularly in areas such as car production and consumer electronics. During the mid 1990s it also became apparent that Taiwanese and Malaysian investments were gaining ground. Compared to these flows, it was widely noted that the EU's investment performance in the Asia-Pacific was weak both in absolute terms and in relation to the activities of the USA and Japan (*The Economist*, 1996). A 'competitive bloc' model of relations would clearly indicate the need for the Europeans to resist further 'invasions' from the East and to increase their presence in the Asia-Pacific region. The latter consideration was certainly part of the basis for the new EU Asia-Pacific strategy as it evolved in the early 1990s.

The realities of globalization and interpenetration, though, make such goals difficult to realize. First, the Asia-Pacific presence in the EU is concentrated in certain countries, such as the UK, who clearly have good reasons to argue for a continuation of a liberal policy on FDI. 'Fortress Europe' is thus difficult to build, not only because there are those within who don't want it, but also because through the development of transnational alliances it is difficult to identify the 'outsiders'. A major book on Japanese investment in Europe was entitled *Does Ownership Matter?*, and for many EU policy makers the answer is at best a qualified 'yes' (Mason and Encarnation, 1994). Apart from any other considerations, it became apparent in the mid 1990s that Asia-Pacific investors might easily be tempted to invest in central and Eastern European countries, where they would have access to the EU but would have markedly lower costs of production.

So, the process of globalization makes it difficult (some would say self-defeating) to build trade barriers against an Asia-Pacific 'invasion' of the EU. But, as noted, many Asia-Pacific countries are themselves resistant to liberal investment policies, usually on the basis that they are at an earlier stage of national economic development and that they need some defences, at least temporarily. In some cases this is undoubtedly true, although aid and development funding can also play the role of a Trojan horse in enabling EU firms to penetrate closed markets. In other cases, such as that of Japan and increasingly Korea, this argument is difficult to sustain. Such an asymmetry is bound to create both economic and political tensions as time goes by.

14.5   Evaluating EU–Asia-Pacific relations

There are two ways in which EU–Asia-Pacific relations might be evaluated for the purposes of this discussion. First, we could ask, 'who is doing what to whom, and what are they getting out of it?' This gives us a means to explore the costs and benefits of the relationship, as well as its overall texture. Second, we could ask, 'what direction is the relationship moving in?' This section looks briefly at each of these questions.

Asking 'who is doing what to whom, and what are they getting out of it?' brings us to the concern with participation, the focus of relationships and the processes they generate, and the complex issues of costs and benefits explored in relation to the Asia-Pacific region in earlier chapters.

On the issue of *participation*, it is clear from what has been discussed that the EU–Asia-Pacific relationship is multilayered; that is to say, participants can be found at many levels and their activities often cross those levels. Apart from the intergovernmental relationships existing between states in the EU and states in the Asia-Pacific region, there is a host of mediating and modifying forces. Some of these are at the regional level, acting through the EU or through channels developing in the Asia-Pacific region. Linked with this, but not the same as it, are the participants at the inter-regional level, including not only the EU and Asia-Pacific countries meeting in ASEM, but also the 'triangle' of relations between the EU, the USA and Japan. Others are at the transnational level, with the activities of commercial organizations and NGOs prominent. Finally, others are at the global level, including the institutions and organizations that form an important part of the context for EU–Asia-Pacific interactions. Diversity and complexity of participation is thus central to the relationship, and will continue to be so.

When it comes to the *focus and processes* characteristic of the relationship, it is clear that EU–Asia-Pacific relations span a number of areas vital to regional development and to global order, but that they do so unevenly. If we take the core of the relationship to be the economic domain, it is apparent that this cannot be divorced from issues of governance, human rights, broader cultural values and international security. Although the latter has not featured strongly in this discussion, it is in a way crucial to an understanding of the relative sensitivities of the EU and Asia-Pacific countries, and to their ability to form a resilient set of relations. In its broadest sense, security encompasses all of the sensitivities about national autonomy and mutual respect that run through the relationship, and extends to the discussion of value-systems and culture. While military security is not central to this relationship, it is impossible to talk about EU–Asia-Pacific relations without encountering the issue of what some have called 'societal security' and its ramifications. In all of these areas we have encountered questions of power: not simply in terms of the shifting balance between the EU and the Asia-Pacific countries, which has been fundamental to the evolution of the EU's new strategy and to the approach taken by ASEAN members and others, but also in terms of the channels through which bargaining takes place and leverage can be exerted. We have also encountered significant questions about institutions and the extent to which the evolving relationship can be expressed through the establishment of formal rules and procedures. You will have noted at many points the divergent assumptions about ways in which inter-regional relationships can be designed and managed.

Finally, there is the question of *results*. Who is getting what out of the development of EU–Asia-Pacific relations? On the side of the EU it seems clear that there was an amalgam of forces and motivations behind the emergence of a new Asia-Pacific strategy in the early 1990s: responses to the end of the Cold War, the threats and opportunities seen as emerging in the Asia-Pacific, and the internal dynamics of the EU and its institutions. There was also a tension – usually muted but sometimes explicit – between the collective EU stance and the interests of specific EU member states. Because of the complex blend of interests lying behind the strategy, it is difficult to point conclusively to winners and losers. It is apparent, however, that the EU has succeeded in creating a more pro-active engagement with the region. On the Asia-Pacific side, there is an equally complex and differentiated set of motivations: the activism of the ASEAN members is especially notable, but has to be placed alongside the longer-standing EU–Japan entanglement and the emerging focus on China.

One conclusion from this evaluation could be that EU–Asia-Pacific relations constitute an experiment in the ways in which inter-regional relations can be conducted in a globalizing world, and in the absence of overt coercive means. To this extent, we can conclude that they have come a long way during the 1990s, and that the development both of strategies and institutions from a low base has been impressive. But where might these relations be going? To a certain extent, the answer to this question depends upon one's initial interpretation of the relationship itself. If one takes a 'competitive bloc' model of the relationship, then it is likely to be very strongly conditioned by the development of relations between the EU, the USA and Japan as the key global bloc leaders. But many would challenge this view, choosing instead to emphasize the ways in which global institutions shape the relationship and also the ways in which EU–

Asia-Pacific relations themselves can become strongly (even if informally) institutionalized. Still others would choose to emphasize the multilayered nature of the relationship, and in particular the ways in which it is penetrated by transnational networks and the broader forces of globalization. The likelihood is that it will conform to none of these models, but it is clear that there are powerful incentives driving the EU, as an 'outsider' to the Asia-Pacific region, in the direction of continued activity and the further development of an Asia-Pacific strategy.

14.6   Conclusion

This chapter set out to explore EU–Asia-Pacific relations as an example of the ways in which the Asia-Pacific both impacts upon and is targeted by 'outsiders'. It has focused on four areas of analysis:

- the growth and focus of the relationship;

- the emergence of an EU strategy for the Asia-Pacific;

- the ways in which this relationship relates to the broader global context;

- the ways in which the relationship might be evaluated.

By doing so it has raised, in a different form, a number of the questions encountered in other chapters, about the nature of regions and inter-regional relations, about the range of participants and strategies deployed in the global arena, about the multilayered nature both of regions and of the global system, and about the ways in which change has taken and might take place. The chapter raises important issues about world order, which are taken up in Chapter 15.

This chapter has also tried to gather together a number of strands in an analysis of EU–Asia-Pacific relations, and to construct an overall evaluation. It should not be surprising that the evaluation is inconclusive, since part of the 'message' is that EU–Asia-Pacific relations are both diverse and continuously evolving. It does seem, though, that the question 'who is doing what to whom, and with what results?' brings us into contact with some central questions in the analysis of international relations and the global political economy, relating to participants, processes and the outcomes of complex interactions. It also forces us to reconsider a central issue of identity, which applies in different ways both to the EU and to the Asia-Pacific: to put it simply, how many EUs are there, and how many Asia-Pacifics? Both are multilayered and multidimensional phenomena, operating not only in relation one to the other but also in relation to a wide range of groupings, both more and less restricted. The interests, motivations, activities and impact of these groupings are illustrated in distinctive ways by the development of EU–Asia-Pacific relations.

References

Acharya, R. (1995) 'The case for China's accession to the WTO: options for the EU' in Grant, R. (ed.) *The European Union and China: A European Strategy for the Twenty-First Century*, London, Royal Institute of International Affairs, pp.54–74.

Agence Europe (1996) *Conclusions of the Euro-Asian Summit of Bangkok,* Europe Documents, Brussels, 20 March.

Allen, D. and Smith, M. (1990) 'Western Europe's presence in the contemporary international arena', *Review of International Studies*, vol.16, no.1, January, pp.19–39.

Allen, D. and Smith, M. (1997a) 'The European Union's presence in the European security order: barrier, facilitator or manager?' in Rhodes, D. (ed.) *The European Union in the World Community*, Boulder, CO, Lynne Rienner.

Allen, D. and Smith, M. (1997b) 'External policy developments' in Nugent, N. (ed.) *The European Union 1996: Annual Review of Activities*, Oxford, Blackwell.

Commission of the European Communities (CEC) (1994) *Towards a New Asia Strategy*, Communication from the Commission to the Council, COM (94) 314 final, Brussels, European Commission.

Commission of the European Communities (CEC) (1995a) *Europe and Japan: The Next Steps*, Communication from the Commission to the Council, COM (95) 73 final, Brussels, European Commission.

Commission of the European Communities (CEC) (1995b) *A Long-Term Policy for China–Europe Relations*, Communication from the Commission to the Council, COM (95) 279 final, Brussels, European Commission.

Commission of the European Communities (CEC) (1996) *Creating a New Dynamic in EU–ASEAN Relations*, Brussels, European Commission.

Dent, C. (1996) *EU–East Asia Economic Relations: Completing the Triangle*, London, University of North London, European Dossier Series No.42.

The Economist (1996) 'Has Europe failed in Asia?', 2 March, pp.63–5.

Eurostat (1996) *Statistics in Focus*, No.2, Luxembourg, Eurostat.

Grant, R. (1995) *The European Union and China: A European Strategy for the Twenty-First Century*, London, Royal Institute of International Affairs.

Hill, C. (1993) 'The capability-expectations gap, or conceptualizing Europe's international role', *Journal of Common Market Studies*, vol.31, no.3, September, pp.305–28.

Hine, R. (1985) *The Political Economy of European Trade*, London, Harvester-Wheatsheaf.

Islam, S. (1995–96) 'EU sets out to write new Asia agenda', *European Voice*, 21 December–3 January, p.7.

Mason, M. and Encarnation, D. (eds) (1994) *Does Ownership Matter? Japanese Multinationals in Europe*, Oxford, Clarendon Press.

The Nation (1996) 'EU, S. Korea agree to cut trade barriers', Bangkok, 2 March.

Smith, M. (1996) 'The EU as an international actor' in Richardson, J. (ed.) *European Union: Power and Policy-Making*, London, Routledge, pp.246–62.

Smith, M. (1997) 'Regions and regionalism' in White, B., Little, R. and Smith, M. (eds) *Issues in World Politics*, London, Macmillan, pp.69–89.

Suthiphand, C. and Erdmann-Keefer, V. (1996) *The First ASEM (Asia–Europe Meeting): Outcome and Perspectives*, Bangkok, Chulalongkorn University European Studies Programme, May.

Thomsen, S. (1991) *The Evolution of Japanese Direct Investment in Europe: Death of a Transistor Salesman*, New York, Harvester-Wheatsheaf.

UNCTAD Division of Transnational Corporations and Investments (1995) *World Investment Report 1995: Transnational Corporations and Competitiveness*, United Nations Publications, No.E.95.II.A.9.

Wise, E. (1996) 'Beijing calls the shots in relations with EU', *European Voice*, 2–8 May, p.9.

Further reading

Commission of the European Communities (CEC) (1996) *Creating a New Dynamic in EU–ASEAN Relations*, Brussels, European Commission.

Grant, R. (1995) *The European Union and China: A European Strategy for the Twenty-First Century*, London, Royal Institute of International Affairs.

Rhodes, D. (ed.) (1997) *The European Union in the World Community*, Boulder, CO, Lynne Rienner.

CHAPTER 15

The Asia-Pacific: what kind of challenge?

Gerald Segal

15.1 Introduction

Readers of the preceding chapters should be in no doubt that what is happening in the Asia-Pacific is of far-reaching importance. What is somewhat less clear is the nature of the challenge posed by these developments, both to the third of humankind that lives in the region, and to the wider world. In this final chapter I will address three aspects of the Asian-Pacific challenge. First, I will ask whether the internal forces that led to the rise of the Asia-Pacific are likely to continue. Second, I will assess whether it makes much sense to talk of a single challenge from a region as diverse as the Asia-Pacific. Finally, I will analyse the extent to which the challenges in the region are leading to a restructuring of international relations both within the region and beyond.

These issues, as you will already know from earlier chapters, are the focus of an increasingly intricate debate. As the people of the Asia-Pacific grow more rich and successful, and as their social and political systems evolve, there is increasing need to understand how this will transform the pattern of regional and global relations. All too often the debates about these trends are cast in terms of simplistic paradigms of international affairs: a realist is said to underestimate the role of interdependence, or those neo liberal-institutionalists who assume the emergence of a regional community misunderstand the continuing role of the balance of power. In the analysis that follows there is an attempt to take a more integrative approach that does justice to the complex story of how the impressive success in the Asia-Pacific is beginning to transform international relations. The change we are witnessing is an impressive but sometimes volatile mixture of new patterns of interdependence, the creation of a regional community and the emergence of a new balance of power. Any one of these threads is merely a necessary, but far from sufficient basis on which to weave a complete analysis (Segal, 1997).

15.2   The sun rises in the east: does the sun also set?

Just as 'where there is smoke, there is usually fire', so where there is sustained hype there is usually some solid evidence of a new trend. In the case of the Asia-Pacific, there has undoubtedly been a remarkable rise of the region to global prominence, and for good reason.

It has only been in the past two generations that the magic of 'modernization' has been managed beyond the 'West' – in the Asia-Pacific. In an astoundingly short period of time a large part of humankind that lives in the Asia-Pacific has been dragged out of the agricultural stage, and in many cases rapidly through industrialization to a modern service economy. Given the enormity of the success, it beggars belief to suggest that such a transformation would not have far-reaching implications for those who have been through the process and others elsewhere in the world (World Bank, 1993).

And yet, before we get carried away with hyperbole, it is worth recalling the raw material with which the people of East Asia began. Until the early nineteenth century China was the world's largest economy and could claim to have been the world's greatest sustained civilization. Japan also had a sustained and glorious tradition. Indeed, many of the peoples of the Asia-Pacific had long experience of independence. Their grandeur was interrupted by Western imperialism, but in comparison to the scale of their historical grandeur, the era of subjugation was a blink of the eye (Segal, 1990).

Thankfully, even in the blink of an eye, one can glimpse a powerful picture. What the people of the Asia-Pacific saw was that the Western imperialists did have a great deal to teach. Some chose to open up to this foreign knowledge – others resisted, for a time, the powerful ideas that came from the West. We now know that by the end of the twentieth century, nearly all people in the Asia-Pacific have surrendered to the essentials of the Western recipe for prosperity.

Some of you will no doubt bristle at the previous sentence, for it suggests that the recipe for success in the Asia-Pacific is Western. That seems to contradict the notion that Asia's success is based on 'Asian values'. But the debate about the importance of 'Asian values' is crucial to our understanding of whether what is going on in the Asia-Pacific is a challenge to the non-Asian world. If you believe that there is something distinctively Asian about the success of the Asia-Pacific, then the challenge for outsiders is how to learn to be more 'Asian'.

At this point it is essential to draw a distinction between 'values in the Asia-Pacific' and 'Asian-Pacific values'. It is easy to argue that there are certain values and social practices that have under-pinned the success of the Asia-Pacific, just as there were values and social practices that lay behind the earlier triumph of the Atlantic world. Hard work, a propensity to save, stress on education, 'family values', even authoritarian government, have all been features of society, economics and politics in successful states in the Asia-Pacific (Campos and Root, 1996; Rohwer, 1995; and Hofheinz and Calder, 1992). But the fact that these were also values in the earlier phases of success in the Atlantic world, suggests that there are values in the Asia-Pacific that explain success, but not specifically Asian values. 'Victorian values' or 'the Protestant ethic' were terms once used to explain success in the Atlantic world.

Some of the most telling evidence in this debate about the values that underpin success, comes from the way in which the supposedly unchanging Asian features are being transformed by the powerful forces of modernization. Japan, and to some extent Singapore, Taiwan, Hong Kong and South Korea, which were the earliest to achieve sustained economic progress, are also the first to show signs of eroding values. After a generation or two of success, values seem to change in Asia as they changed in the West. The drive to work hard decreases. The propensity to save also declines as richer consumers want to spend more. The stress on primary education that was such a crucial platform for industrialization is not sufficient for societies that need to meet the challenges beyond industrialization when 'inspiration' is more vital than 'perspiration' (Krugman, 1995). Traditional values are also eroded as the stresses of modernization lead to higher rates of divorce or drug addiction. Once women are empowered, the extended and nuclear family comes under stress. In such an environment, when power is being diffused from elites to individuals, it is also obvious that authoritarian government is harder to sustain and politics becomes more pluralist. In short, while there were values in the Asia-Pacific, they do not appear to be immutable. Because this trend seems to be similar to that experienced in the Atlantic world, it seems likely that the values that underpinned success are not especially Asian.

If these conclusions are correct – and they are hotly contested – then they tell us a great deal about the nature of the challenge posed to, and by, the Asia-Pacific. If the people of the Asia-Pacific are by and large buffeted by the same sorts of winds of modernization that struck Western societies, then there are serious reasons to worry about the sustainability of rapid rates of economic growth in the East. What made the sun rise in the East in recent decades was a specific package of good policies mixed with good local conditions. But policies and conditions change as people move from a society based on agriculture to one based on a modern service economy. It is already clear that the most economically advanced countries of the Asia-Pacific have no magic formula for sustaining the work ethic, savings rates or family values. They may be able to meet the challenge of an economy that requires more inspiration than perspiration, but they will need to develop a better system of higher education and a more pluralist political system that fosters the kind of sceptical instincts and innovative thinking that makes inspiration possible. In short, the challenge of the Asia-Pacific is an enormous challenge to the Asia-Pacific itself. Having raised expectations in their own societies that they have found a recipe for success, popular aspirations need to be satisfied or else society becomes unstable. This is the 'bicycle theory of history' – if you fail to move forward, you risk falling over. It seems likely that, as Japan has recently demonstrated, economic growth

Symbols of Asia-Pacific rise: the Petronas Towers, Kuala Lumpur

does eventually slow to speeds well known in the Atlantic world. The bicycle need not stop entirely, but it will slow.

If it is correct that growth rates will slow in the Asia-Pacific, then the outside world faces a greater challenge than simply learning from an Asian model. If only life were so easy, then Latin Americans or Africans could sit at the feet of Asian gurus and transplant success. Although there are lessons to be learned from the success in the Asia-Pacific, they might be seen as the old lessons learned from the Atlantic world. Of course, the ingredients for modernization impose major changes on societies that agree to meet the challenge, but the fact that Asian societies have replicated the Atlantic miracle suggests a basic optimism about the ability to do it again somewhere else. In that sense, the challenge from the Asia-Pacific to other parts of the developing world is an uplifting if daunting one. They should also be encouraged by the fact that as the people of the Asia-Pacific become rich, they also vacate certain parts of the production chain, leaving opportunities for others to take their place.

The challenge posed by growth in the Asia-Pacific for the already developed world is very different. In some senses the Asia-Pacific represents a 'blast from the past'. It is a reminder of what underlay past success in the Atlantic world, and to the extent that increased competition requires Europeans or Americans to work harder, then there are useful lessons from the Asia-Pacific. But if the Asia-Pacific is a reminder of the past, then it is little guide to the future of the Atlantic states. There can be no going back to authoritarian regimes or the enclosure of women in the home. The challenge of the Asia-Pacific is to look forward to new solutions to the provision of welfare, creation of cutting-edge educational inspiration or new forms of stable families. And if the already developed world is successful in meeting these challenges, the lessons it learns will be invaluable to the people of the Asia-Pacific who will face similar ones in due course.

15.3   Challenge or many challenges?

It should be clear already that there are many diverse processes taking place in the Asia-Pacific. This is not surprising given the diversity of the peoples and states in the region. Taking all this diversity together, it is obvious that it makes little sense to talk of a single challenge, or even a single set of challenges to and from the Asia-Pacific.

Diversity, especially in increasingly complex and decentralized pluralist systems, is often more a source of optimism than pessimism. For example, the fact that there are very different levels of development and states with very different natural conditions has made it possible to have more of the benefits of comparative advantage that underpins economic prosperity. If all states in the region had started from the same place, and at the same time, rivalry might have been too great. As it was, Japan's role as the leading goose in the flying geese pattern of economic development made it possible for new birds to join the flock. In time they benefited from Japan's positive example, its flows of investment and technology, and its wealthy market as a destination for exports. This process, however uneven in reality, had a powerful demonstration effect on by far the largest player in the Asia-Pacific, China. The Chinese had resisted Western liberal ideas and when it adopted a Western model, it chose the dead-end of Soviet-style Communism. But the fact that other Asians – the people that the Chinese had considered 'civilizationally-challenged' – had sped past China on the road to economic prosperity, was a powerful motivation for the reforms of the 1980s.

When China in effect adopted many of the basic principles of Western modernization, it pretended to do so because it was an Asian rather than a Western process (Overholt, 1993).

China's entry into the pattern of economic growth makes it hard to sustain the pretty oriental picture of flying geese (Rohwer, 1995; Hofheinz and Calder, 1982). Given the fact that China has some two-thirds of the Asia-Pacific's population and territory, this is not so much a goose as an entire new flock. China's own growth has been based on its own version of a flying geese pattern, with several coastal provinces far ahead of inland provinces in their economic, political and social development. Some of China's richest provinces such as Guangdong are already at levels that would qualify them for membership of the first flock of geese, and in some senses it might be best to see the Asia-Pacific region as composed of one large and increasingly spread-out and even scruffy flock.

The diversity of the region, although seen most acutely in economic terms, is also evident in security terms. Measured in crude terms that try to take account of political, economic and military power, there are three main categories of powers (Dibb, 1995). The first category of indigenous great powers has only two members (China and Japan). Russia is a power in the Asia-Pacific, but not an Asian-Pacific power. The USA can be described in similar terms, but it has far less territory in the region and is in fact far more powerful than any of the indigenous powers. China and Japan are the major economies and grandest societies in the region, and they account for well over half the total defence spending in the region. They are clearly the major powers able to shape a regional balance of power.

The second category is middle powers, including the likes of Indonesia, Taiwan, the two Koreas, and Australia. These are states with diverse economies, most of which have had real success in meeting the challenges of modernization. Many of them have tacitly or explicitly close security ties with the USA and are crucial building blocks for any regional balance of power. The third, much looser category of smaller states includes a wide range of powers. Singapore, with its stress on high technology and a small, highly trained force, is in a world apart from the likes of Vietnam with largely poor peasant armed forces.

There is also enormous diversity in the range of challenges to regional security. At the highest level, there is the growing concern with the creation of a balance of power in order to constrain a rising China (Leifer, 1996). The region used to worry about the implications of the Cold War, but apart from the Korean or Taiwanese conflicts (which are best seen as unresolved civil wars), there are only the faintest echoes of a struggle with communism (for example in Cambodia). Some also used to worry about a reprise of Japanese imperialism, but fifty years of a passive Japan has begun to ease those worries. Koreans and Chinese still talk of the risks of a resurgent Japan, but this says more about their deep memories and current domestic politics than about the reality of contemporary Japan.

By far the most dominant current concern is with the implications of the rise of Chinese power. Given its size and history, it is natural for China's neighbours (and China itself) to see a hegemonic China as the natural order of things (Goodman and Segal, 1997). But it is equally natural for the modern states on China's rim to resist Chinese hegemony. The problem is that they do not know how to create an international system that will help ensure their independence of action. Japan, and to some extent South Korea and Taiwan, seek the protection of American power. Many South-East Asians might wish to do likewise, but doubt American resolve and are more resigned to living under China's shadow. Australia and New Zealand have natural affinities to the USA, but in their search for greater acceptance in the Asia-Pacific they are sometimes reluctant to associate themselves too closely with US power. Some states try to make an artificial division between military and economic power and suggest that the Americans can take care of maintaining the military balance of power while others get on with weaving webs of interdependence. In reality, political, economic and military power need to be woven together to create the fabric of international society. Pulling at one thread tends to unravel the entire cloth. Thus, taken together, these diverse motives and diverse sources of power explain why it is so difficult to create an over-arching balance of power in the Asia-Pacific (Shinn, 1996).

The states of the region also tend to see issues on sub-regional as well as a region-wide basis. Obviously crucial sub-regional disputes include those between the two Koreas, Taiwan and China, or between various claimants to the South China Sea. These are all issues with complex political, economic and military elements of power and rivalry. There are other, notionally territorial disputes between China and Japan, China and Korea, and Korea and Japan – all of which carry real risks of conflict and are also made up of complex political, economic and military factors. Thus a key challenge for the region and beyond is whether there is anything that can emerge out of this diversity that can constitute a natural pattern of stable international relations.

15.4   Building regional and global security

In a diverse region, shared identity can be hard to build (Manning and Stern, 1994). But a shared identity can be built if diversities overlap and if participants are less ambitious in the kind of unity they are seeking to establish. The presence of disjunctures and diversities in the Asia-Pacific are not inherent reasons for pessimism about the future pattern of regional affairs. These issues are themes in this book because they will pose complex challenges for some time to come.

It is unfair to expect the people of the Asia-Pacific to find unity across their region. Even the European experiment with a formal union, or the much less ambitious attempts at forming a free trade area in the Americas, includes far fewer people than in the Asia-Pacific. To some extent China alone can be considered an experimental union, for the size of its empire has waxed and waned and comes under special strains in the modern world because of its lack of a federal structure.

If it were not for China looming over the Asia-Pacific, it would make most sense to treat the region as having two halves: a North-East Asia that includes China, Russia, the Koreas, Japan and Taiwan, and a South-East Asia that includes China and the ASEAN states. There are few issues that are best handled at an Asia-Pacific-wide level, and none that do not include a focus on one of its members, China. The conclusion seems to be that the international relations of the Asia-Pacific are in the main about China and its neighbours.

If the Asia-Pacific is naturally Sino-centric, then it makes sense for any discussion about regional identity and the pattern of regional affairs to focus on China's role. This assessment may seem unduly simplistic, but to an important extent it is merely a return to the more traditional pattern of regional relations. While it is true that before the coming of European imperialists the people of Asia never had a sense of themselves as part of a coherent region, it is true that the international affairs of the Asia-Pacific had China as its main player. Our current images of the region are still befuddled by images of the Cold War when an overlay of the struggle with Communism gave a distorted picture of the natural state of affairs. The Sino-Soviet split, wars among communists in Indochina, China's capitalist reforms, and then the death of European communism, resulted in the gradual erosion of the communist overlay in the Asia-Pacific. What emerged from under the overlay still remains unclear.

This lack of clarity has a great deal to do with uncertainty about how much the region will revert to a Sino-centric pattern. The Asia-Pacific has spent the past 200 years without its own natural pattern of regional affairs. The world that Asians now inhabit is one in which state sovereignty is a fading value and interdependence and globalism are increasingly powerful. Unlike the Europeans or Americans, Asians are being asked to create a system of regional relations without having had much time to establish their sovereign characters and to think about how they wish to surrender to the forces of interdependence and globalization. Because they have grown rich, they are expected to act in a sophisticated and mature fashion. The weight of expectation may be unfair.

If I adopt a more tolerant perspective, it can be said that the states of the Asia-Pacific are making progress as 'actors' in international society. This is not to say that they are building their own regional society, for in fact there are several structures under construction. Not all will necessarily be completed, not all will be grand, and not all will last long. In fact, some of the best contributions that the peoples of the Asia-Pacific have to make is to the wider world beyond their home region.

The first construction is a balance of power. This is a building of which its builders dare not speak its name, at least not until its foundations are dug much deeper. The reason for this caution is obvious. There is only one 'non-status quo' power in the Asia-Pacific – China. Its rejection of many of the 'rules' of contemporary international society make it, like Bismarkian Germany, an unsatisfied power. Given the size of the country and the scale of the challenge to build a balance to constrain such a beast, none of the builders can quite believe that they will succeed in their task. They have good reason to be chary. Never has the international community tried to incorporate a state of this size. There must be better than even bets that

China will change the international system more than the system will change China. But the stakes – regional and global prosperity – could also not be higher. There is no more important task for managers of international prosperity and security than the peaceful incorporation of China and its fifth of humankind into the global order (Shinn, 1996).

The nature of the struggle to build a regional balance of power can be seen in the debates about how much to 'engage' and how much to 'contain' or 'constrain' China. The answer is blindingly simple – China needs to be engaged and constrained when it acts in a dangerous fashion. What is far less simple is how to combine engagement and constraint. Should China be allowed into the World Trade Organization without making it play by the rules of the system, or should it be allowed in and then find a way to massage the rules to fit the new member? Should China be allowed to take the islands that it wants in the South China Sea or to regain Taiwan against the wishes of its people? Appeasement of China, as with the earlier version concerning Germany in Europe, has a good rationale for those who believe that there will be no countervailing power and/or that keeping the giant happy will eventually turn it into a benign power 'more like us'.

Hence the centrality of building a regional balance of power. The obvious starting point for such a balance is the existing superpower, the USA (Stuart and Tow, 1995). Assuming that the Americans are prepared to continue to provide the fundamentals for regional security – and that is a big assumption – then the next task is to find the key countries that will form the anchor points for the main spokes of the wheel with an American hub. Japan is an obvious anchor, and its close security relationship with the United States is being modernized with a beady eye on China (Samuels, 1994). At the opposite end of the region, Australia remains another American anchor and one that has an even closer alliance with the USA. In between, another anchor might be tiny Singapore or mightier Indonesia, both of which have a vested interest in creating a regional balance of power. Further afield, under certain circumstances Russia and India might also see the value in sustaining a robust balance of power, but they dislike the image of a system with an American hub.

Both the need for, and the sustainability of, such a balance of power depends on Chinese actions. If China continues to be an assertive power that wishes to see the status quo changed, if it continues to claim and take territory from its neighbours, if it continues to demand major changes in international institutions such as the WTO, then it will ensure there is cement for the construction of a balance of power. Should China join the international system much like the USA a century before, as a proud power but one that was prepared to adapt to the rules in order to adapt them from the inside, then there will be far less need for a balance of power. China not only has its fate in its hands, it also holds the fate of the Asia-Pacific region (Betts, 1993).

A second construction site is that currently called either the ASEAN Regional Forum (ARF) or the Asia-Pacific Economic Co-operation (APEC). The ARF is concerned with building region-wide security while APEC is concerned with enhancing economic co-operation. In truth, the two bodies overlap in their shared concern with 'comprehensive' international security – the notion that economics requires a stable security environment and that military security requires economic prosperity. The two bodies are also still constructing their foundations and plans for the superstructure change every time the leaders gather. Neither arrangement depends on binding commitments, let alone the rule of law. In both cases, North American, Australasian or European members often find themselves frustrated by the determination of most Asian-Pacific states to proceed slowly and in an ad hoc and non-binding fashion. These 'Anglo' members have learned to hold their tongue and see how the Asians make out with their more informal vision.

To date, it is easy for the non-Asians to be cynical about the new constructions. Neither constrain state action. Neither intrude on the ability of national elites to make national policy according to national agendas. Nothing has been agreed at this regional level that has not already been arranged at the global level. Military transparency agreements at the United Nations cannot be agreed at the ARF level. WTO arrangements are more far-reaching than anything agreed at the APEC level. It is not that the ARF or APEC, are useless, but they are far from essential.

Asian architects of these new structures call for less hurried rushes to judgement (Borthwick 1994; Wanandi, 1996). They argue that building regional identity takes a long time. They note the fragility of many states and their continued love affair with state sovereignty. They argue that non-Asians judge such buildings by the strength of their legal structure, while Asians just want to see if it works. So far, judging whether it works can only be done on the basis of whether things have got worse – is the Asia-Pacific less stable or less interdependent since the creation of the ARF or APEC?

The answer is certainly no in the case of APEC, although all of the economic interdependence is due to the economic strategies of corporations or the success of governments negotiating global economic arrangements. At the regional level, government action is far less important than that of corporations or individuals.

In the case of the ARF it probably can be argued that the region has been less secure in the past few years. That is not the fault of the ARF – it is mostly the result of the rise of China. But it can be argued that because the ARF provides the illusion that something is being done about regional security, it actually lulls people into a false sense of security and makes the creation of a robust balance of power more difficult. The jury must still be out on this question. But there must be serious doubt that any arrangement like the ARF, that has the problem member (China) in its midst, can be the best and the only way to agree difficult counter-measures to keep the peace and prosperity. If military security in the Asia-Pacific is to rely on the ARF, then it will have to depend even more on a simultaneous balance of power.

In part because of such concerns, there is some talk of clearing a new building site for the creation of a North-East Asian construct. Japanese, and to some extent, Koreans are conscious that the ASEAN states who set the agenda for the ARF, have little real sense of how to handle North-East Asian affairs. As ASEAN states seem to tack to Chinese winds, the likes of Japan feel they need to look after their own interests more directly. Concern over North Korea's possible economic implosion or explosion with nuclear weapons has also led to calls for a sub-regional economic and/or security mechanism. So far, there are only the sketchiest of plans for such a building, but the increasing discussion of the matter says a great deal about dissatisfaction with current regional arrangements.

The troubled history of regional construction efforts still has some way to go before either the optimists are ground down or the pessimists are proven wrong. There are simply too many disparate forces at work in the Asia-Pacific to make conclusive judgements possible. The disjuncture between continued economic growth and rising signs of regional military tension makes generalization about trends impossible.

15.5   Challenges to the global order

Assuming that these trends continue, what can I say about the nature of the challenges posed to the wider international order? For one thing, the wider world is growing used to paying more attention to the Asia-Pacific. North Americans and Europeans have grown accustomed to doing more trade with the Asia-Pacific than they do across the Atlantic. Europeans and North Americans increasingly rely on financial flows from the Asia-Pacific and even technology is beginning to flow to, and from, these three parts of the global economy in an increasingly heavy torrent. Large European and North American companies have grown accustomed to the challenges and opportunities in the Asia-Pacific.

Government officials (and even academics) have been slower to see these trends. It was only in 1993 that APEC leaders gathered for their first summit. Major academic interest in the Asia-Pacific as a region (as opposed to its constituent states) only began after the end of the Cold War. Although the economic, political and military trends that now exercise the attention of governments and academics have clear roots in earlier decades, many of the main phenomena are only beginning to be seriously assessed for their global impact. I have already touched upon the debate about an Asian model of success that is apparent in both the developing and developed world. In economic terms, there is also little doubt that the impact of the rise of the Asia-Pacific for the global economy is beginning to be well understood. What is least appreciated is the extent to which the political and security pattern of international affairs is also changed by the rise of the Asia-Pacific.

Part of the explanation for this time lag in understanding the political and military nature of the Asia-Pacific challenge has to do with the policies of the Asian-Pacific states. In most cases they have been backward in coming forward as actors in international society. Only China sits on the United Nations Security Council and it has been the most passive of the permanent members. Japan seeks a permanent seat on the Council but has done so with such politeness that the realists at the world's top table feel they are under no pressure to act. Most Asian-Pacific states also suffer from what some have called a 'compassion deficit' – for despite their new wealth they rarely make serious contributions to international agencies or aid efforts. Perhaps they are just *nouveaux riche* and only 'older money' feels it needs to take charity and good causes more seriously. Perhaps there are Asian values that prefer to ignore the disadvantaged (it certainly mirrors the way the disadvantaged are treated in many Asian-Pacific societies). But it is striking that Japan has been the primary exception to the Asian-Pacific pattern of a 'compassion deficit'. Japanese officials have begun to play important roles in UN agencies and it is the world's largest aid donor. Some Asian states such as Malaysia have begun to play a useful role in UN peacekeeping, but in comparison to India or Pakistan, the rich Asians have much more to do before they are considered good 'international citizens'.

So far, the Asian-Pacific states have played a very small role in international security. When there is an international coalition in the Persian Gulf acting under United Nations resolutions, Australia and New Zealand send fighting forces, but virtually no one else from Eastern Asia makes a contribution. When it comes to the global arms trade, only China is among the major exporters of arms. Japan, South Korea and Australia play a part in the global transfer of defence-related equipment, but they are mainly importers of such technology. In fact, the Asia-Pacific is the fastest growing export market for sales of military hardware from Europe and the USA.

The Asia-Pacific is therefore a net consumer of security. Some states in the region rely on outsiders for security, but they contribute little to the world outside. The Asian-Pacific states are developing indigenous arms industries, but so far they are still major importers rather than exporters. Neither are they major architects or even supporters of arms control agreements. Notable exceptions are Australia, and to some extent Japan, both of which have been architects of important arms control initiatives. The rest of the Asia-Pacific is a target of diplomacy, but not an active shaper of the diplomatic agenda.

It is unclear how much this is likely to change. If it is true that Asians are less interested in formal accords of any sort and prefer personal and private diplomacy, then they are not likely to lead international diplomacy. But just as Japan has demonstrated that several generations of wealth and confidence can lead to a greater commitment to international society, so the rest of the Asia-Pacific may simply be on a steep learning curve. It is notable that some ASEAN states (Singapore, Malaysia, Indonesia) now seem prepared to take some of their territorial disputes to the International Court of Justice rather than continuing to pretend that matters can be resolved in ASEAN forums or in 'the ASEAN way' of informal consultations.

Certainly there is no rigid template for international good citizenship. France and Britain may feel that the rich and powerful should be active contributors to international society, but Germany and Italy seem to have been far more passive. Smaller middle powers like Canada or Sweden have been active in 'punching above their weight' in international affairs – something that Indonesia used to do in the non-aligned movement but no longer does. Only Singapore stands out as a smaller Asian-Pacific state with a determination to set agendas despite its tiny size.

15.6   Looking beyond ...

As I look further into the future of the impact of the Asia-Pacific on the wider world, it is possible to see the outlines of major challenges ahead. Even though the Asia-Pacific is unlikely to be a coherent region, the actions of its constituent parts will be more important than they are today. More economic and probably military power will reside in that region than anywhere else. Asians may well play a much more active part in global culture. As the Asia-Pacific grows, it will need far more fuel, food and finance to sustain its growth. Major new buyers in the Asia-Pacific may well drive up the prices of these and other traded goods and services. They will also create new markets for exports for both the developed and developing world.

While the generally rising importance of the people of the Asia-Pacific is obvious, what is less obvious is the more specific impacts of these shifts of power. Will the people of the Asia-Pacific be able to translate their economic prosperity into a greater ability to shape the international political agenda? One might envisage a new Asian hubris that disparages the values of the West and seeks to dictate a new model of development for developing states. Perhaps. But recent trends suggest that because Asians, like Europeans before them, find their values change during the course of modernization, economic prosperity will bring as many challenges to the states of East Asia as they pose for the wider world. As time goes on, we may well grow to understand the impressive diversity of the Asia-Pacific and respect their different struggles with modernity.

Assuming that economic success continues, at least for some time, there will also be major challenges for all concerned. Will energy hungry Asians seek to ensure energy supplies by force or will they leave it to market forces (Calder, 1996)? And even if energy prices do not rise, how will societies cope with the need for a better environment and political discontent that comes from the past policy of economics-in-command? It is far from obvious that East Asians have found solutions to the question of how to balance the need for economic growth and the desire for better living conditions and a more open political system. East Asians may not find the same mix as has been found in the Atlantic world, but they cannot avoid the struggle. Once again, we are most likely to see diverse responses from the peoples of the Asia-Pacific.

In terms of security policy, will the Asia-Pacific become the source of major arms exports just as it now sells cars and microwaves on world markets? Will we see Chinese or Japanese aircraft carriers keeping open the

Gulf oil routes? Such scenarios are possible, but seem premature. One of the most persistent worries about the Asia-Pacific is that it still faces major challenges in building regional security, and as a result the region's states will not be net contributors to global security for some time. It seems most likely that the world outside the Asia-Pacific will worry more about the sustainability of stability in the region rather than the impact that the booming region might have on the world outside.

In the end, nearly all these questions revolve around the uncertainty about the role of China. Given that China is growing faster that any economy has ever managed in the past, and that it constitutes a vast proportion of East Asia, it is a worry that China's future seems so uncertain. Questions about whether Chinese will run the International Monetary Fund or throw their weight around in determining who should be the Secretary General of the United Nations are theoretically interesting, but still some way off. Before we worry about such a powerful China, we need to face the challenges of the next generation when China will have to prove it can sustain its growth.

For the time being, China, and to some extent the Asia-Pacific as a whole, has not yet proven that it can re-shape the world outside. As the countries of the Asia-Pacific grow richer and stronger, they begin to demonstrate complex tendencies well known from the Atlantic world. At the same time as they grow more diverse, they also struggle with common problems of modernization and the management of a complex balance of political, economic and military power. It may be that the very process of growth and prosperity in the Asia-Pacific produces such a complex series of outcomes that we cease to treat the region as a coherent whole. Perhaps we need to remember that we can only guess at the answers. But one thing is sure, these are the kinds of questions we will continue to ask in the twenty-first century.

References

APEC (1994) *Achieving the APEC Vision*, Asia-Pacific Economic Co-operation Secretariat.

Betts, R. (1993–94) 'Wealth, power and instability: East Asia and the United States after the Cold War', *International Security*, vol.18, no.3.

Borthwick, M. (ed.) (1994) *Advancing Regional Integration*, Singapore, Pacific Economic Cooperation Council.

Buzan, B. and Segal, G. (1994) 'Rethinking East Asian security', Survival, vol.36, no.2.

Calder, K. (1996) *Asia's Deadly Triangle*, London, Nicholas Brealey.

Campos, J.E. and Root, H. (1996) *The Key to the Asian Miracle*, Washington, Brookings.

Dibb, P. (1995) 'Towards a new balance of power in Asia', *Adelphi Paper no.295*, London, International Institute for Strategic Studies.

Dobbs-Higginson, M.S. (1993) *Asia-Pacific: its Role in the New World Disorder*, London, Mandarin.

Friedberg, A. (1994) 'Ripe for rivalry: prospects for peace in a multipolar Asia', *International Security*.

Goodman, D. and Segal, G. (eds) (1997) *China Rising*, London, Routledge.

Hofheinz, R. and Calder, K. (1982) *The East Asia Edge*, New York, Harper and Row.

Huxley, T. (1996) 'Southeast Asia in the study of international relations', *Pacific Review*, vol.9, no.2.

Leifer, M. (1996) 'The ASEAN Regional Forum', *Adelphi Paper no.302*, London, International Institute for Strategic Studies,.

Manning, R and Stern, P. (1994) 'The myth of a Pacific community', *Foreign Affairs*, November/December.

Overholt, R. (1993) 'China: the next superpower', *Foreign Affairs*.

Rohwer, J. (1995) *Asia Rising*, New York, Simon and Schuster.

Samuels, R. (1994) *Rich Nation, Strong Army*, Ithaca, Cornell University Press.

Segal, G. (1990) *Rethinking the Pacific*, Oxford, Clarendon Press

Segal, G. (1996) 'East Asia and the "constrainment" of China', *International Security*, vol.20, no.4.

Segal, G. (1997) 'How insecure is Pacific Asia?', *International Affairs*, vol.73, no.2.

Shinn, J. (ed.) (1996) *Weaving the Net*, New York, Council on Foreign Relations.

Stuart, D. and Tow, W. (1995) 'A US strategy for the Asia-Pacific', *Adelphi Paper no.299*, London, International Institute for Strategic Studies.

The Pacific Review (1996) 'Asian values', vol.3, no.9.

Wanandi, J. (1996) 'ASEAN's China Strategy', *Survival*, vol.38, no.3.

World Bank (1993) *The East Asian Miracle*, Oxford, Oxford University Press.

Further reading

Calder, K. (1996) *Asia's Deadly Triangle*, London, Nicholas Brealey.

Dobbs-Higginson, M.S. (1993) *Asia-Pacific: its Role in the New World Disorder*, London, Mandarin.

Goodman, D. and Segal, G. (eds) (1997) *China Rising*, London, Routledge.

Rohwer, J. (1995) *Asia Rising*, New York, Simon & Schuster.

Segal, G. (1990) *Rethinking the Pacific*, Oxford, Clarendon Press.

Acknowledgements

Grateful acknowledgement is made to the following sources for permission to reproduce material in this book:

Figures

Figure 2.1: Kinder, H. and Hilgemann, W. (1978) *The Penguin Atlas of World History*, volume two, Penguin Books Ltd; Figure 2.2: Moore, R.I. (1981) *The Hamlyn Historical Atlas*, figure 2.2 'The Retreat of Imperialism in Asia', Hamlyn (an imprint of Reed Books); Figure 5.4: Valencia, M.J. (1995) *Adelphi Paper 298*, © The International Institute for Strategic Studies, Oxford University Press, by permission of Oxford University Press; Figure 6.2: Calder, K.E. (1996) *Asia's Deadly Triangle*, Nicholas Brealey Publishing Ltd, 36 John Street, London WC1N 2AT; Figure 8.1: World Bank (1995, 1991) *World Tables 1995, 1991*, Johns Hopkins University Press; Figure 8.3: Cohen, S., Paul, J. and Blecker, R. (1996) *Fundamentals of U.S. Foreign Trade Policy*, p.232, Westview Press, Inc.; Figures 14.1, 14.2 and 14.3: Quatro, R. (1996) *Statistics in Focus – External Trade*, Eurostat; Figure 14.4: 'FDI stock among Triad members and their clusters, 1993', *World Investment Report 1995: Transnational Corporations and Competitiveness* (United Nations Publication, Sales no. E. 95.II.A.14) (1995) United Nations Conference of Trade Development.

Tables

Table 3.1: Garnaut, Ross (1989) *Australia and the Northeast Asian Ascendancy: Report to the Prime Minister and the Minister for Foreign Affairs and Trade*, Canberra, AGPS (p.36 table); Table 3.2: derived from the International Economic Data Bank, World Bank Tables, July 1994, Australian National University, Canberra; Table 4.2: Wyatt-Walter, A. (1995) 'Regionalism, globalism and world economic order' in Fawcett, L. and Hurrell, A. (eds) *Regionalism in World Politics*, Oxford University Press, by permission of the author; Table 5.1: George, P., Bergstrand, B.-G. and Loose-Weintraub, E., 'Tables of military expenditure', *SIPRI Yearbook 1996: Armaments, Disarmaments and International Security* (Oxford University Press: Oxford), table A.2; Table 5.2: *The Military Balance*, © The International Institute for Strategic Studies, Oxford University Press, by permission of Oxford University Press; Table 8.2: Cohen, S., Paul, J. and Blecker, R. (1996) *Fundamentals of U.S. Foreign Trade Policy*, p.177, Westview Press, Inc.; Table 12.1: 'Membership in Regional Organizations', http://www.stimson.org/cbm/china/index.html, The Henry L. Stimpson Center.

Photographs

Cover: Hulton Getty; pp.3 (left), 51, 78, 102, 108, 159, 180, 182, 252, 262, 282, 283, 304: Popperfoto; p.3 (right): The Hutchison Library, © Robert Francis; p.15 (top four): Hulton Deutsch; p.15 (bottom): BBC Hulton Picture Library; pp.22, 148: Associated Press; pp.24, 44: AP Wide World Photos; p.63: Sam Greenhill © Sally and Richard Greenhill; p.126: © John A. Norris; p.220: Greenpeace/Morgan; p.319: © Topham Picturepoint.

List of contributors

Baker, Nikki. Currently a researcher at the Defence Studies Institute, Australian National University, Canberra specializing in the defence and foreign policies of the Asia-Pacific medium powers.

Brook, Chris. Chris Brook is Lecturer in Geography at The Open University, UK. His publications include *A Global World? Re-ordering Political Space* (co-edited, 1995, Oxford University Press).

Buzan, Barry. Barry Buzan is research Professor of International Studies at the University of Westminster, London and a Project Director at the Copenhagen Peace Research Institute (COPRI). He was Chairman of the British International Studies Association 1988–90, and Vice-President of the (North American) International Studies Association 1993–94. His most recent books include: *Military Security, Technology and International Relations* (1997, with Eric Herring); *Security: a New Framework for Analysis* (1997, with Ole Wæver and Jaap de Wilde); and *Anticipating the Future* (1997, with Gerald Segal).

Gibney, Frank. Director of the Pacific Basin Institute, Santa Monica, California. An established scholar of US–Japanese relations and author of numerous works on Japan, and US–Asia-Pacific relations.

Herr, Richard. Reader in Political Science in the Department of Government at the University of Tasmania. Recent publications include: 'The United Nations, regionalism and the South Pacific' (*Pacific Review*, vol.7, no.3, 1994); 'Regionalism and nationalism' in K.R. Howe, Robert C. Kiste and Brij V. Lal (eds) *Tides of History: the Pacific Islands in the Twentieth Century* (1994, Sydney, Allen & Unwin); Report of Regional Institutional Arrangements in the Marine Sector Review, South Pacific Organizations Co-ordinating Committee (August 1995, with S. Tupou, Review Panel Chair, *et al.*).

McGrew, Anthony. Senior Lecturer in International Relations at The Open University, UK. Recent publications include: *Empire, The US in the Twentieth Century* (ed.) (1994, Hodder & Stoughton); *The Transformation of Democracy? Globalization and Territorial Democracy* (ed.) (1997, Polity Press, Cambridge).

Mackerras, Colin. Chairman of the School of Modern Asian Studies, Griffith University, Brisbane, from 1979 to 1985 and Head since 1996. Among Professor Mackerras's most recent books are: *China's Minorities: Integration and Modernization in the Twentieth Century* (1994, Oxford University Press); *China's Minority Cultures: Identities and Integration Since 1912* (1995, St. Martin's Press); and *Peking Opera* (1997, Oxford University Press).

Mak, J.N. Director of Research at the Maritime Institute of Malaysia (MIMA) in Kuala Lumpur and Head of the Institute's Centre for Maritime Security and Diplomacy. Recent publications include: *ASEAN Defence Reorientation 1975–1992:*

the Dynamics of Modernization and Structural Change (1994, Strategic and Defence Studies Centre, Australian National University); and, in conjunction with Dr Bates Gill, *Arms, Transparency and Security in South-East Asia* (Oxford University Press, UK and the Stockholm International Peace Research Institute).

Maswood, Javed. Senior Lecturer in the Faculty of Asian and International Studies, Griffith University, Brisbane, where he teaches international political economy and Japanese politics. Recent publications include: *Japanese Defence* (1991, Sydney, Allen & Unwin) and 'Does revisionism work: American trade policy and the 1995 US–Japan automobile dispute' (1997, *Pacific Affairs*).

Pyle, Kenneth B. Professor of East Asian Studies at the University of Washington, Seattle, and President of The National Bureau of Asian Research. He is author of *The Japanese Question: Power and Purpose in a New Era* (2nd edn, 1996, American Enterprise Institute) and other works.

Ravenhill, John. Senior Fellow in the Department of International Relations, Research School of Pacific and Asian Studies, Australian National University, Canberra. His recent publications include: *Pacific Cooperation: Building Economic and Security Regimes in the Asia-Pacific Region*; and *The Political Economy of East Asia* (1994, Allen & Unwin Australia).

Roy, Denny. Research Fellow at the Strategic and Defence Studies Centre, Australian National University, Canberra, until March 1998. Editor of *The New Security Agenda in the Asia-Pacific Region* (1997, Macmillan) and recent articles on North-East Asian security affairs appearing in *International Security, Survival, Asian Survey* and *Security Dialogue*.

Segal, Gerry. Senior Fellow at the International Institute for Strategic Studies (London) and Director of the UK Economic and Social Research Council's Pacific Asia Programme. He is also Co-Chair of the European Council on Security and Co-operation in Asia-Pacific, the European Secretariat for the Council for Asia–Europe Co-operation and has been a 'fellow' of the World Economic Forum since 1995. His most recent publications include: *The World Affairs Companion* (1996, Simon & Schuster); *The Fate of Hong Kong* (1993, Simon & Schuster); *China Changes Shape* (1994, Brassey's for the IISS); and *China Rising* (edited with J. Goodman) (1997, Routledge).

Smith, Mike. Professor of European Studies, Loughborough University, UK. Author of numerous works on the external relations of the European Union and currently engaged in research into its Asia-Pacific strategy.

Woods, Lawrence T. Associate Professor International Studies Program, University of Northern British Columbia, Canada. Recent publications include: 'Rediscovering security' (1997, *Asian Perspective*); 'Economic cooperation and human rights in the Asia-Pacific region: the role of regional institutions' in James T.H. Tang (ed.) *Human Rights and International Relations in the Asia-Pacific Region* (1995, London, Pinter); 'Learning from NGO proponents of Asia-Pacific regionalism: success and its lessons', *Asian Survey* (vol.35, no.9, 1995); and *Asia-Pacific Diplomacy: Nongovernmental Organizations and International Relations* (1993, Vancouver, University of British Columbia Press).

Index